Catholics and Sultans

CATHOLICS
AND
SULTANS

The church and the Ottoman Empire
1453–1923

CHARLES A. FRAZEE
Professor of History, California State University, Fullerton

CAMBRIDGE UNIVERSITY PRESS
London   New York   New Rochelle
Melbourne   Sydney

Published by the Press Syndicate of the University of Cambridge
The Pitt Building, Trumpington Street, Cambridge CB2 1RP
32 East 57th Street, New York, NY 10022, USA
296 Beaconsfield Parade, Middle Park, Melbourne 3206, Australia

© Cambridge University Press 1983

First published 1983

Printed in Great Britain at
New Western Printing Ltd, Bristol

Library of Congress catalogue card number: 82–4562

British Library Cataloguing in Publication Data
Frazee, Charles A.
Catholics and sultans: the church and the
Ottoman Empire 1453–1923.
1. Catholic Church in Ottoman Empire–History
I. Title
282'.56   BX1595
ISBN 0 521 24676 8

NWP

Contents

Acknowledgments

Many people have assisted me in the composition of this study. First of all I should like to thank Dorothea Kenny and Jackson Putnam who read the manuscript in its early stages and made many helpful suggestions. Other contributors include my graduate assistants: Albert Mueller, Joy Pedroja, and Barbara Maroze, and those who helped with the preparation of the manuscript: Kathleen Frazee, Maria Snelson, Millie Thompson, Lee Gilbert, Paulette Woodward and Cheryl Perreira.

I am indebted to the American Philosophical Society and the California State University Fullerton Foundation for research grants.

Introduction

The collapse of the Byzantine state in May 1453 not only ended one of the world's most enduring empires, but also prepared the way for a new confrontation between European Catholics and Ottoman Turks. In one sense, this contest was but a continuation of the Christian–Muslim struggle which began with the Crusades, yet it had aspects which made it unique, since the areas which the Turks had occupied prior to the conquest were inhabited principally by Greek and other Eastern Christians.

Latin Catholics and Greek Orthodox had long been at odds over doctrinal, liturgical, and administrative issues, so that some Western observers saw the Byzantine defeat as God's judgment on heretics, but the majority of Western Christians regarded the Greek collapse and the occupation of 'New Rome' as an unmitigated disaster. Nearly everyone in the West feared that Mehmet II might suppress the Orthodox church just as he had the Byzantine state, but the contrary proved true. Mehmet made the church part of his administration and assured that its leadership, which he controlled, should be noted for its hostility towards Latin Catholicism. The Turkish conquest further alienated the two Christian churches by removing forever the emperors who had often befriended the papacy despite that policy's unpopularity. It also eliminated the influence of the small Greek party which favoured church union, who now had no choice but to live in impotent exile in Italy. The results of the Turkish capture of Constantinople in 1453 resembled those of the Fourth Crusade, for both events shattered the hopes of those who sought a single Greek and Latin Christian church, even though this union would not have included the Slavic or Arab-speaking churches and would have created a new schism within Eastern Christendom.

The period of overt hostility between the Turks and the papacy following Constantinople's fall was remarkably short-lived; within fifty years the Curia and the Porte had entered into negotiations and, in the sixteenth century, when the French and Turks sealed an alliance against the Habsburgs, the position of Ottoman Catholics was secured. Thereafter, a permanent French embassy, established in Istanbul, provided a sheltering wing for Western missionaries making their way into the Ottoman world.

The Catholic community of Istanbul had almost disappeared by the time the missionaries arrived. It soon became evident that these newcomers were not content to serve as chaplains to the Catholic diplomatic and merchant communities, but intended to proselytize actively among the Orthodox and Eastern Christians throughout the Empire. Latin missionaries, at heroic costs and often under very difficult circumstances, laboured at this task until several Near Eastern churches were formed in communion with Rome. Local clergy, who often welcomed the Western religious orders when they first appeared, became hostile once they realized separate and rival ecclesiastical organizations were being created.

The latter part of the eighteenth century was a period of decline due to the suppression of the Jesuits and the rationalist attitudes of the Enlightenment. Then came the French Revolution and the Napoleonic era which further disrupted the Catholic communities of the East. But once these years passed the nineteenth-century Catholic revival joined to papal initiatives provoked new interest in the Orient. Missionaries again poured into the Ottoman Empire to regain what was lost so that, by 1900, the church and its institutions had never been stronger. Yet, the best of times was making way for the worst. The First World War crushed both empire and church. When the Turkish Republic was proclaimed in 1923 there were few Catholics left to cheer.

PART I

After the conquest of
Constantinople

Ottoman gains and the Catholic response

During the Turkish siege of Constantinople, which began in late April 1453, the Catholic community living within the Byzantine capital was divided. Some actively sought to aid Emperor Constantine XI and the Greek defenders; others believed that the only practical course was to remain neutral. Generally speaking, the first point of view was held by those living inside the city's walls, Venetians and those Westerners who had come specifically to aid in its defence. With them stood Cardinal Isidoros of Kiev, legate of Pope Nicholas V, who had announced the decisions of the Council of Florence in the past December, his companion Leonardo of Chios, archbishop of Mitilini, and the Franciscan friars of the convent of St Anthony of the Cypresses. They believed it their duty to support the emperor because he had advocated the union of the churches.

The contrary opinion was held by most of the Latin Catholics who lived in Galata, the thriving Genoese colony on the eastern side of the Golden Horn. There were no romantics in that community of hard-headed merchants whose sentiments reflected the sober assessment that the Empire could not survive. It made little difference to them whether the ruler of Constantinople was Greek or Turk. Their concern was business; they could deal with anyone who allowed them to pursue their commercial interests in the East. While they might sympathize with the gallant struggle of their fellow Christians, they were anxious to be on good terms with Mehmet II. A treaty of several years' standing between the Galatans and the Ottomans defined their relations.

Many of the Latin defenders, like the captain Giovanni Giustiniani, gave their lives in defence of the city. Some were captured after its capitulation on 29 May and had to be ransomed, while others, like the Venetian *bailie* Girolamo Minotto, were executed by the victorious Turks. The Catholic churches of the city survived without major damage. Because of the friars' support of the Greeks only the Franciscan convent of St Anthony was confiscated, and the Venetian church of St Mary was temporarily closed.[1]

Despite the neutrality professed throughout the siege by the Galatans and the security they had been guaranteed by the Turks, many fled the city on the vessels which evacuated the refugees from Constantinople. The governor of the colony, *Podestà* Angelo Lomellino, and his council were embarrassed by this flight, knowing that Mehmet II would not approve. When a delegation from Galata came to his camp to offer the victorious Turkish leader their congratulations and to deliver the keys of their city into his hands they were practically ignored.

Several days later two ambassadors, Babalino Pallavicini and Marco de Franchi, with an interpreter, had better success. They were given an imperial *firman*, a grant of privileges, which set forth the rules for the governing of the colony now that the Turks were the masters. In the *firman* the Galatans obtained the right to trade within the Empire, and were promised security for their lives and property and freedom to practise the Catholic faith. Their sons were not subject to the *devşirme*, the forced recruitment of boys from Christian families for the Janissary corps or the Ottoman civil service, nor were any Muslims to be settled within the colony. On the other hand, the town and its citizens were to be disarmed. The walls and the citadel of Galata were to be torn down and every adult male became subject to the *cizye*, the poll tax levied on non-Muslims in the Islamic world. No bells were to be rung nor clocks strike the hour nor would the construction of new churches be permitted. All such stipulations were consonant with Islamic practice in dealing with a city which voluntarily submitted to Muslim rule.

On 3 June Mehmet crossed the Golden Horn to visit Galata. In an official ceremony *Podestà* Lomellino paid him homage. The *firman* between Mehmet and his Italian subjects was proclaimed. Then a Turkish administrator, a *kaimakam*, was installed as local governor. After this ceremony Mehmet toured the town. He ordered an inventory of property of those who had fled; their houses to be sealed and, if the owners did not return within three months, the buildings and their contents to be transferred to the Turkish government.

In September the former *podestà* left for Genoa. With Mehmet's permission, the Galatans were permitted to choose an Elder to represent them before the Turkish authorities. He was to be assisted by a governing council, the *Serenissima Communità di Pera e Galata*, which met in the sacristy of the small chapel of St Anne on the grounds of the Franciscan convent. This was the site of St Francis Catholic church, the largest in Galata, built during the Western occupation of the Byzantine capital in the thirteenth century.[2]

At the time of the conquest the ecclesiastical government of Galata's Latin churches was complicated by a number of factors. Officially, they were under the authority of the Greek patriarch Gregorios III Mammas, but this prelate had moved to Rome several years before 1453 because of the unpopularity of his pro-unionist sentiments. The acting head of the Latin churches was a vicar appointed by the patriarch. Usually the superior of the Franciscan convent of St Francis was appointed to this office, but the heads of other religious orders might also be chosen. The vicar's actual authority, however, was severely limited. Since the vast majority of Galatans were Genoese, many of them attended St Michael's church where the clergy were Genoese, sent out to the East by the archbishop of that city. The religious orders had their own superiors in Western Europe who took a hand in the affairs of their Eastern communities. Besides the Franciscan Conventuals, who served at St Francis, these included Franciscan Observants, Dominicans, and Benedictines. In 1453 a total of thirteen Catholic churches and chapels were to be found in Galata to minister to the Western Catholics who had settled in the Byzantine capital, and several others were found in Constantinople itself.[3]

The Orthodox populations of the Empire were organized by Turkish law into *millets*, or nations, under their own religious leaders, but Mehmet and his successors always treated Latin Catholics as foreigners. No matter what his national origin, everyone coming from Western Europe was a 'Frank'. The Catholic community of Galata was legally defined by the *firman* of 1453 and, as other Catholic groups entered the Ottoman world, they were required to negotiate individual *firmans* with the Ottoman government to regulate their presence in the Empire. The *Shari'a*, the sacred law of Islam, did not cover the status of foreigners: hence the need for these special arrangements.

THE PAPAL REACTION TO MEHMET'S VICTORY

The Venetians on Crete were the first Catholics to learn that Constantinople had fallen, when a boat filled with refugees reached the island in early June 1453. Other survivors began landing in the Peloponnesus, Cyprus, Euboea, and the Aegean islands closest to the fallen capital. The papal fleet which had been commissioned by Pope Nicholas V to aid Constantinople was anchored in the harbour of Chios when its commanders heard that their mission was now pointless and therefore ordered a return to Italy. By the end of June reports reaching Venice from officials in Greece told of the destruction of Galata as well as Constantinople, the slaughter of every inhabitant over six years of age, and the capture of the papal fleet. The Venetians at once drafted a letter to the pope informing him of the disaster and urging that Italy prepare itself for an attack.

The Venetian messenger who carried the letter to Rome spread the news in all the cities along his route. In Bologna, Cardinal Bessarion, leader of the Greeks at the Council of Florence who had supported union between the churches, was stunned by the announcement. The messenger reached Rome on 4 July to announce to the papal court that the Eastern Roman Empire was no more. Pope Nicholas V and his cardinals convened in an emergency meeting to discuss what should be done.[4]

The Genoese heard the news from Venetian messengers on 6 July and the *Signoria*, shattered by the information, assumed that Galata shared the fate of the capital. A feeling of defeatism spread, for Genoa was already at war with Naples and its resources were heavily taxed. Couriers from Venice reached Emperor Frederick III at Graz. The usually passive ruler was visibly moved. Aeneas Sylvius Piccolomini, then at the court, wrote to Pope Nicholas, 'What is this execrable news which is borne to us concerning Constantinople? My hand trembles even as I write; my soul is horrified, yet neither is it able to restrain its indignation nor express its misery. Alas, wretched Christianity!...of the two lights of Christendom, one has been extinguished.'[5]

During the summer Pope Nicholas began marshalling the forces of Christendom for a counterattack. He commissioned three galleys to sail to Eastern waters and ordered five more to be fitted out in Venice. He then sent legates to the Italian cities summoning them to meet in Rome in October. Late in September he issued a bull to all

Christians urging a crusade against the Turks. In it he called
Mehmet II the cruellest persecutor of Christ's church 'the son of
Satan, son of perdition and son of death, seeking like his father,
the devil, to devour both bodies and souls. He has risen up like a
rabid beast whose thirst is never satisfied by the shedding of
Christian blood.'[6] He encouraged princes to defend their faith with
their lives and wealth, and proclaimed a plenary indulgence to
anyone who would equip a soldier for six months. He promised to
spend still more of the papal income (60,000 ducats had already
been committed) for defence, and announced that both pope and
cardinals had agreed to tithe themselves. All Christians were to
desist from civil wars and enlist in the great endeavour to push back
the Turks.

At the end of November while the meeting of the Italian cities
was in progress in Rome, a ship arrived in Venice bringing more
refugees from the East, among them Cardinal Isidoros who had
managed to escape to the Peloponnesus after having been ransomed
by the citizens of Galata. He had made his way to Crete, accompanied by those Franciscans of St Anthony's who had escaped.
From their personal experience they added to the information about
the conquest already known in Italy. Isidoros set off for Rome to
report directly to the pope. He, and many others who had escaped
from Constantinople, believed that Mehmet planned an attack upon
Italy in the very near future. He composed a letter which was
circulated throughout Italy describing the fall of the Byzantine
capital and urging the need for action. Meanwhile Leonardo of
Chios was also seeking to inform the West of the conquest. In
contrast to Isidoros who claimed that Satan had inspired the Turks
to victory, Leonardo attributed the defeat of the Greeks to their
own lukewarm attitude towards the union of the churches. He
complained, 'Alas what hope is there for a people hardened in
serious iniquity, who have remained for so many years without
spiritual life, cut off, as they were, from their head.' The union was
not a true one, but 'fictitious', and now God's justice had fallen
upon the impious Greeks.[7]

Cardinal Bessarion, head of the Greeks in Italy, sought to mobilize
the Italian states to assist his homeland. He sent a stirring appeal
to the Doge of Venice beseeching the Republic to take action
against the Ottomans. He believed that the united action of the
Italian city states could yet stave off disaster: 'I can no longer,
unfortunately, request help for the salvation of the Empire or of

my fatherland, but I can ask it for the protection and honour of Christendom, for the preservation of the faith of Christ.'[8]

The missionaries sent to announce the crusade throughout Europe were met with indifference, while at Rome the envoys of the Italian states found they had little in common. Actually, while the Venetians in Rome were talking about action to be taken against the Turks, the Republic had dispatched Bartolomeo Minotto, the son of its last *bailie*, to seek out Mehmet and attempt to reach an agreement with him which would protect Venice's commercial interests in the Orient. Bartolomeo did not know that the Turks had executed his father; he hoped to ransom him and to secure the release of the other Venetian prisoners. Since his father was dead, this part of Bartolomeo's purpose could not be fulfilled, but after long discussions with Mehmet II at Edirne, he reached agreement with him on a treaty signed in April 1454. The treaty provided that 'Between Sultan Mehmet and the *Signoria* of Venice, including all its present and future possessions, as far as the banner of St Mark flies, henceforth, as before, there is peace and friendship.' Venice pledged it would never enter into any alliance against the Turks.[9]

The one solid accomplishment of Nicholas' Roman conference was the Peace of Lodi, signed by delegates of Florence, Venice and Milan on 9 April 1454. This brought to a conclusion the internal wars on the peninsula, but nothing was done to recapture Constantinople. The response to Nicholas by the other European powers had been completely negative. The Emperor Frederick did bestir himself into summoning a Diet for 23 April 1454 to discuss the situation. Invitations to come to Regensburg were sent to all European and German princes, but when the time came, hardly anyone had arrived. The Emperor himself was absent and only sent a delegate. The eloquence of Aeneas Sylvius was wasted on empty chairs. Efforts to enlist Alfonso V of Aragon proved futile for, despite this sovereign's repeated assertions of his eagerness to drive back the Turk, his navy remained in port. The best the pope could do was to commission a fleet of five vessels to sail east to encourage the Christian people still living outside Mehmet's rule.[10]

Pope Nicholas V died on 24 March 1455 lamenting his inability to aid the Christian Greeks now under Islamic leaders and unaware that the Christians had won a battle at Belgrade several days before, thereby temporarily checking the Turkish advance. The conclave which met to choose his successor was composed of fifteen cardinals, two of whom were Greek, Bessarion and Isidoros. Eight of the fifteen supported Bessarion for the papal office since he was so well known both for his learning and his devotion to the crusading ideal. The Greek cardinal had apparently done nothing to promote his candidacy, hence the Frenchman, Alain of Avignon, protested. 'Behold the poverty of the Latin church which cannot find a man worthy of the apostolic throne unless it looks to Greece.' The cardinals elected the aged Alfonso Borgia who assumed the name Calixtus III at his coronation on 20 April 1455. He was the first of the Borgia popes.[11] Calixtus was devoted to the Crusade. Not only was he interested in regaining Constantinople but he also believed that Christian arms should be used to regain Jerusalem.

In September 1455, Calixtus began gathering a fleet, commissioning Archbishop Pietro Urrea of Tarragona to be commander. The force was to go into the Aegean to support Chios and the other islands still held by the Christians. King Alfonso V of Aragon was to augment the papal fleet of sixteen ships with fifteen more of his own. Calixtus envisioned a land army led by Philip the Good of Burgundy. This prince had already shown his disposition with a romantic flair when, at the Feast of the Pheasant, held at Lille in February 1454, he and his courtiers had promised to take the cross.

All the hopes Calixtus had for the crusade were thwarted by the actions of those in whom he had placed his trust. Alfonso became embroiled in a war with Genoa in which Archbishop Urrea gladly enlisted the papal fleet to aid his countrymen. The pope dismissed the archbishop because of his partisanship and lack of judgment, appointing a new commander, Cardinal Ludovico Scamparo, on 17 December. Scamparo was made responsible for serving as the pope's legate to all Greek lands and territories in the East Mediterranean. On 13 May 1456 he was given the cross by Pope Calixtus and went off to Istria. Here five thousand men boarded the papal vessels and the flotilla set sail for Naples to join Alfonso's ships. But once more Alfonso delayed so in August the pope ordered his fleet to leave for the Aegean without the Neapolitans.

The papal fleet first visited Rhodes, then Chios, and finally Lemnos and its island dependencies where the family of the Gattilusi ruled as vassals of the Turks. On Chios and Lesbos their reception was polite but cool. The island rulers feared the wrath of the Turks too much to welcome the Christian navy. The fleet expelled the Turkish garrisons on Lemnos and Samothrace in August 1457, and successfully destroyed a Turkish fleet off Lesbos. After this victory, the Christians retired to Rhodes and then returned to Italy. No significant change had been effected in the Aegean but the pope was so enthusiastic over the victory at Lesbos that he caused a medal to be struck to commemorate the event. On it were the words, 'I have been chosen for the destruction of the enemies of the faith.'[12]

Calixtus never doubted that his vision of reconquering the Christian East would be realized. He continued to urge Franciscan missionaries to keep his hope alive among all Christian people. Letters were constantly being sent from Rome to the Catholic princes of Western Europe to rouse them to common action against the Turks. The pope was also in correspondence with the Muslim leader of Eastern Anatolia, the Turkoman Uzun Hasan, who was known to consider Mehmet a dangerous rival. At length Calixtus died in the summer of 1458. He would have been pleased to know his dream for the crusade was shared by his successor, the well-known humanist, Aeneas Sylvius Piccolomini, who became Pope Pius II on 29 August 1458.

PIUS II, THE HUMANIST CRUSADER

Reports of the Turkish occupation of the Peloponnesus during the summer of 1458 confirmed Pius' conviction that action must be taken against Mehmet. On 13 October 1458, less than two months after he had assumed office, the pope published a bull, *Vocavit nos Pius*, summoning the heads of the European states to come to a congress at Mantua to plan for a crusade; he would himself preside.

The optimistic pope left Rome with six cardinals in late January 1459, and after a slow journey through Italy reached Mantua in May. Not a single king or prince was to be found; only minor officials had come, sent as delegates by the European princes. The chagrined pope ordered new messages sent to the courts of Europe, pointing out the urgency of the situation. Despite growing defeatism even within the papal party, he remained convinced that it was still possible to rally Christendom against the Turk, but only Bessarion and Torquemada, the Spanish cardinal, showed any determination.

The Congress at Mantua finally convened on 1 June 1459 with Pope Pius offering a solemn Mass in St Peter's church. Representatives from Naples, Epirus, Cyprus, Rhodes, Trebizond, Bosnia and Hungary were in attendance. The bishop of Koroni delivered the sermon urging Christians to action. Then the sessions were suspended to await the arrival of new delegations. Francesco Sforza at last dispatched a party from Milan and in August a Burgundian embassy arrived. Venice, the key to any successful operation in the East, refrained, arguing that unless all Christian princes were unanimous in their intent to pursue the Holy War, the Republic intended to stand aside.

Having spent the summer in idleness, on 26 September the Congress held its first working session. Pius delivered an address which deplored the indifference of the Catholic West to the plight of Eastern Christians. Bessarion responded to the pope's address on behalf of the cardinals. He seconded every point the pope had made. Then deliberations commenced on the measures to be taken. The Congress heard with dismay that the Emperor Frederick III had proclaimed himself king of Hungary, an action bound to trouble central Europe. At the same time there was some encouragement from France, England, and the Holy Roman Empire, whose delegations finally arrived in late autumn.

By 19 December an agreement was reached. The emperor would provide an army of thirty thousand infantry and ten thousand horse while the Italian states would provide a fleet. A tithe would be levied on the income of the clergy; the laity would pay one-thirtieth and the Jews one-twentieth of their incomes to raise funds for the venture. All that remained was to close the Congress on 19 January 1460 with the official bull. Cardinal legates were sent to the princes and Franciscan friars to the laity to stir up enthusiasm for the crusade. Bessarion went off to Germany, while Isidoros, who had succeeded to the title of patriarch of Constantinople on 20 April 1459, proceeded to Ancona to supervise preparation of the fleet.[13]

While the pope waited for his envoys to return, news of the Turkish conquest of Lesbos arrived in Rome; after only a month's siege Mitilini had fallen. The lord of the island, Niccolò Gattilusi, had surrendered, and announced his conversion to Islam, but was killed by the Turks anyway. Three hundred prominent Italian citizens had been put to death by the Ottomans, by their bodies being sawed in two, while hundreds more became Turkish slaves.[14]

The indifference of the Western princes to his pleas for military action made Pius decide upon a personal appeal to Mehmet II in 1461 hoping that persuasion might prove more effective than force. It is hard to assess the weight and seriousness of this gesture, but apparently Pius thought that the resolution of the Turkish prince might be shaken. Some have argued that the pope was engaged in a flight of fantasy, but perhaps he recognized in Mehmet a leader who compared favourably with the chiefs of state in Western Europe.

The letter was a lengthy one, written in the style of the Renaissance. Its aim was to convince Mehmet that if he had enjoyed success as a Muslim, he would have even greater prospects upon conversion to Christianity. For all of this pleading, Pius received no answer from the Turkish leader. Further to demonstrate his commitment, he ordered the head of St Andrew to be brought to Rome with great ceremony on Palm Sunday 1462. The despot Thomas Palaeologos had left the relic at the papal fort of Narni; now it was transported to the gates of Rome by Cardinal Bessarion. As the procession passed through the Holy City, the ailing Cardinal Isidoros, victim of a stroke which had left him unable to speak, greeted St Andrew, now, like himself, an exile in Italy. The head was at last given to Pope Pius by Bessarion to be placed in a shrine prepared for it in St Peter's.

On 23 September 1463 the pope charged the cardinals that at last the time had come for the leaders of the Roman church personally to take the cross. The pontiff asserted, 'It will be said, of course, "What has this sickly old man, this priest, to do with war? What business have cardinals and officials of the Roman court in the camp? Why do they not stay at home and send a fleet with troops accustomed to fight?" ' He answered his own questions: 'Our cry, "Go forth!" has resounded in vain. Perhaps if the word is "Come with me!" it will have more effect.' He drafted new appeals to the Catholic princes and issued the bull of the crusade on 22 October.[15]

The next few months witnessed strenuous efforts to organize the pope's crusade. In November a special treasury was set up in which 27,000 gold coins were deposited. Legates were dispatched to the various capitals and preachers to the people.

On 18 June 1464 the pope took the cross in St Peter's in Rome and immediately afterwards set out with his party for Ancona. He was not well and the journey became very difficult. Crusaders from the poorer people of France, Spain, Germany and the Netherlands were already gathering at the Italian ports in response to the papal summons. Many were without funds or arms, and the local Italians were anxious to be rid of them. In Ancona, the main centre of activity, the arrival of thousands of would-be warriors had strained the city's resources. Quarrels were frequent among the nationalities; sickness ever present. The archbishop of Crete, named by Pius to put things in order, despaired and asked the poorest and weakest to return home.

Pius got to Ancona on 19 July to find the situation bordering on chaos. Professional soldiers were hard to find; his call to war had been answered only by innocents. Venice, which was to provide the fleet, had still not sent its ships. His already poor health broke down in the heat. Everyone around him saw he was a dying man. On 14 August 1464 he gave his last advice to the cardinal of Pavia, Jacopo Ammanati, 'Keep the continuation of our holy enterprise in the mind of the brothers and aid it with all your power. Woe unto you if you desert God's work.' In a few moments Europe's most dedicated crusader died. The Venetian fleet arrived to learn the news that Pius was gone. It sailed back to port; Pius' soldiers packed their few possessions and left for home. The papal galleys were turned over to Venice and the treasury sent off to the king of Hungary. It was a dismal end for Pius' enterprise.[16]

THE FURTHER SUCCESSES OF MEHMET II

The successor of Pius II was a Venetian, Pietro Barbaro, who took the name of Paul II. The new pope was anxious that the papacy should support his native city since, despite the Republic's efforts to keep on good terms with the sultan, war had broken out between Venice and the Turks.

After seven years in the papacy Paul was dead and Sixtus IV became the incumbent of St Peter's throne in 1471. Sixtus continued the tradition of his predecessors, sending legates throughout Europe to convince the princes of the need for a crusade. He even saw the Russians as allies in the cause. An adventurer named Giovanni Battista della Volpe had convinced Cardinal Bessarion that the Grand Prince of Moscow, Ivan III, might be persuaded to aid Catholic Europe. The bait was to be Bessarion's ward, Zoe Palaeologa, daughter of the now deceased despot, Thomas Palaeologos. Negotiations with Ivan proved a success; Zoe was married to him by proxy in Rome in 1472 and then sent off to Russia. The desired effect failed to materialize, however, since Zoe reconverted to Orthodoxy, taking a new name, Sophia, and Ivan's interest in the crusade evaporated.[17]

Cardinal Bessarion went on his final mission for the sake of his homeland in 1472. Sixtus IV dispatched him to France to enlist the aid of King Louis XI. The meeting with the French monarch went badly, no sign of interest was forthcoming. Discouraged and ill, the aging cardinal had to be carried back over the Alps in a litter; he died in Ravenna before reaching Rome, on 14 November 1472.

In Istanbul Mehmet took the advice of Venice's Italian rivals that he really had little to fear from any alliance formed against him. The Catholic ambassadors of Genoa and Florence took every occasion to urge the sultan to pursue the war against the Republic. Apparently the only Venetian response to counter these stratagems was to resort to attempts upon the sultan's life, none of which proved successful.

In 1472 a Christian fleet composed of papal, Venetian and Neapolitan vessels was made ready to attack the East. The papal navy, twenty-three galleys, was commanded by the Neapolitan cardinal, Olivera Caraffa. The Christian forces harassed the Anatolian cities of the Ottomans and struck Izmir, pillaged and then temporarily garrisoned it. These brief victories were all that was accomplished; Mehmet's power had hardly been challenged. Proof of this appeared the following year when Mehmet attacked and overwhelmed Uzun Hasan at Bashkent on 11 August 1473, and with the defeat of their Muslim ally, both papal and Venetian hopes were crushed and Venice was forced to agree to peace.

Mehmet's gains determined him to inaugurate new moves against the pockets of Christian power adjacent to his empire. His first targets were the remaining Genoese colonies of the Black Sea. A force led by Ahmet Gedik Paşa struck Caffa; for three days there was resistance, but then the Genoese commander, recognizing the hopelessness of the situation, negotiated surrender. The Ottomans agreed to peace provided the Genoese left the Crimea. The Catholics were uprooted from their homes; some returned to Genoa, while others were permanently settled in Istanbul. Several hundred young men and boys from Caffa were forcibly recruited for the Janissary corps.

The expelled Genoese community, numbering almost two thousand people, was placed in the neighbourhood of the Edirne Gate where the inhabitants were permitted to organize themselves along the lines of the Genoese in Galata. This area came to be known as *Kaffa-Mahalessi* (the Caffan quarter), a name which it held until its destruction by fire in July 1919. Mehmet decreed that two abandoned Byzantine monasteries and their churches should be placed at the disposal of the Catholic clergy who came with the Caffans. They were dedicated to St Mary and St Nicholas and were served by Dominicans. St Mary held the Madonna of Caffa, an image which was the most precious of the objects brought with the exiles from the Crimea. St Nicholas became the home of both Latin and Armenian Catholics, who shared the building.[18]

Mehmet then turned his attention towards the island of Rhodes, since this fortress was the strongest bastion left in Catholic hands in the East, garrisoned by the Knights Hospitallers of St John. There had been constant tension between the two states over the refusal of the Knights to pay tribute to Mehmet since his accession, and, at best, an uneasy truce was all that both sides had agreed upon.

The Knights were no longer so numerous as they had been in earlier times, but their discipline and devotion made up for what they lacked in numbers. In 1480 the Grand Master was Pierre d'Aubusson. He was well aware that Rhodes must prepare itself for an eventual attack by the Ottomans. The arrival of a Turkish envoy on the island in the summer of 1479 with a proposal to renew the truce surprised the Knights since they had been informed that preparations were under way for an attack. Although the treaty was renewed the Knights continued to strengthen their defences. Their fears proved well founded when in December 1479 a Turkish fleet appeared off Rhodes and troops were sent to pillage some of the undefended villages. Then on 23 May 1480 another fleet began landing forces on the west coast. Soon the city of Rhodes was invested. The odds against the Christians were great; the Turks had many more men and powerful cannon. The Knights numbered less than three hundred with their sergeants and three to four thousand French and Italian troops. In bitter fighting, however, they turned back every Ottoman assault. Finally the siege was broken off, and to the acclaim of Catholic Christendom, Rhodes was saved.[19]

While the siege of Rhodes was in progress Mehmet struck out in still another direction against the Catholic world. He dispatched Ahmet Gedik Paşa with 140 vessels from the Albanian port of Vlorë to attack Italy. Mehmet may well have had designs on Rome itself. One contemporary, Niccolò Sanguindo, reported that the sultan believed Constantinople to be the daughter of Rome, and having won the daughter he also hoped to gain the mother. In late July Ahmet Gedik landed on the south coast of Apulia. He invested the castle and city of Otranto, near Brindisi, and took it on 18 August 1480. The news that the Turks had an army in the peninsula finally forced the Italians into action. Pope Sixtus IV called for men and money while quietly making plans to flee to Avignon should that prove necessary. King Ferrante in Naples, son of Alfonso V, sent appeals to the sovereigns of Europe for immediate assistance.

The Turkish troops pillaged and burned the countryside and dealt harshly with the captives. They destroyed the Greek monastery of San Niccolò di Casole and led eight hundred Christians of Otranto to a hill outside the city where they gave them the option of embracing Islam or suffering death. Most held to their faith, despite the prospect of execution by impaling or beheading. The archbishop, Stefano Bendinelli, was sawn in two as was the military captain of the garrison. Thousands of townspeople were sent off to Albania as slaves.

The pope and the Roman cardinals donated 150,000 ducats to fit out an army and construct twenty-five galleys. The money was distributed to the kings of Naples and Hungary. The pope also issued a bull to all Christendom on 8 April 1481, asking for assistance. Within the year the Christian forces had rallied, and the Turks were expelled on 10 September 1481. The news gave Rome's citizens occasion to celebrate a three-day holiday. The withdrawal was seen as a major check on the Turks but, in fact, it was only a limited victory over Ottoman ambitions. It was much more important that death, at last, had come to Catholic Europe's most formidable enemy. Mehmet II died on 3 May 1481.[20]

THE PAPACY MOVES FROM FOE TO FRIEND

Mehmet's successor was his son Bayezit, who first had to contend for the sultanate with his younger brother Cem. Bayezit's support proved the stronger and Cem mistakenly sought the assistance of the Knights of St John to obtain his father's throne. He sent ambassadors to Rhodes asking for a treaty of friendship and permission to come to the island. The surprised Grand Master, Pierre d'Aubusson, hardly knew what to make of such a request, but negotiations were concluded satisfactorily when the Knights promised Cem their aid. With this assurance he came to Rhodes. While he was negotiating, the Grand Master sent messengers to Bayezit reporting that Cem was in Rhodes and questioned the sultan's reaction. Bayezit proved to be quite willing for the Knights to hold his brother and in return for their cooperation in acting as Cem's jailors, he offered to pay the Christian order thirty-five thousand ducats annually, and in addition ten thousand more each year in compensation for the damage done by his father's attacks on Rhodes. A secret treaty was signed between them on 7 December 1482.

The unfortunate Cem was transported to the Knights' priory at Nice within the year. News that the son of the terrible Mehmet the Conqueror and the pretender to his throne was now in Western Europe caused many Christians to shake their heads in disbelief. At once a debate began on how best this unexpected turn of events might be used to Christendom's advantage. Cem began composing a poem about his fate, aware now that he was more a prisoner than a guest. He was shunted about the establishments of the order in France, where he had at least one affair with the daughter of a guard, until at last it was decided that a special castle should be built for him. Here he languished for the next several years.[21]

Bayezit II came to power in the last three years of the pontificate of Sixtus IV. While the pope urged upon Catholic Europe the need for the crusade, the appeal had been heard so many times before that it was counted a mere rhetorical formality. Indeed Sixtus' real concerns were closer to home: building the chapel which still bears his name, forming its famous choir, patronizing the Vatican library and its museum.

The situation changed when Innocent VIII succeeded him in 1484. Innocent held real hope for containing the Turks, for he believed Cem could be used to advantage over Bayezit. Two years after his accession he persuaded the Knights to place Cem directly under papal protection. It was another three years before the Turkish prince actually came to Rome, however, since the French King Charles VIII objected strongly to the transfer. He arrived in the Eternal City in the spring of 1489.

Cem was lavishly received. All the ceremonies attendant upon the arrival of a foreign dignitary at the papal court were closely followed. Cem approached Innocent, embraced him and gave him a kiss. He did not, however, remove his turban, which appeared to some onlookers as a breach of protocol, but the pope chose to pay no attention. Cem spoke to the pontiff through an interpreter, recounting the misfortunes of his past, and asking Innocent to aid him in returning to his homeland. After the reception, he was assigned a residence in the Castel Sant'Angelo.

The news that Cem was now in Rome and presumably co-operating with the pope was rightly judged dangerous in Istanbul. The pope was known also to be making overtures to Kait-bey, Mamluk sultan in Cairo, sounding him out on the possibility of an anti-Ottoman alliance. Bayezit took immediate action. In November 1490 he dispatched an embassy to Rome, headed by Mustafa

Bey, his chief gatekeeper. Mustafa brought a gift of 120,000 gold coins, numerous personal items and a letter of friendship as a sign of the sultan's regard for the pope. Innocent greeted the delegation warmly, accepted the gifts and promised to consider the sultan's letter carefully. The Ottoman envoy was allowed to meet and talk with Cem and later a secret audience was held between Mustafa and the Roman cardinals.[22]

Whether the ghosts of Innocent's predecessors were shaking in their graves cannot be known, but certainly many Christians looked aghast at this turn of events. The Italian states were not only amazed at the pope's extraordinary good fortune in having both the Conqueror's sons courting his favour, but they were also envious that the papal finances had overnight increased enormously. Some had their misgivings. Sigismondo dei Conti da Foligno observed, 'It really seemed absurd to many serious and learned men that the pontiff should find himself so easily in alliance with the Turks and could enter into business with them so eagerly.'[23]

Mustafa Bey carried Pope Innocent's acknowledgement of Bayezit's letter back to Istanbul. The pope was pleased that the sultan had protested he intended no hostile action against any of the eastern European Catholic states: Venice, Rhodes, or Cyprus. He was willing to continue keeping Cem a prisoner in Rome, but at an increased price, 45,000 ducats each year. Failure to pay might result in Cem's being 'unleashed.'

In May 1492 Bayezit renewed his contacts with Rome, sending an ambassador with the funds to pay for Cem's confinement. Once again the reception accorded the Ottoman delegation was cordial, for in addition to the payment of gold Bayezit had sent the pope a precious reliquary containing part of the Holy Lance along with several other objects of Christian devotion. Promises of continued cooperation were made. Innocent's special arrangement with the Porte allowed him to spend money as few popes before or after him have done.

Later in 1492 Innocent was dead and Alexander VI, a Spaniard and a Borgia, was elected to the papacy. This same year saw Granada, the last Muslim state in Spain, extinguished, so that, in Bayezit's view, the new pope might indeed return to the papacy's traditional crusading position. That this did not happen is attributable to the fact that the interests of Alexander VI were very much forged by his family and its need of money. He sought to take full advantage of his inherited position as Cem's jailor. No crusader, he actually sought to allay the pressure of the French king, Charles VIII, for a call to arms of all Europe against the Turks.

Alexander commenced a series of letters to Bayezit II which continued over the next several years. He asked that the subsidy paid to Rome should be increased, to the astronomical sum of 300,000 gold ducats. Alexander warned Bayezit that Charles threatened an invasion of Italy because of his claims on the throne of Naples and that this would be only the prelude to French designs on Istanbul. Alexander pointed out that should Cem fall into French hands there would be no end to the consequences. Bayezit paid up commenting, 'Our friendship will grow with God's help from day to day. Do not forget to report to us on your welfare; we, on our part, will be pleased to hear such news.'[24]

At length the pope sent a personal envoy, Giorgio Bucciardo, to Istanbul to put his case for even more funds, as he awaited the imminent invasion of the French king. On his return to Italy in 1494 Bucciardo and the Ottoman ambassador, Assam Bey, bringing 40,000 ducats to the pope, were taken captive at Sinigaglia by Alexander's enemy, Cardinal Giuliano della Rovere, and held prisoner. Charles VIII, having received the correspondence carried by the embassy, expressed his outrage that the head of Christendom was in league with the sultan.

Bayezit responded to these threats by tighter surveillance of those Christians in his empire who might be in collaboration with his enemies. The Venetians, perennial foes of papal policies in Italy, were assumed to be in alliance with the French. Compromising correspondence from the Venetian *bailie* in Istanbul, Girolamo Marcello, had been intercepted by Ottoman officials in 1492 and Marcello had been expelled for spying. Since 1489 Venice had also held the island of Cyprus on a claim that Caterina Cornaro, the widow of the last Luisgnan king, had bequeathed her island to the Republic. Bayezit feared that Venice might very well intend to use Cyprus as a new stronghold in the East Mediterranean to enhance its maritime empire.

The invasion of Italy by the French proved to be a temporary success. Charles VIII took Rome on 11 January 1495, and among other demands forced Pope Alexander to hand over Cem. The unfortunate captive, once more under a new master, was ordered to join Charles for the next four weeks on campaign in southern Italy. Cem unexpectedly died on 25 February 1495 at Capua.

Whatever plans Charles may have entertained for his prisoner
were forever gone. After much haggling the body of the deceased
was handed over to Ottoman officials for burial in the royal
cemetery in Bursa. For Bayezit obviously the death of his brother
came as a great relief. Henceforth his policies toward Catholic
Europe could be pursued from a position of strength.

THE VENETIAN ECLIPSE

Throughout the 1490s Bayezit had concentrated on improving the
Ottoman navy for its inevitable contest with Venice for control of
Eastern waters. In 1497 a Venetian pilgrim ship to Jerusalem was
taken and its passengers killed or enslaved. Open hostilities began
again in 1499 with an attack launched by the Turks against the
remaining Venetian possessions in Dalmatia and on the Greek
mainland. All Venetians in Istanbul were placed under arrest.
Navpaktos (Lepanto) fell to the Turks and the Catholics departed.
In the following year the important ports on the south coast of the
Peloponnesus, Methoni and Koroni, were conquered. The new
Ottoman fleet had proven its worth.

The Hungarian King László VIII together with Louis XII
of France joined Venice in alliance against the Turks. Pope
Alexander VI turned on his former Ottoman friend and
issued a crusading bull on 1 June 1500. A French fleet sailed
into the Aegean, but this did not prevent further losses to the
Christian powers. A treaty ending the war was signed on 14 December 1503. In accordance with its terms, the Venetians gave up
their Greek ports and the few cities of Albania still remaining in
their hands.[25]

The decline of Venetian power in the East Mediterranean over
the next fifty years grew out of that city's inability to cope with the
larger nation states of Europe and the loss of its markets consequent
on the shift in trade to the Atlantic. Commerce with Egypt still
brought the city large profits in 1500 but soon even this would end.
The League of Cambrai which was formed in 1508 by the Holy
Roman Emperor, Maxmilian I, and included France, Spain and
the papacy, aimed specifically at the destruction of Venetian power.
Against such opposition Venice had no chance. In 1509 the Venetians were crushed at Agnadello and never fully recovered. The fact
that Venice, the strongest Catholic power in the East, had been
defeated by a coalition including the papacy, was not lost on the

Ottomans. It proved to the Turkish officials that they need have no real concern about a great Western counterattack.

THE POLICIES OF BAYEZIT II

The sultanate of Bayezit II was a prosperous time for Muslims, but this good fortune did not extend to the Catholics in Istanbul. Their numbers were in great decline – less than two hundred and fifty Caffan Genoese households were counted in the city by the time of Bayezit's accession. In Galata only eight Catholic churches were functioning in 1500.[26]

Bayezit followed his father's policy in keeping the Orthodox Christians of his empire hostile to Catholicism. Patriarch Maximos III Manasses admonished the Venetian Doge against any persecution of the Orthodox in the territories of the Republic. Maximos went so far as to proclaim, 'Although the great and most exalted monarch is of another faith, he leaves the Christians and everyone else complete freedom of opinion and belief...', in contrast, of course, to Venice.[27]

To further the distinction which the Orthodox hierarchy wanted to make between themselves and the Latins, Maximos III summoned a council which was concluded during the patriarchate of Symeon of Trebizond in 1484. The Orthodox hierarchy believed it to the Greek church's advantage to demonstrate both to itself and to the sultan that the church union reached at Florence was dead. The assembly, in which the Melkite patriarchs of Alexandria, Antioch and Jerusalem also participated, drew up a service for those Orthodox who once lived under Italian Catholic rule and had recognized the pope and the decisions of the Council of Florence. Any person seeking to be restored to Orthodoxy was required to condemn 'the terrible and foreign doctrines of the Latins' specifically in those areas in which agreement had been reached at Florence. After swearing his assent and signing a statement to that effect, the convert was then anointed with Holy Oil. The council did not, it should be noted, require re-baptism.[28]

SELIM I AND THE ROMAN POPES

Bayezit's ambitious son Selim I, a contemporary of Pope Julius II and the Medici pope, Leo X, ruled in Istanbul at a time when the Renaissance was in full flower in Rome. Julius had too many

activities in Italy to be troubled by the Ottomans but Leo, a Philhellene, did occupy himself with the East. However, the actions of
a German priest, Martin Luther, were eventually to consume more
of his attention.

Leo worried over the successes of Selim as they were reported to
him in Rome. He had a Greek aide, Ioannis Laskaris, who encouraged him to free his countrymen and, to further interest in
the East, Leo subsidized a Greek College in Rome where Laskaris
and Markos Musurus, another Catholic Greek, taught the Greek
language and its literature. Laskaris was often used by Leo as his
personal envoy. Leo believed that the Christian princes should be
alerted to the dangers to which Christendom was exposed by
Ottoman expansion, and to that end he sent numerous letters to
Europe's rulers. To win the support of France, the pope encouraged
Francis I to think he might be named emperor in the East.

Since Hungary bordered the Ottomans, Leo focused his efforts
in Rome on trying to collect funds for the Hungarian army. But
the Hungarian peasants, armed to fight the Turks, turned instead
on their own nobility. In 1515 a terrible civil war broke out which
ended with the peasants crushed and tens of thousands killed. The
Hungarian Diet, in an attempt to prevent future uprisings, passed
legislation making all peasants permanent serfs.

Early in 1518 Selim addressed a letter to Pope Leo notifying him
that the Ottoman armies were now free of concern in Asia and
that the West would soon be hearing from him. The news brought
panic to Rome. The pope ordered daily processions to St Peter's.
He walked barefoot, accompanied by the ambassadors of the Catholic powers, following Rome's most precious relics. The Venetians
informed the Turks of all this and warned Selim that the pope was
forming a league, the Fraternity of the Holy Crusade, to bring
French, Germans and English into alliance against him.

In the midst of Leo's preparations, word reached Rome that the
sultan had died. The pope ordered prayers of thanksgiving in all of
Rome's churches, and plans for the crusade were suspended. Everyone believed Selim's sole remaining son, Süleyman II, would be a
man of peace.[29]

SÜLEYMAN II AND THE CATHOLIC POWERS

In the autumn of 1520, Süleyman inherited his father's throne at a
time when the Ottoman world was poised to make further political

and military gains against Catholic Europe. During his lifetime he raised the prestige of his empire to its highest point, hence 'Magnificent' has been added to his name by Western authors. He is known as '*Kanuni*', the lawgiver, by the Turkish people, in token of his concern that all in his domain should enjoy fair and equitable justice. Throughout his long reign the empire's economy prospered as never before, and Istanbul, reflecting the magnificence of its sultan, became the most important city of the Mediterranean.

In many ways Süleyman shared the values of his father. He believed it to be his vocation to pursue the Holy War against the Christians so as to extend the borders of Islam, and at the same time to fight against Muslim heresy, which was ever more pressing since Shi'ism had become identified with Persian aggression against his nation.

Süleyman so constructed his administration that military matters received priority over all other concerns of empire. The Janissary corps, his father's pride, was further developed to become the largest and best trained infantry in Europe. In addition, the native Turkish *siphais*, long the most honoured group in Ottoman society, provided a cavalry noted for its ability to sweep through the country-side in support of the main body of troops when on campaign.

There can be little doubt that Süleyman's success was in large part due to the particularly favourable conditions during his reign, which fell at the critical period of the Protestant Reformation, when Latin Christendom was divided into two warring factions. It also coincided with a time of great social unrest in Eastern Europe. There a rapacious nobility sought to enjoy extravagant pleasures wrung from the toil of a suffering peasantry and at the same time to limit the powers of the central government lest it be forced to make some sacrifices for the good of the nation. Finally, the Ottoman sovereign was fortunate that the two strongest Catholic powers of Europe, France and the Habsburgs, were locked in combat for years, dissipating whatever strength a united Europe might have been able to gather to thwart his plans.

The French king, Francis I, in his contest with the Habsburg Charles V for control of northern Italy suffered a stunning defeat at Pavia in February 1525. Charles V captured Francis and confined him in Spain after the battle. While her son languished in imprisonment, an idea was born in the mind of his regent mother, Louise d'Angoulême, for a new coalition against the Habsburgs. With her son's approval, but surrounded with great secrecy, she entrusted a French envoy with a mission to Istanbul. His purpose was to forge an agreement with Süleyman which would provide for concerted action against what both French and Ottomans feared, an un-challenged Habsburg ascendancy in Europe. The first ambassador died en route in Bosnia, but the second, Jean Frangipani, reached the Ottoman capital and made the French plans known.

Süleyman was impressed. He dictated a letter which marks the beginning of French–Ottoman diplomatic affairs.

I, who am the Sultan of Sultans, the King of Kings, the Distributor of crowns to the princes of this world, the Shadow of God upon earth, the Supreme Sovereign of the White Sea and Black Sea, of Roumelia, Anatolia and of the countries which my glorious ancestors have con-quered, as well as the numerous countries subjugated by my own triumphant sword, to Francis, who is prince of the country of France . . .

The French envoy made his presentation and the sultan had been pleased with the message from Francis:

All that he [the envoy] has spoken at the foot of my throne, the refuge of the world, has made me perfectly understand your situation. In these times, it is not rare to see kings defeated and taken prisoner. Do not let your courage lag. In all circumstances, our glorious ancestors have never refused to fight the enemy and make conquests; and I, too, go forth in all seasons against powerful provinces and well-fortified strong-holds.[30]

The newly formed alliance between the French and Turks was put to the test in 1528. While the French under the now liberated Francis I attacked the Habsburgs in the west, Süleyman marched northward to aid his vassal János Zápolya in Transylvania. In the following spring an even stronger force left Istanbul to aid Zápolya's continuing struggle against the Habsburgs. Together they occupied Buda in September. The Turkish sultan then ordered an advance into Austria and besieged Vienna. For three weeks the defenders held on; it was to be long enough, for with the approach of winter Süleyman lifted the siege. He withdrew once more, scouring the Hungarian plain as he headed back to his capital, satisfied that the Habsburgs had been sufficiently warned not to disturb the delicate balance of power in the northern Balkans. He left a Turkish garrison in Buda to support Zápolya. Meanwhile, in the west, a truce had been agreed upon at Cambrai in August 1529 between Francis I and Charles V. The emperor wanted to be free to deal with the Lutheran princes in Germany. The papacy, despite Charles' role as head of Catholic Christendom, was no friend of the emperor, for it feared his pretensions to unite Italy and to submit the Pro- testant problem to a general council. Pope Clement VII paid for his sentiments when Charles' army looted Rome in 1527.[31]

Recognizing that there was little permanence in the European situation as it then stood, Francis I knew better than to give up his understanding with Süleyman. He kept the Turkish alliance secret, lest he, like Zápolya, suffer excommunication. Letters continued to pass between the two sovereigns concerning affairs of common interest. One issue raised in 1528 dealt with the rights of French merchants in Egypt. Since Mamluk times the Catholic merchants of Alexandria, French and Catalans, enjoyed special privileges to trade there, and these agreements were confirmed by Selim I after the conquest of Egypt. Among them was the right of the merchants to own several Catholic churches which were served by Franciscans from the Holy Land. Francis asked Süleyman for permission to make repairs to these buildings and inquired about the loss of one of the Catholic shrines in Jerusalem, apparently a chapel on Mt Zion. The sultan replied that work could begin on the Alexandrian churches, but as for the chapel, 'for a long time it has been a mosque and Muslims have prayed there', hence it was impossible to return it to Christian use. Süleyman pledged, 'The other places, except the mosque, remain in Christian hands; no one, under our benign Sovereignty, will ever molest those who are there.'[32] The importance of Süleyman's renewal of the agreement with the Catholics of Alexandria had broad implications for the future, since this grant of privileges was used as the basis for all further negotiations between France and the Porte during the sultan's lifetime.

In 1534 the first official French ambassador, Jean de la Forêt, was dispatched to the Ottoman capital. His arrival in May 1534 opened the door to increased French influence in the Turkish empire, and with it the possibility of a change in the situation of Ottoman Catholics.

La Forêt's instructions were to seek trading privileges as well as a military agreement with the Turks, and, in addition, to have the religious rights accorded to the Alexandrian merchants extended everywhere in the Ottoman Empire. In effect, this would allow the French merchants and diplomats in the Orient to own Catholic churches and employ clergy to serve them. La Forêt, who carried on the talks with the vezir, Ibrahim Paşa, made significant progress in all these matters. It was further agreed that a joint attack would be made upon Italy: France would strike Lombardy while an Ottoman fleet invaded Naples by sea. The ambassador was also assured that 'merchants, agents, delegates, and all other servants of the king would not be molested or judged by Muslim officials and would enjoy freedom of worship'.[33] One of the articles of agreement would have allowed the pope to join in the attack upon the Habsburgs. Unfortunately, a few weeks after the agreement was negotiated Ibrahim Paşa fell from power and was strangled. As a result, the proposed text of the French–Ottoman treaty was never confirmed by Süleyman. Nevertheless, the proposal did have a positive effect, since Süleyman was well aware of what had transpired and understood what his French ally wanted from the Ottomans in return for their cooperation. Meanwhile in Western Europe, Pope Paul III had brought Charles and Francis together again, so that the projected invasion of Italy was quietly called off by the French monarch.

Apparently unaware of this truce between the Christian powers, Süleyman led his army across the Balkans to Vlorë in Albania where a navy was assembled for the attack upon Italy. After a weary wait for the French strike into Lombardy, he dismissed his invasion force and, in his disappointment, directed that the fleet should be used against the remaining Venetian possessions in the Adriatic, since Venice was a Habsburg ally. Corfu was invested and then his admiral, Barbarossa, sailed into the Aegean against the Venetian-held islands.

CATHOLICS IN ISTANBUL DURING SÜLEYMAN'S RULE

Despite the continued decline in the total population of Latins, in Süleyman's time Catholics still held nine churches in Galata and three in Istanbul itself. A visitor in Galata during this period counted 500 Genoese, 500 freed slaves of various nationalities, and a total of 600 Spaniards, Venetians and Neapolitans. By far the largest number of Catholics were the six thousand slaves, some of whom belonged to the state, others to private individuals. The lot of the public slaves was indescribably miserable, but life in Galata was pleasant and genteel. Men and women were tastefully and stylishly dressed and enjoyed life in a society based upon Italian customs greatly different from Oriental mores. The major complaint of the Galatans came from the settlement of Granadan Moors in their midst. Still resentful over their expulsion from Spain, they often took out their spite on the Catholics of the Ottoman capital.[34]

The Dominicans who had lost their church of St Paul to the Muslims were compensated in 1535 when the church of St Peter was deeded to them by a wealthy Galatan, Angelo Zaccaria. The new residence was called Ss Peter and Paul, since the friars wanted to recall their former convent at their new centre. In 1557, the Dominicans also assumed responsibility for St Benedict's church.[35]

In the middle of the sixteenth century there appeared a number of Orthodox patriarchs without the usual animosity towards the Latin church. In large measure this was due to the return to Istanbul of Greeks who had been educated at Padua and had there lost some of their prejudices. Some of these received Orders and held responsible positions in the church, becoming advisors to the patriarchs. Patriarchs Dionysios II and Joasaph II were known to be well disposed to the Latins and especially Metrophanes III, named to the patriarchate in 1565. Metrophanes, former metropolitan of Caesarea, had previously enjoyed a journey to Italy where he had visited Venice and Rome and was favourably impressed. His own clergy, though aware of his pro-Latin sentiments, took no action against him so long as Süleyman ruled.[36]

The one incident which disturbed Catholic tranquility in the Ottoman capital at this time occurred when two over-zealous missionaries of the newly founded Capuchin Order arrived in Istanbul in 1551. One was a Spaniard, Juan Zuaze of Medina, and the other a Neapolitan, Giovanni of Troia. Having met at Portiuncla in 1550 they had decided, after consulting with the head of their order, on a mission to the Turks. Contrary to the practice of the Catholic clergy in the capital, they saw their mission as an effort to convert the Muslims to Christianity. Once the Turks became aware of what they were doing, the Capuchins were arrested, beaten and thrown into prison. The Catholic community bailed them out with the understanding they would leave the city.

The Capuchins sailed off to visit the Holy Land and afterwards went to Egypt where they imprudently sought once more to make Muslim conversions, preaching in front of the paşa of Cairo. The expected happened: they were thrown into prison and left without food and water. A week later the French consul at Alexandria came to Cairo to bargain for their release, but it was too late. They were found dead in their cells; the first Capuchin missionaries had become the first Capuchin martyrs.[37]

By the end of Süleyman's reign, the Catholics inside Ottoman boundaries enjoyed relative freedom and stability in the practice of their religion. Although the Ottoman sultans, from Mehmet II to Süleyman, could have closed the capital's churches and expelled the Catholic population at a moment's notice, they did not. Toleration continued even in the face of difficult and prolonged conflicts with Western Catholic powers and almost constant papal calls for a crusade. On the other hand, for Eastern Catholics, especially the Hungarians and Bosnians, the gains made by the Turks at their expense were devastating.

2

The Ottoman attack upon Catholics in the Balkans and Greece

MEHMET II ATTACKS BELGRADE

Before the conquest of Constantinople there was a single precedent for relations between the Turkish government and a Catholic community. This was the treaty concluded between Sultan Bayezit I and Dubrovnik (Ragusa) in 1399, which allowed the citizens of that town to pay an annual tribute and recognize the sultan's sovereignty in return for local autonomy and the right of its merchants to travel freely within the borders of the empire.

Dubrovnik was completely Catholic. No Orthodox churches were permitted there and any person seeking to remain in the city had to convert to the Latin faith. Within its wall, churches and monasteries abounded. However, the aristocrats who governed the city saw to it that the church's role was kept subordinate to political interests. To ensure this, they enacted legislation which specified that no native citizen might become archbishop lest he become ambitious and busy himself with municipal affairs. The unique arrangement which the nobility enjoyed with the Turks may have been frowned upon by other Christian states, but it brought prosperity to the Dubrovnik merchants, who formed colonies in all the major cities of the Ottoman world. The continuation of their treaty of vassalage to the sultan was the cornerstone of Dubrovnik's security and it had the highest priority in the city's foreign policy. The treaty was respected and renewed by Mehmet II.[1]

The Orthodox Serbs who lived east of Dubrovnik did not enjoy the same benign treatment. After the conquest of Constantinople, Mehmet II campaigned for several years in southern Serbia, for he feared a possible Hungarian advance down the Danube. The countryside was devastated; fifty thousand captives were taken as slaves, and the Serbian upper class, already weakened by a century of conflict, was extinguished. The few nobles who survived were drafted into the Ottoman army. Djordje Branković, the Serbian despot, was left to rule a truncated state of little importance.

In 1456 Mehmet decided to attack Belgrade, key fortress of the southern Balkans, then held by the Hungarians. Alerted to the danger, the Hungarian Diet voted funds for its Danubian army commander, János Hunyadi, to recruit sufficient men to bring his companies to full strength. These preparations were further assisted by the popular preaching of Giovanni Capistrano, a Franciscan Observant who had dedicated all his efforts to the crusade against the Turks. Pope Nicholas V supported Capistrano in all his work and sent his own legate, Cardinal Giovanni Carjaval, to Pest.

In June 1456 Hunyadi led the army into Belgrade. Since he was uncertain of the size of Mehmet's forces he appealed to Capistrano to reinforce the city with men to whom he had given the cross. On 3 July, the Turkish force came within sight of Belgrade and it was clear that battle would soon be joined. On Sunday 4 July, Capistrano celebrated Mass for the defenders, offered them general absolution, and taught them the chant 'Jesus, Jesus, Jesus' to be used as a battle cry. The Franciscan's enthusiasm and Hunyadi's generalship gave the Christians victory; on 22 July Mehmet ordered a withdrawal. Throughout Europe the news spread that Belgrade was saved and that Christian arms had prevailed against the infidel. Unfortunately for the Christian cause its two heroes did not long survive; within a month Hunyadi was a victim of the plague, and Capistrano died several weeks later.[2]

THE ALBANIAN RESISTANCE

The victory at Belgrade checked Turkish ambitions for the moment, but Mehmet II had no intention of giving up his plans to occupy the Balkans. He was soon making preparations to suppress the lingering rebellion in Albania, where, after the Catholic champion Skanderbeg had raised the flag of revolt in 1443, no Turkish force had succeeded in routing him from the mountains. While most Albanians were Orthodox Christians, those in the north, speaking the Gheg dialect, had become Catholics during the Middle Ages. In the thirteenth century, when Venice controlled the town, Durrës (Dyrrachium) had been made an archbishopric.[3]

Albania had first come under Turkish attack from 1385 to 1395, but its rugged terrain had prevented effective occupation. At the beginning of the fifteenth century, Catholic leadership was in the hands of Gjon Kastriote, chieftain of the Kruijë region, and some other mountain leaders. In 1423 Gjon was forced to accept vassalage to the Ottomans and to send four of his sons to Edirne as hostages. Three of these died in captivity; the youngest, named Gjorgj, survived; he was raised as a Muslim and given a commission in the Turkish army. When only eighteen, he led an army in Anatolia, where he so impressed his soldiers that they gave him the name Iskenderbey, after Alexander the Great.

In 1443 Gjorgj Kastriote was sent with a Turkish company to fight the Hungarian commander János Hunyadi, then operating in the region of the Serbian city of Niš. The battle went against the Turks, so a retreat was ordered. During the confusion, Kastriote was able to obtain from the Ottoman imperial secretary a document which named him lord of Kruijë. With a band of loyal Albanians he then made for home. Once there he presented the document to Zabel Paşa, the Turkish governor, who turned over the fortress and town according to the orders in the rescript. Kastriote then proceeded to Kruijë's cathedral, where he renounced Islam and made a profession of Catholicism. Henceforth, as Skanderbeg, he became the leader of Albanian resistance to the Turks.

On 1 March 1444 the other lords of Albania, the Prince of Montenegro, Stefan Czernowić, and delegates from Venice responded to a call from Skanderbeg to meet at Lezhë. There they proclaimed him 'Chief of the League of the Albanian people', and voted him men and money to wage war against the Turks. While his army scarcely ever numbered more than thirty thousand men, he was able to keep the Ottomans at bay for the next twenty-five years. Three times, in 1450, 1464 and in 1467, his capital at Lezhë was besieged, but it never fell. Constantly in need of money and supplies, he sent frequent appeals to Rome and other Italian cities. The Venetians, seeing him as a possible threat to their cities in Albania, did not always help, but Alfonso of Aragon and the popes often sent money. So much was Pius II his benefactor that in 1461 Skanderbeg brought his army to Italy to assist papal forces in a conflict with the Angevins of Sicily. Pius looked upon him as the best hope of Christendom in the Balkans and prayed that his continued resistance might demonstrate to the West European princes that the Ottomans could be stopped. As long as Skanderbeg lived he fulfilled that promise; before he died on 17 January 1468 he realized that there was no one to take his place, so he left his territories to Venice.[4]

BOSNIA

The other Catholic state immediately threatened by Mehmet II
was Bosnia. Here the situation was complicated by divided religious
sentiments and claims by the Hungarian kings to be the rightful
rulers of the principality. In 1138 the Hungarian king had added
'King of Bosnia' to his titles. Possibly because of the Mongol
invasion, the Catholic bishop of Bosnia and his clergy abandoned
the region around 1230 and did not settle permanently again until
thirty years later, when Dakovo, north of the Sava River in Slavonia,
was chosen for the episcopal residence. A few monasteries and their
monks, left behind in isolation, not only lost touch with the Latin
hierarchy, but also with some aspects of Catholic doctrine. They
became known as the Bosnian church, and had their own distinct
organization and religious life. The members continued to live in
monasteries, called *hižas*, and looked to an ecclesiastical leader
known as the *djed*. The Bosnian nobles supported this church as did
large numbers of the predominantly rural population. Around 1350
when Latin clergy returned to the area they charged that the
Bosnian church was heretical, infected with Manichaeism. In fact,
those teachings considered unorthodox were probably only survivals
of pre-Christian Slavic customs.

The Franciscans were the principal agents employed to reconvert
Bosnia; they set up a vicariate and gained large numbers of converts
through their preaching. Occasionally the Bosnian kings were won
over, although the nobility and a good proportion of peasants
remained loyal to their national church.

In the early fifteenth century when the number of Franciscan
convents had reached thirty-two, Catholic proselytism increased
under the leadership of Tomaš Tomasini, bishop of Hvar and papal
legate to Bosnia. Though the king, Stefan Tomaš, professed Catholicism he delayed receiving baptism: but after several years in
indecision, he gave up his objections and even began a persecution
of his non-Catholic countrymen. In 1459 he offered the clergy of
the Bosnian church the option of choosing Catholicism or exile.
The vast majority of clergy, two thousand persons, chose conversion,
while only forty sought asylum in neighbouring Orthodox Hercegovina. This affair virtually destroyed the Bosnian church. When
Stefan Tomaš died in July 1461, he was buried in the Franciscan
convent of Stujeska.[5]

His son, Stefan Tomašević, succeeded, appearing at a time critical for Bosnia's existence when the Turks were poised to strike at his kingdom. To strengthen his hand, he sought a crown from Pope Pius II, who sent a nuncio to place it on his head at Jajce on 17 November 1461 and recognize him as 'King of Serbia, Bosnia, Hum, Dalmatia and Croatia'. Unfortunately the bearer of such a title was bound to invite action from both Ottomans and Hungarians.

Mehmet attacked Bosnia in 1463. Almost at once Bosnian resistance crumbled. Stefan Tomašević surrendered at Kljuc; he was returned to Jajce where he was beheaded and most of his nobility executed with him. Thousands of Catholics fled the country and more were threatening to leave. Their migration was forestalled, however, because of an appeal made by the Franciscan friar, Angelo Zvijezdović, who obtained from the Turkish commander in Bosnia a *firman* guaranteeing the right of Catholics to practise their faith in freedom and the recognition of Franciscan property as *mulk*, land freely held by its possessors. Yet, although the Franciscans had permission to remain and the Bosnians were allowed to practise their religion, the number of friars declined and thousands of peasants, fearful of Muslim rule, emigrated to Habsburg territory. This depopulation enabled Turks and Serbs to settle the abandoned land and so to change considerably the religious profile of Bosnia. Among the remaining Catholics conversion to Islam or Orthodoxy became frequent and it was estimated that by 1515, 150,000 Catholics had abandoned their faith.[6]

A number of Catholic prisoners were taken from Bosnia and northern Albania and brought to Istanbul as slaves. One of these was Andreas of Chios, who was accused before the Turkish authorities of having once been a Muslim. The penalty for apostasy from Islam was death, to be avoided only by a return to one's former faith. Despite the fact that Andreas had been mistakenly charged, he was tortured each day for over a week, parts of his body being cut away until the bones of his arms and legs were exposed, in order to extract from him a denial of Christianity. Yet, he remained constant: 'Do with me whatever you like; only one thing I ask, that you don't harangue me with your speeches.' At last, on 29 May 1465, he was beheaded and his body taken by the Catholics in Galata to be buried in St Mary's church.[7]

Toward the end of his life, when fighting the Venetians, Mehmet made further gains at Catholic expense. In 1477 he besieged the Venetian-held city of Shkodër (Scutari). For fifteen months the garrison held on until forced to capitulate due to exhaustion. Then

Kruijë fell and Venice was forced to recognize that further attempts to resist the Turks in Albania would be impossible. By a treaty of peace, signed in 1479, Venice turned over its Albanian territories to the sultan and ended the sixteen-year-old war.

MEHMET II AND THE CATHOLICS OF GREECE AND THE AEGEAN

After the fall of Constantinople all the Christian rulers of the small states adjacent to Ottoman borders had hastened to Mehmet's court at Edirne to congratulate him on his victory and to accept vassalage. The single exception was the delegation of the Knights of St John from Rhodes; its members claimed it was impossible for them to recognize any sovereign other than the pope. This rejection of his authority irritated Mehmet and convinced him of the need to subjugate Rhodes as soon as possible.

In 1455 the moment had arrived and an Ottoman fleet sailed into the Aegean to attack the island fortress. On the way the Muslims stopped at Chios to make a demand that the *Mahona*, the Genoese ruling body of the island, pay 40,000 gold coins to a friendly Italian merchant who claimed the Chiotes owed him this debt. When the *Mahona* refused, Turkish soldiers plundered several areas of the island, and upon embarking let it be known they intended to return. On appearing before Rhodes, the Turks found the task of taking the island too great, so they returned to Chios, which had decided to pay its obligation rather than risk a fight. In the next few years Chios kept the sultan away by agreeing to raise to 10,000 gold coins the amount of tribute paid to the government of the Porte. The Genoese on the mainland, at New Phocaea, were not so fortunate. A Turkish expedition took their city, enslaved the merchants, and brought an end to that colony.[8]

In the following year, 1456, Mehmet ordered an expedition to move against Athens, where a Catholic prince, Duke Franco Acciajuoli, held power. His family of Florentine merchants had held the city for several decades. While still a young man he had lived in the sultan's court at Edirne and there had become friendly with Mehmet; afterwards, in 1455, Franco had been allowed to return to Greece where be believed himself secure. On hearing of the Turkish advance, the duke barricaded himself in his palace, the Propylaea of the Acropolis, from which he negotiated with Mehmet's general, Omar. On the latter's promise that he might leave peacefully for Thebes, the duke surrendered the town on 4 June 1456. The Latin archbishop, Niccolò Protimo, left with him and was later appointed bishop of Chalkis, where he remained until forced once more into exile after the conquest of Euboea.[9]

When war had broken out in 1463 between Venice and the Turkish empire, one of the major issues was the lingering conflict over the possessions of the Republic in the Peloponnesus. At first the Venetian armies had been successful against the Turks; Argos and Corinth had fallen to them early in the campaign, and in July 1466 the Venetian commander, Vittorio Capello, took Athens. This marked the high point of the Republic's fortunes. Later that same year and again in 1467, while Mehmet himself was on campaign in Albania, Turkish forces won victories over the Venetians. Three years afterwards, the sultan's army invaded Euboea and invested Chalkis, the island's main city. An Ottoman force under Mehmet Paşa, a former grand vezir, blockaded the channel between Chalkis and mainland Greece with a fleet of three thousand vessels. For seventeen days the city was struck from both land and sea, then it capitulated and slaughter of the Venetians took place. Every male over eight, an estimated six thousand persons, was killed; those under age were shipped with their mothers and sisters to the slave-markets of Istanbul. The Venetian governor, Paolo Erizzo, was cut in two. His head and those of the other prominent men of the colony were displayed in the Piazza de San Francesco, the public square.

The loss of Euboea to the Turks sent a shudder through Catholic Europe since, as had happened with the threat to Constantinople, no one had believed it could happen. The Grand Master on Rhodes, Baptiste des Orsini, sent the West a description of the final battle, imploring the European princes to respond with men and supplies lest all the Catholic territory in the Aegean be lost. On 13 December, Cardinal Bessarion wrote an impassioned appeal to the Italian princes asking them to unite in their determination to fight the Ottomans. He argued that Mehmet II could never be satisfied unless he expanded his empire to its limits: 'Truly he cannot keep it unless it continues to grow, for it will decline unless he adds more territory; it will become enfeebled unless it is always increasing. What more proof does anyone need? Daily his army grows, he who already has the largest of forces – he must invade foreign lands lest he lose his own.'[10]

The loss of Euboea caused the Republic to increase its efforts

to form alliances with potential victims of the Ottomans. Throughout Italy the princes were assured that every Catholic state was
endangered, for Turkish raiding parties, operating out of Bosnia,
had already penetrated into Austrian territory in Styria. Diplomatic
missions went off to Uzun Hasan, Mehmet's most serious rival in
Anatolia, and negotiations were opened with the Bey of Alanya.
Old Venetian difficulties with Cyprus and the Knights of St John
were forgotten; a grand alliance against the Turks was envisioned.
The Venetian counterattack succeeded temporarily, but the Republic's resources were insufficient to save the Venetian empire in the
East. Without the aid of other European powers, the struggle against
the Ottomans was simply too difficult.[11]

SÜLEYMAN CONQUERS RHODES AND THE AEGEAN ISLANDS

When Süleyman became sultan one of his ambitions was the conquest
of Rhodes, since the warships of the Knights and their allies constantly preyed upon Ottoman shipping. Preparations were under-
taken in the winter of 1521 after he had made certain of the
diplomatic isolation of Rhodes. The Grand Master, Villiers de l'Isle
Adam, was alerted to the possibility of an attack when he received
a menacing note from Süleyman in the summer of 1522. Several
weeks later, Turkish ships were sighted hovering near the island.
Inside the city all preparations were made for a long siege. The
majority of the population, including the Greek Metropolitan of
Rhodes, cooperated with the Knights in strengthening the defences.

The Ottomans soon landed and their powerful cannon ham-
mered at the walls for four months, after which the exhausted
defenders, pushed to the limit of their resources, asked for terms.
Süleyman was magnanimous: he guaranteed the remaining Knights
that they could leave the island with their personal possessions.
Other inhabitants wishing to depart might also go, but as an induce-
ment, those who would remain were promised freedom of worship
and a five-year exemption from taxation. The grand master accepted
and the Knights and three thousand Catholics, including the Latin
bishop, sailed to the West. The majority of Rhodes' Greek population remained and their clergy soon transferred allegiance from
Rome to Constantinople. Upon his entry into the captured city,
Süleyman prayed in the Catholic church of St John, thus making

it a mosque. The same destiny subsequently befell all the other Latin churches on the island. For the next four centuries there were no Catholic churches on Rhodes.[12]

While Süleyman was at war with the Habsburgs, he sent his admiral, Khair ad-Din Barbarossa, to strike at Christian bases in the Western Mediterranean. But Charles V had been preparing for such an eventuality; he had taken the Knights of St John under his wing and settled them on Malta and at Tripoli on the Libyan coast. Then he had enlisted the able Genoese admiral, Andrea Doria, to lead the Christian Mediterranean army. The fleets of Barbarossa and Doria stalked each other throughout the length of the Mediterranean, stopping in enemy territory only long enough to plunder the hapless citizens. Doria landed at Methoni in the Greek Peloponnesus, sacked the town and captured the Turkish garrison of eight hundred men. Then he was aided by a Christian uprising in Koroni that expelled the Turks; later the fleet seized Navpaktos on the Corinthian gulf. All these towns had been Venetian ports and were eager to throw off Turkish rule. The Christian occupation, however, could not be sustained, and after two years an evacuation was ordered. Large numbers of the native population, Greeks and Albanians, including an Orthodox bishop, joined the exodus and were later settled in the Kingdom of Naples. Tunis, which Barbarossa had won from the Habsburgs in 1534, was retaken by Doria a year later, in a victory Charles V considered the most important ever won over the Muslims.[13]

In 1537 Süleyman sent Barbarossa into the Aegean to wrest control from the Catholic princes who had ruled those islands since the time of the Fourth Crusade. On nearly every island the Turks could count on many in the Greek majority who resented the rule of the Latin aristocracy and on a clergy alienated by Latin prelates who treated them as second-class Christians. In order to hold office, Greek priests, and bishops where they were permitted, had to acknowledge Latin superiority and pray in their Eucharist for the pope rather than for the patriarch in Istanbul. The Greeks spoke of Latin policy towards them as offering only 'a little bread but a lot of wood'.[14]

The Latin secular rulers of the islands were an inbred group living in their own villages or in certain sections of the larger towns. Their wealth came from their country estates or from shipping; their greatest problem was piracy, the scourge of the Aegean. The spiritual rulers, except on Chios, were never natives, but Italian-born prelates sent from the West to what was considered Europe's eastern frontier. Bishoprics were to be found on Naxos, Siros, Mikonos, Tinos, Thira (Santorini) and Chios whose origins extended back to the first Latin occupation. Naxos had become an archbishopric after the conquest of Rhodes in 1522 when that island's exiled hierarchy settled there.

The largest of the Catholic states in the Aegean in 1537 was the Duchy of Naxos. Conquered in 1207 by an Italian raiding party led by Marco Sanudo, the Duchy became a private fiefdom for his descendants for the next century and a half. In 1383 the Sanudi were replaced by a new dynasty, that of the Crispi, which continued to hold power into the sixteenth century. At the time of Barbarossa's attack, the ruler was Duke Giovanni II Crispo. Naxos, impossible to defend, surrendered to the Muslim fleet and in return for his confirmation as duke, Giovanni agreed to pay an annual tribute of 5,000 gold coins. He also agreed to the appointment by the patriarch of Constantinople of a Greek Orthodox bishop to the see of Naxos. Later, when a Latin bishop appeared on Naxos in 1540 without receiving permission from the Turkish authorities, he was arrested. The Ottomans wanted no one to doubt that they were in charge in the Cyclades.[15]

Throughout the following year Barbarossa pursued his policy of subordinating the Catholic islands of the Aegean to Istanbul. He razed the Cretan coastal cities and other Venetian ports. The Turkish admiral's activities at sea, and Süleyman's menacing position in East Europe, roused Pope Clement VII to form yet one more Western coalition against the Turkish menace. Calling it the Holy League, he proclaimed it in Rome on 8 February 1538.

The League's force, captained by Andrea Doria, advanced to Preveza on the Epirote coast of what was then considered Albania and attacked the city. News of its difficulties brought Barbarossa to the defence and the Christians withdrew. Venice's Adriatic ports bore the heaviest brunt and it was not surprising that the Republic was the first to sue for peace. On 20 October 1540 Süleyman signed a peace treaty according to which Venice had to turn over its few remaining possessions in the Peloponnesus to the Turks and agreed to increase its indemnity to the Porte for trade rights in Ottoman territories.[16]

SÜLEYMAN'S BALKAN CAMPAIGNS AND THE
HUNGARIAN DEFEAT

The Balkans also became a scene of serious conflict during Süleyman's rule. The sultan's goal was to capture the stronghold of
Belgrade, the fortress city which had eluded the conquest attempted
by his great-grandfather Mehmet II. On this occasion when the
Turkish armies encamped beneath its walls, the Christian defenders
of Belgrade had neither a Capistrano nor a Hunyadi. After a short
siege, in which the Serbian contingents of the Hungarian army
showed little spirit, the city fell in August 1521.

The Ottoman–Hungarian boundary was always in flux, with
Christian and Muslim feudal lords battling against each other in
interminable skirmishes. And now, heartened by his success at Belgrade, Süleyman determined to press on against Hungary, and so
forestall any attack launched through that nation by Charles V. A
further excuse for Süleyman's intervention in Hungary grew out
of the marriage of the sister of the Magyar king to the brother of
Charles V. A child born of this marriage would bring the Habsburgs to the very borders of the Ottoman state.

In 1526, as was his custom each year, Süleyman opened the
Turkish campaigning season in April, leading an army of 100,000
men and three hundred cannon out of Istanbul. Hungary, despite
knowledge of its danger, had made little preparation against an
Ottoman attack. King Lajos II rose at noon and spent the day
hunting, devoting scant attention to readying the royal army,
despite papal subsidies sent to provide increased manpower. The
bulk of Magyar forces consisted of levies furnished by the nobles,
jealous of the king's power and reluctant to commit themselves.
János Zápolya, a man of great personal ambition, was leader of
the nobles' party and *voivode* of Transylvania. Upon learning of
Süleyman's advance the king named the archbishop of Kalcosa, Pal
Tömöri, to lead the royal army of twenty-four thousand southwards.
At Mohács on 29 August the disciplined Janissaries rolled over the
Magyar foot-soldiers while concealed cannon massacred a charge
by the cavalry. In two hours, the battle was over. Lajos II, twenty-
two of the Hungarian magnates and seven bishops including
Tömöri were dead. No prisoners were taken alive; all survivors of
the Hungarian army were beheaded. Süleyman had won an overwhelming victory.

Moving on, the Turkish army occupied Buda, the Hungarian

capital, by 10 September; Süleyman made its royal castle his head-
quarters there. All churches and houses of the wealthy citizens in
Buda and its neighbourhood were plundered and many set on fire.
The famous library of Matthias Corvinus, the best in Eastern
Europe, was destroyed. The Ottoman cavalry swept through the
countryside taking whatever people remained to be sold as slaves.
Only in the far north and west did any security remain, where an
Austrian army defended the region.

Meanwhile, Zápolya's partisans, who had refused to join the
royal army, met at a diet in Tokaj and chose the *voivode* to be
their sovereign. He quickly made contact with Süleyman, promising
loyalty in return for recognition of his title. Since he did not then
contemplate permanent occupation of Hungary, Süleyman agreed
that Zápolya, like the princes in Wallachia and Moldavia, should
become a tributary. In western Hungary, however, the surviving
nobles chose a stronger candidate, Ferdinand of Habsburg, the
emperor's brother. Ferdinand's army descended on Zápolya, who
was really no match for the Austrians, and defeated him badly. At
a new diet, called at Pozsony (Bratislava) on 17 December 1526,
Ferdinand was unanimously elected King of Hungary but Zápolya
was allowed to remain in Transylvania.

In 1530 Süleyman again marched north, this time to support
his vassal against Habsburg interference. His huge army moved
through devastated central Hungary while columns of cavalry struck
into areas of southern Austria and Croatia. Süleyman's goal was to
draw out Ferdinand's army and settle the issue of Hungary once
and for all, but the Habsburg king would not give battle. Moreover
the sultan experienced an unexpected delay during the siege of a
Hungarian fortress on the Raab river, wrecking the Ottoman time-
table. The army withdrew to winter quarters without accomplishing
its mission.

Three years later negotiations between Ferdinand and Süleyman
brought temporary peace to the Danube. The Habsburg king agreed
to pay Süleyman annual tribute and to renounce his claims on
Zápolya's Transylvanian lands, provided Süleyman's attacks upon
Hungary should cease. This truce allowed both sides to fortify positions and prepare for the next inevitable conflict. Süleyman established *siphais*, Ottoman cavalrymen, in the countryside and permanently garrisoned the larger towns with Janissaries. The civilian
population of central Hungary had been practically exterminated.[17]

THE STRUGGLE FOR HUNGARY CONTINUES

At the conclusion of the War of the Holy League in 1540, for a period of months, Süleyman rested. He wanted to consolidate all of the gains he had made and to reform the administration of the Empire, but this rare interval of quiet was broken by information received that Hungary was once more endangered by the Habsburgs. His vassal Zápolya had no heir; hence the direction of the kingdom in the *voivode*'s later years had fallen into the hands of his chief minister, the bishop György Martinuzzi. It was quietly agreed by the Transylvanian nobles in concert with Martinuzzi, that upon the *voivode*'s death they would transfer their allegiance to Ferdinand of Habsburg. This plan was upset when Zápolya remarried and produced an heir whom he now wanted to succeed him. Nevertheless Martinuzzi took up residence in the royal castle at Buda in order to welcome Ferdinand.

Later in 1540 Zápolya died and the projected drama began. Ferdinand came to Hungary to be proclaimed sovereign, while Zápolya's widow and her infant son, Sigismund János, asserted their claim to Transylvania, appealing to Süleyman for aid. The sultan at once recognized Sigismund János, moved the Ottoman army into central Hungary, and annexed the area outright to the Empire, as the province of Buda, while Sigismund János' state was limited to Transylvania.

Inside Buda Süleyman installed a vezir with greater authority than any other governor of Ottoman provinces. Although Süleyman promised the inhabitants of the region that no harm would come to them, there were few Hungarian survivors. In Buda the Christians comprised only 238 families, so few that both Catholics and Protestants shared the single church left open, St Mary Magdalen. Other churches became mosques or were left to decay. When the imperial ambassador of the Holy Roman Empire, Busbecq, passed through Buda several years later, he noted that the city was in the last stages of decline, the population housed in the meanest huts and cottages. Slaves were still being exported chained together in long lines like horses being taken to the fair.[18]

Ferdinand did not accept his defeat; he continued military action until, by a peace signed in 1547, the Habsburg king relinquished claim to Buda and agreed to pay tribute to the Porte for those areas of Hungary in his possession. The final scene was played in 1551 when Ferdinand attempted to send an army into Transylvania to assist Sigismund János in throwing off his vassalage. Süleyman would not allow this to happen; his army under Mehmet Sokullu marched on Transylvania and restored Ottoman sovereignty. The next few years were marked by naval action against the Habsburgs in the West Mediterranean, but the abdication of Charles V in 1555 meant that Süleyman's principal enemy was at last giving up. His legacy was carried on, however, by Ferdinand and Charles' son, Philip II.

THE SIEGE OF MALTA AND THE CAPTURE OF CHIOS

Even in these last years, Süleyman regretted that his conquests were not finished. He dearly wanted to dislodge the Knights of St John from Malta as once he had flushed them out of Rhodes. Their ships were a menace to him at sea and a scourge to the coastal settlers of Ottoman lands. In 1565 he commissioned the admiral Piyale Paşa to sail against Malta with an armada of 190 ships and an army of 30,000 men. Once landed, the Turks pounded the Christian positions, but did not prevail. Finally months of fighting and heavy casualties had to be written off as the Ottoman fleet abandoned the siege and sailed for Eastern waters.[19]

In 1566, seeking compensation for its defeat, Süleyman ordered the navy to an easier target, the island of Chios. An excuse for intervention was provided by a delay in payment of the annual tribute owed by the Chians to the Porte. The Ottoman fleet arrived in the harbour of Chios the night before Easter. The *Mahona* invited Piyale Paşa to come ashore, only to find their guest demanding an immediate transfer of funds. The *Mahona*'s members asked for a six-month grace period, but the admiral refused; he jailed the *podestà* and twelve of the council, and ordered his army to occupy the island. He seized all property belonging to the *Mahona*, plundered two of the nine Catholic churches, and ordered several Genoese families to be taken to Istanbul as captives.

On Chios, the Catholic bishop along with several Franciscan and Dominican friars went into exile. The churches of St Mary of the Castle and Our Lady of Grace were converted into mosques and the Ottomans sent a trusted metropolitan from the patriarchate to receive the submission of the Greek population to Orthodoxy.[20]

In the spring of 1566 while Chios was being incorporated into the Ottoman domain, Mehmet Sokullu, his vezir, persuaded Süleyman to make one more march into Hungary. It was to be his last.

He died on 7 September 1566 outside the Hungarian city of Szeged, having kept intact his reputation as the greatest of Ottoman sultans.

The years extending from Mehmet II's to Süleyman's rule were ones of constant aggression against Eastern Catholic princes and nations. Pope after pope encouraged the Western sovereigns to help their brothers, but nothing could apparently be done to stir them into action. The monarchs of Western Europe were much too busy with their own affairs to be persuaded that the far-away Balkans concerned them. Much closer to home was the contest between Catholic and Protestant or between Habsburg and Valois. Eastern Christendom would have to await the settlement of these issues, and since none was forthcoming, a vast desert was created in the Eastern reaches of the Catholic world.

3

The Catholics of Armenia and Syria come under Ottoman rule

SELIM I AND THE ARMENIANS

In 1515 Sultan Selim I with the support of the Janissaries, and over the dead bodies of his brothers and their children, came to power. He at once set about an aggressive policy against the Turkoman Shi'ites in Eastern Anatolia and their patron the Persian shah, Ismail Safavi. By 1517 he had suppressed the Shi'ites and for a time occupied the Persian capital of Tabriz.

The presence of Ottoman armies in Eastern Anatolia affected principally Armenians and Greeks; the Catholics less so. The situation of Armenian Christians at this time in history presents a confusing picture because of the wide dispersion of that people throughout the Near East and the variety of cultural influences that had been at work within the nation. A majority of Armenians recognized the catholicos at Echmiadzin in the Causasus as their head, but another hierarchy depended upon the catholicos of Sis, who was ruling prelate of Cilicia and northern Syria. Two lesser catholicates existed, one at Akhtamar, an island in Lake Van, and the other in Jerusalem, where the abbot of the monastery of St James claimed the title. On his own initiative, ignoring the other Armenian leaders, Sultan Mehmet II had established a patriarchate in Istanbul. There was also a Catholic Armenian church located in Azerbaijan and Nakhichevan, whose ministers belonged to a religious order known as the Unitor Brothers, following the rule of St Dominic. At their head was the archbishop of Nakhichevan.

In the early sixteenth century the largest, most conservative and nationalistic group of Armenians followed Echmiadzin, for monastic influence was strongest in this region and contacts with other churches minimal. A smaller Cilician church recognized the catholicate of Sis, which had grown out of the eleventh-century Armenian immigration into that region. For two hundred years the Armenians

46

had enjoyed political independence here and their kingdom was an important base for Christian military activity during the Crusades. Since the Cilician Armenians had discovered that the Western knights shared their distaste for Turks and Greeks, and since both groups needed support against the Muslims, it had made both religious and political sense for Rome and Sis to reach accommodation. The catholicate at Sis had therefore operated within the Catholic community for several centuries, but in 1382 the Kingdom of Cilician Armenia was destroyed by a Mamluk invasion which left the church in tragic circumstances. For the next century Egyptians, Kurds and Turkomans took turns at despoiling the Armenians. Nevertheless, the catholicate survived, with a tenuous attachment to Rome, although by the early sixteenth century this was more a memory than a reality.[1]

The Nakhichevan Catholics had originated in the fourteenth century when a Dominican bishop, Bartolomeo of Podio, arrived in Maragheh during the time of Mongol rule. Bartolomeo lived in an Armenian monastery, where his Western education and austere way of life attracted a number of disciples. One of these invited him to his monastery of Qrna in Nakhichevan. The Armenian monks subsequently converted to Catholicism, thus forming a centre for missionary activity throughout Nakhichevan and Azerbaijan. In 1344 the Catholic Armenian monks, calling themselves Unitor Brothers, adopted the Dominican rule and dressed in the white habit of St Dominic. Bartolomeo had become archbishop of Nakhichevan in 1344 because of the strong growth of the Unitors and the congregations they served, then numbering 15,000 people. During Selim's war with Shah Ismail, Catholic Armenians, caught in the middle, suffered severe losses. During the next few decades their territory passed back and forth between Persians and Turks, and ordered religious life became extremely difficult.[2]

The depredations caused by the constant warfare on Armenian soil had also affected the catholicos of Echmiadzin. In 1547 Catholicos Stefon V of Salamas resigned in desperation over the harsh treatment of his people by Muslim rulers. He then summoned a convention of ecclesiastical and lay leaders at which it was decided to seek Western assistance in alleviating the distress of the Armenians.

Stefon himself was one of the delegation which arrived in Rome in 1548. Here, though he willingly professed his faith in Catholicism, Pope Paul III could do little more than offer him moral support. Back in Echmiadzin, he encouraged his successor, Mikael of Sebastea,

to continue the dialogue with Rome. In 1562 Mikael sent a second
delegation to Rome. It had three members: Abgar of Tokat, his son
Sultan and a priest, Agheksanter. They carried a profession of the
Catholic faith by the catholicos, a list of the churches and monasteries
of his jurisdiction, a copy of a medieval forgery which recounted a
meeting between Pope Sylvester and the Armenian apostle, Gregory
the Illuminator, and a letter imploring the pope to come to Armenia's
assistance. The catholicos confided to Pope Pius IV, 'the time is near
when we will be freed from captivity through your efforts'. He also
sent gifts to the pope: relics of St Theodore, a ring, a cross, and a
vial of Holy Myron, the sacramental oil consecrated on special
occasions. Abgar was to learn the customs of the Latins so that he
might teach them to the Armenians.

Pius IV, delighted by his conversations with the Armenians, made
up a delegation to Echmiadzin and also to the Catholic archbishop
of Nakhichevan. A Maronite bishop from Cyprus was put in charge;
he was to make sure of the orthodoxy of the Armenians before reconciling the church to full communion. The mission was dispatched
to the East, but nothing more is known of it, for it evidently never
reached its destination. Abgar, on the other hand, went off to
Venice where he had the Armenian psalter printed in 1566; it was
not the first book printed in Armenian, but it was an accomplishment
significant in the history of Armenian letters.

SYRIAN CHRISTIANS

Having disposed of the Turkoman revolt and checked the Persians
on his frontier, Selim now turned to settle with the only other
Islamic power in the East Mediterranean, Mamluk Egypt, ignoring
that its sovereign, Kansawhal-Ghawri, had been strictly neutral in
the conflict between the Ottomans and Persians. The most serious
threat to Egypt at that time, the presence of the Portuguese in the
Red Sea, was an irritation to Selim also, and it is likely that one
factor in his decision to attack Egypt was the conviction that his
own army was better equipped to repeal the Western Christians.
The war with the Mamluks began when Selim struck Dulkadir, one
of their vassal states. Sultan al-Ghawri mobilized his army and
marched northward to meet the Turks outside Aleppo in Syria. On
24 August 1516 battle was joined; the Egyptians were crushed and
the sultan killed.

Selim's conquest of Syria and Lebanon meant that the three

Syrian Christian churches were now incorporated into the empire: the Melkite, distinguished by acceptance of the seven ecumenical councils looked upon in the East as Orthodox and in communion with the patriarch of Constantinople; the smaller Jacobite church, which recognized only the first three councils and was regarded by the Melkites as monophysite, therefore heretical; and a still smaller Maronite church, based upon Mt Lebanon and in full communion with Rome. Each church had its own patriarch and hierarchy, though all were now Arab-speaking and all followed the ancient liturgical rite of Antioch. Together they represented about thirty per cent of the total population of Syria and Lebanon, where, during the slow, steady erosion of Christian communities, the Muslims had become a majority around 1400.

Under the Mamluks, the Melkite patriarchs had continued to reside in Antioch, whenever conditions permitted, despite the decline in population of their see. At the time of the Turkish conquest, however, the patriarch Dorotheos II was living in Istanbul. His successor, Joachim III, returned to the Near East only in 1530, but he changed his residence to Damascus after Antioch had been once more destroyed in 1529. In the early sixteenth century there were twelve Melkite bishops in Syria and one in Diyarbakir, while in Palestine and Jordan Melkites were the only Eastern Christians to be found. Two monasteries fell within the patriarch's jurisdiction: Balamande in Syria and St Saba in Palestine. From the few extant records of this period it is possible to learn that heads of the Melkite church were always in communion with Constantinople and sometimes in correspondence, if not in union, with Rome. At the Council of Florence the Melkite church was represented by a delegate, but Patriarch Dorotheos was ambivalent about the council's actions. His successor, Michael IV, however, renewed communication with Rome, and his delegate, Archdeacon Moses, had been received by Pope Pius II in 1460 and returned to Syria carrying letters of mutual recognition. His successor, Theodoros, also corresponded with Rome. It is probable that at the time of Selim's conquest some of the Melkites considered themselves in union with Rome.[3]

The position of the Syrian Jacobite church was somewhat different. This church, formed from Syrian dissenters from Chalcedon, originated in the fifth and sixth centuries. Byzantine persecution was pushing the church toward extinction, when it was saved, almost single-handedly, by the bishop Jacob Baradaeus, whence the name, 'Jacobite'. Jacob was a Syrian monk in Constantinople when called to the episcopate in 542. For the rest of his life he travelled back and forth through Syria and Mesopotamia consecrating bishops and providing a clergy for his church. The head of his community was called patriarch of Antioch, but could never live there, even during his church's greatest prosperity in the Middle Ages. Due to contact with the Franciscan friars in Syria an episcopal delegate of Patriarch Ignatius IX had come to Florence in 1444 and had there accepted a reconciliation with Rome. But, plagued by factions and by losses to Islam, the church was no longer strong when the Turks occupied Syria. Ignatius XII Noah was patriarch at that time, living at the monastery of Dair al-Za'fran, near Mardin, which had become the usual patriarchal residence. As with the Melkites, communion with Rome was hardly a vital consideration in 1516.

It was an altogether different story with the third Syrian church, the Maronite. The Maronites take their name from a late fourth-century hermit whose tomb was located on the Orontes river near ancient Apamaea (Qala'at el-Mudig). The grave became a shrine and by it a monastery was built, Bait-Maroun, to guard the relics. The monastery grew so large as to provide the neighbourhood with a religious identity all its own. During the fifth and sixth centuries, the monks and the people they served were noted for their Chalcedonian convictions, but in the seventh century they adopted the Emperor Heraklios' monotheletism. After the Arab conquest of the Near East, the monks of Bait-Maroun were further isolated from the rest of Christendom, and around 740 they began speaking of their abbot as 'patriarch of Antioch' since from 702 to 742 the Melkite patriarchate was vacant. Naturally, once the Melkite patriarchate was restored, efforts were made, but unsuccessfully, to integrate Bait-Maroun into the orthodox church.

Another event occurred in the eighth century which proved to be of special significance in Maronite history. Exhausted by Bedouin raids and Muslim armies, Maronite clergy and people began to emigrate from their exposed position on a major road leading to Damascus, to seek shelter on the northern slopes of Mt Lebanon. The first recorded monastery on the mountain, St Mammas, was founded in 749 at Idhin. The immigration continued until practically the whole of the Maronite community had settled on the mountain or on Cyprus. The old monastery of Bait-Maroun was destroyed in the tenth century.

At this time the Maronite situation forced the church to develop its own peculiar type of religious and civil authority. At the head of all Maronites an abbatial patriarch enjoyed absolute ecclesiastical and political authority. His seven or eight synodal bishops, also abbots of monasteries, enjoyed no independent power. They were simply patriarchal assistants. Civil authority was delegated by the patriarch to the heads of the feudal landowners of the mountain, the *mouqaddamin*.

Maronite isolation from the Christian world was complete from the ninth to the eleventh centuries. Then into their seclusion came the Western Crusaders, Catholics from France and other lands of Europe, and suddenly the Maronites discovered Christians who were not hostile to them. The Latins were equally pleased to find that the Maronites, although different in language and culture, did not consider them heretics. When the County of Tripoli was set up in 1107 by the Crusaders, the bulk of the Maronites were included within its boundaries. Finally, in 1181, William of Tyre records, the patriarch and his church of forty thousand members came to Antioch and there, before the Latin patriarch, Amaury de Limoges, pledged allegiance to the Catholic church of Rome and its head, Lucius III.

Rome was naturally pleased with this turn of events. For centuries the popes had had no inkling of the existence of the Maronites, but immediately the bond between the churches was sealed by correspondence. When the Fourth Lateran Council was summoned by Pope Innocent III in 1215 a special invitation was sent to the Maronite patriarch to come to Rome. Patriarch Jeremiah al-'Amshiti received a pallium from the pope and a letter confirming him in his office.[4]

Unfortunately for the Maronites, the Crusaders were not to remain a power in the Near East. Mamluk and Turkoman raiding began in the late thirteenth century. From 1289 to 1291 the Western Christians were forced back from the coast; Acre, the last Latin fortress, fell to the Mamluks in 1291. This brought an end to the Crusading period and the Maronites were left to fend for themselves. Many who had taken up city life now fled back to the isolation of mountain villages, but were not always secure even there. Kisrawan, the major Maronite region, was devastated; its monasteries, churches and villages were attacked time after time.

While the Mamluks ruled, the Maronites suffered intermittent persecution. The Turkoman tribe, Banu 'Assaf, was made their policeman, charged with keeping them under surveillance and seeing to it that their taxes were paid. In addition, the Druzes, a heterodox Islamic sect which had also settled in Lebanon to find security from persecution, began to exercise a kind of feudal sovereignty over the Maronites in their midst. During these years of isolation only the rare visit of a wandering Franciscan or Dominican from the Holy Land kept alive the contact between the Latin Church and this small church of the Near East.

In the fifteenth century official contacts between Rome and the Maronites were renewed. Pope Eugenius IV sent a Franciscan friar to invite Patriarch Yuhanna of the Maronites to come to the reunion Council of Florence. The patriarch declined the invitation but assured the papal envoy that the Maronites would agree to whatever was decided for the good of Christendom. He asked the Franciscan to tell the pope he would like to receive a pallium such as his predecessor had worn and to receive recognition of his title from Rome. In October 1439 the pallium arrived.

These embassies exchanged between Rome and the Orient brought suspicion upon the Maronites. The Mamluk governor of Lebanon ordered his soldiers to destroy the monastery of the patriarch, then at Miefuq; Yuhanna had to flee to a Maronite settlement in the Kadisha valley where he established his residence in the monastery of Qannubin. This move made communication with Rome still more difficult, but intrepid Franciscan couriers continued to pass back and forth between patriarch and pope.

In 1455, when the popes were seeking allies against the Ottomans, a Flemish Franciscan named Gryphon was entrusted with the Lebanese mission. Once a doctor of theology at Paris, Gryphon was a master linguist and had already served many years in Palestine. For almost twenty years he travelled the paths of Mt Lebanon, everywhere encouraging monks and people to hold tightly to their Roman allegiance. He was a good friend of Patriarch Butrus al-Hadithi who always supported his efforts.[5]

Later in the century, Gryphon's Franciscan successors convinced a Maronite monk, Jibra'il ibn al-Qila'i, to go to Rome for theological studies – the first of his church to travel to the West for an education. In Rome he mastered Latin and learned as much as he could of Western theology and canon law. With this knowledge, he began translating some of the major religious works of the Latins into Arabic and in subsequent centuries these translations became the basis for the Latinization of the Maronite church.

In 1492 the patriarchate was assumed by Shim'un IV ibn-Hassan, like his predecessor a native of Hadith. Despite the urging of the Franciscans, for many years he did not seek either the pallium or confirmation of his election from Rome. Only in 1513 did he finally dispatch an envoy from Beirut to ask Leo X for recognition. The patriarchal message arrived while the Fifth Lateran Council was in progress, and pope and bishops, having almost totally forgotten the Maronites, requested that more information about their church be forwarded to Rome before they would take action.

In response to this request, Shim'un sent a formal profession of his Catholic faith to Rome on 8 March 1514. It was accepted by the curia and two delegates were dispatched to Lebanon to bring Shim'un the pallium and confirmation of his office. The delegates, Gian-Francesco da Potenza and Francesco da Rieti, were charged not only to recognize the patriarch but also to remind him of Rome's displeasure that the Maronites had not conformed with Latin practice on the conferring of Baptism and Confirmation. The papal mission returned to Rome with three Maronites who were introduced to the Council and apprised of its work. It was at the time of the Ottoman conquest, therefore, that close relations between Rome and the Maronites were revived.[6]

At the time Selim occupied Syria, a group of Druze chieftains appeared before him in Damascus pledging him their support. At their head was Fakhr ad-Din al-Ma'in, lord of the Shuf region. The sultan confirmed them in their possessions, requiring only that the tribute they had formerly paid the Mamluks should now go to him. This meant that the local Christians were also left undisturbed by the conquest and the Maronite *mouqaddamin* remained in control in the villages. Patriarch Shim'un, also, could continue his patriarchal rule as before, although his authority received no recognition from the Ottomans.

SYRIAN CHRISTIANS DURING SÜLEYMAN'S RULE

The conditions of Syrian Christianity did not appreciably change during the rule of Selim's son, Süleyman. While the ordinary Melkite Christian layman was indifferent to Catholicism, party strife and family ambition so frequently marked the hierarchy's activity that it was always possible to find, at that level, groups favouring Rome. Patriarch Joachim IV was to be accused of being favourable to Catholics after he made a long journey visiting the churches of Poland. The Antiochene hierarchs were at a great disadvantage since their sole means of access to the government in Istanbul was through the patriarch of Constantinople. This meant that the Greek clergy of Istanbul, rather than native Syrians, were at the centre of power, and saw to it that Greek interests were served.

In 1555 a movement towards Rome was initiated within the Syrian Jacobite church. At that time the patriarch, Ignatius Ya'kub XIV, sent a priest, Musa of Mardin, to Rome to have some of the Syriac liturgical books printed. While there, Musa made a profession of faith before Pope Julius III. He found a patron in Ferdinand of Habsburg, who paid for the publication of the New Testament, the first book ever to be published in Syriac.

A few years later, in 1560, Ni'matallah, patriarch of the Jacobites, dispatched Bishop Yuhanna Cacha to Rome with a letter affirming that he sought to be in communion with Rome and to conform his faith with that of the Latin church. Trusting the patriarch's sincerity, letters were returned with Yuhanna welcoming Ni'matallah to the Roman communion.[7]

Throughout Süleyman's time the Maronite patriarch was Musa Sa'adah of Akkari, elected to that office in 1524. Musa sent his aide Antun, archbishop of Damascus, to carry news of his election to Rome, and to return with the pallium and certificate of recognition. But Antun's ship was taken by pirates; and having lost everything he arrived in Rome happy to be alive. Without his official documents and unable to communicate very well with the cardinal who was commissioned to deal with him, Antun returned to Lebanon empty-handed.

In 1557 Musa summoned what has become known as the first council of the Maronite church. He used the occasion of the consecration of the Holy Oil at Rizqallah to call an assembly of eight archbishops, four hundred priests and a large number of Maronite chieftains. He still lacked the pallium and confirmation from Rome, since no one was anxious to take on the risks of the journey until a Cypriot priest, named Jirgis, volunteered to go to Italy. He arrived in 1567, obtained both the pallium and decree of confirmation, but betrayed his trust by presenting a forged letter from the patriarch asking the Roman authorities to name him to a bishopric. They complied; Jirgis was consecrated and sent back to Lebanon as a bishop, but along with the patriarchal gifts was included a profession of faith for Musa to sign and return to Rome.

Needless to say, the patriarch was doubly upset, both because of Jirgis' uncanonical consecration and the implied doubts about his orthodoxy. The rest of his patriarchate was overshadowed by Musa's feelings that his leadership was looked upon unfavourably at Rome. He died in 1567, outliving many popes, and Sultan Süleyman himself by a year.[8]

THE ORIGIN OF THE CHALDEAN CHURCH

During Süleyman's reign, Ottoman authority was extended over the whole of Iraq. In the northern part, modern Kurdistan, lived a Christian community which had its genesis in the fifth century. Its proper name is the Church of the East. However, since the members of this church shared the theological view of Nestorius, the patriarch of Constantinople accused of heresy at the Council of Ephesus, their opponents have always called them Nestorians. Their own writers correctly point out that Nestorius had had nothing to do with the founding of their church, which arose among the Syrian population of Edessa (modern Urfa), whose theological school had also rejected the decisions of the Council of Ephesus. The main Christological doctrine of the Church of the East makes a distinction between Jesus who is man, suffers and dies, and the Logos, who is God. The fathers at Ephesus contended that this theology created a human person in Jesus and destroyed the unity of Christ, the God-man.[9]

The Edessan theologians migrated into Persian territory rather than change their views, and eventually persuaded the Persian Christian church to accept their opinion. A separate head of the Persian church, called the catholicos, was established at Ctesiphon, and bishoprics were set up throughout most of Mesopotamia and Persia. At the time of the Islamic conquest, the Church of the East flourished all the way to Korea, with centres in most major cities of Central Asia as well as in India. Once Baghdad had become the capital of the Abbasid caliphate, only one Christian chief was allowed in the city's walls. This was the catholicos of the East.

In the thirteenth century, the Christians of the Church of the East were, for the first time, made aware of the church of Rome when Dominican friars arrived in their midst. For a century and a half intermittent messages passed back and forth, but then came their church's overwhelming destruction at the hands of the Mongol chieftain, Timur. Almost overnight the Christians were reduced to a handful of survivors who retreated into the security of the triangular area between the Tigris, Lake Van and Lake Urmia. Here they organized themselves into fiercely combative mountain tribes.

At the time of the Council of Florence, representatives of their church from a small community on the island of Cyprus appeared in Italy and subscribed to the council's decrees. Those who joined the Catholic communion at that time were given the name Chaldean by Pope Eugenius IV.

Because of their isolation, the Christians of the Church of the East developed some unique liturgical and administrative customs. Among these was the tradition of hereditary succession to church offices, a practice which extended to the catholicate itself late in the fifteenth century during the catholicate of Shim'un III Basidi bar-Mama. Since the catholicos was always required to be a monk, hereditary succession in this case meant passing on the leadership to a nephew in the bar-Mama family.

In 1551 the catholicos Shim'un V died, survived by only one nephew, a boy of eight years. Three of the metropolitans of the church who were to be his consecrators rebelled at giving the leadership of the church into such immature hands. They assembled a synod of like-minded clergy and notables at Mosul, and, determined to break with tradition, chose Yuhanna Sulaqa, abbot of the monastery of Rabban Hormizd, located near Al-Qosh, to be catholicos. Meanwhile the metropolitans following the hereditary principle acclaimed the young nephew of the former catholicos as Shim'un VI Denha. Faced with double leadership, the supporters of Sulaqa decided on an appeal to 'the Western fathers' to legitimize his election

Sulaqa, with three notables and a party of seventy made their way to Jerusalem where they met with the Franciscans. The friars were assured that what the group wanted was to profess the faith held by Rome and receive approbation of Yuhanna's election. The Franciscans provided the party with a letter claiming that 'we are orphans, without father or guide or anyone to lead us, not even a metropolitan, but only two or three bishops. We do have a kind of patriarch but for a hundred years no one has been made metropolitan unless he is from his family and kin, or his relations, and for a hundred years to the present, his family has unlawfully determined that this must be the rule.' Sulaqa and one noble left for Rome while the rest of the party returned to Iraq.

The two reached Rome in November 1552, announced the purpose of their journey, and were examined by church authorities on the soundness of their faith. Pope Julius III appointed a commission, which, after some time, satisfied itself that Yuhanna had been elected legitimately and that his faith was orthodox. At a public consistory held on 20 February 1553 Sulaqa made a profession of his Catholic belief and promised to recognize the pope as his ecclesiastical superior. The record in the Vatican archives reads, 'since all the Oriental people of Assyria, both clergy and laity, according to their ancient custom, have acclaimed for their patriarch the monk Simon Sulaqa, superior of the house of Hormizd, of the order of St Basil, in the diocese of Mosul', he may now take his place as head of the church, 'since Simon Mannae, of blessed memory, is deceased'. There was no mention that Sulaqa had a rival or that the method of his election had violated tradition. Yuhanna was consecrated bishop on 9 April by Pope Julius himself, who later bestowed the pallium on him and the title 'patriarch of Mosul'. This, the first investiture of an Eastern catholicos by a pope, made the Chaldean church a direct beneficiary of Roman initiative.

Sulaqa left Rome for the Near East accompanied by two Maltese Dominicans. They reached Diyarbakir in November 1553, and were welcomed. The catholicos moved on to Mesopotamia, and during the following months created five metropolitans, thus providing a hierarchy for the Chaldean church.[10]

The partisans of Shim'un VI Denha were chagrined at the schism created in the Church of the East. They prevailed upon the paşa of Diyarbakir to summon Yuhanna Sulaqa for an investigation. The unsuspecting prelate was put under arrest, tortured, and finally strangled. His body was tied in a sack and thrown into a river in January 1555.

Upon his death, the Chaldean church rallied behind one of his metropolitans, 'Abdiso' (Ebedyeshu'), and proclaimed him their new head. Several years later, following in the footsteps of his predecessor, 'Abdiso' took the long journey to Rome for confirmation of his title. Here, in separate ceremonies in 1562, he received the pallium and recognition of his title. Pope Pius IV suggested he might like to visit Trent, where the Latin bishops were now in council, but 'Abdiso' preferred to return to his congregation in the Near East. He lived the rest of his life, until 1578, in the monastery of St James the Recluse.[11]

Paradoxically the Turkish occupation of Syria and Iraq proved a boon to Catholicism in those regions. It brought new people and new ideas into a world marked by lethargy before the arrival of the Ottomans, and, in spite of itself, allowed Christianity to make progress there. Christians who wanted to contact Rome were permitted to do so, and by such contacts Catholic influence spread over a much wider area than it had ever done before. A new Eastern Catholic church, the Chaldean, had been established and the ties between Rome and the Jacobites opened up the possibility of significant gains for the future.

4

The Ottoman advance into Palestine and Egypt

THE TURKS IN PALESTINE

Several months after his victories in Syria, Selim I had led his armies into Palestine. Jerusalem was taken in early December 1516, and his troops were in Gaza by the end of the year. The occupation of Palestine involved the Ottomans with the Latin Catholics located in Jerusalem and Bethlehem, whose antecedents extended back to the Crusaders' Kingdom of Jerusalem. The clergy was composed of Franciscan friars, first established in Palestine in 1219, when they were assigned to the Church of the Holy Sepulchre.

The Franciscans of the Holy Land flourished, along with several other orders, so long as the Latin Kingdom of Jerusalem was extant, but upon its destruction, were ousted with the Crusaders. Only a few years elapsed, however, until they and the Dominicans were able to return with the permission of Mamluk authorities. The Franciscans were sponsored by Robert of Anjou and Sancha of Aragon, king and queen of Naples, who promised to pay the expenses of twelve friars to go to Palestine and remain there as guardians of the Holy Places. The Mamluk sultan offered them the site of the Cenacle and two chapels on Mt Zion. Subsequently, other properties purchased by donations from Western Christians were obtained on Mt Zion, and in 1341 the Franciscans returned to the Holy Sepulchre. Five years later they took possession of the grotto of the Nativity in Bethlehem and later extended their custody to Gethsemane.[1]

Throughout the two hundred and fifty years of Mamluk rule, the Franciscans had difficulties in maintaining custody of the Holy Places. Rapacious governors and unruly soldiers continually menaced the lives of the friars. Little wonder that the Palestine Franciscans developed a siege mentality which caused them to guard their churches with fierce tenacity.

Most of them came from Italy and a few from Spain. They were headed by a Custodian; under him was an advisory council which assisted in daily administration. In addition to their liturgical activities, the friars provided a hospice for Catholic pilgrims and served as guides to the Holy Places. Their work was supported by alms from the Christian princes of Europe, especially the kings of France.

Within the decade prior to the Ottoman conquest, the French monarch Louis XII had shown renewed interest in the Holy Land, dispatching two ambassadors to Cairo. These were to seek from the Mamluk sultan guarantees for Catholic possession of the Holy Places and their recognition as protectorates of the French crown. Catholics were also to have free access to the shrines in Melkite or Armenian possession. The Mamluk sultan agreed to this arrangement, hence at the time of the Ottoman conquest the Franciscans were enjoying a rare moment of peace. When Selim arrived, the Franciscans, under Custodian Zenobius of Florence, were confirmed as protectors of the Holy Sepulchre and Mt Zion, and, according to one source, the sultan donated 500 gold coins for their support. Selim, following earlier Ottoman policy, ordered that the Melkite hierarchy should enjoy precedence in the Holy Land, and guaranteed the possession of their monasteries and churches.[2]

Since Palestine was economically poor, the Ottomans were principally concerned to protect the shrines sacred to both Islam and Christianity and to keep open the pilgrim road to Mecca. It was difficult for Ottoman officials to provide good government due to their inability to check the excesses of local officials or to curb Bedouin raiders on the eastern frontier. In Bethlehem, for example, the marble which had covered the walls of the Church of the Nativity since Justinian's time was torn off by Muslims who claimed it was needed for the Haram-es-Sherif mosque in Jerusalem. In the following century, the roof of the chapel lost its lead and the Franciscans had to stand by in silence at the despoliation of their shrine. Christian pilgrims still came to Jerusalem, but the fees charged for their entry escalated, the revenues so gained going to pay the salaries of professional reciters of the Koran.[3]

THE CONQUEST OF EGYPT

Selim's success in Syria and Palestine had not assured him of complete victory over the Mamluks. He was willing to negotiate terms with the governor, Tuman Bey, but Tuman foolishly sought to decide the matter by force. Leading the Ottomans across the Sinai, Selim met and vanquished him on 23 January 1517. Tuman Bey was taken prisoner and then executed; Ottoman control was extended over Egypt, and the Caliph, religious head of all Sunnite Muslims, who had been living in Cairo, was sent by sea to Istanbul, the new Islamic capital. In acknowledgment of the passing of leadership to Selim, the governor of Mecca surrendered the keys of his city to him.

The Christians of Egypt now became part of the Ottoman world. As had happened to Christians in Syria and Palestine, their lot under the Mamluks had often been extremely hard while, at other times, they enjoyed long periods of peace with the Muslims. Always there was insecurity, so, as in the Levant, social pressure and hopes of bettering their position led many to abandon their Christian faith and accept Islam.

The largest of the Christian communities was the Coptic church, distinguished by its native Egyptian population and its doctrinal position in opposition to the Council of Chalcedon. The Coptic patriarch, with the title of Alexandria, lived in Cairo and sought to avoid notoriety during Mamluk times. Bishops and clergy were forced to make large payments to the Mamluks for church appointments, so the church remained extremely poor. In all affairs, social or religious, the Copts were extremely conservative.[4]

The activist policy of Pope Eugenius IV toward the Eastern churches in the early fifteenth century had included the Copts. After centuries of isolation the Roman and Egyptian churches renewed contact as a result of the pope's letter of invitation to the Coptic patriarch Yuhanna XI to come to Florence. The patriarch had declined the invitation to attend in person, but did send a delegate, the Abbot Andreah of St Anthony's monastery. Andreah went to Florence, addressed the council fathers in Arabic, and agreed to sign a document, *Cantate Domino*, restoring relations between Rome and Alexandria, simply demonstrating what he considered to be good manners. But, at the time of Selim's conquest, the Copts had completely forgotten about union.[5]

There was also a small Melkite church in Egypt, ethnically Greek, with a patriarch in communion with his brothers of Antioch and Constantinople. At the time of Florence, the Franciscan envoy to the Copts also called upon Philotheos, Melkite patriarch of Alexandria. Like his Coptic counterpart he declined to come to Florence, but cordially agreed to whatever might be done there and promised that henceforth the pope's name would be commemorated at the Eucharist.[6]

The Latin faith was represented in Egypt by French, Catalan and Venetian merchants who had come there to trade. The Mamluk sultans had given them special privileges, capitulations, which guaranteed them security in this alien land and allowed them to own small churches served by the Franciscans from the Holy Land. Before Selim returned to Istanbul he renewed these capitulations. The Latin Catholics lived in Egypt for the sake of profit. Most were young men without families who intended to spend only a few years in the Orient before returning home. Their interest in religion was not high. For them, the Sunday Eucharist was more a social than a religious event, which allowed them to learn the latest news from Western Europe, and to discuss the arrival and departure of ships and the prices obtained for cargoes.[7]

SÜLEYMAN'S POLICIES IN PALESTINE

In the sixteenth century, the small Latin community in Palestine suffered a number of reverses in its effort to retain its shrines. At the very outset of Süleyman's sultanate, rumour had it that he intended to oust the Franciscans so that, in an ecumenical gesture prompted by apprehension, the friars temporarily transferred their rights to the Armenians. Once that threat had passed, in 1523 new problems arose over the alleged discovery by some Muslims of King David's tomb directly under the Church of the Cenacle on Mt Zion. Pressure was put on the Franciscans to leave their Mt Zion convent and they were accused of want of respect for the sacred place, but at that time they succeeded in holding on.

The high point of the year for Latin Catholics in Palestine came during Holy Week when the Franciscans conducted a great procession into Jerusalem, the Custodian riding an ass. Pilgrims were amazed at his courage, for Muslims sometimes attacked the group and pulled the friar from his mount. On Good Friday, the reenactment of Jesus' journey to his crucifixion along the *Via Dolorosa* also brought out Muslim hecklers.[8]

The native Arab-speaking Melkite church came to be governed by Greeks at this time. In 1543, Germanos, a native of the Peloponnesus, was named by Istanbul to the Jerusalem patriarchate. He took up residence in the Greek Orthodox monastery of Ss Constantine and Helena and there formed a Confraternity of the Holy Sepulchre, the Agiotaphites, in membership entirely Greek. The overt purpose of the Confraternity was to guard the Holy Places held by the Orthodox, but Germanos saw to it that only his country-men should hold positions of importance in the church of Jerusalem. To this end, he constructed the Agiotaphite constitution that stipu-lated that only Greeks hold the position of Melkite patriarch of Jerusalem.

Germanos was bitterly opposed to the Latins and lent his aid to the local Muslim campaign to force the Franciscans from the Church of the Cenacle. In 1551 patriarch and Muslims succeeded; the lower storey of the Church of the Cenacle became a Muslim shrine and a *shaykh* with his dervishes moved into the buildings. Four years later, after the Franciscans had made repairs in the Holy Sepulchre, Germanos demanded that they be ousted from here, too; later, he sought to expel them from Bethlehem. His patriarchate opened a conflict over the Holy Places which to this day has not been resolved.[9]

A JESUIT MISSION TO THE COPTS

In the sixteenth century the city of Rome had its share of Oriental churchmen who came to the West, some in permanent exile, others on embassies or alms-raising ventures. Their costumes and language marked them as exotic creatures, and many of the Roman clergy were apt to believe almost anything they said. One such was a Coptic cleric named Ibrahim who appeared in Rome announcing that he was an emissary of Jibra'il VII, Coptic patriarch of Alex-andria. He convinced large numbers that the Copts were anxious for communion with Rome and in response Pope Pius IV dispatched the first Jesuit mission to Egypt.

Two members of the Society were chosen for the task: Cristobal Rodrigues and Giovanni-Battista Eliano. Rodrigues was a Spaniard who had entered the Jesuits in 1554; Eliano had a quite different background. He was born Elias, of Jewish parents, in Alexandria. His association with the foreign merchants there apparently led him to accept Catholicism and proceed to the West, where he eventually joined the Society in 1551. As a student of Oriental languages he was an obvious choice for a mission to his native land.

In November 1561 the two Jesuits arrived in Alexandria, where, under the protection of the Venetian consul, they proceeded to the residence of the patriarch in Cairo expecting a hearty welcome. Instead they met with but cool courtesy and an indifferent offer by the patriarch to discuss their mission. It was obvious that Jibra'il had no intention of changing his religious views on Chalcedon or Rome's authority in the East, but for several months the Jesuits doggedly pursued their task. At last they made their way back to Alexandria, where Eliano was imprisoned on charges that he was an apostate. After his ransom by the Catholic merchants, the Jesuits sailed out of Alexandria only to suffer shipwreck on their way back to Rome, adding one more frustration to their journey.[10]

By the time of Süleyman's death, Catholic prospects in Palestine and Egypt were hardly promising. The Franciscans had been undisturbed in their shrines for centuries only because they could count on the local Muslim respect for keeping past agreements. The change in leadership of the Melkite church now brought a more aggressive foreign Greek hierarchy to the fore and threatened their security. Centuries of conflict were to follow this development. In Egypt, a Catholic mission met with failure, hardly surprising when missionaries from Europe confronted the Coptic world-view, nourished by years of isolation and self-containment.

PART II

---

*The golden age of
the missions*

5

The growth of French influence in Istanbul

THE CAPITULATIONS

In the autumn of 1556, when the army bearing the corpse of Süleyman reached Belgrade, his heir, Selim II, came to pay final respects to his father and receive the homage of the troops. To gratify the soldiers, especially the Janissaries, Selim distributed a bonus to each man, a dangerous custom which, once begun, could never be omitted by his successors.

The politics of Istanbul were dominated in the early part of his reign by Mehmet Sokullu who held the office of grand vezir. He, in turn, was supported by the financial power of several wealthy Sephardic Jewish families of the capital, especially Doña Gracia and her son Joseph Nasi. Another, less influential group, dominated by the sultan's principal wife, opposed Mehmet Sokullu and sought to increase Venetian interests over French in Selim's council.

Since Sokullu hoped to revive the French alliance, inoperative since the death of Francis I, new talks were commenced between the vezir and the French ambassador in Istanbul. These resulted in an agreement known as the Capitulations of 18 October 1569, the first of a long series of such agreements between Paris and Istanbul which made France the most important ally of the Turks as long as the Empire existed. The implications for the future of Catholicism in the sultan's domain were most important, for under the shield of the Capitulations it was possible for the church to send missionaries into Ottoman lands to provide for Catholic Christians.

Charles IX of France, Selim's contemporary, employed Claude du Bourg as his negotiator at the Porte. This ambassador skilfully gained privileges which, while appearing to be part of reciprocal agreements, were actually heavily weighted in favour of the French. They granted extensive trading rights to France, permitting its merchants and ships to go wherever they pleased in the Ottoman state without interference or payment of custom duties. Any other European merchantman flying the French flag was granted the same right. The 'Franks' were guaranteed freedom of worship and permitted to employ sufficient clergy to make religious services available to all Catholic merchants and diplomats. The French ambassador and the various consuls scattered throughout the Empire were to monitor the behaviour of Ottoman officials in this regard. Finally, the status of the king of France was elevated to the level of 'brother' of the sultan, far ahead of all other European heads of state.[1]

The Capitulations placed the French ambassador to the Porte in a commanding position in matters involving Catholics, overshadowing the Venetian and Genoese officials who had previously served in that capacity. Henceforth when Catholic bishops needed a *berat* of appointment, they looked to the French envoy to procure it, and, very often, to provide the fees – always necessary for attainment of any office in the Ottoman world. If a church official had a grievance, this was also transmitted to the Porte by the French minister. Since these concessions allowed French merchants to settle in Balkan and Near Eastern cities the influence of the Latin church reached into areas never before entered in the Orient.

France and the Ottomans were brought together because of their common fear of the Habsburgs. Over the years the Turks would capitalize on the division between the two principal Catholic powers in Europe, to ensure that no united crusade would be possible. Thus Selim II attacked Cyprus in order to add it to the Empire, judging that efforts to save the island for Christendom would collapse over rivalries in Western Europe. The formation of the coalition composing the Christian fleet at Lepanto, therefore, came as a surprise.

More than even Pope Pius V could have hoped for, the fall of Cyprus brought a concerted response from the usually disorganized members of the Holy League. The conscience of the West had been outraged when it learned of the heroic defence of Famagusta, the last Venetian stronghold of the island. In the autumn of 1571 the League's navy, commanded by Don Juan of Austria, the son of Charles V, sailed into the Mediterranean. It reached the waters off Patras in the Peloponnesus to find that the Ottoman navy had anchored in Lepanto (Navpaktos) for the winter. Many of the Ottoman sailors, a majority of them Greeks, had already been dismissed, yet the Turkish admirals decided to contest the sea with the Christians.

The battle took place at the mouth of the Corinthian Gulf on 7 October 1571. The Christians, more numerous and better led than the Turks, won the day; there were thirty thousand Ottoman casualties but only nine thousand Christian. Upon the announcement of victory the *Signoria* of Venice went to St Mark's in joyful procession, all the city bells ringing. Three days of holiday were proclaimed and an arch of triumph crowned the Rialto bridge. Pope Pius V was so elated that he began planning a crusade to retake Jerusalem.[2]

However, the significance of Lepanto was seriously exaggerated by the Christians. It did not mean that Turkish naval power was permanently damaged; on the contrary, Ottoman losses were made up within a year and the Turkish fleet, as strong as ever, was at sea again in 1572, raiding the coasts of Italy and Sicily and capturing Tunis from an independent Moroccan ruler. Philip II had to withdraw his fleet in order to seek out the French or Dutch whom dynastic politics made more dangerous than the Turks; Lepanto's victory was never pursued.

Venetian euphoria soon turned to reality as the Republic was left to carry on alone against the Turks. Shortly afterwards, Venice, without a struggle, lost the important city of Bar on the Montenegrin coast when its commander, upon the threat of a Turkish siege, took the garrison out of town. The four Catholic churches and the thirty monasteries and convents were all plundered. The archbishop was captured and put to death. In March 1573 the Republic sued for peace and the Holy League collapsed. Venice accepted the loss of Cyprus and promised an increased tribute to the Porte in return for permission to retain its remaining trading privileges.[3]

THE FORMATION OF THE GREEK COLLEGE IN ROME

Prodded by his interest in the East and his hopes that the battle of Lepanto signalled a new era for Christians in the East Mediterranean, Pope Gregory XIII set about making Rome a centre of Hellenic studies once more. Leo X's sixteenth-century college – whose goals had been dictated by humanistic concerns – survived only a few years. Gregory XIII, on the other hand, had a much more practical aim for his Greek college; he wanted it to train missionaries for the Ottoman Empire now that French protection made that task so much easier. Recruits would come from both

Latin and Greek-rite Catholics of the islands, and possibly from the
Orthodox as well. He had formed a commission of three cardinals,
entitled '*de rebus Graecorum*', in 1573 specifically to study the
Greek situation and advise him on the matter. Without doubt the
formation of the college grew out of the commission's deliberations
as well as the order to print twelve thousand Greek copies of the
catechism of the Council of Trent.

The college opened in November 1576, its endowment established
with the bull of confirmation two months later. It occupied a building on the Via Babuino beside the church of St Athanasius, where
it still stands. The Jesuits declined an invitation to staff it on the
grounds of an already great involvement in other missions and a lack
of personnel. As a result the four cardinals who made up the
directorate chose one of their members, Giulio Antonio Santori, to
be in charge with the title of protector. He, in turn, delegated his
authority to the first rector, a secular priest, but personally drew
up the college's constitution.[4]

The opening of the Greek College was a landmark in the history
of Rome's efforts to win over the Orient. Here for the first time
Greek students from the East were trained in Western Catholic
traditions. Some welcomed the experience and were assimilated;
others, once they had left Rome, rejected it completely. In the next
century the alumni of the college, both Catholic and Orthodox,
were scattered throughout the Ottoman world, with results dependent on how little or how much each individual had received from
his Roman education; for although the Greek College produced
the papacy's strongest promoters, it also graduated some of its
strongest enemies.

POPES AND PATRIARCHS

After the death of Süleyman, Patriarch Metrophanes' Catholic
sympathies were no longer ignored. Members of the synod and
several powerful laymen, especially the Kantakuzenos family,
thought he departed too far from the anti-Western tradition of his
predecessors, and he was ousted from the patriarchate in 1572.

His successor, Jeremias II Tranos, was a native of Larissa and an
accomplished church leader. Shortly after his accession, Jacob
Andreae and Martin Kraus, Lutheran theologians from Tübingen,
wrote to him explaining Protestant views on Christian theology.
The letters were conveyed to the patriarch by the Protestant chaplain

to the Habsburg ambassador at the Porte, Stephan Gerlach. Jeremias making no response, the Lutherans wrote again in November 1574. This time Jeremias replied, expressing his belief that there were serious differences between Orthodox and Lutheran points of view. Nevertheless, over the next few years, a lively correspondence continued between them. Jeremias later confided to Pope Gregory XIII that he had 'rightly judged the Germans to be heretics'.[5]

Gregory XIII was anxious for Jeremias' cooperation in promoting his favourite project, the new calendar, so he paid great attention to the Oriental churches; nothing since Eugenius IV's invitation to the Eastern churches to come to the Council of Florence is comparable. For the difficult journey to Istanbul the pope chose Pietro Cedulini, bishop of Nona on the Dalmatian coast; Cedulini was to meet Jeremias and tell him of the new calendar and to make a visitation of all the Latin churches in the Balkans and Anatolia. He would be the first apostolic vicar appointed for such a formidable task since the fifteenth century. Despite difficulties in obtaining passage to the Orient, he arrived in Istanbul in October 1580 and remained until April 1581.

Cedulini stayed with the Franciscans in Galata as he pursued his visitation. His meeting with Jeremias went well. The patriarch brought the matter of the calendar before the synod, but it was rejected there and the Orthodox patriarchate continued to follow the Julian calendar. Jeremias wrote to Gregory explaining his church's position, and sending him a relic, the finger of St John Chrysostom, in token of his esteem. Despite its rejection by the Eastern churches the Gregorian calendar came into use in Rome from 15 October 1582. It was adopted by the church of Constantinople, with modification, only in 1924.[6]

In 1579, after angering the synod, Jeremias found himself ousted and excommunicated while his predecessor, Metrophanes, returned. The ouster had lasted only a short nine months when Jeremias took up his duties as patriarch a second time, but once more, with the connivance of officials at the Porte, he was rejected, though he again returned in 1587. It was during his third term in office that he travelled to Moscow to seek funds for his hard-pressed church in Istanbul. Having arrived when Boris Godunov was acting as regent for Tsar Fedor, Jeremias was invited to make the Russian capital the patriarchal see for all Orthodox Christians. In January 1589, after many long months of consideration, he agreed to allow Metropolitan Job of Moscow to take the patriarchal dignity, while he returned to Istanbul. The patriarchate of Moscow dates from this time; so too the disaffection of the Ukrainian hierarchy towards Jeremias, which led to its union with Rome in 1596.

CATHOLIC LIFE IN CONSTANTINOPLE

The number of Catholics in Galata declined during the rule of Murat III, who succeeded Selim II in 1574. Economic prosperity had shifted to the Atlantic, and Italian merchants no longer made fortunes in the Orient. Many of the old Galatan families had left for Italy. According to Cedulini there were still three churches in Istanbul proper and nine in Galata, but the total Catholic population was only five hundred citizens and five hundred freed slaves. He counted six hundred merchants temporarily in the Ottoman capital from Western Catholic countries, plus one hundred people on the staff at the French and Italian embassies. By far the largest group of Catholics, as many as two thousand, were slaves, prisoners of war or captives from piratical raids along the Mediterranean coasts. Of the total Greek population only seventy-five, emigrants from the islands, were Catholic.

The Galatans told Cedulini that their greatest lack was a school. Promising forty ducats to pay for their expenses, the chief officer of the *Magnifica Communità*, Bernardino Frediano, asked 'in the name of all', that Jesuits be sent to Istanbul.[7]

When the British traveller, Harry Cavendish, visited the Ottoman capital in 1589, his reflections on the city were negative:

> ...I se yt evell buyld and inhabitants rude and proud and veary malyshyous toward Crystans, tearming of them doges and offering them many abuses. Many them wear so malyshyous to Crystans that they would not sell us ther ware but waft us from them wythe ther hand.[8]

Anti-Christian sentiment was partly the result of apocalyptic warnings circulating among the Muslim masses predicting dire happenings at that time. Many dervishes and *shaykhs* forecast doom since Christians still existed both inside and outside the Islamic world, a doom about which the superstitious Sultan Murat III was easily convinced. The Franciscans bore the brunt of the popular agitation. One was tied to a cross outside St Francis'; later several were imprisoned on the excuse that they had aided a Christian slave to escape. In 1585 St Francis, the largest church in Galata, was closed.

This had been foreshadowed when a Catholic procession, led by the French ambassador Jacques de Germingny, was forced back to the church as a result of hostile crowds. St Anne's, the small chapel on the grounds of St Francis, and the church of St Sebastian were also threatened, and only the strongest protests by de Germingny preserved them from confiscation. The Orthodox suffered, too; the patriarchal church of Pammakaristos was transformed into the mosque of Fetheye Cami, so named by Murat III because of his victories over the Persians in Azerbaijan.[9]

THE FIRST ARRIVAL OF THE JESUITS AND CAPUCHINS

Acting upon the Galatans' request for educators, Pope Gregory XIII and the Jesuit general, Claudio Aquaviva, agreed to dispatch five members of the Society to Istanbul in 1583. At the head of the mission was Giulio Mancinelli, a priest, who was accompanied by two other clerics and two brothers. They took possession of the church of St Benedict, which the *Magnifica Communità* transferred from the Dominicans. Soon, with assistance from both the French and the Venetian ambassadors, the Jesuits opened their school and began preaching at St Benedict's. A very valuable memorial, *Concerning the Mission of the Fathers of the Society of Jesus Sent by Gregory XIII to Constantinople from the Year 1583 to 1586,* composed by Mancinelli after his return to Italy, provides documentation for the event.[10]

The memorial begins by describing the impression made on the Jesuits by the large number and varieties of Christians found in the Ottoman capital. Each had its own distinctly garbed clergy; there were even some clergy who apparently had no congregations whatever. There were wandering bishops who administered the sacraments, ordained priests and performed marriages without the least concern for faculties or jurisdiction, something shocking to the Tridentine mind. Mancinelli claimed that monks were a plague in the city and that the married clergy spent all their time caring for their wives and children. He could discover only one Greek and seventeen indigenous families in the whole of the Catholic population at the capital.

Despite his pejorative view of the Oriental clergy in Istanbul, Mancinelli commented favourably on the efforts of the churches to provide basic education for the young people. General religious

instruction he found insufficient, consisting as it did of stories
about the saints with emphasis on the miraculous and little concern
for accuracy. Catechism, as taught in the West, did not exist.
Faith, the Jesuit noted, was kept alive by the Eucharistic liturgy
and the frequent feasts and fasts. Churches were dirty, vestments
torn and old, yet Sunday Eucharists were well attended. Mancinelli
regretted that some Orthodox churchmen were more anxious to use
the power of excommunication than to administer the sacrament of
penance.

The Jesuit liked Patriarch Metrophanes, whom he described as
a 'modest man with a good reputation'. Metrophanes had told the
Jesuits, in secret, that he believed the pope to be the 'true supreme
head of the whole church of God', and had promised to forward a
profession of Catholic faith to Rome. Mancinelli received similar
assurances from Patriarchs Michael VII and Joachim IV, both
former heads of the Melkite church of Antioch, and from many
other bishops and monks. When Mancinelli and another Jesuit
were on a return visit to Rome in 1583, pestilence struck the city
and the remaining three missionaries died, wiping out the first Jesuit
establishment in Istanbul.

At their general meeting in 1587 the Capuchins also agreed to
recommence missionary activity in the Orient. Four Italian friars
volunteered to go to Istanbul, whence a request for chaplains had
come from the new French ambassador, Savary de Lanscome. Once
in the Ottoman capital they were given a house next door to the
ambassador's and were counted as official members of his staff – a
fiction which allowed them freedom to travel. In less than a year,
two, one of whom was the superior Pietro della Croce, were dead
from pestilence, while the others, falling foul of popular prejudice,
had been arrested. In prison, one of these, Giuseppe de Leonessa,
was strung up on ropes and suspended for three days while a slow
fire burned beneath him. Finally he was cut down and he and his
companions were ordered to leave the city. The Capuchins' mission,
like that of the Jesuits, had ended in failure.[11]

THE MISSION OF LEONARDO ABEL TO THE
EASTERN CHURCHES

Paralleling the commission of Pietro Cedulini to the Greek church,
Pope Gregory XIII sent another emissary, Leonardo Abel (Abila),
a Maltese fluent in Arabic, to the heads of the Oriental churches

to promote the new calendar. Abel, consecrated titular bishop of Sidon, began his journey in 1583.

Abel's first destination was Diyarbakir to meet with the Syrian Jacobite church hierarchy. He carried with him letters and reports from the former patriarch, Ni'matallah, who had come to Rome seeking refuge from his persecutors. During his tenure in the patriarchate Ni'matallah had been so harassed by problems in his church that he had appeared before the Ottoman governor of Diyarbakir to announce his conversion to Islam. The Jacobite community was, of course, shocked by his apostasy, and his brother Ignatius Dawud Shah quickly took over his office. But Ni'matallah found no peace as a Muslim, and in 1577 he fled for sanctuary to Pope Gregory in Rome. After an examination by Cardinal Santori he was recommended to the pope as a sincere convert who should be admitted into the Roman communion. It was due to information supplied by this Ni'matallah that Bishop Abel felt confident he knew the Jacobite situation well. Abel had brought a pallium to confer on Patriarch Ignatius Dawud since he understood that the latter wanted union with Rome. When Abel arrived in Diyarbakir, however, Dawud Shah would not even meet with him. The monastic community, where the patriarch lived, had decided that the purpose of the papal delegation was 'to change their faith and to condemn their holy fathers', and they would have none of it.[12]

At last, however, a delegate was sent by the patriarch to meet Abel in the monastery of Mar-'Abiahi near Gargar. Abel delivered his message from Ni'matallah and told the Jacobite that their former patriarch had made a profession of faith. Then documents concerning the decisions of the Council of Chalcedon were examined by Abel and the Syrian. On examining these the Jacobite delegate became outraged, especially when he read that Dioscoros, the chief proponent of monophysitism at Chalcedon, was a heretic: 'Dioscoros excommunicated! He is not damned, but a saint and the chief father of our Jacobite church!' he cried. Abel brought up the issue of accepting the Gregorian calendar, only to have the Jacobite profess the need for greater study on the issue. At this point, reports filtered into the monastery that Abel had brought arms and money to start an insurrection, and Turkish authorities began to grow anxious. This provided an excuse for adjournment of the meeting and for the Roman mission to move on, the pallium still in Abel's baggage.[13]

Abel travelled on into Kurdistan, where several Chaldean Catholic communities were located. He was never able to meet the catholicos Shi'mun IX, since Shi'mun lived in the Mar Hanna monastery in Persian territory. Abel sent him a pallium, vestments and liturgical ornaments and received in return his profession of Catholic faith.

The Roman party did reach the catholicos of the Church of the East, who lived in the monastery of Rabban Hormizd, outside Mosul. Catholicos Iliyas V welcomed Abel and agreed to sign a statement of belief composed by himself and his counsellors. This was dispatched to Rome by a personal messenger, 'Abd al-Masih, but when examined there it was considered unacceptable and communion between Rome and the Church of the East remained only a hope.[14]

Abel's next visit was to the catholicos of Sis; here at last he obtained some success. Before the visitation, Catholicos Khatchatour had corresponded with Gregory XIII, addressing him as 'sovereign pontiff of Rome, courageous and vigilant pastor of pastors, you who are made chief of the flock, who hold the place of the holy apostles Peter and Paul, the honour of all Christians'. It was his successor, Azarias of Tchougha, who met with Abel. Their talks were harmonious; Azarias recited for Abel a prayer he had himself composed: 'Deliver us from the tyranny under which we live, then we shall become Latins; you may guide both our bodies and souls, and we shall do whatever you say.'[15]

At the end of their discussion, the catholicos signed a profession of the Catholic faith in the presence of four bishops of his synod. Abel, in return, offered him funds for the repair of his churches and told him, to his delight, of Gregory XIII's plans for an Armenian college in Rome. So encouraged was Abel by this meeting that he thought that, were it not for Ottoman opposition, all Armenians could be won for Catholicism. In fact, Azarias was later called to Istanbul to face charges of having betrayed his church by signing Abel's profession of faith.

The Roman envoy also sought to communicate with the Catholicos Krikor in Echmiadzin, but the war along the Persian frontier precluded a personal visit. Abel believed that the Armenians served by the Unitors of Nakhichevan were the strongest Catholics in the Orient; unfortunately, the Unitors were now so few that in 1583, just before Abel's visit, the archbishop of Nakhichevan had the order directly incorporated into the Dominicans.[16]

When Abel sought out the Melkite patriarch of Antioch, he was proceeding on the supposition that this prelate was in communion with Rome. Such was certainly the view which Antonio Possevino, Jesuit expert on the eastern churches, had expressed in Venice: 'The patriarch of Antioch recognizes the primacy of the pope and asks for confirmation of his office.' Possevino was referring to Patriarch Michael VII and, in fact, when Abel found him in retirement at Aleppo, he willingly declared his loyalty to the Catholic church and the pope.

It was a different story, however, when the papal nuncio met with the then ruling Melkite patriarch, Joachim V. Their talks took place at Aitakh, a village outside Damascus. Joachim argued that he had never heard of any council of Florence; he 'marvelled' at the decisions taken there, and confessed no action could be taken on the Gregorian calendar until the other patriarchs were consulted.

Abel recognized that he had got nowhere with Joachim, but he was consoled by his welcome in Tripoli, where members of the Melkite church gave him a good reception and respectfully listened to his views. Seven laymen signed a letter, written in Arabic, for him to take back to Rome, in which they professed that their 'Catholic-Orthodox' faith was identical with that of the papal envoy. They excused Joachim for the rebuff he had dealt Abel, noting that he was under tension due to the appearance in Istanbul of a rival who was seeking to unseat him.[17]

In Egypt Abel met with the Coptic Patriarch Yuhanna XIV. He had already been host to a Catholic visitor when the Jesuit Giovanni-Battista Eliano had passed through Egypt a second time, two years earlier, on his journey home from Lebanon. Abel persuaded Yuhanna that the Catholic faith and Gregorian calendar should both be accepted, and the patriarch agreed to summon a synod in Babylon, Cairo's suburb to the south, to study the matter.

The meeting in Babylon proved to be a stormy one, with a large number of the bishops wanting nothing to do with the proposed changes. Yuhanna died in the midst of the deliberations, and Abel and his companions were placed under arrest for disturbing the peace and had to be ransomed by Coptic merchants. Needless to say, nothing of their work with the Copts remained. Abel returned from Egypt to Rome in 1587 after a four-year absence. His effort to contact all the Oriental churchmen he could find was accomplished, although with disappointing results. At least he had learned that signatures on professions of Catholic faith in the Orient meant very little to the signers, even if they counted for a great deal in Rome.[18]

THE PLANS OF POPE CLEMENT VIII

When Clement VIII ascended the throne of St Peter in 1592 he brought with him a strong interest in the Eastern churches. He dispatched numerous delegations to the hierarchy there, exhorting them to communion with the Roman see and possible alliance against the Turks. The Serbs, Maronites, Copts and Armenians were all recipients of his embassies. His interest was whetted by the success of the negotiations between Rome and the Ukrainian episcopate which culminated in that church's corporately joining Rome at the Union of Brest in 1596. To further missionary activity, Clement established a 'Congregation for the Affairs of the Holy Faith and the Catholic Religion' with Cardinal Giulio Santori at its head. It was the predecessor to the Congregation for the Propagation of the Faith.

The pope was especially concerned to preserve Catholicism among the Greeks. He forwarded generous sums to the Aegean bishoprics and urged the Jesuits to establish more Eastern foundations on the model of their house on Chios. One of Clement's plans was to win over the Ottoman grand vezir to Catholicism. This was Cagalazade Sinan Paşa, a Genoese originally named Scipione Cicala, who had been taken prisoner in a raid on the Italian coast and brought to Istanbul where he converted to Islam. He had risen rapidly through the ranks of the Ottoman civil service until he reached the pinnacle of the Turkish bureaucracy. It would be a noteworthy success for Christendom if this man could be won back to his original faith, so Clement sent two members of the Cicala family who were Jesuits along with his brother to Naxos, where, it was hoped, the delicate conversations necessary for the reconversion were to take place. The Cicalas brought with them an emotional letter from his mother appealing to him to return to Italy. Contacts were made with the vezir, but none bore fruit. Sinan remained a Muslim and the commander of the Ottoman armies on the Persian front; he died, still faithful to Allah, at Diyarbakir on 2 December 1605.[19]

THE FRENCH ASCENDANCY

The latter part of the sixteenth century saw France and the Ottoman Empire come closer in their interests. Frequent consultations took place between the French ambassadors and the officials of the Porte. Charles IX had appointed François de Noailles ambassador in 1571, a remarkable choice since de Noailles was a cleric, bishop of Acqs, and the first Latin ecclesiastic to reside in Istanbul since the thirteenth century. In 1581 the ambassador de Germigny, an extremely vigorous man, had succeeded in representing French interests by obtaining, first, reconfirmation of the earlier Capitulations, and then, still more concessions. The renewal came at an opportune moment, for new rivals to the French had appeared in Istanbul when British merchants had sailed into the Golden Horn.

Henry IV's ambassador was the able Savary de Brèves. Due to his efforts the church of St Francis was reopened and a renewal of the Capitulations was signed in 1597. Church authorities in Galata acknowledged French predominance, assigning de Brèves a special seat of honour in front of the whole congregation at Sunday Mass. Once begun, this tradition, although several times contested, remained in force until 1914. In 1599 de Brèves was instrumental in warding off a new Orthodox attack on the Franciscan position in Jerusalem's Church of the Holy Sepulchre. His timely intervention with Ottoman authorities in Istanbul preserved the Catholic holdings.

When war broke out again between the Habsburgs and the Turks at the end of the sixteenth century and continued into the sultanate of Ahmet I, de Brèves' gains were consolidated and a new draft of the Capitulations was agreed upon in 1604. Article V confirmed the earlier privileges given to Catholics:

for the honour and friendship of the king we declare that the religious who live in Jerusalem, Bethlehem and other places may continue to serve the churches which have been built there as in times past, and may reside there in safety, and may come and go without any difficulty or hindrance and shall be well received, protected, helped and made secure under all circumstances.[20]

The year after the signing of the Capitulations, the Austrian war ended with the treaty of Zsitvatorok; this allowed the Ottoman vassal Istvan Bocsaki to rule in Transylvania and recognized Turkish sovereignty over Moldavia and Wallachia. The Habsburg emperor was to be recognized as 'brother' of the sultan. After this, Ottoman–Habsburg relations improved, and in 1616 the Emperor Matthias was granted his own Capitulations. The articles in this document regarding Catholics were similar to those of the French grant with the exception of a special clause concerning the Emperor's protection over the Society of Jesus. This permitted the Jesuits 'to build churches in our domain, to read the gospel there and perform the divine services according to their customs'. Though the Jesuits had only one church in Istanbul and one on Chios, they never took advantage of the permission. They realized that any attempt to exercise the religious rights there designated would rouse violent resistance in the Muslim community.[21]

GALATAN SOCIETY IN THE EARLY SEVENTEENTH CENTURY

The early seventeenth century was a time of friction between the Galatan laity and the clergy who resented their authority. The *Magnifica Communità*, heading the Galatan community, often sought to have the dominant voice in matters which were beyond its competence. Thus in 1606 it protested against the adoption of the Gregorian calendar and sought to delay its implementation. In 1608 the Dominicans at SS Peter and Paul requested and received a *firman* which made the French ambassador their protector to escape the vexations of the local procurators. Nor did the complete prohibition of intermarriage between Orthodox and Catholics issued by the patriarchal vicar, Guglielmo Foca, do much to endear him to the Catholic laity of the capital.[22]

Travellers to Galata at this time were always impressed by the wealth of its merchants, by the shops and warehouses, and the numerous taverns serving wine and arak. Latin and Greek women were sumptuously dressed in Turkish fashions with silks and jewels. They used cosmetics extensively and, according to Pierre Lescalopier, 'spent all their wealth on clothes, wore many rings on their fingers and jewels in their hats, most of which were false'.[23] The same traveller recounts how the religious life of the city reflected contemporary Italian spirituality: the magnificent Corpus Christi procession typically provided an occasion for lavish street decorations. Most Catholic men, sent out by companies in Italy and France, left their families at home, so Galatan society was male-oriented and both its pleasures and its business centred around the embassies. The British observer George Sandys noted that the Galatans 'live freely, and plentifully, and many of them will not lie alone where women are so easily come by'. It was possible to purchase a wife from Greek Christian families who sent their daughters to Istanbul from the islands. Sometimes these unions lasted only as long as the tour of duty which kept the Western merchant in the Turkish capital; others were permanent, the children being considered 'Franks'.[24]

Life was usually pleasant, although attacks from fanatical Muslims sometimes occurred and sudden changes in Ottoman foreign policy always had to be expected. The difficulties of dealing with Turkish officials required patience and generosity in the matter of 'gifts'. Indeed, most of the ambassadors' work consisted in sorting out problems which arose between Turkish bureaucrats and Western merchants.

THE RETURN OF THE JESUITS

For many years Henry of Navarre had been the champion of French Calvinism, but ambition to become king of France had dictated his conversion to Catholicism in 1594. For a year longer he remained excommunicated, but was then absolved by Pope Clement VIII. Henry had always considered the Jesuits as agents of the pope and of Habsburg Spain so it was not until September 1603 that he allowed the Society to return to France. No sooner were the Jesuits reconstituted than their novitiates filled with earnest young men. After only seven years there were forty-five Jesuit houses and 1,300 men enlisted in the Order.

At Henry IV's behest, the French ambassadors to the Porte, de Brèves and, after his recall, Jean de Gontant-Biron, baron de Salignac, sought the Porte's permission to introduce Jesuits as French embassy chaplains in Istanbul. In 1608 the Turks agreed and Henry personally selected five members for the appointments, placing François de Canillac in charge. Before the Jesuits left France, the king met them and outlined what he considered the duties of their assignment.[25]

The Jesuits left Paris for Italy on 21 January 1609, then travelled to Istanbul with stops at Corfu, Mikonos and Chios, and reached the capital in early September. Ambassador de Salignac was on holiday but on hearing of their arrival he immediately sent members of his staff to provide whatever they needed. The French were alone in welcoming the Society, for the Venetian *bailie*, the English ambassador, and even the bishop of Tinos, then serving as apostolic visitor to Istanbul, were all disturbed by the appearance of Jesuits in their midst.

The French were protectors of St Sebastian and St Benedict, two Galatan churches, and hoped they would be available to their protégés. The former Jesuit mission had used St Benedict's, but now, although the church stood empty, the bishop of Tinos – to the disappointment of de Canillac – would not allow them to use it, and the smaller St Sebastian's was made their headquarters. When de Salignac returned from his holiday, he escorted the Jesuits to the camp of Grand Vezir Murat Paşa to present them as the new French embassy chaplains. Murat gave them a cool reception, saying he already knew too much about the Society to give them any welcome.

Immediately, de Salignac let it be known that he intended a complete break in diplomatic relations if his chaplains were ousted. The grand vezir relented, the Jesuits remained, and the next few months saw their situation improve considerably. St Benedict's was transferred to them and there the services – conducted in Italian in the morning and French in the evening – began to attract large congregations.

While working with individual Orthodox Christians, the Jesuits never lost sight of a more ambitious goal, the corporate union of the Greek church with Rome. While in retrospect such an aim appears to have been impossible, the Jesuits were enthusiastic in their attempt to win over the heads of the Eastern Christian churches, thus preparing the way for the reestablishment of full unity between the churches.

At the time of their arrival in Istanbul, the Greek Orthodox patriarch was Neophytos II. He was favourably disposed to Catholicism, having quietly dispatched a profession of faith to Rome on 1 August 1608. His predecessor, Raphael II, had also been in secret correspondence with Rome as a result of conversations held with Ioannis Mendonis, a Catholic from Chios. Mendonis was an alumnus of the Greek College in Rome whom the patriarch had welcomed to Istanbul and established in a Galatan church. De Canillac, the Jesuit superior, and Neophytos were on excellent terms and the patriarch told him that he wished to send his nephew to the Jesuit school, but hesitated for fear of possible public reaction.

In the autumn of 1610 the Jesuits lost their great patron when ambassador de Salignac died. The Ottoman authorities ordered their arrest and they remained in confinement until the next ambassador reached Istanbul. This was Achille de Harlay-Sancy, only twenty-five at the time of his appointment, but considered an excellent choice by the court officials of Louis XIII. One of his first tasks was to obtain the release of the Jesuits.

By 1612 the Society's work was again in progress and Neophytos II even invited the priests to concelebrate the Eucharist with him at Epiphany. They were also able to make many friends among the

Armenians. In addition, the influence of Mendonis continued to rise; the patriarch gave him permission to preach in all the Orthodox churches. De Canillac noted 'he is very much loved and respected and openly preaches the Catholic truths, not without regret on the part of some of the Greeks'. Later, however, de Canillac had to report that the Holy Synod ordered him silenced and Kyrillos Loukaris, then holding the office of Melkite patriarch of Alexandria, had him excommunicated.[26]

Despite this setback to the Catholic cause, the Jesuits remained optimistic; late in 1612 de Canillac returned to the West to persuade the papacy and the French court to increase their number. He wanted Jesuit houses, financed by the French, in all the major Ottoman cities. Pope Paul V and King Louis XIII encouraged him, but his superior-general, Claudio Aquaviva, regarded the proposal as too ambitious.

Neophytos II died in January 1612, and for twenty-one days the patriarchal office was held by Kyrillos Loukaris as *locum tenens*, after which time the synod rejected him for Timotheos II, former metropolitan of Patras. In 1615 de Canillac could write to Aquaviva that the patriarch had privately confided to him that he accepted the Catholic faith and recognized the pope as head of all Christendom. Timotheos excommunicated Loukaris because he was believed to have converted to Calvinism.

A dramatic change in the Catholic fortunes in the capital occurred in the summer of 1616 with the appointment of a new grand vezir, Halil Paşa. Seeking to disrupt the advance of Catholicism and the spread of French influence, Halil charged that a captured Polish officer had escaped from Seven Towers prison with the assistance of employees of the French embassy. Furnished with information handed to him by the Venetian *bailie*, Halil Paşa ordered the arrest of Harlay-Sancy and all of his staff. The Jesuits at St Benedict's were herded into prison on the unlikely pretext that they were in contact with Russian Cossack forces in the Ukraine and the Habsburg emperor. They were also charged with having secretly baptized Muslims, an accusation which was probably true. The sweep of Catholics extended even to the patriarchal vicar, the Franciscan Giovanni-Battista Sangallo, who was thrown into prison and died there, drowned or strangled by his guards.[27]

KYRILLOS LOUKARIS, PATRIARCH OF CONSTANTINOPLE

The stage was now set for fresh confrontations between the various powers seeking to determine the future of the Greek Orthodox church. In 1620, a new ambassador, Philippe de Harlay, Comte de Césy, had been sent out from Paris to demand full satisfaction for the Catholic losses and for the insult to the former ambassador, a task he ably accomplished. Césy befriended the Orthodox patriarch, Timotheos, and counted him a friend of France. One evening in the autumn of 1620, Patriarch Timotheos dined at the house of Cornelius van Haag, Dutch ambassador to the Porte. A few hours later he was dead. Césy was convinced that Timotheos had been poisoned, his death part of a conspiracy hatched by van Haag and the English ambassador, Thomas Roe, to win the patriarchate for their ally, Kyrillos Loukaris. He was proved correct in the latter assumption, for on 4 November Kyrillos was chosen by the synod to become patriarch once more.[28]

Kyrillos Loukaris was the most interesting of all those who held the Greek patriarchate in Ottoman times. Seven times elected and seven times deposed, his fortunes reflected the turbulence surrounding leadership of the seventeenth-century Greek church. He was born 13 November 1572 in Candia (Iraklion), Crete, and like many other bright young Cretans went for his university education to Italy. After taking orders he joined the staff of the Melkite patriarch of Alexandria, Meletios Pegas, in 1595. This involved him in the work of the patriarch who was then the most prominent Orthodox polemicist in the Ottoman world. He was sent to the Ukraine by Meletios as Orthodox spokesman during the negotiations which preceded the entry of the Ukrainian church into communion with Rome.

Despite what must have been a strong commitment to Orthodoxy, Kyrillos moved to a pro-Catholic position after succeeding Meletios as patriarch of Alexandria in 1602. On 28 October 1608 he addressed a letter to Pope Paul V including a profession of faith and a pledge of obedience to the Roman church: 'We want to adhere to the head and to live and work most obediently under your authority.'[29] But this flirtation with Catholicism soon passed and by 1620 no one doubted his anti-Roman sentiments. Césy lamented, 'Soon after he was established, he began sewing the evil doctrine of Calvin and several other heresies.' Sir Thomas Roe, on the other hand, rejoiced that

The patriarch of the Greek church here is a man of more learning and witt than hath possessed that place in many years, and in religion a direct Calvinist; yet he dares not shewe it: but it were an easy worke upon any alteration here, to settle that church in a right way...[30]

On the other side, the French ambassador sought, with the aid of the Jesuits, to enlist against Kyrillos the pro-Catholic members of the synod. These were grouped around Gregorios, metropolitan of Amasia, excommunicated when Kyrillos got wind of the plot. The grand vezir, Huseyin Paşa, was told that Kyrillos, in league with the Muscovites, intended to hand over the island of Chios to the Jesuits. The English ambassador's Anglican chaplain was aware of the Catholic attempt to replace Kyrillos by Gregorios, so that he 'should little by little save the Romish doctrine, and privately subscribe the pope's universality, and in tyme subject the Easterne church wholy to his holyness'.[31]

Kyrillos' downfall was finally achieved when Césy paid Huseyin Paşa an amount which Roe said was equal to £40,000. In the spring of 1623, Kyrillos was dismissed and ordered into exile on Rhodes while Gregorios of Amasia replaced him. Gregorios lasted a brief two months. He proved to be incompetent, but, more damagingly, could not raise sufficient funds to make the required 'gifts' to the Porte's officials. He was replaced by Anthimos, metropolitan of Adrianople, who not only had Latin sympathies and therefore enjoyed French support, but also had the necessary financial resources. But the Dutch ambassador also had funds for rewarding Ottoman officials and Anthimos' tenure, in consequence, was short. In October 1623 he abandoned his office for the security of the French embassy and Kyrillos Loukaris, thanks to van Haag, returned in triumph, while Césy vowed to continue fighting him to the 'last dropp of his bloud'.[32]

THE CAPUCHINS COME TO THE ORIENT

The reign of Louis XIII in France coincided with an outpouring of Catholic zeal unknown in that nation since the thirteenth century. The reforms of Trent had borne fruit in all areas of religious life, especially in drawing recruits to the Jesuits as well as to the second great missionary order of the day, the Capuchins.

The architect of the French Capuchin advance into the East was Joseph le Clerc du Tremblay, whom history knows as 'the Grey Eminence' because of his influence at court during Richelieu's time.

Born into a noble family in Paris on 4 November 1597, he had received a broad education and had travelled in both Italy and England. He then joined the Capuchins and was ordained as Father Joseph in 1604. His talents were so extraordinary that he was soon elected superior of the convent of St Honoré and subsequently passed from one office to another until he became provincial of his order.

Father Joseph was a visionary as well as an administrator and he dreamed of a great crusade led by his native France to regain the Orient for Christianity. The plan called for Charles de Gonzague, duke of Nevers, a relative of the last Palaeologos and therefore with a distant claim to the throne of Byzantium, to lead the expedition. Orthodox prelates in the Peloponnesus, believing that the duke intended to claim his inheritance, had commissioned a delegation, two archbishops and three bishops, to go to France to pledge him their support. Messages came from Albania and Serbia as well, but the duke was preoccupied with problems closer to home. He did, however, form a group known as the 'Order of Christian Militia', and he fitted out a small expeditionary force which landed in Albania in 1616 only to be quickly overcome by the Turkish militia.[33]

Father Joseph hoped also to interest Philip III of Spain, the Italian princes and Pope Paul V in aiding Charles in his crusade; he visited the courts of these rulers, laying before them his carefully nurtured project, but his hopes were dashed when the Thirty Years War erupted, distracting the attention of the Western European powers, and he was forced to devise a new project to replace his goal of a military victory over Islam in the East.

His alternative was spiritual conquest of the Orient: he would so flood the Ottoman and Persian empires with missionaries that Eastern Christians could not help but be convinced of the Catholic faith. His own French Capuchins, free from the Venetian hostility which hampered the Jesuits, would lead the way. The martyrs of the earlier Capuchin mission to the Orient, Juan Zuaze and Giovanni of Troia, would provide the inspiration.

In 1622 he sent a scout, Pacifique of Provins, to the Orient to seek out the best places to establish Capuchin houses. Pacifique was an able observer; he went to Istanbul, Egypt, Palestine and Syria, visiting all the Latin communities. His report is a remarkable source of information on the status of Catholics in the Ottoman empire in 1623. In Galata, when he visited St Francis church, he was pleased to note that the mosaic of the Franciscan founder pictured him in a Capuchin habit. At St Anthony's church he witnessed several healings of both Muslims and Christians when the priest placed the gospel of St John on the heads of the sick.[34]

Returning to the West, Pacifique reported to Pope Gregory XV and his officials, then carried his information to Paris. Rome conferred the title 'Prefect of the Missions' upon Father Joseph with a charge to him to provide Capuchin missionaries for 'England, Scotland, Constantinople and other diverse places of the East'. The Capuchins were limited only by an admonition they should not establish houses where Franciscan Observants were already in residence. After considerable preparation the first three groups of Capuchins were ready to set off in February 1626.[35]

The mission to Istanbul consisted of four members, led by Archange of Fosses, a relative of the French ambassador, Comte de Césy. Upon Césy's request, the vacant church of St George was put at their service.

The missionaries were welcomed by their fellow countrymen, the Jesuits, who assisted them in beginning their language study in Greek and Armenian. As soon as possible, the Capuchins opened a school which attracted a large Armenian clientele. Césy reported to Paris, 'It is almost unbelievable how the Capuchin fathers have been so well received here by all the nations...They have a very handsome church and an old house with six rooms, a good refectory, a gallery, kitchen and small storeroom.' Within several years the Capuchin community rivalled that of the Jesuits in Istanbul as the best representative of Catholicism in the city.[36]

The early seventeenth century began the golden age of Catholic missions to the East Mediterranean. Fired by the religious renaissance of seventeenth-century France, the Jesuits and Capuchins led the way into the East anxiously seeking individual conversions, especially among the hierarchy in Istanbul and elsewhere. Apparently, the French religious believed that once a patriarch had signed a profession of Catholic faith, it would only be a matter of time before his church followed him. Such optimism was shared neither by the Ottoman Catholic laity nor by the older religious orders working in the East, who must have been highly critical of the contest for the patriarchate during these years. The popes, for their own reasons, supported the French dynamism – although Gregory XII, for one, probably would have been content to see a conversion to his calendar.

6

The missions come under the Congregation for the Propagation of the Faith

THE FOUNDING OF THE CONGREGATION FOR THE PROPAGATION OF THE FAITH

The Catholic church's missionary activity throughout the sixteenth and early seventeenth centuries depended on the several Catholic monarchs of Western Europe and their willingness to underwrite expenses. Missionaries were expected to be agents of their home countries in return for such patronage, and religious from one nation might, as a result, look upon those from another nation or order as rivals rather than fraternal cooperators in a common enterprise.

From Rome's point of view, centralization of missionary activity under a congregation reporting directly to the pope was badly needed, and to this end, during the brief pontificate of Gregory XV 1621–3 by a bull of 14 January 1622 the Sacred Congregation for the Propagation of the Faith (usually called '*Propaganda*' to simplify its title) was created. By constitution and structure it became one of the most efficient and constructive organs of the modern Catholic church. All missionary lands lacking resident bishops came under its jurisdiction, so all the Ottoman territories except Albania and the Greek islands fell within its purview.

The first secretary of the Congregation was Francesco Ignoli, an able administrator who used his office to circumvent the monarchical claims of the kings of the Catholic nations of Western Europe by appointing regional apostolic vicars with episcopal titles, thereby thwarting any appeal to past traditions which left the direction of foreign missions in secular hands. During its formative years, the Congregation leaned heavily upon the advice of the Capuchin Father Joseph, regarding his plan for the Orient as a model for the missions of the East.[1]

One of the Congregation's major concerns was reform of the

Greek College in Rome, which had not lived up to the expectations of its early years. Enrolment remained small and the regime too strict. (Students were required to keep both their own and the Latin feasts and fasts. Failure to obey the rules was punished by beatings and even confinement in the college cellar.) The rectors were at a loss how to proceed: between 1576 and 1591 no less than eight men had tried their hand at the task. Finally, in September 1591, six Jesuits arrived to reform the institution; the new rector emptied the college cellar of recalcitrant students and instituted the Byzantine liturgy on a regular basis.

Dominating the life of the college in this formative period was the Jesuit missionary, Antonio Possevino. An able translator and author, experienced from years of work on the Catholic–Orthodox frontier in Bielorussia and the Ukraine, he often served as adviser to the faculty and staff. In 1592 he composed a new set of rules for the college.

When a new cardinal-protector appeared in 1604 the Jesuits were ousted in favour of the Dominicans, but the change did not seem to affect the educational improvements at the college. By this time alumni were undertaking missions to the Ukraine and the East. The first distinguished alumnus was Pietro Arcudio, from Corfu. He spent many years in the Ukraine, and at the Council of Brest in 1596 brought that church into communion with Rome. He published a comparative liturgical study, *Concerning the Harmony Between the Eastern and Western Churches in the Administration of the Seven Sacraments.* Paralysed in 1609, he spent the remaining twenty-four years of his life in the college library, carried into his study during the day and back to his room each evening.[2]

The importance of the Greek College for the Catholic missions in the Orient increased in the seventeenth century as more and more celebrated graduates were produced. Giorgio Matteo Cariofilo from Crete spent a good portion of his life after ordination back on his native island. He was consecrated titular bishop of Iconium (in the Latin rite, although he preferred to use the Greek liturgy). Francesco Cocco of Naxos travelled to Istanbul to meet the Orthodox patriarch and Niccolò Alemmani of Andros later became director of the Vatican Library. But of all the graduates of the Greek College during this period, the most brilliant was Leon Allatios (Leone Allacci).

Allatios was born on Chios about 1587, son of an Orthodox father. His uncle, Michael Neurides, an alumnus of the Greek

College in Rome, had taken him to Italy to enter him in the college when he was only nine years of age, but the authorities wisely suggested that he delay his entrance until he was older. Young Leon spent the next four years in Naples and Calabria and commenced his studies in 1600, spending the next ten years at the Greek College. At some time during this period he made a private profession of the Catholic faith, but refused to accept ordination.

Allatios completed his studies in exemplary fashion, standing for the doctorate in both theology and philosophy. He spent the next five years in Sicily and in 1615 returned to Chios as Bishop Massone's vicar general. Here he became involved in much litigation and personnel problems; at the same time he developed a strong antipathy towards Calvinism, possibly because of reports concerning Kyrillos Loukaris. Tired of contention, he left Chios to study medicine in Italy, and, after receiving his degree, had hardly begun his medical career when he abandoned it to teach rhetoric at his alma mater. There, unfortunately, he met with difficulties from other faculty members which caused him to accept an appointment, offered by Pope Paul V, as professor of Greek at the Vatican and *scriptor* at the Library.

During Gregory XV's pontificate he was sent to Heidelberg to bring to Rome the 32,000-volume library of the deceased elector, Maximilian of Bavaria. Until his death his fortunes at the Vatican Library rose and fell with the various papal changes of policy. In 1661 he was named to head the administration with the title Custodian of the Vatican Library where, happily, when funds were short, he enjoyed the patronage of the wealthy Barberini family. He died in 1669.

During his tenure he was often consulted on affairs dealing with the Orthodox, and the fruits of his research on such matters was published in *Three Books on the Lasting Agreement Between the Eastern and Western Churches*. While many Orthodox writers have accused him of harshness towards the Eastern church, a careful reading of his work does not support this contention, but rather shows him to be a man of ecumenical spirit, something unusual in seventeenth-century Italy.[3]

THE CONGREGATION AND THE MISSIONS

The Congregation believed that it should bring the missions of the East Mediterranean as closely as possible under its control. Despite

their own lack of experience in Ottoman affairs its members showed
no hesitation in legislating for Latin missionaries there. In general,
missionary questions were decided by men of extremely narrow
views who regarded Orthodoxy and Protestantism alike as the
'enemy'. Thus, contrary to traditional practice, the Congregation
in 1627 forbade Capuchins and Jesuits to offer Mass in Orthodox
churches since these were sometimes used for 'profane and sacrilegious rites'.[4] The new Eastern converts to Catholicism were now
strictly forbidden to attend the services of their former co-religionists,
a custom which had been tolerated for decades. Since Islamic law
did not allow the construction of new Christian churches, Latin
clergy and their small congregations, wherever churches did not
exist, were now forced to worship in the missionaries' homes, often
in chapels which were simply domestic rooms outfitted with an
altar and a minimum of ornament. Here priest and people crowded,
hot and uncomfortable, on Sunday mornings for the Eucharist.

Comparing this to the beautiful music and lavish decoration and
ceremonies of their former churches, Catholic converts must have
been sorely tried to believe that worship in these poor surroundings
represented a change for the better. A Capuchin missionary,
Agathangel of Vendome, wrote of the difficulties experienced by the
Ottoman Catholic convert as a result of Rome's legislation:

It seems to me that one should leave the decision in this matter to the
missionaries, who for a long time have held the opinion that converts
should not be forbidden to attend common services. The opposite
opinion destroys every possibility and hope of doing any good in this
mission and will lead to disastrous consequences.[5]

Propaganda also drew up a creed to be administered to converts
upon reception into the Catholic faith. It was a long statement,
beginning with the Nicene Creed and continuing through various
other conciliar statements up to the Council of Trent. The pope's
role as head of the church was made a central issue, the most
fundamental point of 'conversion' – all this ignoring the fact the
Roman primacy was the most difficult tenet of Catholicism for the
Eastern Christian to accept. It speaks well for the devotion of the
Latin missionaries in the Orient that in spite of the obstacles made
for them by both Ottoman and Roman authorities they continued
in their vocation with remarkable perseverance.

The work of *Propaganda* was followed with great interest by
Pope Urban VIII. Only a year after he commenced his pontificate,
in 1624, his concern for the Orient resulted in the promulgation of

a new constitution for the Greek College limiting enrolment to
Eastern-rite students. The intent was to attract more ethnic Greeks
from the Orient; Italo-Greeks were given only ten positions and
Ruthenians four.

The regime set up by Urban's constitution appears extraordinarily
harsh. The days and nights of the students were completely filled
with periods of study, alternating with periods of prayer. All meals
were to be eaten in the college refectory except for two days a year
when the boys might eat outside with visiting relatives. Overnight
absence was never permitted. It is easy to imagine why some of the
alumni, once freed from its discipline, became Rome's severest
critics in the East.

Urban's grandest enterprise was the foundation of a college
under the auspices of the Congregation for the Propagation of the
Faith to train native clergy for missionary regions throughout the
world, especially the Near East. A building on the south side of
the Piazza di Spagna was donated to the pope for the institution in
1627 and opened with scholarships for twelve students; two each
from convert Georgians, Persians, Nestorians, Jacobites, Melkites
and Copts. In addition, a press attached to the college soon became
a major source of printed liturgical and religious books. The school
still exists and bears the name of its founder, the Urban College.[6]

THE CONTINUING STRUGGLE OVER THE PATRIARCHATE

In 1627, while Kyrillos Loukaris was in his third term in the
patriarchate and Murat IV was sultan, an Orthodox monk from
Kefallinia, Nikodemos Metaxas, brought the first Greek printing
press to Istanbul. It was set up in a house near the English embassy
and began its publications with anti-Catholic polemical works, since
the growing presence of French missionaries was deemed a serious
menace to the Orthodox faithful. The Latins were keenly interested
in limiting the activities of the press or having it destroyed. The
Greek press thus became a major concern to both parties.

When word reached Rome of its operation, church authorities
commissioned a Greek Catholic, Canachio Rossi, to proceed to
Istanbul to dissuade Patriarch Kyrillos from supporting the venture.
The Rossi mission, predictably, failed and tracts attacking Catholic
doctrine continued to appear. Unfortunately for Kyrillos, one of
his own works which had been printed by Metaxas contained some

passages which could have been interpreted as contrary to Koranic teaching. This gave the Catholics an opening; the French ambassador, Comte de Césy, hurried to the grand vezir, Husrev Paşa, to point out the offensive sections. The vezir ordered the arrest of Metaxas on the feast of the Epiphany in January 1628, when he and Patriarch Kyrillos were at dinner at the British embassy. Metaxas managed to escape but the Janissaries destroyed the press.

Sir Thomas Roe, along with the Venetian and Dutch ambassadors, descended on the vezir to protest vigorously at the Janissary action, which was blamed upon a French Jesuit conspiracy. Husrev Paşa was persuaded that he had been duped; he ordered Rossi and the three Jesuits then residing at St Benedict's church to be jailed for having unlawfully plotted against Patriarch Kyrillos and the government of Murat IV. Two months later the sultan issued an order expelling the Jesuits from the capital. They were forced to leave for Chios where they remained in exile for the next three years.

For a single month, in October 1630, the French and Austrian ambassadors were able to have Kyrillos Loukaris removed, but he then returned to hold office for the next three years, after which he was replaced by Kyrillos Kontaris, a native of Veroia in Macedonia, who had been a student of the Jesuits. Kontaris had come to Istanbul in 1618 and had taken up residence at St Benedict's while attending classes. Eventually he became well known among influential Catholics, some of whom were willing to sponsor him in his quest for higher office in the Orthodox church, just as the Protestants supported Kyrillos Loukaris.

The Capuchin superior in Istanbul, Archange of Fosses, in 1630 carried to Paris a letter from Kyrillos Kontaris asking for the protection of Louis XIII. Afterwards, in Rome, Archange received papal authority to absolve him 'of every censure of schism and heresy', but it is unknown whether Kyrillos made a formal conversion to Catholicism at the time. For eight days in 1633 Kontaris held the patriarchate, but the English and Dutch ambassadors were soon able to restore Loukaris.[7]

Twice Kyrillos Loukaris was deposed due to the accession of prelates furnished with Bourbon and Habsburg funds. In 1634 Athanasios III Patellaros held office for a single month. After his expulsion from the patriarchate he went off to Italy and sought papal support for a more lasting tenure. In March 1635 Kyrillos Kontaris returned for several months, only to be deposed by the synod and exiled to Rhodes. Kyrillos Loukaris did not immediately return to the patriarchate; instead Neophytos III held office for several months until he resigned in Loukaris' favour. In 1637, for the seventh and last time, Loukaris assumed the patriarchate, but within the year several bishops, including Kyrillos Kontaris, complained to the Porte that Loukaris was engaged in stirring up revolution. Loukaris was imprisoned and later killed by Janissaries who were taking him to a place of confinement in June 1638. His death was a great loss to Orthodoxy, for despite his Calvinist bias, he tried to meet the challenge of Catholicism with an intellectual response. It was unfortunate that he lived at a time when rivalry between Catholics and Protestants in Western Europe had made the offices of the Orthodox church a prey to the cupidity of both Greeks and Turks.[8]

Upon Loukaris' final deposition, the synod elected Kyrillos Kontaris for a third time, but his hold on the patriarchate was tenuous, threatened by many enemies. To cement his Catholic support, on 15 December 1638 he signed a formal profession of the Catholic faith which had been composed for him by the Congregation for the Propagation of the Faith. This act did not go unnoticed. At the end of June 1639 he was ousted, placed under arrest by the Turkish authorities, and ordered into exile in Tunisia. He died in Tunis on 24 June 1640, strangled by his guards after he refused to become a Muslim.[9]

The struggle between Greek factions and their allies over the control of the patriarchate continued its tragic course until 1648 and beyond. In 1644 Parthenios I died of poisoning and was replaced by Parthenios II, former metropolitan of Chios. In earlier times, Parthenios had corresponded with Rome, but during his two years in office made no commitment to Catholicism. In 1646 he was exiled and replaced by Ioannikios II, a cleric sympathetic to Catholicism.[10]

A BISHOP FOR ISTANBUL AND THE RETURN OF THE CAPUCHINS

After the bishop of Thira, Pietro Demarchis, made an apostolic visitation to Istanbul in 1622, he recommended that the patriarchal vicar should be replaced by a titular bishop who would be a suffragan of the Latin patriarch of Constantinople. Roman authorities agreed, and allowed the cathedral chapter in Candia to proceed to an election. Their choice fell upon a cleric named Livio, head of the chapter, but the candidate never went to Istanbul. He may very well have been aware that the *Magnifica Communità* was very much opposed to having a bishop in their midst, the members realizing that one of the prelate's functions would be to regulate more strictly their control of the patronage of the Galatan churches. Livio died on Crete in 1643.

In 1629 the Congregation for the Propagation of the Faith, frustrated by Livio's inaction, itself named a vicar for Istanbul, Giovanni Francesco d'Angani; his immediate superior was Demarchis, now archbishop of Izmir since its reestablishment as a Catholic see in 1624. He arrived in the capital and, following Rome's instructions, began the unpopular task of centralizing Galatan church administration under his immediate jurisdiction. The procurators of the *Communità* were most reluctant to allow the revenues and properties of the churches – which had been in lay hands for centuries – to be turned over to the vicar, and every kind of objection was put forward to delay his plans. The French ambassador was also displeased at seeing his role of protector of the capital's Catholics threatened by d'Angani's presence.

At the time of Bishop d'Angani's appointment the number of Latin Catholics was estimated at 1,500 permanent Galatan residents and 400 foreign merchants. Five churches were functioning: St Francis, held by the Franciscan Conventuals, St Mary Draperis, served by the Franciscan Observants, SS Peter and Paul, held by the Dominicans, St Benedict, the residence of the Jesuits, and the Capuchins' St George. There were eight Franciscans, six Dominicans, four Jesuits and four Capuchins resident in the capital. All the other churches and chapels of the city were used infrequently or had been converted to secular purposes by the *Communità*.

Contemporary travellers report that despite the good reputation enjoyed by the missionaries, Turkish hostility towards Christianity remained as constant as ever – 'the condition of a dog is better than ours' – yet, Henry Blount noted, each ethnic group was intensely jealous of its position: 'Each loves the Turke better than they doe each of the other, and serve him for informers and instruments against one another.' With a perceptive eye Blount noted that there were many converts from Christianity to Islam, for 'many who professe themselves Christians scarce know what they mean by being so; finally, perceiving themselves poore, wretched, taxed, disgraced, deprived of their children and subject to the intolerance of every Raschall, they begin to consider, and prefer the present World, before that other which they so little understand'.[11]

Evliya Çelebi, the seventeenth-century Ottoman traveller, believed Galatan Christians to be morally degenerate, since the town had over two hundred taverns with music and dancing, and prostitutes walked the streets. He claimed that no one there cared for anything except making money. It was not a safe place for a devout Muslim. On the other hand, he was impressed by the churches, 'painted inside and outside with wonderful figures that seem to breathe'.[12] In March 1639, however, a great fire swept through Galata and the church of St Francis, with its mosaics, was almost destroyed. Although Césy received permission to have it rebuilt, the church lost its distinction as the most beautiful building of the town.

Another facet of Galatan life involved the role of the French ambassador, especially while that position was held by the vigorous Comte de Césy. From his residence, 'the palace of France', which dominated the hills of Pera, he sought to make the Catholic church in the capital an adjunct of French policy. The church did reap some advantages from its close connections with France for, in the words of Louis XIII, 'the principal business of the ambassador of the King to the Porte is to protect, in the name of the king and the authority of His Majesty, the religious houses established in the different locations in the Levant, as well as the Christians who come and go in order to visit the sacred places of the Holy Land'.[13]

On French holidays, the Galatan aristocracy, although mainly Italian, was expected to be present at commemorative masses in St Francis. When the news of the king's victory over the Huguenots at La Rochelle reached Istanbul in 1629, a Solemn Mass was offered and the *Te Deum* sung at St Francis. Césy gloated that there had been a procession, 'with cross, banners, and torches just as in Paris, and a large number of people from many nations were in attendance'.[14]

Several years later, at Easter in 1632, after Césy had been replaced by Henri de Gournay, Comte de Marcheville, an unseemly brawl broke out between the new French ambassador and the Imperial internuncio. The animosities of the Thirty Years War had reached the Orient. Two years later Marcheville was expelled by the Ottomans and Césy resumed his former position until 1639. While the office of French ambassador was vacant and Catholic influence at a low ebb, the two remaining Catholic churches in Istanbul, St Nicholas and St Mary, were confiscated by the government. In time, the Church of St Mary became the Odalar mosque.

In 1639 Césy was replaced by Jean de la Haye, Seigneur de Vantelet. Louis XIII was anxious for renewal of the Capitulations, something that, despite all his diplomacy, Césy had never been able to effect. At the suggestion of Father Joseph and Richelieu, de la Haye was instructed, 'as his first concern to protect and assist the Christians of the Levant in so far as that is possible, interposing the name and authority of His Majesty whenever it is judged opportune'.[15] Even though he failed to have the Capitulations renewed, the Ottomans continued to tolerate French intervention in ecclesiastical matters. This may be explained by the confidence the Porte authorities had in their own authority. It would be their decision, not that of Paris, which ultimately determined the fate of Latin Christianity in the Levant. Possessed of that entirely correct notion, the Porte could afford to be tolerant of French activity which would otherwise have been unthinkable.

In 1631 Rome replaced Bishop d'Angani with a new appointee, Giovanni Mauri, to take up the task of supervising Istanbul's Catholics. In a report to Rome, Mauri lamented the decline of Galata's old Catholic families. The rest of his flock, freed slaves, foreign merchants or diplomatic personnel, totalled two thousand people. Diplomatic staff, being only temporary residents, had little concern for the Catholic community. Mauri's successor, a Franciscan, Angelo Petricca, arrived in 1636. He witnessed the final deposition of Kyrillos Loukaris and the ascendancy of Kyrillos Kontaris, and it was he who received the latter's profession of Catholic faith. In a memoir written upon his return to the West in 1639, he claimed that Murat IV had lost control of the armed forces and that the opportunity was open for a united Christian Europe to push the Turks back into Asia. It was an old refrain, but making it in the midst of the Thirty Years War says something about the author's political acumen.[16]

In 1645 the Ottoman sultan Ibrahim I opened hostilities with Venice over possession of Crete, and a long, bitter contest continued for the next decade and a half. Despite the strain this caused to relations between the Porte and the Italian Catholic families living in Istanbul, the French missionaries in the capital, regarded as representatives of an ally, were allowed to serve the religious needs of the resident Latins without hindrance. They also established conferences for Greek and Armenian clergy at their churches, and ultimately, some who attended were won over to Rome. Principally, it was their education which gave the Catholic clergy an edge over the Orthodox and Armenians. Paul Rycaut, Protestant chaplain to the British ambassador to the Porte, a man with no love for the Catholics, noted, 'so far indeed have the Latins the advantage over the Greeks, as Riches hath over Poverty, or Learning over Ignorance'.[17]

In 1651, through the mediation of the Catholic ambassadors in Istanbul, the Congregation for the Propagation of the Faith received permission to name a new bishop as patriarchal vicar in Istanbul. They chose Giacintho Subiano, a Dominican friar who was co-adjutor to the archbishop of Izmir. He received his confirmation by decree of Pope Innocent X on 6 March 1652.

Subiano's stay in Istanbul was brief. He soon returned to his former residence on Chios where the climate was more favourable for Italian Catholic prelates. He named the resident superior of the French Capuchins, Thomas of Paris, to be his vicar general in Istanbul.

Propaganda then chose a Franciscan Conventual, Bonaventura Teoli, to take the vicariate. Not surprisingly he became embroiled in disputes with the *Magnifica Communità*, but managed to persevere until 1662 when he left for Italy. Apparently Istanbul's local Catholics had little interest in maintaining him, and providing funds to support an episcopal appointment in the Ottoman capital had already become a serious problem when the revenues from church lands on Crete were lost after the conclusion of the war there.[18]

The final settlement of the dispute over church properties in the capital was made in 1682 during the tenure of Bishop Gasparo Gasparini. This prelate had requested a decision from Rome on the ownership of the churches. Hardly surprisingly, the Congregation, by a decree of 17 October 1682 ruled in favour of the bishop. The *Communità* sought in vain to reverse this ruling, since its effect was to end the economic basis of its organization, but soon afterwards accepted the inevitable and was dissolved, only its spiritual association continuing to function as the Confraternity of St Anne. For Istanbul's Catholics a new era had begun which would see increasing control of the city's ecclesiastical life exercised by Roman authorities.[19]

THE PATRIARCHS AND ROME IN MID-CENTURY

Good relations between the Eastern patriarchs and French ambassadors in Istanbul were sought by all parties during the sultanate of Mehmet IV. On one side, there was need for protection against the often unpredictable policies of the Porte towards the Christians of the Empire; on the other, there was a presumption that the good will of the sultan's Christian community provided both political and religious benefits to Paris. In 1651, when the government in Istanbul was passing through a crisis, a group of rigidly orthodox Muslims called *Kadizadelar* became so influential in the capital that Orthodox Christians felt threatened. Patriarch Ioannikios II found asylum in the residence of the French ambassador for ten months. Later he was deposed and left for Venice.

In 1656, at the time when Mehmet Köprülü assumed office as grand vezir, Parthenios III Parthenakes became patriarch. The unfortunate Parthenios became an object of suspicion because of his correspondence with Russian and Romanian princes. Seeking to avoid disaster he contacted the French embassy in late October to request that the minister, Jean de la Haye, write on his behalf to the pope and to the French king detailing his friendship and his need for assistance. He also asked that, if the need arose, he might come to live at the embassy. He never obtained his wish, for on 21 March 1657 he was hanged and his body burned, by orders of the grand vezir, for having been a traitor to the Ottomans. His immediate successor, Gabriel II, was also hanged for disloyalty that same year after having been exiled to Bursa on orders of Mehmet Köprülü. The arm of the French king obviously did not reach far enough.[20]

THE GREAT FIRE OF GALATA

A great disaster struck the Latin Catholic community of Galata in 1660. In early April a huge fire roared through the town, burning out of control for two days. Hundreds were killed, thousands of homes destroyed, and of the six Catholic churches in use, five were gutted: St George, St Francis and its chapel of St Anne, St Mary Draperis and SS Peter and Paul. The sole surviving Catholic church in the Ottoman capital was the Jesuits' St Benedict, but the Jesuit residence was lost and some of the priests had to live in the church tower.

Since this occurred after Mehmet Köprülü had come to power and after the French ambassador had been dismissed, the heads of the religious orders were in a poor position to bargain for permission to restore their lost churches. Despite the setback, none of the orders wanted to abandon its mission. The Franciscan Conventuals began gathering funds to rebuild St Francis while they took up temporary residence in other parts of Galata. The Capuchins found a welcome in the French embassy where they were serving as chaplains. The Dominican convent was spared complete destruction and its refectory was converted into a chapel. Almost a decade went by before sufficient funds were gathered to finance the reconstruction and make the necessary 'gifts' to obtain official permission for the rebuilding. Then, in 1685, the church of St Benedict, sole survivor of the great fire of 1660, burned in another of the frequent disasters which befell Galata during this period.[21]

FRENCH DIPLOMACY AT THE PORTE

At the beginning of the rule of Mehmet IV in 1648, the French ambassador was Jean de la Haye, Seigneur de Vantalet. Along with the Venetian *bailie* and the Habsburg internuncio, de la Haye formed the triumvirate of diplomatic protectors of Catholicism in Ottoman territories. The Cretan war meant that the *bailie*, when not actually under arrest, had no influence at all, while the frequency of Habsburg conflicts with the Turks forced the imperial embassy to be closed for many years. The French were assured of precedence.

De la Haye's situation, nevertheless, was a delicate one, since the French were known to be aiding the Venetians on Crete. When, in 1656, Mehmet Köprülü was named grand vezir, the French ambassador neither sent him the usual gifts upon his accession nor called upon him to offer congratulations on behalf of Louis XIV. Eventually de la Haye did meet with him, but the atmosphere was frigid. Later, a letter from Venice to the French envoy, intercepted by the Turks and handed over to Köprülü, revealed such compromising material that the ambassador sent his son to Edirne to explain the matter, but the grand vezir was not impressed and the boy was imprisoned as a spy. Finally in 1660 de la Haye himself was jailed in the Seven Towers on an accusation that he had defaulted on a debt. After being ransomed by the French merchants in the Turkish capital, he left for France while one of the local Frenchmen was put in temporary charge of the embassy.[22]

In 1661 Louis XIV began his personal rule in France. Because of the hostility shown the French by Mehmet Köprülü, he did not immediately move to repair the breach in relations with the Porte. On the contrary, he stepped up French assistance to the beleaguered

Venetians on Crete and in 1664 dispatched a French contingent of several thousand men to fight with the Habsburgs. This army was present at the battle of St Gotthard, a fact which greatly embittered the Turks.

Nevertheless, after the Peace of Vasvar brought an end to Habsburg–Ottoman hostilities, Louis sent a new envoy, Denis de la Haye, Seigneur de Vantelet, son of the elder de la Haye, accompanied by a French Capuchin, Robert of Dreux. Their mission was to restore good relations and to assure the position of French merchants in the Turkish realm. Louis XIV's minister, Jean Baptiste Colbert, had set up a special department in his ministry to oversee the conduct of Ottoman trade. Marseille was designated a free port and its Chamber of Commerce given charge of all merchants leaving France for the Orient.

De la Haye made some progress with the Ottoman authorities only to incur the wrath of the local Catholics. The patriarchal vicar was Bishop Andrea Ridolfi, who had come to Istanbul in 1663 when French influence was minimal and the disaster of the great fire was still everywhere evident. Ridolfi was not prepared for de la Haye's demand to resume the custom that the French ambassador should kiss the book of the Gospels at Mass before the celebrant read the selection of the day and be incensed before all other dignitaries attending the Eucharist. A tempest began over the bishop's refusal, and Rome, asked to settle the affair, decided that the French ambassador was out of order and that the rubrics of the Mass should be strictly followed. Again in 1669, replying to reports that the French clergy were apt to accede to the ambassador's insistence on his traditional rights, Rome ordered that clergy who violated the rubrics would merit a suspension whose remission would be reserved to the pope.

The French clerics proposed to mollify the ambassador by offering a second gospel book for his reverence, while reserving to themselves the one used at the Mass. De la Haye would not agree, and continued to demand the same privileges his predecessors had had. To this the religious replied, 'They would give their lives for the king, but they must obey God.' The ambassador threatened to close St Benedict's and the embassy chapel, but Rome wisely compromised and allowed an exception to the rubrics. The loss of support by Catholic Europe's most powerful ambassador in the Orient was too great a risk.[23]

In 1670 there was a change at the French embassy upon the

arrival of the Marquis de Nointel, Charles-François Olier. He came with orders to seek better understanding with the Turks and, if possible, renewal of the Capitulations. At first the vezir Fazil Ahmet treated Olier coolly but relations eventually improved. Aided by an extraordinary minister sent from Paris, Olier renegotiated the Capitulations, signed at Edirne in June 1673 for the fifth time.

With these Capitulations Olier succeeded in bringing all Latin clergy in Ottoman lands under French protection, having them considered subjects of Louis XIV. Article II reads as follows:

Bishops who depend on France and other religious who profess the religion of the Franks, of whatever nation or place, as long as they act in that capacity, shall not be troubled in the exercise of their duties within the boundaries of our empire where they have lived for a long time.[24]

The articles dealing with religion confirmed the right of pilgrims to visit the Holy Land and guaranteed the presence of the French Jesuits and Capuchins in Istanbul. A year after the signing of the Capitulations, Olier made a tour of inspection which took him to the Greek islands, Syria and Palestine.

Another incident, however, troubled Ottoman–French relations at the close of Mehmet IV's sultanate. This grew out of the bombardment of Chios in which a French admiral was involved during the War of the Holy League. Only large donations to Turkish officials kept the ambassador of that period, Gabriel-Joseph de le Vergne de Guilleragues, from imprisonment. De la Vergne was later responsible for securing permission to construct the first new Catholic church built in the capital since the time of the conquest. It was set in the grounds of the French embassy and was dedicated to St Louis. Staffed by the Capuchins, it subsequently became the official church of the French embassy.[25]

By the late seventeenth century, two important institutions were at work in the Ottoman capital for the advancement of Catholicism: the bishops appointed by the Congregation for the Propagation of the Faith, and the French ambassadors. Both sought to enhance their position at the expense of other European powers and religions. Despite some temporary setbacks, for the most part, their efforts succeeded. Catholicism was a force to be reckoned with in the Ottoman capital.

7

The Balkans and Greece

AFTER LEPANTO

When word of the Christian victory at Lepanto reached the subject peoples of the Balkans some of them believed their moment of deliverance was at hand. Several Albanian chieftains took up arms against the Turks, at the same time seeking a Western leader for their armies. They sent envoys, first to Charles Emmanuel I of Savoy and then to the Prince of Parma, offering the crown of Albania to the one who would come. Nothing, however, came of it. The *uskoks*, Christian Slavic pirates who preyed upon Ottoman shipping in the Adriatic, were emboldened by Don Juan's victory to strike further afield. On land four to five thousand Serbs moved from Bosnia into Croatia in 1573; they brought clergy with them and set up an Orthodox bishopric in Marča.

On the Greek mainland scattered revolutionary activity occurred. Archbishop Makarios of Monemvasia pleaded with Don Juan to bring his fleet to his fortress city, where an army of twenty-five thousand infantry and three thousand cavalrymen was promised. Don Juan did not arrive. The Ottomans did, however, and the rebellion was extinguished with the total loss of the Greek army. An interesting note survives, addressed by an official in Istanbul to the *sanjak-bey* of Skopje, asking him to investigate a certain Nikola Leko. The official has information that on the news of the capture of Cyprus, Leko had closed his shop to cry. Now, the official inquires, has he shown any joy over the results of the Turkish defeat at Lepanto? If so, he is to be arrested, sent to Istanbul and his property confiscated.[1]

In 1577 thirty-eight chieftains of the Orthodox Himarë region of Albania appealed to Pope Gregory XIII for arms and supplies sufficient to fit out an army of ten thousand. They promised to transfer their religious allegiance to Rome and to recognize Philip II of Spain as their sovereign. They asked only that their priests be allowed to retain their Eastern liturgical customs, 'since the majority of the population is Greek and they do not understand the Frankish language'. Philip II also received a personal communication from them, but was hardly willing to become king of Albania. From this time the Himaréns accepted the pope as religious head and identified themselves with the Catholic church.[2]

Throughout the early seventeenth century, Albanian Catholics, both Latin and Eastern, remained remarkably firm in their Roman allegiance wherever they were in the majority. Their loyalty was strengthened when, after 1628, the first graduates of the College of the Propagation of the Faith were assigned to Albania; at about the same time Basilian monks from Italy began to appear in their midst. There were few native Albanians in the Catholic clergy, and the bishoprics were so frequently vacant that in some places the Orthodox had taken over episcopal properties. In an effort to offset conversions to Islam, Rome allowed the missionaries special privileges in confessing and reconciling Catholics who had apostasized.

When the Cretan war began, the Latin archbishop of Bar sought to betray the city of Shkodër to the Venetians, and the discovery of his plan resulted in persecution of the Catholic community in his diocese. Three thousand Latins fled to Venetian territory while another sizable group went over to the Muslim faith. In 1645 Venetian agents were able to persuade the Albanian Catholics once more to take up arms against the Ottomans. Preoccupied with the Cretan war, the Turks were at a disadvantage, but, the war once over, they appeared in force; the small Venetian contingent which had supported the rebellion withdrew, and with them, fearing for their lives, went many of the Catholic clergy. Again in 1689, when the Holy League was at war with the Ottomans, an imperial fleet cruised the coast seeking to stir up Albanian Christians. But this time there was no response.

Since Latin missionaries had enjoyed such success among the Eastern-rite Albanians of the Himarë, other converts from Orthodoxy were welcomed there, and the Himarë became a refuge for dissident Orthodox prelates. One of these, in 1660, was Archbishop Athanasios II of Ochrid, and another Simeon Laskaris, who had been an archimandrite in Istanbul. Athanasios came to be recognized by Roman authorities as bishop of the region. While he lived the attachment of the Himaréns to Rome remained strong, but when he retired to Italy in 1685 the union's strength began to wane.[3]

VISITATIONS OF BISHOPS CEDULINI AND BIZZI

Information on the Catholic church in the Balkans and Anatolia in 1581 is found in the report of Bishop Pietro Cedulini. After his departure from Istanbul he had journeyed to Caffa in the Crimea, where he found a handful of Latins with a small church dedicated to St Peter. He noted with amazement that the Catholics now spoke Tartar as their native language. Cedulini called at the residence of the Armenian bishop to discover that this prelate still considered himself in communion with Rome. Farther on, he found small Catholic merchant communities in Trabzon and Bergame, but in Bursa the former Catholic church had been converted into a mosque. In the Greek islands, with the single exception of Andros, he was favourably impressed by the life of the church. In Gallipoli he found a small church caring for nine Catholic families and served by a Franciscan from Istanbul. In Edirne, one hundred and fifty Catholics, mostly from Dubrovnik, but Bosnians and Hungarians too, gathered at the house of a wealthy town merchant for Sunday Mass. In Plovdiv, Sofia and Novi Pazar the bishop encountered more Catholics, including some converted Bogomils. His travels into Moldavia and Wallachia were depressing; there, the Catholics, known as Saxons, were all ethnic Germans. One priest had married, another hardly ever offered Mass. In Iaşi he saw one church 'made of wood, very small, rude and desolate'.[4]

In other parts of the Balkans, where Cedulini did not always have the opportunity for first-hand information, the life of the church was marked either by prosperity, as in Dubrovnik, or by heavy losses, as in Bosnia. While in 1587 the former city counted forty-one churches, two large friaries of Franciscans and Dominicans and eight convents of nuns, the rural areas of Bosnia frequently had no churches or priests. The attrition of the Catholic population continued, and, as if conversions to Islam were not sufficiently troublesome, the efforts of the Serbian Orthodox clergy to obtain tithes from the Catholics made conditions even worse. Appeals were sent to Istanbul by the Latins asking the intervention of the authorities at the Porte to have the practice stopped. Usually the Turkish officials agreed that the practice was illegal, but local prelates were difficult to convince.

In 1610 the bishop of Bar, Marino Bizzi, received a *berat* from the Porte allowing him to make a visitation of the Balkan Catholic churches. The status of his own church was none too promising:

the former cathedral was now a mosque while only a few of Bar's smaller churches were still held by Catholics. One part of the episcopal residence was the residence of the *kadi*; another section had become a stable. Bizzi undertook the visitation knowing that Catholicism still survived in Bosnia, Albania and Macedonia; but he had no illusions that Muslim rule was anything less than a disaster for the churches located there. The results of the Turkish occupation varied from town to town: one small village of twenty-five Catholic families had become completely Muslim, yet in other places the Catholic population remained intact. In some locations, Bizzi discovered that Catholics had become nominal Muslims in order to avoid paying the *cizye*. In general, he found the clergy ignorant, some even illiterate; many kept concubines and lived a life indistinguishable from that of the peasants to whom they ministered. The bishop's advice to the Catholics was to emigrate either to Italy or north to Habsburg territory where they might practise their religion in better circumstances. Such advice did little to strengthen the Catholic communities which still remained in their old homelands. In the 1620s the number of Bosnian Muslims was estimated at 700,000, many of them former Catholics. The Franciscans still occupied thirteen convents which were rapidly becoming Christian islands in a foreign sea. The demands of Muslim landowners, further emigration and the isolation of the Catholic villages all contributed to the decline. The worst was yet to come. At the end of the century, in the war between the Ottomans and the Holy League, Bosnia became a battleground. So destructive was the conflict there that scarcely 30,000 people were alive at its conclusion and two generations would pass with no ordered Catholic life.[5]

The Catholics of Dubrovnik suffered a major setback because of a great earthquake which struck their city on 6 April 1667, levelling the palace, the churches and all the monasteries. Six thousand people were killed and the entire population left homeless. Only twenty-five noblemen survived to form a provisional government and these dispatched appeals to the sovereigns of the Western Christian nations for reconstruction funds, yet they spurned an offer to move Orthodox families inside the city walls to repopulate the town.

In the midst of their rebuilding the citizens of Dubrovnik received word that Kara Mustafa, the Turkish grand vezir, intended to increase their tribute to the Porte. At once the government dispatched two ambassadors to Istanbul in an attempt to dissuade him. Kara

Mustafa was adamant; he jailed the delegates and spoke of annexation. He failed to pursue the matter only because he turned to a more important project: an attack upon Vienna. The failure of this expedition and the vezir's subsequent execution saved the city; the ambassadors were freed and Dubrovnik continued to enjoy its traditional privileges.

In 1684 the states comprising the Holy League demanded that Dubrovnik become a member, and in August of that year a treaty was agreed upon by which Vienna promised that an imperial fleet would aid the city in the struggle against its Muslim masters. Citizens and government alike were reluctant allies. Their participation in the war against the Ottomans was minimal and, the conflict over, Dubrovnik hastened to patch up its differences with the Turks and to resume payment of its regular tribute.[6]

There were some Catholic gains among the refugee Serbs in Habsburg territories. Bishop Simeone Vretanjić who lived in the Marča monastery in Ivanić Grad had converted to Catholicism along with his monks and had gone to Rome; there, he was given the title 'bishop of the Serbs in Rascia and the Kingdom of Croatia'. Later Bishop Pavel Zorvić, successor of Vretanjić, inaugurated a seminary to train priests for missionary work among his fellow Serbs. In 1688, Rome established a second Serbian bishopric with an episcopal residence at the Hopovo monastery.[7]

Correspondence, and even personal visits, between individual Orthodox bishops and Rome continued throughout the seventeenth century. The Metropolitans Porphyrios of Ochrid and Hieronymos of Durrës, delegates of eighteen Eastern bishops, sought papal assistance for their churches during personal visits to Rome in 1624. Porphyrios' successor, Abram, subsequently sent a profession of Catholic faith to the pope. The Balkans' most active prelate in search of allies against the Turks was Archbishop Gabriel of Ochrid. In this quest he travelled widely, also going to Rome to enlist papal help. Similarly the Croatian, Aleksandar Komoulović, and Nikolaos Mouriskou, son of the protopapas of the rugged Peloponnesan area, Mani, sought freedom for the Balkan Christians. Mouriskou went to Rome asking the pope for aid in equipping six thousand Maniote soldiers for battle against the Turkish enemy.[8]

CATHOLICS IN BULGARIA

In the ninth century, Boris, Khan of the Bulgarians, decided to lead his nation into Christianity. Seeking to avoid the political difficulties which a religious conversion might involve, he first dispatched a mission to the Franks asking for Latin missionaries to preach to his people. He avoided inviting the nearby rival Greeks because he feared that acceptance of Eastern Christianity might very well threaten the independence of his country, already indebted to the Byzantines for much of its culture and perennially threatened by Constantinople's foreign policy. But before the Latin missionaries could arrive, agents of Photios, patriarch of Constantinople, successfully convinced the Bulgarian prince that he had acted precipitately and persuaded him to receive their baptism. So, in 865 Boris was baptized according to the Byzantine rite and accepted the Christian name of Michael, because the Emperor Michael III acted as his godfather. His countrymen followed him into Eastern Christianity.

Since the Middle Ages, in addition to the Eastern Christian majority, there had also been a group of Bulgarians who lived outside the faith and jurisdiction of the national church. These were the Bogomils, named after the tenth-century founder of their sect. Bogomil had developed his doctrines from the teachings of certain Paulician heretics, Armenian and Syrian, settled in Bulgaria a hundred years before by order of the Byzantine emperor. The Bogomils were metaphysical dualists, had little use for hierarchy or liturgy and, as appears from the few extant sources concerning them, were considered social radicals and political revolutionaries. The imperial church strove to eradicate them but in no way succeeded in destroying their doctrinal allegiance.

From the period of the Turkish conquest until late in the sixteenth century, the Orthodox and Bogomil populations were practically undisturbed by the presence of Latin Catholics except for a few small communities of Italian merchants. In 1581 when Bishop Cedulini made his visitation, he found the Latin communities in Bulgaria made up almost entirely of foreign merchants.

Cedulini reported that, for various reasons, a few native Bulgarians, such as the employees of the Catholic merchants, were drawn to the Latin Catholic faith. This happened, especially, in the case of Bogomil families who were alienated from the rest of their countrymen. Some Bulgarians expressed interest in the Latin church because they believed that the Ottomans could be expelled from the Balkans if only the Catholic states of the West, especially Habsburg Austria, could be enlisted in their cause.[9]

Late in the sixteenth century Catholic influence in Bulgaria increased considerably as a result of immigration of German miners to the northwestern corner of the country. Their main settlement was at Chiprovtsi, a town located fifty miles northeast of Sofia. The Germans, for the most part, were Catholic Swabians who had been settled along the Danube and in Serbia for several centuries. With them came Franciscan friars who opened the first Catholic convent in Chiprovtsi. Rome, always sanguine about new missionary settlements anywhere, in 1601 named one of the Franciscans, Pietro Solinat, to be bishop, giving him the titular see of ancient Sardica.

The Franciscans were not content to minister to the Swabians but pursued a policy of proselytization, especially among the Bogomils. By 1623, the time of Bishop Solinat's death, several thousand former Bogomils had been baptized Latin Catholics. The number of Franciscan friars in Chiprovtsi, some of them native Bulgarians, had increased to twenty-five.

A year later, in 1624, the recently formed Congregation for the Propagation of the Faith commissioned a visitation of the Bulgarian church by Bishop Pietro Marsarechia. He reported that Bulgaria now held eight thousand Latin Catholics. This information prompted Pope Clement VIII to choose Elias Marinov, a Franciscan and native Bulgarian educated in Rome, to become bishop and successor to Pietro Solinat. Marinov's task of organizing the church was beset by difficulties caused by local Ottoman officials unsure how to react to a Catholic bishop in their midst, by Orthodox churchmen who found his presence a serious irritant, and even by the Catholic archbishop of Dubrovnik who considered him an interloper in his diocese. On the other hand, Marinov enjoyed certain advantages, the first of which was that he was a native Bulgarian. This gave him an advantage over the Greek hierarchs sent out from Constantinople's patriarchate, men often isolated from the local clergy, unable to speak Bulgarian or write in Cyrillic. Marinov was strongly convinced that the formation of an autonomous Bulgarian Franciscan province would assist the work of the church, but he died before he could accomplish this.[10]

In the mid-seventeenth century, the Latin church made still more gains. Petur Bogdan Bakšić, a native of Chiprovtsi who had been named bishop in 1641, so held the confidence of the Ottoman governor that in 1653 he was allowed to open a Catholic church in Sofia. Local sentiment, however, soon forced it to close and the building was converted into a mosque. Pope Alexander VIII was visibly impressed by Bakšić's work and in 1660 named him archbishop and supervisor of all the Franciscan convents of the central Balkans, including the Principalities.

A contemporary of Archbishop Bakšić was Filip Stanislavov, a secular priest who had graduated from Rome's Urban College. Stanislavov, like most native Catholics, came from the Bogomil tradition. His work with his former coreligionists gained numerous converts, but it also aroused the ire of the Franciscans, who felt he was detracting from their own labours. Rome named Stanislavov to the bishopric of Nicopolis but his ministry continued to be controversial. When, after 1680, both Bakšić and Stanislavov, the two most dynamic personalities of the church, were dead, the number of Bulgarian converts declined and the church lost much of its vigour. Apparently many of the converts had expected conversion to better their status either socially or politically, and when this did not happen, their interest in Catholicism waned.

At the end of the 1680s, when the Habsburg armies of the Holy League advanced into the Balkans, a new and tragic episode in the history of Bulgarian Catholicism opened. The Bulgarians were encouraged to think the days of Ottoman rule were numbered. The townspeople of Chiprovtsi joined their countrymen and expelled the Turkish garrison. They were soon to realize that the rebellion had been premature: the Western armies withdrew and the Peace of Karlowitz returned Bulgaria to the sultan. In a matter of weeks the Turks reoccupied Chiprovtsi and destroyed the Franciscan convent. Catholics became refugees, fleeing to Wallachia or to the cities of the Siebenburgen in Transylvania. Bishop Biagio Koičev settled with a number of the exiles in Cioplea. Since Bulgarian Bogomil converts had held aloof from the revolution, Catholicism was able to survive in the country, but the losses of the ill-fated rising of 1688 were not easily repaired. Chiprovtsi was never again the Catholic centre of the country.[11]

SELIM II'S CONQUESTS IN THE GREEK LANDS

Upon his accession Selim II sought to enhance the dignity of Joseph Nasi, who had become his friend and confidant. An opportunity presented itself when, on the island of Naxos, a revolt broke out against Duke Giacomo IV Crispo. Selim, on the excuse that order must be restored, dispatched the admiral Piyale Paşa to occupy Naxos and depose Giacomo. This done, Selim appointed Nasi to the dukedom, with all its revenues, an office which he held until 1579 when the island became a regular province of the Empire.

At the time of the fall of the house of Crispi in 1566 the Catholic population had numbered about five hundred people. Although Nasi made no effort to supplant the Catholic secular aristocracy's authority, the Latin archbishop, Antonio Giustiniani, was prohibited from residing on the island, a prohibition which continued to the end of the century. With the extinction of the Crispis only one Catholic family dynasty remained in the Cyclades, that of the Gozzadini on Siphnos and Kithnos.[12]

Joseph Nasi was an ambitious man whose vision extended beyond Naxos. While the title 'duke of Naxos' rang well in his ears, that of 'king of Cyprus' sounded even better, and he envisioned that the occupation of the island might provide a homeland for his fellow Jews. An opportunity for him to realize this plan presented itself after Mehmet Sokullu had blundered. Sokullu had sent an Ottoman army into the Caucasus area to take Astrakhan and to bolster Istanbul's allies, the Crimean Tartars, by digging a canal to link the Black and Caspian seas. Despite a mighty effort, when the Tartar khan withdrew his support the enterprise became a Turkish debacle; the grand vezir fell into disgrace and Nasi assumed the role of chief adviser to the sultan. At his suggestion Selim directed preparations be started for an attack on Cyprus.

The Latin Catholic church had first been established on Cyprus in 1191 as a result of the conquest by Richard the Lionheart. Richard had taken it from a self-proclaimed independent governor who had broken his ties to the Byzantine emperor. Eventually, the island was passed on to the Lusignans, the dynasty of the crusaders' Kingdom of Jerusalem. To serve the Western crusaders, a Latin hierarchy was established, the Greek church being placed in subjection to it. Many Latin religious orders settled here, building great monasteries and convents. Under Lusignan rule, the island had passed through periods of prosperity and privation, but after an Egyptian Mamluk invasion in the early fifteenth century, it had not succeeded in restoring its economy. Still, even impoverished, Cyprus was the largest Christian bastion in the East Mediterranean and had always provided a haven to persecuted Eastern Christians. The Maronites were the oldest of these refugee groups and on occasions had even their own bishop; in addition, there were Armenians and members of the Church of the East.

The Venetians had come to Cyprus when the last widowed queen on the island, Catarina Cornaro, herself a citizen of the Republic, returned to Italy in 1489. Venetian rule had caused few changes in the social order; wealthy landowners, both Latin and Greek, had large estates, served by peasant labourers, growing grapes, sugar cane and cotton. The Catholic clergy, enjoying a privileged position, were often at odds with the Greek bishops and priests, who were only reluctantly united with Rome, as the Catholic hierarchy well knew. The moral life of the Latin clergy seems to have been pitiful, as many were careless about clerical discipline and often absent from their churches. By 1570 the Dominicans were the largest religious order on Cyprus with four convents; the Carmelites, Augustinians, Benedictines and Franciscans were also represented, but none seems to have been flourishing.[13]

Venice assumed its role in Cyprus knowing full well that the island was in an exposed position, liable at any time to Turkish attack. The authorities tried to keep friction with the Ottomans to a minimum by acknowledging the sultan's sovereignty of the island, and by faithfully sending tribute to the Porte. However, when word reached Istanbul that the Venetian arsenal had suffered a major fire, the time seemed opportune for redressing the setback recently suffered in the Caucasus, so in February 1570 a Turkish ambassador arrived in Venice to demand that the island be surrendered to direct Ottoman control.

Preparations for war commenced on both sides. Selim requisitioned church revenues in the Ottoman Empire, while Venice sought papal assistance in raising funds from the Western monarchs. Pope Pius V did more than expected: he announced to all of Europe the formation of one more Holy League. The French cardinal in Rome, de Rambouillet, reported that the pope had ordered galleys to be built, and that he was already selecting commanders for the fleet: 'The Pope is strongly resolved to aid the Venetians in every way he can in this war against the Turks.'[14] As the summer days passed, the pope chided the French cardinal that his king, the first son of the church, had not responded to his appeal. In fact, Pius could count only on Genoa and on Philip II of Spain to furnish ships and men for his enterprise.

Meanwhile the Turks had landed on Cyprus at Larnaca early in July. Aided by the Greek peasant population, who rose against their landowners, the army advanced on Nicosia, besieged it for six weeks, assaulted and captured it. The defenders, including two Latin and three Greek bishops, along with the superiors of the Latin religious orders, were killed. Prayers to Allah, intoned in the cathedral of the Holy Wisdom and most other churches in the city, confirmed their future use as mosques. The army then marched off to the remaining Venetian stronghold of Famagusta. By this time the forces of the Holy League sent to aid the defenders had reached Crete, and moved into Cypriot waters, but on hearing of the collapse of Nicosia, the commanders ordered the fleet withdrawn. No effort was made to assist Famagusta which was abandoned to its fate.

The Christians in that city held out through all of the next year until late in the summer of 1571, when there was no choice but surrender. The commander, Marc Antonio Bragadino, met with the Ottoman general Lala Mustafa to arrange the transfer of his small force to Italy. But once the surrender had been effected the disarmed Venetians were arrested and claimed as slaves. A worse fate was reserved for Bragadino, who was taken to the public square and there was flayed alive. His skin was stuffed with straw so that it might be put on display throughout the cities of the Empire.

A commentary on the fate of Cyprus, written by the Dominican Angelo Calepio, demonstrates the bitterness between the Latin and Greek communities on the island:

This was indeed a punishment and act of justice upon the Greeks of this kingdom, many of whom, while they were under the rule of the Latin Christians, abhorred the limpid water of the Holy Roman obedience, and despised the lifegiving stream of its Head; for these Greeks preferred to be subjects to that gangrened limb, the Patriarch of Constantinople, because he and his fellow patriarchs, especially the Patriarch of Jerusalem, when the poor Cypriot merchants and pilgrims went to their churches, held aloof from them, considering them excommunicate...[15]

Lala Mustafa brought in twenty thousand Anatolian Turks to confirm the Turkish presence on the island, thus providing a major change in its total ethnic composition. Some Latin families who had hidden in the mountains were eventually allowed to return home only to find that their former Greek servants were now in a position to be their employers. Catholics were forbidden to own property and, as a result, many converted, if only nominally, to Islam. Those who remained Christians had to attend Greek churches, which

were now in communion with the patriarch of Constantinople. Only
the Maronites, still found in thirty-three villages, were left as a
Catholic community, but under Orthodox prelates. The Catholic
converts either to Islam or Orthodoxy got the colourful name of
linovamvaki, meaning 'linen-cotton', since they sought to combine
their old Catholic faith with their present religion.

Because of the Capitulations which the French had obtained from
Selim II, a number of Frenchmen, after the Turkish occupation,
moved to Larnaca where the agreement with the Porte allowed them
to have Catholic ministers, and where, therefore, they requested and
received Franciscan priests from the Holy Land. Thus from the
ashes of the terrible destruction of the previous year, a Franciscan
convent, aptly named St Lazarus, was established in Larnaca in
1572. This establishment also served as a station for pilgrims on
their way to Jerusalem.[16]

THE GREEK ISLANDS IN THE SEVENTEENTH CENTURY

In the early seventeenth century, after a thirty-eight-year vacancy
in that office, the Naxian Catholic community received a resident
archbishop once more. Thanks to a delegation from the island and
the diplomacy of the French ambassador, de Brèves, the Porte
issued a favourable *firman* which allowed Dionysios Rendi to
proceed to Naxos and to reclaim from the Orthodox both the church
of St Anthony on Naxos and the cathedral of Milos. It also fixed
the taxes paid on each of the Catholic churches at a definite figure.
By now, out of a total population of four thousand, the Catholics
numbered less than four hundred. Bishop Rendi held the cathedral
and three churches in Naxos itself and four in the countryside, and
he was also responsible for the twenty-two Catholics on Paros. For
this work he had nine secular priests in his archdiocese and a single
Franciscan in the friary of the Observants.

The church at Naxos benefited from the misfortune of two Jesuits
who, when on a voyage to China, were forced by a storm into the
harbour of Naxos. Upon an invitation from the French consul and
Archbishop Raffaele Schiattini, they were installed in the former
chapel of the dukes of Naxos, and Rome gave its permission for
them to take up permanent residence there. The chapel contained a
famous statue of Mary, to which the islanders often had recourse in

times of emergency. As custodian of 'Our Lady of the Chapel' the Jesuit church attracted a large number of people.[17]

The Orthodox clergy and people on Naxos, excited over the arrival of the Jesuits, frequently called upon their services, and this made a pleasant change from the island's usual bitterness between Catholic and Orthodox. Ambassador Césy wrote to Louis XIII that the French Jesuit presence caused 'the *fleur-de-lis* and the name of the king to be held in the same reverence on Naxos as in France itself'.[18]

The Jesuits were invited to preach in the Catholic cathedral, where they delivered sermons in both Greek and Italian to congregations which included Orthodox monks as well as numerous clergy and laity. During Holy Week and on the feast and octave of Corpus Christi, they organized processions which involved all the Catholics of the town. They also established confraternities for the laity, who gathered on special occasions for prayers, instruction or works of charity.

The missionaries made an effort to reach the villages of rural Naxos. A public crier was sent ahead of the priests to announce their coming; then the Jesuits, arriving, would gather a congregation in the public square. Often the village priests, both Catholic and Orthodox, would invite the missionaries into their churches where instruction in Christian doctrine was given and confessions heard irrespective of the penitent's religious allegiance. The Jesuit practice was simply not to ask questions concerning doctrinal matters. After a few days in one location they moved on. Everywhere they were welcomed by the people, who had few opportunities to hear sermons of quality.

When any Orthodox individual was judged sincere in wishing to convert to Catholicism, the Jesuits required a private profession of faith. They recognized that centuries of hostility between Latin and Orthodox families on Naxos could not be dissipated overnight. Although the arrangement was contrary to Rome's instructions, converts were allowed to continue worshipping in the Orthodox church. Social pressure from family and friends would not have permitted any other course of action. Rome's demand that converts must make a public profession of faith was guided by the early Christian experience and by its more recent dealings with Western medieval heretics and converted Protestants. The Jesuit practice was based upon a realistic assessment of the situation which recognized a significant difference between formal and material heresy. In the

case of Orthodox Greeks within an isolated island community such
as on Naxos, the missionaries would find very few of the former –
therefore, the private administration of the sacraments could be
allowed and little done to disturb the consciences of those who,
because of cultural demands, could not afford a public pronounce-
ment of allegiance to Catholicism.

In 1634 there occurred on Naxos an event rare in the Ottoman
Empire: the assembly of a Catholic synod, the first since the Turkish
occupation. Summoned by Archbishop Schiattini, it began on
30 April and lasted for two weeks. Here, the Catholic clergy of
Naxos divided their attention between doctrinal, liturgical and disciplinary matters. In most cases, the synod did little more than
reaffirm its allegiance to the documents of Trent, but some of the
canons dealing with church life on the island provide an insight
into the practice of seventeenth-century Catholicism there.

According to one stipulation, parish church bells had to be rung
three times daily for the Angelus and once to announce the death
of a parishioner, but the cathedral bells had priority and parish bell
ringers had to wait until these had been heard. The hiring of
professional mourners by families of a recently deceased person was
forbidden. Anyone who had been the victim of a sorcerer was to
be exorcised.

Clergy were ordered to wear clerical dress both in public and
private, to confess and communicate weekly and, as part of their
Sunday observance, were to attend conferences where moral problems would be discussed.[19]

Another insight into Naxian Catholicism comes from a letter of
1643 written by the Jesuit Mathieu Hardy to his patrons in France.
After recounting the activities of the mission, he describes in detail
some of the activities of the island peoples. Carnival time immediately before Lent had once been filled with 'excesses', so the Jesuits
had instituted the Forty Hours' Devotion during these days. The
church was decorated and the Sacrament exposed. The archbishop
offered Mass in the ducal chapel each morning, then a sermon
followed. Upon its conclusion, the Office of the Blessed Virgin was
sung and confessions were heard. Throughout the day people took
turns assisting in worshipping the Eucharist in the church. In the
afternoon, classes on Christian doctrine were held, followed by
public recitation of the rosary, and the day ended with Compline
and Benediction.

Hardy was pleased to report that while in the past wealthy women of the island would send friends or servants to represent them on Ash Wednesday, they now attended in person. Holy Week brought the Catholic community's worship to its climax. A procession of uniformed men and women belonging to the confraternities, bearing candles, walked through the streets. Children, dressed in white, carried pictures of Christ's mysteries and of the saints, while two choirs sang appropriate hymns. Orthodox Christians sometimes joined in these activities also and, Hardy noted with satisfaction, 'The Turks are at the windows of their houses in such a way that they can view the solemnity.'

The Jesuit school offered classes taught in both Greek and Latin, but students usually lost interest before progressing very far and they left school to find work. Hardy had yet to discover a student whom he would consider an apt candidate for the clerical life. He found great difficulty in getting his Naxian parishoners to observe the laws of fasting and in persuading the women to sing in church. In their silence they contrasted with the women on Tinos and Chios who held their own rosary devotions with hymns on Saturday evenings.

The Jesuits were on good terms with the Orthodox metropolitan, Germanos Barbarigo, who had once attended the Greek College in Rome. Barbarigo encouraged his people to make their confessions to the Jesuits and to attend their catechetical instructions. Once, when Hardy was preaching in an Orthodox church and Vesper time had come, the Greek clergy began the service in an adjoining chapel lest he be disturbed, a gesture which, the Jesuit felt, characterized the Society's good relations with the Orthodox clergy. Despite the work of the missionaries, however, the lack of employment continued to drain Catholics from the island, thus keeping their number static.[20]

CHIOS

The situation of Catholics on the island of Chios had been improved by a *firman* of 1578 allowing the reestablishment of the Catholic bishopric which had been vacant for the twelve years since the island had come under direct Ottoman rule. The Catholics, though still numbering several thousand people, were served only by a single Latin priest when Bishop Benedetto Garetto landed. He soon discovered that his residence and cathedral were near collapse, necessitating a long rebuilding project which was finished only years later.[21]

The most promising event for the Catholics of Chios was the arrival in 1587 of the Jesuits. They opened a school on the grounds of the former Franciscan church of St Anthony, and within ten years the school enrolled two hundred students, eighty of whom were Orthodox. Just when the situation appeared to be so favourable, the grand duke of Tuscany, Ferdinand I, embarked on an Aegean adventure to 'liberate' the island from the Turks. In 1597, troops landed by the Florentine navy marched on the island's main fortress. There were no Catholics around to be liberated, since they had all been jailed on news of the expedition's approach. When the fleet withdrew, it left a climate of suspicion against the Catholic Chians, who were suspected of having collaborated with the Italians. Harsh measures were introduced by the Turks to limit Catholic activities, and Bishop Hieronimo Giustiniani was expelled.

Eventually, the animosity against the Catholics declined, allowing the French ambassador Césy to provide two Capuchins with papers permitting them to settle on Chios. The church of St Rocco was obtained by Césy for a residence where, in a short time, three more brothers joined them and a school was opened.[22]

The Dominicans were also active on Chios. They made St Sebastian's convent into a centre of study for their missionaries to the Orient. One superior on Chios, Jasques Goar, edited and published the Greek *Eulogion*, the ritual used by the Eastern church. A fellow Dominican stationed on Chios, Alessandro Baldrati, became a martyr for his faith in February 1645 when he was falsely accused by some Muslims of being an apostate from Islam. His accusers demanded that the Turkish authorities arrest him, so he was taken before the *kadi* who told him he had three days to abandon Christianity. Baldrati replied:

If you want my honest answer, I have no need of the three days. I have told you and once more repeat that nothing will ever make me renounce the faith of Jesus Christ...Your prophet is a false teacher and your law is the work of the father of lies.

His statement earned him a beating; then he was hauled away to prison and thrown down the steps to an underground cell.

Rumour swept through Chios that all the Dominicans of St Sebastian's were under arrest, and the Catholic bishop, Marco Giustiniani Massone, ordered all the churches to hold special services to strengthen Father Alessandro's resolve. For three days the friar remained alone in his cell; then he was brought out before the *kadi* to give his answer. As expected, he denied ever having been a

Muslim and assured the judge that he did not want to become one now. The *kadi* ordered him burned alive. A large crowd gathered to witness the event; a slow fire was lighted beneath him and his agony began. Before he died of suffocation, the soldiers charged with the execution beat him senseless and plunged a knife into his chest. The shocked Christians, both Catholic and Orthodox, went home convinced they had witnessed the death of a saint.[23]

In 1664 the Orthodox metropolitan, Ignatios Neochori, attacked the Catholics on Chios before the Turks, accusing them of illicit correspondence with Venice. According to the Anglican chaplain in Istanbul, Paul Rycaut, the true reason for Ignatios' action was his hope of gaining the Latin church properties for himself. The Latin bishop, Andrea Soffiano, was vulnerable because his *berat* had not yet been sent from Mehmet IV. Ignatios gained the support of several high-ranking officials in Istanbul who were willing to rule that the Greek metropolitan should henceforth hold jurisdiction over the Latin laity and control the churches. Soffiano was ordered to be expelled from Chios and the revenues of the Latin churches to be deposited with the Ottoman *kadi*.

Bishop Soffiano left for the court of Kara Mustafa at Edirne to appeal against the decision against him. Here he and his delegation were imprisoned on a charge of treason and the bishop was actually put in chains for fifteen days until a ransom could be raised to free him. Kara Mustafa ruled that any church which had been held by Catholics for less than sixty years should be transferred to Metropolitan Ignatios. Over sixty churches were therefore lost by the Chian Catholics to the Orthodox. Immediately, the French applied diplomatic pressure on the Turks and a new *firman*, issued on 4 January 1665, reversed the earlier decision. Only a few rural churches were not regained. Soffiano secured his *berat* and returned to his post. The tempest passed, and in 1667 a traveller reported that the eight thousand Catholics of the island were prospering. Later, Metropolitan Ignatios had so changed his views toward Catholicism as to be in correspondence with Rome.[24]

In 1681 the famous monastery of St John on the island of Patmos sought to enter the Catholic communion at a time when the Capuchin missionary quest was at its height. The monks here had frequently, in the past, looked to the West for assistance, requesting papal intercession with the Latin bishop of Chios. Three years after their allegiance to Rome was made, two French Capuchins took up residence on Patmos, bringing to the community a greeting from the pope. After hearing it the monks responded, 'May he have many years and many blessings!' The two Capuchins opened a small school and dispensary which was supported by revenues from the monastery.

On the night of 6 June 1684 a landing party of Turks came onto Patmos, ransacked the Capuchin residence and held the priests captive. The friars argued that they were Frenchmen, but the Turkish chieftain contended that they were Spaniards, and therefore enemies of the sultan. Finally, a ransom was paid to which the monks of St John contributed and the Capuchins were freed. They returned to their teaching and took up residence in the monastery itself where a small chapel was given them for offering the Latin Mass. They stayed only a few more months, however, and then left for other destinations. It is not known why the Patmos mission was abandoned.[25]

The church of Siros had an episcopal martyr in 1617 when its bishop, Giovanni-Andrea Carga, was put to death on the orders of the *Kapudan-paşa* of the Ottoman fleet. Carga was a Venetian Dominican who had been superior of the order's convent in Istanbul. In July 1607 he had been named bishop of Siros and for the next ten years had governed the Catholics of the island while living at the old Venetian cathedral of St George in Ano Siros. In October 1617 a fleet under Ali Paşa sailed into the harbour and accused the authorities of allowing Christian pirates to obtain provisions from the islanders. Since Muslim law held Christian bishops responsible for the good behaviour of the laity, Carga and two hundred others were placed under arrest. The bishop was further charged with espionage for the pope. He was given the opportunity of conversion to Islam in order to save himself, but he declined and on 18 November 1617 he was hanged. For three days his body was exposed; then the Catholics cut down the corpse and buried it in the cathedral.[26]

When Bishop Antonio Demarchis visited the island several years later he found that Carga's death had done nothing to weaken the faith of Siros' four thousand Catholics. One hundred and seventy Latin churches and chapels still functioned on the island as testaments to Catholic fidelity. Only seventy Orthodox were to be found in this Catholic preserve. Demarchis reported to Rome: 'The island of Siros is the only one in all the Levant which belongs to the Latin rite and because of its reverence for the Roman Church and the Supreme Pontiff, it is known as the island of the pope.'[27]

In 1600 Thira had a Catholic community of five hundred people in a total population of approximately five thousand. At the cathedral of St John the Baptist located in the town of Phior (Skaros), the Catholics were served by a bishop and two priests. Bishop Antonio Demarchis had arrived at his post after a long vacancy in the episcopate, for his predecessor had been denied a *berat* to take up residence on the island. During this period, the Orthodox laid claim to many Catholic properties, causing difficulties for Demarchis when he attempted to retrieve them.

In 1595 Demarchis, himself a Dominican, founded a community of Dominican nuns at Kartharatto – the first convent of women in the Ottoman Empire. After his death, the convent and the Catholic community as a whole were left in good condition for his successor, Bishop Pietro Demarchis. The Latin clergy were numerous; six canons were attached to his cathedral chapter. In 1642 the arrival of Jesuits further augmented the number of clergy.[28]

But on some Aegean islands the Catholic church was in serious decline. On Andros, for example, by 1600 there were only sixty Catholics. Capuchin efforts at revival ceased when the friars were expelled at the outset of the Cretan war. By mid-century, the Catholics had become even more sparse, only twenty-eight people remaining – two for each of the fourteen Latin churches on the island. On Siphnos and Kithnos the Gozzadini dynasty, the remaining Catholic princely family in the Aegean, held on until 1617. Their fall meant the end of Catholicism on these islands.

The French became much more involved in the Aegean after 1669 as a consequence of the Venetian defeat on Crete. The islanders welcomed the Capitulations agreed to between Istanbul and Paris which allowed them to claim French protection. These were widely promulgated throughout the islands to inform everyone of the special relationship that existed between Greek Catholics and the French sovereign. The French flag was now flown before the Catholic churches on the islands to warn both Muslims and Orthodox that the French monarch considered these churches and their congregations as his charge.[29]

During this period the Roman religious authorities continued to legislate for the Greek Catholics in a way meant to draw lines of distinction ever more sharply between them and their Orthodox neighbours. They emphasized that adult converts to Catholicism must make an explicit confession of the faith which emphasized obedience to papal power. A decree issued in 1669 made valid but illicit the marriage of a Catholic to an Orthodox, witnessed before an Orthodox priest. Several years later another decision forbade the baptizing of a child born to Catholic parents by an Orthodox minister except in an extreme emergency.[30]

Once the Ottomans gained Crete, they were anxious to recruit workers for the quarries located there. French protection was unable to prevent hundreds of island men, Catholic and Orthodox alike, to be commandeered for the task. For example, Siros' Catholic population was only two thousand in 1678, about half what it had been at the beginning of the century. Another cause of the depopulation of the islands was the raiding of Christian pirates who recognized no truce with the Turks and continued to ply their trade in the Aegean, wreaking havoc upon the population. After 1683 their activities were sanctioned by the war of the Holy League. The island of Ios was so infested with Christian corsairs that the Turks called it 'Little Malta'.[31]

CRETE

At the time of Sultan Ibrahim's invasion in 1645, Crete had been Venice's most important colony, with a Latin archbishopric in Candia (Iraklion) and four suffragan sees ministering to the island's four thousand Catholics. The Greek clergy were theoretically required to be united with Rome; their highest cleric was a *protopapas*, for no Orthodox bishop was allowed to reside there. In 1630, a visitor counted thirty-two Latin churches and seventy-seven Greek churches on the island. But in the outlying regions there was a constant flow of Catholics to Orthodoxy since few priests were willing to live away from the larger towns.

Religious on the island included Dominicans, Franciscans and Capuchins, but none of their establishments was flourishing in the seventeenth century. Native candidates to the orders were few and the lack of discipline in the Dominican and Franciscan houses made it difficult to obtain recruits from Italy. The decline of clerical religious life was reflected in the spirituality of the laity. The Jesuit Girolamo Dandini on his journey to Lebanon in 1596 noted some of the Cretan church's problems:

The custom of the women on the island is not to go out of their houses in the day, nor to go to hear Mass or sermons, yet they run around the streets in great numbers all night long, frequently accompanied by men, and go into the churches which have been left open for them.[32]

When the Turks landed on Crete, their first act was to besiege Canea (Khania). The Greek population was divided on whether to support the invaders; people in rural areas tended to join the Ottomans while those in the cities remained loyal to Venice. While Canea fell to the Turks in the first several months of the conflict there was slow progress elsewhere since the Venetian fleet dominated the sea. Only when Candia capitulated after many years of conflict did the Turks become undisputed masters of Crete. Upon the island's surrender all Latin churches were converted into mosques with the exception of two which were sold, one to the Orthodox and one to the Armenians. The peace treaty allowed the Venetians to retain only two footholds on Crete, at Grabusa and Soudha. Here Capuchin missionaries stayed on to provide religious services for the small Venetian garrisons. Some of the Catholic landowners on Crete converted to Islam in order to retain their estates, as did a number of Orthodox, so that by the late nineteenth century, almost half the island's population had become Muslim.[33]

CYPRUS

The church served by Franciscans from the Holy Land at Larnaca, and a small chapel reopened in Nicosia, were the only Catholic places of worship on the island in 1600. When Dandini stopped on Cyprus, he visited the chapel in Nicosia to find an old priest, 'very ignorant', serving the Italian merchants living there. The Maronite villages, a dozen in number, were shockingly poor.[34]

Two French Jesuits came to Cyprus in 1627 with a merchant from their homeland. The Italians informed the Turkish authorities that they were spies of the Spanish king, thus ensuring their arrest and expulsion. Despite this setback, the Congregation for the Propagation of the Faith decided to restore a Catholic bishopric on Cyprus just two years later, with Paphos as the see city, and a Carmelite, Pietro de Vespis, as bishop of the Latin and Maronite churches on the island. Since de Vespis had no sympathy for the Maronites, he began a vigorous campaign to have them conform to Latin usages.

Later the Capuchins arrived, establishing houses in Paphos and Larnaca, but when the merchant colonies declined, they could not remain. In 1684, Bishop Leonardo Paoli died, and there was no attempt to replace him, for only two hundred and fifty Latin Catholics remained on the island.[35]

THE GREEK MAINLAND

In 1640 two French Jesuits, François Blaizeau and René de St
Cosme, were dispatched to Navplion and Patras. These were the
first Catholic clergy for almost two hundred years on the Greek
mainland. The Jesuits turned up some Catholic merchants in both
towns, but found the largest number of Latins among the slaves
quartered in Navplion. Here almost five hundred prisoners, drawn
from many nations, rowed the galleys of the bey. Blaizeau reported:
'Some Latin individuals have passed over to the Greek rite, since
they have not had any priest of the Latin. They promised to return
to the Roman church if a permanent priest could be procured for
them here.'[36]

In early December 1641 Blaizeau went to Athens to canvass the
possibility of establishing a Jesuit house there. He met with the
Ottoman municipal officials and the local Orthodox clergy, who
were so impressed by his plans for a school that they wrote to
Istanbul asking the government to allow him to remain. Blaizeau's
school was begun in 1645, but there were too few students to
warrant its continuation. It moved to Chalkis in Euboea where the
seven or eight Catholic merchant families in residence provided
sufficient students to make the venture worthwhile.

Blaizeau was a temperate man and followed the Jesuit tradition
of seeking out the Orthodox clergy to dissipate their fears. He
asserted: 'I do all that I can to show the Greeks that we love them
and respect their rite.' The Turks were impressed with the Jesuits
because they were considered to be well-versed in astrology.[37]

It was the French Capuchins, however, not the Jesuits, who
established the first Catholic mission in Athens in the year 1658.
Simon of Compiègne, the second priest stationed there, purchased a
house which incorporated the ancient choregic monument of Lysi-
crates, then known as the 'Lantern of Demosthenes'. News of the
transfer brought some remonstrances from the neighbourhood, and
an appeal to the Turkish governor to annul the sale. Instead he
confirmed the transaction, but ordered Simon to be sure that the
monument would be kept open to any visitors who might want to
see it. The Capuchin agreed and his residence, with its famous
antiquity, became a Catholic possession. He opened a school and
when other friars appeared, they served the cause of archaeology
by making a map of Athens and its ancient monuments. They also
helped the cause of agriculture by introducing the tomato to

Greece.[38] In the autumn of 1672 the Jesuit Jacques-Paul Babin visited Athens and composed a description of the city which was subsequently published in Lyon. Among other anecdotes, he relates the Capuchins' discovery of a marble statue of Mary in what was regarded at that time as the house of Athens' famous saint, Dionysius the Areopagite. Since Orthodox tradition forbade the use of sculpture, Babin claimed that the Greek metropolitan ordered it to be destroyed lest Dionysius' reputation be damaged.[39]

During their campaigns in the Peloponnesus, during the war of the Holy League, the Venetians brought Latin clergy with them and, as they occupied the cities of the area, Catholic priests were restored in some churches. In others, Orthodox clerics were not displaced but continued to serve their congregations. A single restriction was imposed on them by Venice: not to communicate with the patriarchate. When Francesco Morosini held Athens for a short time in 1687 he confiscated all the city's mosques and made them into churches.[40]

In addition to their work in the Peloponnesus and central Greece, Western missionaries also journeyed north into Macedonia to visit the centre of Orthodox monasticism on Mt Athos. Wandering Greek monks from the monasteries were sometimes bearers of information to Latin clergy even in Rome itself, whetting the interest of Western churchmen to make the Holy Mountain a field for Catholic missionary activity.

The Latins often busied themselves gathering professions of faith, easy to obtain from those dissatisfied with their situation for one reason or another. One Catholic priest, Josaphat Azales, an alumnus of the Greek College in Rome, made several important contacts there. Upon the request of Ignatios, abbot of the Vatopedion monastery, Pope Urban VIII commissioned Nicholas Rossi to go to the Holy Mountain and open a school at Karyes. The Ottoman authorities eventually grew suspicious of Rossi's school and forced its closure after five years in operation. Undaunted, Rossi began his institution once more in Salonica, but both he and his school succumbed soon afterwards.

Meanwhile the monks of Pantelemon wrote to the pope expressing their devotion to the see of St Peter, and in 1643 the Holy Synod of the monasteries requested that a hospice be established in Rome for their pilgrims; they promised to reciprocate by setting up a guest house on Mt Athos for visiting Italo-Greeks of the Catholic Basilians.[41]

Late in the seventeenth century the vexation of Turkish rule had so frustrated some of the Orthodox on the Mani peninsula in the Peloponnesus that they determined to emigrate to the West. One group settled in Tuscany and were absorbed into the Latin church. Another, larger emigration of seven hundred set out from the village of Iotilion, having received an assurance of welcome from the Genoese authorities. The first of these, including Bishop Parthenios Kaklandes, sailed for Genoa in September 1675 aboard a French ship. On their arrival, the authorities directed them to Corsica. Parthenios was told to report to the Latin bishop there, who was to be considered his superior. In March 1676 they arrived in Corsica and were assigned lands in Paomia. Over the next decades the community flourished, having several churches and even a monastery.[42]

The seventeenth century in the European part of the Ottoman Empire may be assessed in different ways. In some areas there was certainly progress – especially among the Bulgarians, for whom the introduction of Catholicism helped to abet their nationalist tendencies. On the other hand, the War of the Holy League at the end of the century was a disaster for Venice, and hence a disaster for Italian Catholic interests. The bright spot on the horizon was a growing French Catholic presence. The Turks thought of the French as allies while the Venetians were their traditional enemies. As long as such distinctions were made in Istanbul, the church would be able to survive.

8

The Orient and the Latin missions

In line with the policy of the Congregation for the Propagation of the Faith to reinstate former Christian sees in the Orient, Izmir was established as a bishopric in 1624. The bishop of Chios, Pietro Demarchis, appointed to this office, also received jurisdiction over the Istanbul vicariate. At the time of his appointment, Izmir had two Catholic churches: the Immaculate Conception, served by Franciscan Observants, where the Italian merchants worshipped, and a chapel which had just been started for the French community by the Jesuit, Jérôme Queyrot. Demarchis lived most of his time on nearby Chios where the Catholic community was much larger. In September 1644 he was given as coadjutor another Dominican, Giacintho Subiano, who was named titular bishop of Edessa with the right of succession.[1]

Within three years of the reconstitution of the Izmir episcopate, two Capuchin missionaries, Pacifique of Provins and Louis of Rheims, came to the city as chaplains to the French consul. In 1630 they dedicated their church to Izmir's patron, St Polycarp, with considerable solemnity. When Bishop Subinao later transferred to Istanbul the small Catholic community at Izmir no longer enjoyed an episcopal resident, but henceforth the apostolic vicar was chosen from among the religious who served in the town. The majority of Catholics were French and Italian merchants, often at odds with each other. One of the latter, Niccolò Caseti, was promoted as a martyr by his countrymen after his death in 1657. Caseti had been charged with embezzlement and in order to avoid punishment, for his defence was apparently very weak, he announced that he wanted to become a Muslim. Several days afterwards, regretting his decision, he sought the advice of the missionaries, who encouraged him to return to the Catholic faith. He replaced a Christian turban on his head, was arrested by the Turks as expected, and paid with his life the penalty for apostasy from Islam.

Izmir's Greek Catholics were emigrants from the islands who sought employment on the mainland. There was also a community of Catholic Armenians, merchants from Nakhichevan who made a living from the caravan trade which passed through their country to the Aegean. Many of these adopted the Latin rite in the absence of Armenian Catholic clergy.[2]

THE ARMENIANS

As the seventeenth century opened, the incessant warfare between the Turks and Persians was causing the Armenians untold grief. At that time the catholicate at Echmiadzin was held jointly by the catholicoi Melchisedech and Tavit IV. During their tenure in office, after Latin missionaries visited their residence, both leaders sent professions of faith to Rome. Melchisedech was effusive in his admiration for the Roman see which, he asserted, was illuminated 'by the sun of Peter and the moon of Paul'. His envoy to Rome, Vardapet Zacharia, returned to Armenia with an acknowledgment from the pope of his Catholic faith, accompanied by a request for several liturgical changes in the Armenian rite.[3]

When Shah Abbas incorporated Echmiadzin and its surrounding territory into Persia the situation of the Armenians became more difficult. Ruinous taxes were imposed upon the Christians and thousands, including many of the Catholics of Nakhichevan, were ordered to leave their homes for settlement in Persia. Outside Isfahan an Armenian city, New Julfa, was created by these exiles. From 1600 to 1612 the number of Dominican Unitor monasteries in Nakhichevan fell from nineteen to twelve and the number of Catholic laity was reduced to 19,000.[4]

The situation of the Armenians on the Turkish–Persian frontier was in contrast to that of the Armenians of the capital, whose population increased in numbers, wealth and importance. The Armenian cathedral, dedicated to St George, was the richest in the capital, and eight other churches of the Istanbul region had become the property of the Armenians. Unfortunately, the incumbents in the Armenian patriarchate experienced the same kind of turnover as befell the Greeks, since the same forces were at work: ambitious clerics who wanted to enjoy the revenues attached to the patriarchate, and laymen who were willing to finance their favourites. Turkish officials interfered in the Armenian elections with equal interest.

Little was heard from the catholicate of Sis, whose prelates were often forced to wander about Cilicia seeking residence in monasteries. The catholicoi often found refuge in Aleppo, the most prosperous city in the orbit of the catholicate and in which Christians felt most secure. Accounts left by Western missionaries to the Orient are always full of praise for the hospitality of the Ottoman Armenians. Missionaries found them anxious to hear of church developments in the West, and their clergy expressed little hostility to the papacy. In Istanbul, the patriarch, Hovannes III the Deaf, often welcomed the Catholics in the capital to his residence. After twenty years in office, he resigned and went off to live in the Armenian colony in Lvov where he made a profession of the Catholic faith in 1632. His successor in Istanbul, Zacharias of Van, was also sympathetic to the West in marked distinction from his Greek contemporary, Kyrillos Loukaris.[5]

In 1640, the most successful of the Latin missionaries to the Armenians, Clemens Galano, arrived in Istanbul. Galano was a Theatine religious, who had studied both Armenian and Georgian before arrival in the Orient four years earlier. His first assignment was to the Caucasus region; then he was transferred to the capital where he was welcomed by the then ruling patriarch, Kyriakos of Erevan. The French ambassador, de la Haye, joined Galano and the Dominican missionary Paulo Piromalli in persuading Kyriakos to sign a profession of faith and submission to papal authority in 1641.

Galano dressed in the costume of an Armenian vardapet and was appointed to teach in the patriarchal school as long as Kyriakos was head of the church. But when the patriarch died, a victim of the plague, to be replaced by Khatchatour of Sivas, also a friend of the Catholics, a reaction to the pro-Catholic sentiment of the patriarchs appeared among the more conservative members of the Armenian *millet*. Khatchatour was ousted and a traditional candidate installed. This was Tavit of Aleppo, who dismissed Galano from his post in the patriarchal school and brought charges against him before Porte officials that he was disloyal to the government. Galano was arrested, but released upon the appeal of the French ambassador. He returned to Rome in 1643 to become professor of Armenian at the Urban College. Here he composed his great work, *The Concordance of the Church of Armenia with Rome taken from*

the Writings of the Fathers and Doctors, published in 1658. This
volume was, thereafter, the handbook of Western missionaries sent
to the Orient to work among the Armenians. Galano died in 1662
in Lvov where he had been sent to confer with the Armenian community on behalf of the Roman authorities.[6]

Meanwhile the Armenians of Echmiadzin were in frequent correspondence with Rome, important among them the catholicoi Movses
III and Pilibos. Affairs in this part of the world were in a continual
state of flux due to the interminable wars between the Turks and
Persians. The catholicoi were often refugees, and sometimes prisoners, on suspicion of leanings toward the enemy. In fact, Shah Abbas'
son Sufi had promoted the elevation of Movses of Datev because he
was considered to favour the Persians. Prior to his appointment
Movses had been active in reforming the monasteries and he had
been instrumental in making Datev a centre of intellectual activity.
As Movses III, he and twelve of his bishops forwarded a profession
of the Catholic faith to Rome.

The Catholic Armenians were assisted by the Dominican missionary Piromalli, who came to the convent of Abaraner in 1632.
For the next twenty-five years he devoted his ministry to the
Armenians in Nakhichevan and in other parts of the Near East.
For two years he was imprisoned, but at other times he so enjoyed
the favour of Armenian churchmen that he was invited to teach
at Echmiadzin. In 1638 he went to Rome to oversee the publication
of Armenian texts and liturgical books, and after his return to the
Orient in 1642 reached the height of his missionary career when he
was named archbishop of Nakhichevan in 1665; he held this position for the next five years. Piromalli was responsible for obtaining
a confession of faith signed by Catholicos Pilibos, twenty-five bishops
and eight vardapets of the Armenian church.

The French traveller Jean Baptiste Tavernier, who visited Nakhichevan in 1650, found that Latinization had so thoroughly penetrated this remote corner of Christendom that Armenian religious
chanted the Dominican office in Latin and offered the Latin Mass.
Tavernier estimated the number of Catholic laity as less than six
thousand. During the next decade Catholic numbers, both religious
and lay, declined, so that a French traveller in 1673 found only a
few Catholics still living along the road from Nakhichevan to New
Julfa.[7]

In 1662 when the Armenian catholicos at Echmiadzin was Hagop
IV of Julfa, he and twenty-five other Armenian bishops began a

journey to seek assistance for their church from the Western Christians. The delegation reached Istanbul, where Catholicos Hagop was received by the Dominican prior at SS Peter and Paul, then acting apostolic vicar. Hagop made a commitment to the Catholic faith which was subsequently brought to Rome.[8]

Meanwhile, in Istanbul an Armenian Catholic patriarch, To'vma of Aleppo, had ruled for two years, from 1657 to 1659. To'vma's accession had come about through negotiations with the officials of the Porte. He promised a significant increase in payments by the Armenian *millet* if he were appointed patriarch. Once he had obtained this goal, he added the catholicate of Jerusalem to his own jurisdiction so as to increase the revenues of Constantinople. His deposition came on a charge that he had become a 'Frank'; he was first imprisoned, then poisoned and his body thrown into the Golden Horn by his enemies.

Toward the end of his catholicate the aged Hagop IV once more made his way back to Istanbul to visit the Catholic representatives in residence there. He made another confession of Catholic belief and of submission to the authority of the pope before Bishop Gasparini and the Jesuit superior François Gili. He died while in Istanbul. A member of his party, Israel Ori, went on to Rome to plead the cause of the Armenian church and, meanwhile, the Armenian clergy elected Eleazer of Glai Hagop's successor.[9]

The French Jesuits became especially concerned with missions to the Armenians in Eastern Turkey and Persia; in the latter part of the seventeenth century, they established centres in Erzurum, Bitlis, Isfahan, New Julfa and Erivan. From their residence in Erivan, they visited Catholicos Eleazer at Echmiadzin to speak of religious matters and to hold out the prospect of French protection for his nation. At one time Eleazer would be sympathetic, at another time, persuaded by his more nationalistic advisers, he would have nothing to do with them and would order his people to avoid the Latins under pain of excommunication.

In 1685 the Jesuit missionary Roux arrived in Echmiadzin. He had earlier been stationed in New Julfa whence his good reputation preceded him to Echmiadzin and won him a welcome from the catholicos. He was given permission to visit the neighbouring monasteries and to preach to the monks. When he fell ill, the catholicos often visited him. His sickness proved fatal; he died on 11 September 1686 and Catholicos Eleazer agreed to officiate at his funeral.

His successor, a Jesuit named Dupuis, continued to call upon

the catholicos, but his efforts to persuade him to sign a formal profession of faith were unavailing. Eleazer told Dupuis that such a
gesture was unnecessary since he knew that he and the bishop of
Rome shared the same Christian faith. On one occasion, the Jesuit
gave him a portrait of Louis XIV which the grateful catholicos
had placed on the door of a church, believing, perhaps, that the
French king might prove to be an important addition to his collection of icons.[10]

SYRIA

In the early seventeenth century no Syrian city was as prosperous as
Aleppo. Here there was a large European Christian merchant community along with native Syrians and Armenians who profited from
the silk and spice trade which passed through the city. The whole
northeast quarter was inhabited by Eastern Christians who acted on
their own behalf or served as managers for European firms. The
Christian quarter had its own walls with gates which were closed at
night to prevent disturbances, and in the heart of the quarter were
the churches, grouped around a large square.

Early in the seventeenth century the Franciscans of the Holy
Land sent one or two missionaries to live in Aleppo to serve the
Latins of the town and solicit alms from the wealthy Catholic
merchants. They were not overjoyed when they learned that other
religious orders in Europe planned to make Aleppo a headquarters
of missionary activity in Syria. Almost simultaneously, Jesuits,
Capuchins and Carmelites sought permission to open houses in
Aleppo.

The Jesuits enjoyed the support of both Louis XIII and Pope
Urban VIII; the French ambassador de Brèves was told to represent
them before the authorities at the Porte. The ambassador did not
relish this task; he feared that the coming of the Jesuits might work
against French interests in Syria. Nevertheless, he obtained from the
Turks a *firman* allowing the Society to settle there.

In August 1625 two Jesuits, Gaspard Maniglier and Jean Stella,
arrived in Aleppo and obtained the French consul's aid in finding
lodgings. A solid front of opposition to their presence was put
together, however, by the English and Venetians. The local authorities were alerted to the danger that the Jesuits presented and the
kaimakam ordered their arrest; they were beaten and expelled to
Alexandretta where they were imprisoned until the governor put
them aboard a ship bound for the West. When they put into Malta

the persistent Jesuits changed vessels and took passage to Istanbul, where they sought official support. After several months of negotiations and payments made by the French embassy to appropriate officials, the Jesuits received new and more effective documents permitting them to return to Aleppo in April 1627.

This time their entry was taken more calmly. When Jérôme Queryot arrived on the scene several months later, the hostility of the town's Christians had turned to admiration, especially when the Jesuits expended all their resources to assist the sick during an outbreak of plague.

The Melkite bishop of Aleppo, Meletios Karmi, like many of his episcopal confrères, sought to keep on good terms with both Catholics and Orthodox. Offering them every consideration, he invited the Jesuits to hold classes in his residence. Soon Queryot could report: 'This school grows from day to day, so quickly that there are now almost thirty children in it who are instructed in Greek, Arabic, and Italian.'[11]

In 1633, upon a change of government officials, the Jesuit community once again came under fire. The two priests and brothers then in Aleppo were jailed for having converted their residence into a church where public worship was conducted. The paşa ordered them to be put into chains and tortured. They were rescued by protests from the French consul, joined on this occasion by the English and Dutch representatives, and resumed their educational work. The French representative subsequently sent a request to Istanbul to arrange for the Jesuits to be named chaplains to the consulate, thus providing them a sanctuary from Ottoman vexations.

The Jesuit presence in Syria was subsequently extended to Damascus. Soon afterwards, Meletios Karmi, who had been on good terms with the Latins for a long time, was chosen to be Melkite patriarch. He invited the Jesuits to staff a school in the patriarchal grounds in Damascus, but an anti-Western group within the church objected. Eventually, this faction prevailed; Meletios was ousted and a Chian, Euthymios III, replaced him. While he too was a friend of the Catholics, he urged the Westerners to avoid notice because of the 'spies' of the patriarch of Constantinople. His successor, Makarios III Za'im, secretly sent off a profession of the Catholic faith to Rome while publicly appearing to be in the Orthodox camp.[12]

In the same year that the Jesuits had established their house in Aleppo the Capuchins also came, led by the indefatigable Pacifique of Provins. They received a better welcome than the Jesuits and were especially befriended by the Maronites. Pacifique met with the Ottoman Vezir Khalil Paşa, when the latter passed through Aleppo, to obtain a guarantee of the rights of the French Franciscans. The Capuchins reported on their work in Aleppo:

At present we live peacefully; our residence is founded on a firm rock; we celebrate Mass in our poor church, we chant the divine offices and we preach in public to the great joy and happiness of all the nations and thus the Lord God rewards the obedience of his servants.[13]

The Spanish Carmelite, Prosper of the Holy Spirit, first appeared in Aleppo on a journey from Persia. He remained in the town, intending to make Aleppo a staging post on the road to the Carmelite missions in Persia. Three priests and a brother were accordingly stationed in the town. Since there were now four Latin religious communities in Aleppo, the Congregation for the Propagation of the Faith decided to name a bishop for Syria. In 1645 a Franciscan Observant was named to the office, but apparently never visited his see.[14]

The Catholic cause received its greatest impetus when Paris commissioned François Picquet consul to Aleppo in 1652. Picquet let it be known that any Oriental Christian who joined the Roman communion would enjoy the king of France's protection and every possible support. Picquet viewed the Jacobites, smallest and politically weakest of the Christian groups, as the most promising field of missionary activity. The Jacobite patriarch was far away, living in his monastery outside Mardin and isolated from his Aleppan flock. His absence had allowed the Catholics to make inroads into the Syrian church even before Picquet's appointment.

In 1656 a Syrian Jacobite convert to Catholicism, 'Abdul-Ghal Akhijan, having studied at the Maronite College in Rome, returned to Lebanon and took up residence with the Maronite patriarch at Qannubin. Picquet suggested that he be consecrated bishop by the Maronite patriarch and sent to Aleppo as head of those Jacobites who had become Catholic. So on 29 June 1656 Akhijan was consecrated bishop by Yuhanna Safraoui, taking the name Andreah. He then went to Mardin to explain the situation to the Jacobite patriarch. This prelate questioned how he could consider himself anything but a Maronite bishop since no one in the Syrian church had elected him? Undaunted, Bishop Andreah transferred to Aleppo, where he had neither a church nor any Jacobite cleric willing to accept him, but only Picquet and the Latin religious, and perhaps two hundred and fifty Catholic Syrians.

His position was so untenable that he left Aleppo within the year. Nevertheless the French Capuchins in the city persuaded him to return in March 1658, promising him a guard, a pension, and a guarantee that the Ottoman officials in the city would acknowledge him as head of the Syrians there. Andreah returned, although his position with the Jacobites remained ambiguous.

In 1662 word arrived in Aleppo that the head of the Jacobites had died and that an election for a new patriarch was pending. Andreah's French sponsors at once began contacting the members of the Jacobite synod, seeking to have him chosen patriarch, and furnishing twenty thousand *sous* to convince the electors of his worthiness. Andreah's bid was successful, not only with the Jacobite synod but also with the Ottoman officials in Istanbul who furnished him with a *berat* written in gold, calling him 'Patriarch of the Syrian Catholics'. Andreah received recognition from Rome only in 1667 when Pope Clement IX forwarded a pallium and confirmation in his office as head of the Syrian Catholic church. Despite the fact that his unquestioned jurisdiction was really limited to a few Catholic converts from the Jacobites, approximately eight hundred in all, he is recognized as the first patriarch of the Syrian Catholics. He died peacefully on 18 July 1677.[15]

There was only one possible Catholic successor to Bishop Andreah, the Syrian bishop of Jerusalem, Butrus, the single convert Andreah had gained among the Jacobite hierarchy. On his way to Aleppo, Butrus fell ill and, in the interim, the monophysite Syrians gained the upper hand. An election resulted in the choice of a Jacobite, 'Abdul Massih, for the patriarchal office. 'Abdul Massih claimed the allegiance of all the Syrians, but the Catholic party refused to recognize him, held their own synod, and elected Butrus of Jerusalem as Patriarch Ignatius Butrus Gregorius.

Since the outcome of the divided election depended upon Ottoman recognition, the Capuchin missionary Justinian of Tours, disguised as a Bedouin and furnished with several hundred *sous*, slipped off to Istanbul. His mission was successful: the Porte gave a *berat* to Butrus Gregorius. Meanwhile the Jesuit Michael Nau went off to Rome to present the case of Butrus Gregorius to the pope and to convince Rome that prompt recognition of his claim was essential for the Catholic Syrian cause. Nau was successful: a pallium and confirmation of Butrus Gregorius was handed to him on 2 April

1678. He then travelled to Paris where Louis XIV's government promised the Catholic patriarch an annual pension of two hundred *sous*. Meanwhile Butrus Gregorius consecrated one of his priests, Risqallah Amin-Han, to be bishop of Homs (Emesa), thus assuring a Catholic succession among the Syrians. Throughout his tenure in office Butrus Gregorius was constantly under attack and without continued French support his tenure would have been impossible.[16]

The high point of Catholic success in Aleppo came in 1658 when Consul Picquet was able to confirm that three of the patriarchs resident in Syria – Andreah of the Syrians, Khatchatour of the Armenians and Makarios of the Melkites – were now Catholics. He secured documents from all of them stating that they would be loyal to the pope. A joint letter was sent to King Louis XIV begging his assistance:

The condition of the Christians of the Orient, living under tyranny, is so wretched that men have apostasized with their wives, others have sold their children to pay their taxes, still more are dead from starvation or lie in prison. Such a terrible situation has never ever been seen.[17]

In 1662 Picquet was replaced as consul by an equally fervent Catholic, François Baron. Upon his arrival he found a tempest brewing in the Armenian community between the Catholic faction and those holding to the national church. An estimated thirteen of the twenty-two Armenian clergy had converted to Catholicism, so rousing the ire of the national party. This group reported to the Turkish *kadi* that many of the clergy had become 'Franks' and one of the supposed converts stepped forward to admit he had lodged at the consul's house where he had been urged to promote rebellion among his people. Baron quelled the disturbance by obtaining Patriarch Khatchatour's testimony that such was not the case. This was easy to get since Khatchatour, as has been seen, favoured the Catholics.

The Catholics in Aleppo suffered only one setback, in 1650, when a Catholic priest announced his conversion to Islam, stating 'I have found my salvation in the Koran.' Such conversions were not common, but when they happened they plunged the other Christian missionaries into despair.[18]

In addition to Aleppo the Jesuits had stations at Antakya and several other places in Lebanon and Syria, wherever the number of merchants was large enough to warrant their presence. They served the French communities by conducting schools and administering the sacraments. While the arbitrary action of Ottoman officials sometimes impeded their work, Orthodox hostility was even more difficult to tolerate. One Jesuit superior in Syria, Antoine-Marie Nacchi, complained in a letter to France:

There is much to suffer from the schismatics. The schism inspires them with an implacable hatred against Catholics and particularly against the missionaries. They use lying, calumny, perfidy, and false witness to bring down the wrath of the Turks upon them as often as they can.[19]

Since Damascus was the residence of the Melkite patriarchs, the Jesuits stationed there had the delicate task of cultivating their friendship while seeking converts from their flock. For several decades this responsibility fell to Jérôme Queyrot, who proved adept at gaining the good will of the Eastern clergy. When he died in 1676 all the Oriental bishops of the city attended his funeral. The Melkite Patriarch Makarios III, one of his closest friends, led his clergy in mourning.

In 1688, after Makarios III's tenure, two claimants to the patriarchate appeared: Athanasios III, supported by the Melkites in Damascus, and Kyrillos V, who represented Aleppo. Both were sympathetic to Catholicism, but the most outspoken of Rome's friends among the Melkite hierarchy was Euthymios Saifi, metropolitan of Tyre and Sidon. Euthymios was a native of Damascus whose pro-Catholic sentiments arose from his antipathy toward Greek prelates who sought to dominate the native Syrians. In 1680 Euthymios officially converted to Catholicism and then became head of the Catholic party among the Melkites.[20]

THE MARONITES

In 1567, Mikha'il al-Risi was elected Maronite patriarch, but he was slow to send a delegation to Rome to ask for confirmation and the pallium. Ten years passed before Pope Gregory XIII heard from him. He sent a delegation to the Maronites to ascertain the state of the church and, to represent him, chose two Jesuits, Giovanni-Battista Eliano, who had the previous experience of a mission to the Copts, and Tommaso Raggio. They were to carry a letter from the pope to Patriarch Mikha'il and an instruction from Cardinal Caraffa, the cardinal-protector of the Maronites, containing twenty-three articles which the patriarch was called upon to consider. These were based on the decisions of Trent which attempted to make uniform the liturgical practices in the Western church. Specifically, the Maronites were requested to change the formula of the *Trisagion* of the Eucharist, the manner of making chrism and of administering confirmation. They were further asked to stop the practice of giving infants the Holy Eucharist immediately after baptism and to accept the Latin reckoning of degrees of kinship for valid marriages. In effect, the Maronite church was to be required to become more western and less eastern in order to stay in the good graces of Rome.[21]

After a year in Lebanon, the Jesuits returned to Rome believing they had gained the acquiescence of the Maronite church. Eliano carried a list of propositions upon which the Maronites would act so as to come closer to the Latin practice of dispensing the sacraments. Pope Gregory XIII was delighted with the report, composed a letter to Patriarch Mikha'il and commissioned the Jesuits to return to Lebanon so that a full council of the church might ratify the propositions.

Eliano and a new Jesuit companion, Fabio Bruno, once again took ship for the Levant, carrying liturgical gifts for the patriarch and messages from the pope and Cardinal Caraffa. Having arrived at Qannubin, they prevailed upon Patriarch Mikha'il to summon a council for 15 August 1580.

This synod of Qannubin was dominated by the Jesuits. A Roman catechism written by Bruno and translated into Arabic by Eliano was proposed and accepted for the religious education of the Maronites. Then a number of canons, based upon the patriarchal propositions and Cardinal Caraffa's instructions, were adopted. Only three days of meeting were required.

At the conclusion of the synod, Eliano and Bruno travelled around the Maronite villages explaining the actions taken at the council. During their journey, they received word that Patriarch Mikha'il had died, and his brother, Sergieh al-Risi, had been chosen as his successor. Family interests were strong in Lebanon, and the patriarchate could not easily be detached from a powerful family.[22]

According to custom, Sergieh journeyed to Tripoli to profess his loyalty to the Ottoman governor, and then requested that Bruno go to Rome for papal confirmation and the pallium. Gregory XIII sent both in March 1583. Meanwhile, Eliano had returned and persuaded the pope that the Maronites, as well as the Greeks and Armenians, should have a college in Rome. The Maronite College was opened in February 1584 with a staff of Jesuits.[23]

This college became an important source of contact between

Rome and the East, for students soon arrived from the Orient to be immersed in Latin theology and liturgy as well as devotion to the church of Rome. Publishing became an activity of the college after the establishment of a press by Ya'kub Kamar. The first books in Arabic included the office of the dead, the four Gospels, and eventually a missal. All of the Maronite manuscripts were altered to conform to Latin practices when the rubrics appeared in printed form.

During the pontificate of Clement VIII complaints had come to Rome that alumni of the Maronite College were not always welcomed on their return to the East. As a result, Clement VIII returned to what had become the usual means of communicating with the Maronite church: a Jesuit mission to Lebanon.

Once more Fabio Bruno was pressed into service, and since Eliano had died, Girolamo Dandini, a philosophy professor at Perugia, was chosen for his companion. In his memoir, Dandini explains: 'The Maronites had now, for a long time, been badly represented to the Pope and Cardinals; they were also accused of different errors and considerable heresies...'[24]

The Jesuits appeared in Lebanon in 1596, when the political power on the mountain was held by Fakhr ad-Din al-Ma'in II, grandson of his namesake who had first greeted the Turks on their arrival in Lebanon. Unlike so many Druze chieftains, Fakhr ad-Din was interested in European affairs, welcomed contacts with the West, and dreamed of the day when Lebanon might be free of Ottoman rule. Hence, the Maronite western alliance was looked on favourably by the prince as opening the door for the fulfilment of his plans.

When Bruno and Dandini reached Qannubin they were greeted by monastery bells, but inside they found Patriarch Sergieh very ill. He was also in bad humour, complaining that he had been treated poorly by Rome. Instead of a solemn document of his confirmation as patriarch, he had received only an unimpressive letter. He also resented being pressured into summoning a council which, he felt, was contrary to Maronite tradition.

Over his objections the Jesuits insisted that he call together the Maronite bishops, clergy and *mouqaddamin* to meet in September. In the interim Dandini sought to learn exactly the content of the Maronite 'errors'. Finally, the day for the council arrived with but two bishops present, although a larger number of clergy and chieftains were in attendance. The former Latinizing legislation was dusted off and presented to the group; so was the Maronite missal printed in Rome. The council gave its approval. Then, in October, Patriarch Sergieh died and, despite objections from the papal party, his nephew, Yusuf al-Risi, was elected to be his successor. Dandini believed a new synod should be called for November, because of the change in the patriarchs.

When this synod opened, only three bishops were present in addition to the patriarch. Of the three, two were recently consecrated graduates of the Maronite College. Once more the canons previously adopted were reaffirmed and the Jesuits believed their task had been accomplished. To be certain, Dandini dictated a personal memorandum to Patriarch Yusuf on what other measures might be taken to reform the church. At the council, Dandini had tried to convince the Maronites to accept all of the Tridentine legislation, as well as the Gregorian calendar. The patriarch argued that if the Maronites were going to adopt Latin modification in their administration of the sacraments, then they should also change their rigorous rules on fasts and abstinence. Dandini failed to see the patriarch's logic and argued that this could not be done, because it involved changing the Maronite tradition![25]

In 1598, Patriarch Yusuf held his own council, without Jesuits, at Bait-Musa. He waited until 1599 to send a delegation to Rome to ask for papal confirmation and the pallium. The three-year delay in making his request may well have been a symptom of his chagrin over the high-handedness of the Jesuit mission.

In 1603 Fakhr ad-Din II organized an abortive revolt against the Ottomans, and was subsequently forced to raise the tribute he sent to the Porte. Nevertheless, his ambition did not rest. He expanded his control into the region around Ba'labakk by attaching a large number of Maronite districts to his emirate, and to the south he contested Galilee with the family of Ahmet Ibn-Turbai. Christians were anxious to join his army, and thousands emigrated to his lands in the south which had once been populated exclusively by the Druzes. His ambitions were frustrated, however, when the Ottoman navy blockaded the Lebanese coast and an army of the paşa of Damascus struck his forces on land. In 1613 he was forced to leave Lebanon and he was evacuated with his court to Livorno in Italy where he lived under the protection of his friend the duke of Tuscany. While in Italy, the Druze emir visited Rome and talked with the pope, telling him of his belief that the Druzes were descendants of the Crusaders.

Eventually he returned to Lebanon where he received a great welcome from his people. Officially he took up the post of 'adviser' to his son, but everyone knew where the real power lay. Once again his troops moved out of Ma'in territories and occupied the region of Kisrawan, the homeland of the Maronites.

Fakhr ad-Din strove to cement good relations between his own Druze people, the Maronites, and the Western powers, but the coalition he envisaged was not strong enough. In 1623 a combination of Ottoman and Arab armies from Galilee brought him down. As a result of this setback he fell seriously ill and the Capuchin Adrien of la Brosse privately received him into the Catholic faith. He later recovered, only to be arrested by the Turks, taken to Istanbul, and, with his sons, beheaded on 13 April 1635. He died wearing a crucifix and making the sign of the cross. The conversion of one of their most active rebels to Catholicism frightened the Turks and confirmed them in their suspicion that to become a Catholic meant to become a 'Frank' and a potential enemy of the Ottoman state.[26]

During the patriarchate of Yuhanna Safraoui, a Maronite delegation was dispatched to France asking for the protection of the young Louis XIV. A document was composed by Cardinal Mazarin, acting in the king's name, which granted the Maronite petition on 28 April 1649. It guaranteed that the French monarch would protect the patriarch and his people, and, as far as possible, their religious liberty. France also assumed the task of overseeing the travel of Maronite merchants and students to Western Europe. Although the effectiveness of such a guarantee might be questioned, the delegation left France satisfied. Copies of the document were distributed among the Maronites in the Orient, who used them to prove their 'rights' to Ottoman officials, if any could be found, who would honour the decree.[27]

The arrival of Jesuit missionaries among the Maronites in the middle of the seventeenth century strengthened the church. In 1656 a Jesuit, shipwrecked on the Lebanese coast near Juniyah, was brought before the chieftain of Kisrawan, Abu-Nawfal, who offered him and the members of his order a parcel of land at 'Ayn Turah, a village between Beirut and Jubayl. A house was constructed here to be the first permanent Jesuit mission. Other centres were founded later at Saida and Tripoli. The Jesuits were enthusiastic over their work with the Catholic Maronites in contrast to other Oriental Christians. They dressed like Maronite priests and one, Giuseppe Besson, in

1660, composed a book, *Soria santa*, designed to stir up interest about Lebanon in Europe. The only complaints about the Maronites concerned their ignorance of Christian doctrine, the lack of devotion among women, who only attended the Eucharist two or three times a year, and the rampant practice of usury. Political instability was at the root of many of the Maronite problems. When a French visitor came to Qannubin in 1660 he had to make an extended search for Patriarch Jirjis who was then hiding in a cave to avoid the Ottomans roaming Mount Lebanon seeking to suppress a rebellion of the mountain clans.[28]

When Patriarch Estfan Douaihi was chosen to lead the Maronites in 1670, the church obtained a man of quality and considerable experience. Estfan was a Roman graduate, having spent fourteen years in Italy. Some members of the church complained the patriarch was, in fact, too beholden to Rome. They also resented his reforms, designed to raise the level of education among the clergy, and the modifications he made in the traditions of the twenty-one Maronite monasteries. Patriarch Estfan was a serious student of Maronite history. During his tenure he composed several works, in which he put forward the theory that Maronite origins could be traced to the Mardites, a Christian tribe of the seventh century. He also popularized the life of St John Maron, reputed to be the first Maronite patriarch.[29]

Estfan's patriarchate was troubled by both the Ottoman authorities and the general economic and political disarray of Lebanon. Those Maronites who had emigrated into the Druze area of the Shuf sorely missed the favour of Fakhr ad-Din, while Kisrawan was often the scene of skirmishes between rival clans and Turks. The Orthodox treated the Maronites so badly that in a dejected mood Estfan once wrote to Pope Innocent XI, 'We suffer very much because we support you.'[30]

THE CHALDEAN CHURCH

Affairs between the Sulaqa line of patriarchs and the hierarchy of the Church of the East became even more confused in the seventeenth century. In 1600 Shim'un X, the Chaldean catholicos, lived at Urmia, and like his predecessors sent a request to Rome for confirmation in his office along with a personal statement of his faith. His representative, Metropolitan Tuma of Diyarbakir, came to Rome but found that the authorities there did not believe *ge.*

mbridge ... Ed. by
London, Macmillan

. 1, p. [79]–140.

rs. Appendices. General
o 1800. 1911.—**iv.** 1801 to

alter William Rouse, 1850–
mp, Alfred Edward, 1870–

17–6219

Shim'un's profession of faith was sufficiently clear on the matter of the unity of Christ in his two natures. Tuma had to return to the Orient without Roman approval for his superior. The difficulty was cleared up by a visit of the Holy Land Franciscan, Tommaso Obicini, to Shim'un. Obicini secured a new and explicit testimony of the catholicos' belief in a profession which the Franciscan probably drafted himself so as to assure its acceptance at Rome.

Meanwhile at the catholicate of the East, where Iliyas VIII, successor to Bar Mamas, lived in the monastery of Rabban Hormizd, a movement sympathetic to Catholicism began to emerge as a result of contacts with the Maronites. Consequently in late 1613 the catholicos sent his archdeacon, Rabban Adam, to Pope Paul V bearing a statement of Iliyas' faith. For two years Rabban Adam remained in Rome explaining to various churchmen his catholicos' exact doctrinal position. The pope commissioned several Franciscans to return to Iraq with him to investigate the status of his community.[31]

Upon Adam's return, a council was summoned to Diyarbakir in 1618 by Iliyas IX (since, in the interim, Iliyas VIII had died, and Adam now held the office of bishop of Diyarbakir). Tommaso Obicini attended the synod to represent the Catholic church. After lengthy discussion and the prompting of Adam and Obicini, the bishops of the Church of the East drew up documents uniting their community with the Roman church. To the report sent to Rome the bishops appended a note asking that they be allowed to continue commemorating Nestorius in the liturgy and to keep him in their calendar of saints as one who shared their faith. This proviso doomed the review of the synod's acts as far as the Roman authorities were concerned. The proceedings of the Diyarbakir synod were returned and Obicini was asked to make a new attempt at convincing the hierarchs of the Church of the East to accept all Catholic doctrine, which included a condemnation of Nestorius.

Contacts between Rome and the catholicoi of Rabban Hormizd continued, despite the difficulties of communication. Iliyas X sent a letter to the pope, cosigned by three of his metropolitans, asking that a college be established in Rome for his students and that a chapel be set aside for worship in one of the Jerusalem churches for members of his community.[32]

In 1667 there came to Diyarbakir a Capuchin, Jean-Baptiste of Saint-Aignan, who had already spent six years in the Orient, mastering all of its major languages. He made many friends among the congregants of the Church of the East and in 1670 won over the local bishop, Yusuf, to the Catholic faith. With the enthusiasm of a recent convert, Yusuf encouraged his priests to omit the liturgical commemoration of Nestorius at the Eucharist and to add 'Mother of God' to the titles of Mary. Catholicos Iliyas X did not look favourably upon these modifications. He ordered Yusuf to come to his residence, then the monastery of Tell Eskot. Yusuf, having no wish to see the catholicos, sought and received permission from the Ottoman governor of Diyarbakir to break his ties with Iliyas. When the catholicos heard this news, he was so distraught that he decided to leave Tell Eskot and seek out the rebellious bishop. According to a member of his church: 'The departure of Mar Iliyas from his monastery caused everyone to wonder, for he never had the custom of leaving. Some believed he was going out to make the world Christian.'[33]

When Iliyas got to Diyarbakir, he removed Yusuf and restored the name of Nestorius to the liturgy. The Christians of the Church of the East hurried to the cathedral, but his sermon was in Syriac, a language unknown to the majority of his flock. Finally, as a result of a bribe given to the Ottoman authorities, Yusuf was imprisoned and only released upon the payment of ransom, after which he left for Rome, arriving in the middle of 1675 and staying for the next two years. Rome was loath to grant his request to be named catholicos, since, presumably, there was already a Catholic catholicos in the Shim'un family. When Yusuf returned to the East, however, the local governor allowed him to assume the title 'patriarch of Diyarbakir'.

On 8 January 1681, at the suggestion of the Congregation for the Propagation of the Faith, Pope Clement X fulfilled Yusuf's dream, giving him permission to be acknowledged patriarch-catholicos and sending him a pallium. Since this, in effect, created two heads of the Chaldean church, one can explain it only by pointing to a rupture of communications between Rome and the Shim'uns – the latter now so isolated that the Latin missionaries could not find them.[34]

9

Palestine, Egypt and North Africa

PALESTINE IN THE EARLY SEVENTEENTH CENTURY

The Franciscans' position in the Holy Land in the early seventeenth century was a difficult one. The friars, as Father Custodian Francesco Manerba complained to Clement VIII, suffered constantly from 'injuries and affronts, lies and beatings' and from 'the haughty attitude' of both Arabs and Turks. Journeying abroad, they were harassed by enemies, both Muslim and Christian, while at home, at any time, day or night, they had to face Muslims who would appear at the convent door demanding wine, vinegar, candles or clothes.[1]

Palestine Orthodox frequently complained of Franciscan transgressions to Turkish authorities in Istanbul. Patriarch Theophanes III charged the Franciscans with forbidding the Orthodox to hang lamps in the church of the Nativity in Bethlehem and with needlessly closing the well outside the church. The sultan's government, siding with the Orthodox, ordered the Latins to desist, and in obvious reference to the Franciscans, instructed the *kadi* of Jerusalem to 'record and report those who display obstinacy and opposition'.[2] Affairs became critical when, in 1611, the Armenians demanded possession of the Rock of the Anointing in the church of the Holy Sepulchre as well as a chapel in the church of Bethlehem. The Franciscans first appealed to ambassador Harlay-Sancy in Istanbul to intercede for their rights, and then unwisely tried to argue that the Armenians had no rights at all in Jerusalem and should be packed off to Cyprus. It was unfortunately evident that the Franciscans had merely over-reacted, and the government ruled for preservation of the status quo.

But in 1620 Harley-Sancy returned to the attack, obtaining from the Porte a *firman* recognizing the Franciscans 'the ancient and exclusive guardians of the Holy Places'. The Venetians, considering it *their* responsibility to protect the Franciscans, resented what seemed to them French intrusion; there resulted a bitter quarrel between the two Christian protectors. Not content with his ambassador's success, Louis XIII sent a personal envoy, Louis Deshayes de Courmenin, to Palestine, there to ascertain how well the sultan's orders were being enforced and to arrange for the opening of a French consulate in Jerusalem. Deshayes de Courmenin arrived in 1621, entering the city in solemn procession, armed and on horseback. His action was ill-advised, and almost sure to jeopardize the status of the Latins once he was gone. He recommended establishing a consulate and suggested that French Jesuits be sent to the Holy City despite the problems this might raise with the Franciscans.[3]

The Franciscan Custodian Tommaso Obicini used the authority of the new *firman* to extend his order's jurisdiction to Nazareth. Fortunately for him the Druze emir, Fakhr ad-Din II, a friend of the Christians, was then ruler of Galilee; in 1620 he ordered the *kadi* of Saphet to relinquish to the Franciscans the grotto which local tradition identified as the site of the Annunciation.[4]

It was really as a participant in the battle for control of the Holy Places that Jean Lempereur, the new French consul, arrived in Jerusalem in 1624. He had been there only a few months when he announced his intention to invite Jesuits to Jerusalem; the incipient move was denounced by Franciscans and Venetians with equal vigour, and when the friars and the Venetian envoy joined forces against him, France found it necessary to recall Lempereur after less than a year's residence.

Seeking to avoid similar conflicts, the Franciscans urged the Congregation for the Propagation of the Faith to prohibit other religious orders from establishing houses in their three locations, Jerusalem, Bethlehem or Nazareth, for the future. But while the friars were thus eliminating the Jesuit threat, they were losing a major battle to the Orthodox in Jerusalem. Lempereur once gone, the Jerusalem Greeks persuaded local Ottoman officials – as usual by bribery – to oblige the Franciscans to share altars with them in the Churches of the Holy Sepulchre and the Nativity. This time, Louis XIII could do nothing; despite his protests, one a personal remonstrance, the order stood.[5]

Then in 1630 the Franciscans were again quarrelling with the Orthodox – this time because Patriarch Theophanes III and his archdeacon Gregorios had asserted additional claims to the shrines in Jerusalem. Both were thought to have Catholic sympathies; they had visited Rome and it had been understood that relations between the churches would improve when Theophanes became patriarch. The Franciscans, seriously dismayed, fought back, but debate over the claim went on, in both Jerusalem and Istanbul, for years until in 1634 Murat IV, under Phanariote pressure, expelled the Franciscans completely from their churches in the Holy Land. When ambassador Césy learned of this, he threatened the vezir that, unless the order was reversed, he would himself go to Palestine to defend the Franciscans. Relations between Paris and Istanbul, he pointed out, would be irreparably damaged. He won the day; the order was reversed and, two years later, the Venetian consul was able to win back for the Franciscans their exclusive rights over the Jerusalem churches. 'We give thanks to God', the Franciscan procurator exulted, 'that after so many difficulties we have won a victory, regaining the Holy Places...'⁶

His rejoicing was premature; Patriarch Theophanes left for Istanbul, where he placed the Melkite cause before the officials of the Porte. Again, in 1637, the government ruled against the friars, considerably reducing their rights in the Church of the Holy Sepulchre and at Bethlehem. Eight years later, Catholic interests were left unprotected when the Cretan war broke out; the Greeks seized the opportunity, sought confirmation of their possession of the principal shrines in the Holy Land, and got it.

During the war in Crete Latin-rite Catholics benefited from French insistence that no restrictions be put on European pilgrims to Jerusalem, but French prestige, especially when relations were strained between Paris and Istanbul, could not always hold the line for the friars. In 1669 a company of English pilgrims reported that:

The Greeks and Latins are the two powerful Religious in the temple, and with greater sums of money and credit they have at Constantinople, they continually buy these places out of another's hands; the other parties are poor, and are therefore squeezed into a small part of the temple.⁷

In 1669 the able Dositheos was appointed patriarch of the Melkite church in Jerusalem. Dositheos was a builder, an organizer, and a vigorous polemicist against both Catholics and Protestants. He sought and received permission from Mehmet IV's government to repair the edicule of the Holy Sepulchre and he renovated the Church of the Nativity in Bethlehem, importing workers to labour on the project.

In 1672 Dositheos summoned a council (called the Council of Jerusalem, though it was actually held in Bethlehem) to reexamine the Calvinist theology of Kyrillos Loukaris, patriarch of Constantinople. Here works attributed to Kyrillos were condemned, but on the ground that they were forgeries. Kyrillos himself was exonerated: 'The Eastern Church has never known Kyrillos as his enemies claim and has never recognized the chapters as his work.' This remarkable decision henceforth became the standard apology for Kyrillos in Orthodox tradition.

Some time afterwards, the French ambassador de Nointel visited Jerusalem at Easter time, arriving to find himself in the Church of the Holy Sepulchre in the midst of a battle between Franciscans and Greeks which left many injured and one, a Greek, dead. After the conflict, he was introduced to the ceremony of the Holy Fire which the Orthodox celebrated on Holy Saturday. During the proceedings the patriarch of Jerusalem solemnly excommunicated the pope and drove a stake into the ground to symbolize how seriously the anathema was to be taken.[8]

Yet one more time, in 1678, a new arrangement between the contending parties was worked out in Istanbul, dividing church properties in Palestine. The Greek cause was considerably enhanced by the patronage of the Chian, Alexandros Mavrokordatos, who had served the sultan's government as *Dragoman* of the Porte, chief translator to the sultan's government. Although an alumnus of the Greek College in Rome, Mavrokordatos was steadfastly Orthodox and on the question of his church's rights in Palestine refused to give an inch to the Latins.

EGYPT

Relations between the papacy and the Coptic church of Egypt were theoretically restored just before the seventeenth century opened when Pope Sixtus V sent Gian-Battista Vechetti as his emissary to Patriarch Jibra'il VIII. After a series of discussions and the passage of considerable correspondence between Rome and Cairo, Jibra'il's profession of faith was forwarded to Rome in January 1597. With it came a delegation of Copts who were warmly received by Pope Clement VIII, then reigning, and were welcomed into the Catholic communion. But Jibra'il's conversion was never communicated to the Coptic church as a whole and remained strictly a personal decision.

His successor was Mark V, a man known to be opposed to Catholicism. A Capuchin mission sent to him in 1605 realized that he had no intention of keeping ties with Rome; therefore a pro-Catholic group of Copts formed a cabal with the aid of the French consul in Cairo to have Mark removed from office. The conspiracy succeeded; on an appeal to the paşa of Cairo Mark was dethroned, publicly beaten and exiled. Kyrillos, a candidate more acceptable to Rome, was chosen patriarch by the Catholic faction in the church, and in October 1608 he dutifully sent off his profession of Catholic faith. The illegal removal of Mark V, regarded by many Copts as the legitimate head of the church, soured many Egyptian Christians against further dealings with the papacy. Yet when the English traveller George Sandys visited Egypt in 1611 he could report 'a multitude of late have been drawne to receive the Popish religion (especially in Cairo) by the industry of the friars'.[9]

The Capuchins opened their mission, the first Egyptian foundation, in 1630 under Gilles of Loches, who was replaced some years later by Agathangel of Vendôme, a veteran priest from Lebanon. Fluent in Arabic, Agathangel obtained the patriarch's permission to preach in Coptic churches. He also attempted evangelization of the European communities in Egypt which, in consequence, soon turned hostile because of his denunciation of their religious slackness. Agathangel visited several Coptic monasteries, even living in St Anthony and St Makarios for several months, and some monks agreed to become Catholic as a result of his efforts. Eventually he went off, with another Capuchin, to Ethiopia, where both were martyred.[10]

The Dominican friar J. M. Wansleban, from his personal experiences on a visit there in 1660, has left us a vignette of life in mid-century Egypt:

As soon as the Turks see a Frank in a Village or Country, chiefly where they never saw him before, they imagine immediately that he is laden with Diamonds and Pearls. They take therefore notice of all his steps, to find out some occasion to quarrel with him; and of all places of Turkie, this happens most frequently in Egypt.

Wansleban was introduced to the Coptic Patriarch Matta, who invited him to dinner. The patriarch, out of fear of the Turks, had not left his residence for over a year.[11]

Late in 1684 the Franciscans obtained a profession of faith from a bolder patriarch, Yuhanna XVI, to whose conversion Pope Innocent XI responded with a letter of congratulations. Correspondence between Rome and Cairo increasing, the pope asked the Palestine Franciscans to spend two thousand gold ducats on the support of Egyptian Catholics. In 1687 he commissioned a special apostolic prefecture for Egypt, separating it from the Custody of the Holy Land and naming Francesco Maria de Salemi as its first chief. The centre of Franciscan activity was in Cairo, where the order already had missions. From here an extension was sent out to upper Egypt, to Akhmim, where the friars had established a convent.[12]

NORTH AFRICA

Ottoman interest in the North African cities first developed during the sixteenth century, when the Habsburgs were attacking the principalities there. The Turkish sultans took the Muslim rulers under their protection and so added the area to the Ottoman domain.

Catholic Europe's major interest in North Africa lay in getting help for the thousands of Christian slaves taken by Barbary corsairs. Two religious orders, the French Trinitarians and the Spanish Mercedarians, had been formed in the Middle Ages specifically to ransom such Christians. The Lazarists added their efforts to this campaign in the seventeenth century.

The Congregation for the Propagation of the Faith encouraged new religious orders to go to North Africa and participate in this difficult work. To this end, Paschal Compte, a Franciscan Recollect, was sent as bishop to Algiers, and later Phillipe Le Vacher, a Lazarist, was named vicar apostolic of Tunisia. Since Le Vacher was also French consul, it was often easier for him to ransom the slaves. His position could not, however, save his brother Jean, who, on the orders of the bey of Algiers, was killed by being shot out of a cannon.

In Libya the Franciscans were in charge of Catholic missions. The friar Jean-Baptiste of Pont Canavese was martyred there is 1653 on the charge of having converted a Muslim. Later, graduates of a Franciscan school in Rome arrived at Tripoli in Libya and at Sfax and the island of Djerba in Tunisia. The North African mission, remote from Istanbul, tended to be regarded as an autonomous field of labour by those missionaries who worked in the Ottoman heartland.[13]

PART III

The eighteenth century

The eighteenth century in Istanbul

THE FRENCH AND THE CATHOLIC MISSIONARIES

At the close of the seventeenth century the Ottomans were at war with the Holy League led by the Austrian Habsburgs. On the Danube frontier the Turkish army suffered severe reverses; after 145 years of occupation Hungary was regained by Christian forces. The Habsburg armies moved southward, taking Belgrade on 8 September 1688, and in the following year penetrated as far as Niš, encouraging many of the Balkan Christians to rise against the Turks. While Louis XIV might consider himself the champion of Catholicism in the Orient, his wars against the Habsburgs did irreparable harm to that cause elsewhere, and even now troops had to be detached from Habsburg armies and sent to Western Europe to meet his menaces against Austrian possessions there. As a result, in 1690, a successful Ottoman counterattack led by the Köprülü, Fazil Mustafa, reestablished Turkish control of Belgrade and restored the lands south of the Danube to Sultan Süleyman II's control.

Since only Fazil Mustafa's leadership had been the cause of Ottoman victories after 1689, his premature death brought an end to Ottoman gains. Both Habsburgs and Ottomans skirmished along the Danube during the four years of Ahmet II's reign, and his successor Mustafa II personally took to the field in campaigns meant to bring an end to Austrian possession of the northern shore of the Danube. Unfortunately for the sultan, in the autumn of 1697, he suffered a great defeat at the hands of the able Prince Eugen of Savoy at Zenta.

Two years later the Turkish government had no choice but to accept the peace negotiated at Karlowitz, for the Ottomans were now faced with a new rival, an invigorated Russia under Peter the Great. The peace of Karlowitz had placed all Hungarian lands, except the Banat of Temesvar, under Emperor Leopold I. Transylvania, so often contested between Vienna and Istanbul, was to become an autonomous province within the Austrian orbit, while the province of Podolia was transferred to Poland. Karlowitz marks the first step in the Turkish retreat from Europe.

The Habsburg emissaries also used the peace-making process at Karlowitz to win concessions for Ottoman Catholics. By Article XIII of the treaty the sultan guaranteed free exercise of the Catholic religion, and the Habsburg ambassador was empowered thenceforth to seek redress of injuries to Catholics in Ottoman lands, especially Palestine. The Emperor was allowed to commission a group of Austrian Trinitarians to serve as chaplains to the Habsburg internuncio in Istanbul. Thus Karlowitz had a second major effect: it forced the French ambassador to share the responsibility of Catholic protection with his Habsburg colleague.[1]

The episcopal head of the Catholic church in Istanbul during this period was Bishop Gasparo Gasparini, who had first arrived in 1678 and held this post until 1702. It was during his tenure that a great fire swept Galata in May 1697, destroying hundreds of Christian homes and businesses. The fire caused so much damage to the rebuilt St Francis church that the Porte officials ordered the building razed. In its place was built a mosque which Sultan Mustafa II dedicated to his mother. Thus the Validé cami of Galata stands upon the site of what had been the most important Latin church of the Christian East. The displaced Franciscan Conventuals obtained permission to move into a new convent and church, dedicated to St Anthony of Padua, constructed close by the French embassy.[2]

In 1692 French merchants in Istanbul were sufficiently numerous to incorporate themselves into a 'nation' along the lines of the Ottoman *millets*. The new nation elected officers, summoned assemblies, and established rules for settling disputes among its members – all despite the fact that Turkish officials gave it no recognition. This body grew in importance throughout the eighteenth century and began to challenge the authority of the Marseille Chamber of Commerce for actual control of French economic affairs in Ottoman lands.

The French ambassadors had traditionally busied themselves in religious affairs in the capital. But Jean Louis d'Usson, Marquis de Bonnac, Louis XV's ambassador, departed from tradition. His predecessors had held that every French cleric in the Orient was an asset to French strength in Ottoman lands; he argued that there were too many missionaries, that they made the Turks uneasy, and that many of them acted as though the Capitulations gave them the right to do whatever they pleased. He reported to Paris:

I am convinced that the great and holy enterprise of the reunion of the Greeks and Armenians is not done as it ought to be; that those who occupy themselves with the task lack the talent and do not have sufficient command of the languages, that almost all those living in the Orient hold on to the prejudices of their native countries and their orders, which may be tolerable when dealing with European heretics, but make them quite inept in dealing with the schismatics of the East...It seems to me that it is not a question of destroying an enemy fortress; the Greeks and Armenians are really old friends who have separated from our communion and now form a distinct group... There is a great difference between being in union and obedient to the head of the visible church and being dominated by him. If the first is enough, why is everything presented according to the latter sentiment, thus upsetting and destroying all good will? Is it not better, perhaps, to speak of negotiation and of compromise rather than to act as if one was engaged in combat.[3]

That d'Usson was right became clear enough in 1722. As a result of a division in the Antiochene Melkite church, the Greek patriarchate in Istanbul, under the influence of wealthy bankers and merchants of the Phanar (the Greek section of the capital), succeeded in obtaining a *firman* on 14 September of that year which forbade all conversions to Catholicism. Catholic converts were ordered to return to their traditional faith and Latin missionaries were commanded to confine their attention to 'Franks' living in the Orient.

Louis XV ordered d'Usson to exert all his efforts against this attack upon the Western clergy:

I want you to use every means to obtain the revocation of the edict of the Grand Seigneur, making it known that it does not harmonize with the observation of the Capitulations between me and that prince. You must know that nothing could please me more concerning your embassy than a successful conclusion to the order I have given you.

Despite the king's urgency, d'Usson hesitated before taking inopportune action which would most likely diminish further France's influence at the Porte.[4]

The *millet* system, which registered every Ottoman citizen into the nationality of his birth and continued throughout his lifetime to determine the rules which affected his life, did not and could not provide for converts to Catholicism and still function. For an

Ottoman Christian to convert to Catholicism openly would amount to changing his citizenship, while still living in the country in which he was born. With keen accuracy the Porte officials recognized that religion and political allegiance were intertwined, and they were not at all prepared to have their Christian subjects become 'Franks'.

The ambassador prevailed upon Bishop Raimondo Galani, patriarchal vicar, to set limits upon the Latin missionaries. On 26 November 1722 the bishop issued a pastoral letter to all religious superiors in the Empire telling them that henceforward no significant change or expansion of missionary activity would be permitted without the approval of both the vicar's office and the French ambassador. D'Usson was pleased by this turn of events, which forced the Latin clergy to abandon some missions and to curtail their activities in others. Neither he nor any of his successors, more loyal to the dynasty than to the church, were ever able to have the *firman* of Ahmet III cancelled; understanding better than Louis XV what the national interests of France in the Ottoman world demanded, they never had much enthusiasm for the task. In 1731 Louis-Sauveur, Marquis de Villeneuve, complained to Paris that he was consulted by the clergy only when 'they have received some bad treatment from the Turks or schismatics'. Some missionaries, especially Franciscans, made their appeals through the Austrian or even the Dutch embassies.[5]

Since the French were instrumental in bringing to an end the Austro-Turkish war in 1739, Mahmut I's government rewarded them in 1740 by a renewal of the Capitulations. The document, signed by the Marquis de Villeneuve on 28 May, marked the high point of French influence in Istanbul. Of its eighty-five articles, nine dealt with religious matters including the right of the French to provide protection for Catholic pilgrims to the Holy Land. It also specified that all Catholic bishops and religious, regardless of national origin, were to be represented by the French ambassador.[6]

Catholic life in Istanbul in the early eighteenth century is described in a long letter written in Paris by the Jesuit Father Tarillon in March 1714 after he had returned from the East. Though the Jesuit believed the Latins were respected by both Ottomans and Orthodox in the capital, he quoted a contemporary proverb: 'In Pero sono tre malanni: peste, fuoco, e dragomanni.'[7] Tarillon estimated that Istanbul then held two hundred thousand Greeks and eighty thousand Armenians; in comparison he counted only three to four hundred Latins in Galata, most of them employed as *dragomans* for the various Western embassies, others practising medicine. Foreign merchants and the staffs of Catholic embassies brought the number of Latin Catholics to three thousand. Tarillon also estimated that twenty thousand Catholics were enslaved in the households of wealthy Ottomans, and another four to five thousand, belonging to the sultan, worked the Ottoman galleys.

Tarillon reported that St Benedict's was the most beautiful church in Galata, a fact attested by the number of important Catholics who chose to be buried there. He was especially proud that recent burials included those of two Hungarian women, Princess Tököly and the wife of Ferencz Rákoczi, who had accompanied the prince into exile at Izmit after his unsuccessful rebellion against Leopold I. Services at St Benedict were conducted in four languages: Greek, Turkish (for the Armenians), Italian and French. While men stood in the body of the church during services, women worshipped in a separate part of the building surrounded by a screen in 'the Oriental manner'.

Tarillon claimed that the Jesuits were welcome visitors at the Greek Orthodox patriarchate. There the patriarch 'gives us his thoughts and without leaving the bounds of respect, we tell him ours'. Greek parents were eager to enrol their children in the Jesuit school; even two sons of the bey of Walachia were in attendance. But Greek converts were few, Tarillon confessed, because of 'national pride'. The Jesuits enjoyed their greatest success with the Armenians, who were so eager for instruction that they would listen for two or three hours and complain that lessons ended too soon. Father Jacques Cachod in a single year converted four hundred persons, and Tarillon estimated that forty-two thousand of the Armenians in Istanbul were now Catholic.

He describes in detail the apostolate among the most wretched Catholics of the capital, the slaves of the Bagno, where two priests were permanently assigned to the mission. In summer at 3 a.m., and at 4 a.m. in the winter, Mass was offered in the prison before the slaves were marched off to work. Only one chain was worn as they attended the Eucharist, and alms, used to buy additional rations, were distributed at the chapel door as the men departed. Every night the fathers toured the cells, sprinkling the prisoners with holy water and leading them in an examination of conscience and evening prayers. Whenever the plague struck, the prisoners were quarantined and one of the Jesuits was then locked up with them rather than risk spreading the disease to his confrères.

Tarillon does not say anything about a ministry to the household slaves. Perhaps some were allowed to practise their faith, but the majority, whose duties were confined to private homes, must have been denied access to the churches and in time have drifted away from Christianity.

The Jesuits were always seeking to expand their missions. François Bracconier went to Salonica in 1706 to supervise the construction of a chapel in the grounds of the French consulate. From here he journeyed through Macedonia and the northern islands, visiting isolated Catholic merchants. It was on one of his trips that he – the first to do so – identified the site of ancient Philippi.[8]

In 1730, shortly after Mahmut I came to power, a new Catholic patriarchal vicar took up residence in Istanbul. Girolamo Bona, a native of Dubrovnik, was expected to follow the long-standing tradition of his countrymen and get along well with the Turks. Bishop Bona was a secular cleric and brought with him his own staff of secular priests, which created a new element in the Ottoman capital where heretofore there had only been members of religious orders as clergy. On 15 April 1742 the bishop's prestige was considerably enhanced when Pope Benedict XIV named him vicar apostolic of the East. The pope wanted to further centralize missionary activity in the Orient, and Bona was given charge of all the religious superiors working in the Ottoman Empire.[9]

The papacy of Benedict XIV, from 1740 to 1758, meant a renewed Roman interest in the affairs of Latin and Eastern Catholic churches in the Ottoman Empire. While Benedict's primary concern was the preservation of the Italo-Greeks of southern Italy and Sicily from complete assimilation into the Latin church, his activities extended far beyond the problems there. He was especially concerned that the colleges of the Eastern rites in Rome become more vigorous in their training of native clergy. In addition, he sought to stop the passage of Eastern Catholics into the Latin rite by issuing a firm injunction prohibiting it:

No Latin bishops may molest or disturb them (Eastern Catholics) in any way, and they are forbidden to denigrate, reprove or cast aspersions upon the rites of the Greeks which were approved both at the Council of Florence and elsewhere.

Despite his solicitude for the Eastern rites, he shared the typical Roman prejudice that Latin Catholics enjoyed precedence over all other Christians. In the document *Esti pastoralis* he spoke of the

Latin rite as enjoying *praestantia*, a 'primacy' over the ancient Oriental churches.[10]

In the letter *Allatae sunt* of 26 July 1755, Benedict issued new directives to Latin missionaries in the Orient at the very time that the Greek controversy over rebaptism was at its peak. In this document he cautioned missionaries to avoid unenlightened zeal for the conversion of Orthodox or Eastern Christians, admonishing them that although the church hoped all should become Catholic, it was not desirable that all should be Latin. Moreover, nothing foreign to the Eastern rites should be introduced by clerical converts from those churches:

Whenever a Greek or any other separated Eastern Christian seeks to return to the unity of the Catholic church, it is never, for any reason, permitted to a missionary to encourage him to leave his own rite.

Allatae sunt is a long document, for it attempts to trace the history of papal protection of the Eastern churches. In it the pope claimed that Rome had always sought to keep the Eastern rites whole and intact, free from any Latin admixture. He pointed out that although Eastern Catholic priests had been given permission to offer the Eucharist in Latin churches wherever they had no places of worship of their own, they had been instructed scrupulously to follow the liturgical law of their own rites.[11] It is surprising that this pope, so well versed in Eastern Christianity and honestly concerned about its future, saw no contradiction between what he wrote and the Maronite synod of al-Luwayzah, which he sponsored, and which sought to bring that church into complete conformity with Latin practice even on small details.

The churches in Galata enjoyed a period of relative prosperity while Benedict XIV was pope. However, SS Peter and Paul, the Dominican church frequented by the French community, had to be rebuilt after a fire. In 1731 St Benedict's was also damaged and required reconstruction. The Capuchin church of St George was the Italian parish and many of the Armenian Catholics worshipped there. German-speaking Catholics attended services in their own language at the Trinitarian church of the Austrian Embassy.[12]

So open was Catholic life in this centre of the Islamic world that visitors always were amazed. One missionary wrote to his sister, 'Would you believe it, even in the heart of Constantinople, Catholics make solemn processions as peacefully and freely as in the centre of Paris?' The Holy Saturday procession, according to this report, lasted for two hours, the Confraternity of St Anne taking the leading position. Members marched solemnly around a relic thought to be a spine from Jesus' crown of thorns. Banners and candles were carried by the marchers while musicians blowing trumpets and playing stringed instruments completed the colourful scene. The Catholic ambassadors participated along with their courts. When the procession passed the Armenian churches, the clergy were in attendance, and some broke into the procession to venerate the relics carried by the Catholics.[13]

Christians living in Galata believed themselves the elite of the Ottoman world. A constant swirl of social activities, including public dancing, went on at the embassies. Staffs of servants and officials numbered in the hundreds, so these events had a glamour not found in any other Ottoman city. In addition to their 'palaces' in Istanbul the ambassadors had country villas to which they repaired whenever pestilence was abroad in the city. Although the Greek Phanariotes and the Armenian *amiras* (the wealthy banker and merchant families) were also aristocratic societies, the fact that they were the subjects of the sultan forced them to be more discreet. Apparently, they found few things in common with the 'Franks' who lived on the other side of the Golden Horn.[14]

THE TRUE SCHISM BETWEEN THE CHURCHES

While 1054 is traditionally accepted as the date of the permanent schism between the Greeks and the Latins, many arguments show that events in that year were too unimportant to cause the break. While the Byzantine Empire survived, so numerous were contacts between Rome and Constantinople that the eleventh-century excommunication of Patriarch Michael Keroularios counted as a rather unimportant occurrence in their relationship.

If, indeed, a schism between the Greek and Latin churches occurred, it was in 1755, when for the first time doubt was cast upon the validity of baptism administered by Latin Catholics. This truly marks a serious division, for sacramental unity, which forms the body of Christendom, is far more important than any unity imposed by ecclesiastical government. When sacramental validity was denied to the Western church, as happened in the patriarchal decree, the *Oros* of 1755, then a true schism came to exist.

The events which led to the *Oros* are rooted in the preceding decade, when the Latin church came under attack from Eugenios

Boulgaris, the leading Greek philosopher-bishop of the century. He was a writer of extraordinary skill, which he used to attack the Latin church. On the popular level a monk named Auxentios preached on the same theme, going about the countryside and condemning the 'heresies' of the Western church and its activities. He especially insisted that the Latin method of baptism by infusion rendered the sacrament invalid. He developed a large following of ordinary people and some highly placed prelates in the Phanar. A Chian layman, Eustratios Argenti, agreeing with him, affirmed that immersion was necessary for validity. Auxentios proved so troublesome that a plot was laid to have him drowned, but the conspiracy failed, leaving him more influential than ever.[15]

Patriarch Kyrillos V and several members of the Holy Synod joined Auxentios; Kyrillos began preaching that converts from the Latin and Armenian churches needed more than chrismation, the usual form of admission for other Christians into the Orthodox faith, and a number of Orthodox converts, especially women, sought rebaptism. According to Baron François de Tott, an aide at the French embassy, converts 'ran in crowds to the holy ceremony'.[16] While the party supporting rebaptism had many adherents, another group within the Greek church opposed it and were strong enough in 1752 to have Kyrillos deposed and to elect a moderate, Païsios.

Païsios was soon under attack by many opponents, especially Auxentios, who argued that, since he was willing to admit the validity of Catholic baptism, he must be a friend of the Latins. One day a crowd formed outside the patriarchal residence shouting,

We do not want you any more. You are an Armenian! You are a Latin! Why don't you baptize the Armenians and Latins? Why do you want to exile the saint (Auxentios)? We do not want you any more.

They rushed into the patriarchate, seized Païsios and dragged him into the street. Only the arrival of his Janissary guards saved the patriarch from further harm.[17]

Although the leaders of this attack were put to death, the grand vezir demanded Païsios' resignation and, on payment of a large gift, Kyrillos V returned. Once settled in his former position he ruled that the Latin and Armenian administration of the sacraments was sufficiently defective as to be invalid. When other synodal members protested that this violated the canons, Kyrillos argued that the laws were ambiguous. On 28 April 1755, when a majority in the synod voted against Kyrillos' position, his response was to exile his opponents and assemble his supporters in order to publish a new and definitive statement on rebaptism. Thus the *Oros* of 1755 came to be issued.

The document argued that the sacraments have been entrusted to the one orthodox church and its ministers; only this church teaches and acts according to apostolic tradition. Hence unless the sacrament is given by a believing Orthodox and according to the rite established by the church, baptism – and by extension all other sacraments – is invalid. The decree was issued in the name of Kyrillos V and the two Melkite patriarchs in Istanbul, Mattheos of Alexandria and Parthenios of Jerusalem.[18]

A protest was raised against the *Oros* by Kallinikos, metropolitan of Amasia. When he was ordered into exile on Mt Sinai by the synod, he fled instead to the grounds of the French embassy. There the ambassador, Gravier, Comte de Vergennes, worked for his restoration and his appointment to the patriarchate. To this end, de Vergennes' aide, Baron de Tott, obtained a large sum of money, new coins freshly minted, personally putting them into the hands of Sultan Osman III. The action had the desired effect. The grand vezir, who supported Kyrillos, was ousted along with his client in January 1757. Kyrillos was put on a barge by a company of soldiers and taken into exile.

The synod voted to elect Kallinikos patriarch, and he left the security of the French embassy to take office. Baron de Tott noted that he followed his Janissary bodyguards as if they were his executioners, for he was well aware that he was very unpopular with a large segment of Istanbul's Greek community. During his enthronement shouts rang out, 'Let the Frank get out.' At the end of the service he was seized by his enemies and beaten until Turkish soldiers intervened. Six months later, his position became so untenable that he retired and a new patriarch, Seraphim II, assumed office on 27 July 1757.[19]

THE SUPPRESSION OF THE JESUITS AND THE MISSIONS

Upon the death of Benedict XIV in 1758, Clement XIII was elected to succeed him. The great issue of the day was the role of the Jesuit order. All of Western Europe's statesmen appeared in alliance against them, and during the 1760s they were ejected from Portugal, Spain and Venice. The most severe blow against them was struck in France: the state took over supervision of all religious orders there after 1768 and systematically enacted legislation to suppress the Jesuits and Reformed Franciscans, to limit the number of novices allowed in the surviving orders, and to restrain their activities in many areas. The troubles of the religious in Western Europe meant that the missions in the Orient could no longer be effectively staffed.[20]

In 1773 Clement XIV issued a decree suppressing the Jesuit order. His capitulation to the enemies of the Society, the strongest institution then found in the church, has no adequate rationale beyond the pope's own reasoning: he believed it was necessary for the peace of the church. The three thousand Jesuit missionaries scattered about the world were ordered to disband and turn over their properties to secular clergy. In the East, at the time of the dissolution, the Jesuits had twenty-five members working in Istanbul, the Greek islands and in Anatolia, while seventeen others were stationed from Syria to Egypt. In some places delegates came from Rome to supervise the closing of the churches and schools and to investigate possible infractions of canon law.[21]

The French ambassador, Comte de Saint-Priest, wrote to his government expressing his amazement at the order; he pointed out that in the Orient there was, in fact, no large body of secular priests to whom Jesuit property might be given and that to leave the Society's lands and buildings vacant was to invite confiscation by both local and national groups. Although a law of 24 March 1774 was issued against the Society in the area of Saint-Priest's jurisdiction, the ambassador closed his eyes to the Jesuits who sought to remain active. The French envoy often encouraged them to take ambiguous titles, such as 'temporary agents', so as to allow them to function. Meanwhile, the dispossessed among the Jesuits appealed to the Minister of Naval Affairs for pensions to tide them over while negotiations in France sought to get clergy from the Congregation of the Missions, the Lazarists, to replace them in the Orient. But though the Lazarists inherited the Jesuit missions and properties they were too few to man all of the Society's stations, and by 1782 had replaced the Jesuits only in Istanbul, Izmir, 'Ayn Turah, Aleppo and on some of the Greek islands. In less conspicuous places former Jesuits continued to serve their old congregations as secular clergy.[22]

THE FRENCH REVOLUTION EXTENDS TO THE
ORIENT

The condition of Catholicism in the Ottoman Empire was further severely tested during the French Revolution and the period of Napoleon's rise to power. Events in France disrupted missionary activity as never before, and for the first time in centuries Ottoman Catholics were placed in an ambiguous position *vis-à-vis* their traditional protector, the French ambassador. When Napoleon invaded Egypt and war was declared between France and the Ottomans, even more confusion spread among those who had depended on a permanent state of friendship between Paris and Istanbul.

At the start of the revolution in 1789 the French 'nation' in the Ottoman capital was divided: some joined in the demand for change; others opposed it. The religious community fell almost entirely inside the latter group when they realized the implications of the revolt in Paris. In October 1789 the French government seized all church property, and the 1790 Constitution, which was drawn up by the National Assembly and accepted by the king, dissolved all missionary religious orders, provided for the election of priests and bishops, and stripped the church of its traditional privileges. The immediate effect bore heavily upon the government subsidies which supported the French Capuchins and Lazarists. The Istanbul clergy subsequently refused to take the oath to the Republic which was required by the government in Paris.

Despite its anti-religious sentiments, the National Assembly and the revolutionary governments which followed did not want to destroy the missions completely since the religious orders represented France in the Orient. Orders from Paris to French consuls directed that the missionaries, if at all possible, should be kept at their stations. Only during the heady days of the Convention, when anti-clerical fever was at a peak, was it suggested that the church properties should be sold.

In October 1792 the royalist ambassador in Istanbul, the Comte de Choiseul-Gouffier, was replaced by Citizen Descorches, a former marquis, who held the title of minister plenipotentiary. His orders were to inform the Porte that Paris intended to maintain its protective role over Catholic missionaries. Conflict was inevitable. In October 1793 the vicar of Archbishop Antonio Frachia refused to allow the church marriage of a local Catholic with a member of the French embassy staff. Descorches insisted that the Lazarists at St Benedict schedule the service or face the loss of their church. The clerics of St Benedict then announced they were no longer under French protection and had transferred their allegiance to the Austrian internuncio. Acting upon this development, the French 'nation', in spite of the protest of the Habsburg emissary, seized all of Istanbul's church properties. Ottoman government officials intervened, announcing that the Porte would hold the assets of the church until the disposition of the properties could be settled. Descorches complained it had all been the fault of the 'fanaticism of the priests'. It was not until 1802 that the missionaries regained title to their churches and residences.[23]

Rome had great difficulty communicating with Istanbul during the revolutionary period, since Italy itself was under attack from the French. The paralysis of Archbishop Frachia in 1791 complicated the situation further. Rome was forced to deal with an administrator who, for the next three years, aided by apostolic visitors sent out from Rome to ascertain the church's status, fulfilled Frachia's duties.

The French embassy continued to contest the protection of the Ottoman Catholics with Austria until war broke out between France and the Ottoman Empire following Napoleon's invasion of Egypt in 1798. The French *chargé d'affaires* was sent to the prison of the Seven Towers, an action which allowed the missionaries publicly to profess their Austrian loyalty. The newly arrived vicar from Siros, Bishop Giovanni Battista Fonto, made the Austrian church of the Holy Trinity his cathedral.[24]

Several months after the cessation of hostilities between France and Great Britain, the French–Ottoman war was ended by a treaty in March 1802. Article II of the treaty provided for the complete restoration of the Capitulations. First Consul Bonaparte, who had signed a Concordat with Pope Pius VII a year earlier, intended that France should resume its role as Catholic protector in the Orient. His first ministerial appointee to the Porte, Maréchal Marie-Anne Brune, was instructed 'to take under his protection all the establishments and all the Christians of Syria, Armenia and all the pilgrims seeking to visit the Holy Places'.[25]

The eighteenth century was marked by remarkable change: from a position of general prosperity at the beginning to one of confusion and disarray at the end. The anti-religious feelings of West Europeans were so foreign to both Muslims and Christians in the East that the events of the Revolution and the Napoleonic era were incomprehensible. The role of France, traditional protector of Ottoman Catholics, must have been especially puzzling. The suppression of the Jesuits, the strongest missionary organization in the East, indeed in the world, demonstrated a papacy unable to understand where its own interests lay. Only the persistent work of the local missionary enabled the Catholic church to pass through this difficult period.

The Balkans after the Peace of Karlowitz

THE HABSBURG ADVANCE INTO THE BALKANS

The Habsburg advance into the Balkans during the War of the Holy League precipitated several significant changes in the lives of Christians living there. Agents of the Austrian armies were anxious to get help from both Catholics and Orthodox, and when Belgrade fell to the Habsburgs, the Orthodox Serbs committed themselves to battle against the Turks only to discover that the Austrians could not occupy the region permanently. So, rather than face the wrath of the Turks, the Serbian patriarch, Arsenije III, and forty thousand families retreated with the Western armies into Croatia and southern Hungary. Arsenije, no friend of the Catholics, requested the Emperor Leopold to grant him jurisdiction over all Serbs in Habsburg lands. This, of course, brought him into conflict with the Catholic Serbian bishops and the Latin bishop of Zagreb. He gained a partial victory: the Serbs in Sirmium returned to Orthodoxy but those in Croatia remained Catholic.

In Dubrovnik, where the citizens had struggled painfully to dissociate themselves from the war, Karlowitz was greeted with a sigh of relief. During the negotiations, Dubrovnik asked that a strip of Turkish-held land should separate it from any Venetian possession, and, to demonstrate loyalty to the sultan, the city at once resumed payment of tribute.

The Albanian Catholics likewise had been encouraged by the Habsburg advance to attempt political change, but their revolutionary efforts also failed, and in consequence the paşa of Peć ordered the deportation of large numbers of them to Serbia. Here, many converted either to Orthodoxy or to Islam. In the Himarë the Eastern-rite Catholics apparently persevered although with varying degrees of commitment.

When Clement XI assumed the papacy in 1700, interest in

Albania increased, since the pope was of Albanian ancestry (demonstrated by his family name of Albani). Concerned about diminishing Catholic strength, Clement asked the Albanian bishops to meet in synod to discuss their common problems. A major concern was the condition of Catholics who had publicly announced conversion to Islam but secretly brought their children to baptism and themselves sought confession. In Shkodër, then, in 1703, under the presidency of Vincenzo Zmajević, bishop of Bar and apostolic visitor of Albania, an Albanian synod considered action on the matter. It was decided that crypto-Catholics should not be allowed communion and that their families should be excluded from the churches so long as they pretended to be Muslims. This decision reflected the consistent policy of Rome that public profession of faith should be required of all Ottoman Catholics. However harsh this might be, it at least gave clear direction to local clergy in cases which, on their own authority, it might have been difficult to decide.[1]

The Ottoman victory over Peter the Great of Russia in 1711 encouraged Ahmet III to plan a campaign against the much weaker Venetians in the Peloponnesus. The Venetians were few in number and their colonial rule had done nothing to ingratiate them with the local Greeks. The only true Catholics in the Peloponnesus during the occupation were the Venetian soldiers. They were stationed principally in Navplion, Patras and Methoni and worshipped in Latin churches that had once been mosques. Here they were served by religious orders: Franciscans, Dominicans and Carmelites.

Not till 1699 did a Latin archbishop, Leonardo Balsarini, formerly metropolitan of Chios, arrive. He assumed the title of archbishop of Corinth but made Navplion his residence. He entered his cathedral on 26 July, amid great pageantry and ceremony in which the Orthodox clergy participated. It had been many years since a Latin prelate had taken office in this part of the Greek world.

In 1715 the Ottoman invaders had reached Navplion and the episcopal incumbent, Angelo Maria Carlini, died in the defence of the Palamedes fortress during the siege. His church, St Anthony of Padua, was confiscated and only a few chapels, in port cities where there were French merchants, survived the reconquest. Another victim was the Catholic Armenian monastery of Abbot Mekhitar; several monks were killed in the siege of Methoni, but the majority escaped by ship to Venice.[2]

The Ottoman fleet scoured the Aegean to dislodge the Venetians from the few possessions they still held. When the most important

of these, the island of Tinos, was taken, the last Latin bishopric of
the Aegean became subject to the Ottomans. Happily for the future
of the remaining Balkan Catholics, the Habsburgs signed a treaty
of alliance with the Venetians before the Ottomans, confident of
victory, marched north. Prince Eugen of Savoy, the most able of
the Habsburg generals, was waiting for them. Over the next two
years he not only turned back the invasion but regained Belgrade,
all the Hungarian territory the Ottomans had retained after Karlowitz, most of Serbia and part of Wallachia. By the terms of the
Treaty of Passarowitz, signed on 21 July 1718, the exhausted Turks
relinquished all these to the Austrians, but were allowed to hold the
gains they had made at Venetian expense.

Among the provisions of Passarowitz, the Porte confirmed
Austria's role, first stated in the Peace of Karlowitz, as guarantor of
the security of Ottoman Catholics. Article XI made this explicit:

All the stipulations of earlier treaties and edicts concerning the exercise
of Christian worship by those of the Roman Catholic faith are confirmed. Religious of any kind and wherever they may live enjoy
Imperial protection, and the ambassador of the Emperor of the Romans
will have complete freedom to perform his mission in all that concerns
religion in the Holy Places of Jerusalem and all other places where the
religious have churches.[3]

The treaty gave the Imperial internuncio a degree of prestige which
theoretically equalled that of the French ambassador in Istanbul.
However, the French were considered friends, the Habsburgs
enemies, in Istanbul, so that the precedence enjoyed by the French
ambassador was never seriously challenged.

THE BALKAN MISSIONS IN THE LATE EIGHTEENTH CENTURY

The Austrian empress, Maria Theresa, wanted to sustain Catholicism
among the Serbs, but not much could be salvaged. Even in Dubrovnik, the Catholic citadel, the cause of the Latin church suffered
from a civil war which broke out in 1763. The old nobility resisted
the merchants who had made fortunes after the earthquake of 1667
and now sought their share of political power and social prestige.
During the Russian–Ottoman conflict, in the 1768 campaign, the
admiral Count Aleksei Orlov menaced the city, notifying the citizens
that the Russians could reach deep into the Adriatic.

The city at last lost its special status as a result of Napoleon's wars. In 1797 the Treaty of Campo Formio divided the Venetian inheritance between Austria and France. As a result of later conflicts with the Habsburgs, the French assumed control of Dalmatia, which they called the Illyrian province. Then in January 1808, by a decree it had no way to resist, the republic of Dubrovnik, a victim of the changing pattern of European politics, was incorporated into France's Adriatic empire. Already in 1802 the barrier against Orthodox churches had been relaxed; now, by French law, the citizens of Dubrovnik were never to legislate for themselves again.[4]

The mid-eighteenth century was a difficult time for the northern Albanians because of endemic war between Mehmet Bushatli and his rival chieftains in the Shkodër region. Some Catholics resorted to dissimulating their faith, while others, encouraged by church leaders, fled. In 1765 the Basilian missionaries in the Himarë were expelled and the Himarëns began a return to Orthodoxy under the patronage of Catherine the Great. By 1774 the Albanian Catholic population was severely diminished and in many areas ordered church life was practically non-existent.

As the central government in Istanbul weakened local landlords built up personal territories, recruiting private armies and conducting their own foreign affairs. Many of these princes started out in the Ottoman civil service, but in response to the enfeeblement of authority, carved out independent states of their own fashioning. The most famous of these was Ali Paşa of Tepelen, the governor of Ioannina since 1788. An expert politician, Ali encouraged both Orthodox Christians and Albanian Muslims to regard him their champion. All were welcome in his forces. In northern Albania Mehmet Bushatli and his son Kara Mahmut generally had Catholic support, and Catholic tribal units enlisted in the army alongside Muslims in a war against Venice and Montenegro. The Catholic Mirdites were especially helpful; an alliance formed with Austria, who became the Mirdites' protector in 1791, significantly enhanced their position with the Bushatlis.[5]

It was not until 1759 that the Franciscans felt they could safely return to Bulgaria. The Congregation for the Propagation of the Faith named a vicar apostolic for Sofia with residence in Plovdiv, the city which then held the largest Catholic community. The dearth of Franciscan missionaries, however, made Rome decide to attach the Baptisan order of Genoa to the mission in 1763. Later, in 1781, Pope Pius VI transferred the vicariate to the Passionist Order.

None of these missionary attempts was able to restore the momentum of the seventeenth century, and the few Latin clergy in Bulgaria had to content themselves with serving small and powerless communities.[6]

In 1700 the French traveller Joseph Pitton de Tournefort made a circuit of the Greek islands and later published a journal of his impressions. Since he was concerned about the religious life of those who lived in the Orient, he provided important information on the situation of the Catholics there. At Canea in Crete he found two Capuchins, the only remaining Latin clergy on an island once so important a part of the Venetian empire. The missionaries were very poor, living on a small pension from Louis XIV's treasury supplemented by contributions from the dozen Catholic merchants in the town. Tournefort explains the dearth of converts by local poverty: 'Our missionaries have great difficulty in leading the Greeks to the true faith, for all the villages are far from the coast where the charity of the king cannot easily reach them.'[7]

On the island of Kimolos the French traveller came across a handful of Latins and a single priest. The Capuchins on Milos, as on Crete, were very poor. Their chapel had recently burned but funds from France had enabled them to restore it. When the bishop of Milos died, before Tournefort's arrival, it was necessary to sell his chalice, mitre and vestments to pay off his debts. Only a few Catholics still lived on Paros, but their number was stable.

On Naxos Tournefort found that there were so few Catholic women that the Latin men were forced to marry their cousins or take Orthodox girls from the countryside. The position of the church on this island in 1700 is further illustrated by the report of a visitation made that same year by Bishop Antonio Giustiniani. He found three hundred and fifty resident Catholics served by secular priests, Capuchins and Jesuits, the latter of whom opened a small seminary in the hope of encouraging a native clergy.

Tournefort also visited Siros, 'the pope's island', where six thousand Catholics lived. He, and later Bishop Giustiniani, were impressed by the vigour of their religious practice and the number of clergy: thirteen secular priests, two Capuchins, twenty-seven Franciscans and nineteen Dominicans. The Orthodox numbered but seven families, served by a single priest.

Of all Catholic island communities the five thousand Latins of

Chios were to endure the most serious reverses at the end of the century. Prior to 1694 everything had seemed to be going well. Relations with the Ottoman authorities were friendly, and Catholic and Orthodox churchmen often shared churches just as the principal nobles shared seats on the island council.[8]

The tragedy which befell the Catholics was a result of the continuing struggle of the Ottoman Empire against Venice and her allies of the Holy League. Francesco Morosini, the Venetian commander in Greece during the occupation of the Peloponnesus, encouraged his countrymen to extend their territories into the Aegean. Before much could be accomplished, however, Morosini died and his lieutenant Antonio Zeno was left in charge. Zeno was a soldier of doubtful ability but undiminished enthusiasm. He decided to make Chios his target because of its economic and strategic importance to the Turks. It was Zeno's belief, encouraged by information received from the island, that the Catholics would assist a Venetian landing and make his task an easy one. However, according to Demetrios Cantemir, an observer of the situation in Istanbul, many Orthodox opposed the project and even sent agents to alert the vezir, Husein Paşa, that rebellion was in the wind.[9]

The Venetian fleet, carrying ten thousand soldiers, reached Chios on 8 September 1694 and made an unopposed landing. The Turkish garrison dispersed and the island's Christian leaders announced their satisfaction at the ouster of their Muslim masters. The Catholics of Chios were sincere, but few Orthodox could have regarded the Venetian deliverance as an unmixed blessing. Zeno set about establishing a Christian government of the island and worked closely with the Latin bishop, Balsarini.

Before long it was obvious to the Catholic leaders that the Orthodox were reluctant to commit themselves to Venetian rule. Greek clergy were discovered to be sending messages to Istanbul; some were jailed and their churches closed. No wonder, as it happened, that the Orthodox were anxious over their situation, for the Ottoman navy was known to be preparing an attack. At last in February 1695 the Ottoman fleet came up and engaged the Venetians. Although the battle was insignificant Zeno announced he intended to evacuate the island. The Chian Catholics were now in a dilemma: to leave with the Venetians or to remain and bargain with the returning Turks. Bishop Balsarini had no taste for martyrdom and packed his bags. So did twenty of his clergy and sixty prominent Catholic families. They were on the Venetian ships which sailed away for the Peloponnesus. Within a matter of days, the Turks had reoccupied the island.

Despite the protests of the remaining Catholics that they had been the victims of circumstances over which they had no control, Ottoman officials believed none of them. Turkish soldiers broke into all the churches, smashed altars and statuary and pillaged the vestments and sacred vessels. A Jesuit eyewitness lamented, 'Nowhere was such desolation ever seen.'[10] A single exception was made for the Capuchin chapel in the grounds of the French consulate.

Four of the Catholic lay leaders were hanged; others, convicted of lesser offences, were condemned to the galleys and their property confiscated. The wives of the men executed appeared before the Ottoman commander along with their children, asking that they, too, be put to death: 'We are also of the same religion and we refuse to change.' The commander rejected their plea, arguing, 'Don't blame me for killing your husbands. It was not me, but the Greek leaders who were responsible for their deaths.'

The French consul acted on behalf of the Catholics. Since the Latin churches were all damaged beyond use, he notified the Turks that Catholics would be content to attend Orthodox services if they were allowed to remain in their homes. The Turkish officials agreed and for the next two decades no public Latin Mass was offered. The remaining Catholic priests quietly offered the Eucharist in private homes. When Tournefort visited Chios, he found twenty-five Catholic priests still living on the island. French citizenship protected two remaining Jesuits and a single Dominican. When the Roman authorities later named a new bishop for Chios, Daniel Duranti of Skopje, the candidate was wisely content with the title, and made no attempt to take possession of his see. Unfortunately the events surrounding the Venetian occupation and its aftermath destroyed much of the good will which had once marked relations between the two Christian communities of Chios.[11]

As a result of the Treaty of Passarowitz, the position of Venetian Catholics in the Aegean was dealt a major setback. The two ports which they had retained on Crete had to be abandoned. As partial compensation, French Capuchins were allowed stations at Canea and Candia to serve the Western merchants located in those cities. The Catholics on Tinos, eight thousand in a population of eleven thousand now under Turkish rule, were served by thirty-two churches with a bishop, sixty secular Catholic priests, a convent of Franciscans and a house of Jesuits. Greek Christians of the Byzantine rite, assigned to the jurisdiction of the Latin patriarchate of Constantinople while Venice controlled the island, had become members of the Orthodox church.

In 1719 Bishop Niccolò Cigala made a visitation on Tinos. He complained that although freedom of worship for the Catholics had not seriously diminished, several churches had been destroyed and the episcopal residence lost. An Orthodox bishop living on the island had forbidden members of his community to confess to the Jesuits as had once been common practice. Orthodox priests, settling there, often spoke against the Latins, notable among them a Russian monk who was especially abrasive in his anti-Catholic charges and did little to keep the peace between the two religious communities.[12]

On some of the other islands which once had sizable Catholic communities the number of Latins was in serious decline. Paros and Andros between them had less than fifty, Mikonos one hundred and thirty. The Capuchin mission on Milos still had two friars, but the number of Catholic was negligible. Only on Thira and Naxos was the Latin church still enjoying relative prosperity.

A major gain for the Catholics of Naxos was made in 1717. The four hundred Catholics of the island, responding to appeals made by Archbishop Antonio Maturi, pledged funds for the construction of a convent on the island, and the archbishop persuaded the French Ursulines to send sisters to Naxos. Once established, the sisters opened a school for women. It was the single educational institution for women in the whole of the Ottoman Empire for the next century.[13]

On Chios, once the pride of island Catholicism, the effects of the disaster of 1696 still lingered. The Greek hierarchy continued to stir up trouble for the Catholics, at one time suggesting to the Ottoman authorities that all Catholics, being potential or actual traitors, should be sent into exile. A French Jesuit complained: 'Our great opposition does not come from the Turks, who have a natural esteem for the French; it is altogether the fault of the Greek leaders.'[14] When a Dominican came to Chios in 1709 he reported that the state of Catholicism could best be described as 'total desolation'. Many of the Latin churches, including the cathedral, had been remodelled as mosques.[15]

The Treaty of Passarowitz had guaranteed to Catholics the right to practise their religion, and this now brought about a change in the Catholic situation on Chios. In early 1720 the bishopric was restored when, under Austrian protection, Bishop Filipo Bavestrelli arrived on the island, and, in his wake, Dominicans and Jesuits. He had funds to build a new cathedral and legal advice with which to apply for restoration of confiscated church properties. His efforts met with little success. It was almost impossible to regain properties that had been in private hands for a generation. Then, in February 1722 the *kadi* of Chios ordered a halt to the construction of the new cathedral and destruction of the few reopened churches. In another few days the bishop, with most of the Western clergy, was arrested on a charge of treason. After thirty-five days in a Chian jail, they were sent to Istanbul, but there, thanks to the good offices of the Dubrovnik representative, and a large 'gift' to officials, they were set free.

They returned to Chios and the cathedral of St Nicholas was completed. All other Catholic churches, except the consulate chapel served by French Capuchins, remained closed. As time went on, Bavestrelli, in his efforts to increase church income, angered the Dominicans and a number of other clergy, who sent off petitions to Rome asking for his removal, but he survived, and by 1730 the Catholics of Chios, though still under pressure, enjoyed a freedom they had not experienced for decades.[16]

A visitation of the Greek islands in 1747 by the Capuchin Arturo Marturi on behalf of Benedict XIV provides further information on this portion of the Catholic Orient. He found that conditions varied considerably from island to island. On Thira times were hard, taxes high and the cathedral in danger of collapse with neither permission from the Turks nor sufficient money to have it restored. The Dominican nuns, on the verge of destitution, were considering dissolution of their convent. Siros, solidly Catholic a century earlier, had had an influx of Greek Orthodox settlers who now held three of the churches. On the other hand, the situation on Chios had considerably improved: three small churches in the countryside and the cathedral in the capital were open, and two thousand Catholics could be counted.[17]

Chios received a new bishop, also named Bavestrelli, in 1755. Giovanni Battista Bavestrelli was consecrated in Istanbul on 29 June but could not immediately secure his *berat* of appointment. Only after the French ambassador had applied both skill and money was it possible for him to assume office. He arrived to find unsettled conditions caused by the conversion of thirty-four Orthodox, employees of Catholic families, to Catholicism, an event which brought down the wrath of the Orthodox hierarchy upon the Catholics.

It was announced by Muslim authorities that henceforth Orthodox servants would not be permitted to work in Catholic households.

Despite the ban, a trickle of converts continued to enter the Latin church and that brought new restrictions upon the missionaries in 1766. Henceforth no foreigners would be permitted to live on the island and only the Orthodox bishop was to enjoy jurisdiction there. Bishop Bavestrelli, one French Capuchin and two Jesuits were deported, leaving the church in the hands of native clergy.

In 1770 the Russian fleet under Count Orlov appeared in the Aegean en route to its victory over the Ottomans at Çeşme. Several of the islands received Russian garrisons which added a new element to their religious life. On Tinos, although the Russian commander ordered a new chapel constructed for his personal use, the Orthodox Albanians in his employ simply seized a Catholic church for their worship. The Albanians on Naxos were even more destructive: they smashed the altar in one church, and, after looting them, destroyed the Capuchin church and convent. Almost all the Latin churches suffered some damage, so that the Catholic archbishop had to make a personal appeal to the Russian commander to hold his soldiers in line. When the Russians withdrew from the Aegean, after signing the Treaty of Küçük Kajnarca, they left many scars.[18]

The Greek Catholic islanders, in addition to what they had endured as a result of the Russian presence, were struck by an even greater blow when the Society of Jesus was suppressed. On some islands the Jesuits, although divested of property and public recognition, continued their work, dressing in secular garb and generally seeking to avoid attracting attention. In this way they kept in touch with their friends while ecclesiastical authority, coached by the French ambassador, looked the other way.

Piracy in the Aegean caused both a loss of island prosperity and continuous emigration to the mainland cities. Bishop Giovanni Battista Fonto, when stationed in Siros, complained to Rome that his diocese was so depopulated that only two thousand people remained huddled behind the city walls, fearful of both the pirates and the Turkish naval patrols sent to suppress them – the one as great a menace as the other. Since most members of the French religious orders were now gone, the bishop reported, he could no longer provide religious education for his people. He asked that the Congregation for the Propagation of the Faith send him some former Jesuits from Russia, for, he said, 'in default of these, the Catholic religion will disappear on this island'.[19]

On Naxos, where pressures begun during the Russian occupation were still being felt, the Catholic community had declined to a mere three hundred and thirty people. Only four French Lazarist priests and two brothers were still in residence. When the French ambassador, Marie Gabriel Choiseul-Gouffier, visited Thira, he was discouraged to find animosity between Catholics and Orthodox so strong. He commented:

It can be observed that the two religions, Greek and Roman, are more in opposition from mutual hatred than from differences of opinion, like two brothers who are always flying into a rage, finding new reasons for their disagreements in recalling their former closeness.[20]

When he called upon the Latin bishop, the latter came in full episcopal robes to meet him, an act the ambassador thought a bit extreme, since the bishop's house was a small, simple structure where his sisters did the housekeeping.

Choiseul-Gouffier found Chios to be the most beautiful and most prosperous of the Greek islands. However, the situation of the Latin church was unhealthy. The damage done to church government by the exile of Bishop Bavestrelli in 1766 had been only partly repaired by the arrival of a new bishop in 1773. The Catholics continued to emigrate, although the number of clergy remained high. In 1783 Bishop Antonio Vuricla counted only eleven hundred faithful, but he had twenty-five native secular priests and three religious in his diocese. During the period of the French Revolution, the Spanish consul on Chios saved church properties which Ottoman officials anxiously sought to confiscate.

The once flourishing French Capuchin missions were lost one after the other in the Aegean. Andros and Milos went first, then Chios and Izmir. A single friar managed to hold on in Athens' Lantern of Demosthenes and another at Candia on Crete. An Italian Lazarist, at times the only Catholic in all the city, kept the Catholic church open in Salonica.[21]

Overall, the situation of the Catholics of the Balkans and especially of those on the Greek islands during the eighteenth century was not a happy one. They were simply too isolated from Western Europe, the core area of Catholicism, to receive the support they required. Confronted by an environment marked by indifference or hostility, the strength of these communities was on the wane even before the French missionaries, their main patrons, disappeared in the wake of the Enlightenment and the French Revolution.

12

The Catholic Armenians

THE ARMENIAN CATHOLICS IN ISTANBUL

Of all Ottoman Christians, Western missionaries won most converts among the Armenians – principally because of the education provided by the Jesuits and Capuchins. One by one, families from among the *amiras*, the wealthy bankers and merchants, converted to Catholicism once their children were enrolled in the religious schools. A number of Armenian priests, through contacts with the missionaries, did the same.

Armenian Catholics suffered several disadvantages. They had no churches of their own and had to worship in Latin churches or in the private homes of priest converts. Either way they were open to accusations of committing treason by becoming 'Franks'. Since, according to the rules of the Armenian *millet*, all baptisms, marriages and burials of those in its jurisdiction had to be conducted by the national church, Armenian Catholics were in a precarious position.

A report made after an apostolic visitation there in August 1700 recorded eight thousand Armenian Catholics in Istanbul, so far exceeding the French and Italian in number that the word 'Catholic' was reserved for them, while Westerners were known as 'Franks' or 'Latins'.[1]

Three Armenian converts, Gomidas Kemurjian, Khatchatour Arakelian and Bedros Manuk, better known by his monastic name Mekhitar, were principally responsible for the Catholic movement among their countrymen. Keumurjian was a married priest attached to St George's church in Galata and had become a Catholic in 1694, the same year that Arakelian arrived in Istanbul, after completing his studies in Rome's Urban College. A native of Erzurum, Arakelian had been won over to Catholicism by an Armenian monk sympathetic to the West. He had then gone to Rome for study and ordination. Mekhitar, most famous of the three, was born in Sivas and had taken vows in the nearby monastery of the Holy Cross. While on pilgrimage to Jerusalem, coming under the influence of the Jesuits in Aleppo, he had converted to Catholicism. In 1698 he received an appointment to one of Istanbul's Armenian churches where he attracted a number of disciples whom he led into the Catholic faith.[2]

In 1701, disturbed by the growth of Catholic sentiment within the Armenian community, the former patriarch, Ephrem of Ghafan, then bishop of Edirne, accused the incumbent patriarch Melchisedech of secret correspondence with the pope and of refusing to act against the Catholics. Ephrem also charged three Armenian priests with having become Franks and he reported them to the authorities so they would be arrested. Ottoman officials, easily convinced of possible conspiracy, issued orders for the arrest of all Armenian Catholics and the exile of Patriarch Melchisedech.

Ephrem then resumed the patriarchate with the Porte's blessing and issued an edict that all Armenians make a public profession of faith. Confessors were told to deny absolution to anyone who refused. The patriarch further demanded that Armenian contacts with Latin missionaries must cease.

This legislation put Armenian Catholics in jeopardy. Some fled the city. Others, like Mekhitar and his disciples, took refuge with the Capuchins in the grounds of the French embassy. However, in spring 1702 Ephrem was ousted, and his vicar, Avediq of Tokat, took over his office. Avediq was even more hostile to Catholics than his predecessor so the converts' situation did not improve.

The French ambassador, Charles de Ferriol, offered to mediate the dispute. He summoned the Latin Catholic religious superiors to meet Mekhitar and Arakelian to discuss possible solutions. The product of this meeting was a compromise authored by Arakelian by which the Armenian Catholics promised to attend the national churches on Sundays and Holy Days, to receive the sacraments from the national priests, and to observe the traditional fasts. In return, the national church agreed to remove the condemnations of Pope Leo I and the Council of Chalcedon from its teaching. The compromise envisaged a later statement from both parties affirming that the faith of the Armenian and Roman churches was in harmony. The proposal of Arakelian, however, was not supported by either the national hierarchy or the more conservative Catholics.[3]

Mekhitar and his community did not wait for a solution. They left Istanbul, travelling in disguise to Izmir whence they took ship

for Italy. Storm forced them into the Venetian-held port of Methoni
in the Peloponnesus, where, because their welcome was so warm,
Mekhitar decided to stay.

While the Catholic Armenians in Istanbul were still under pressure
to conform to the national religion, Latin missionaries were making
new gains in Anatolia. By 1695 the Jesuits had missions directed to the
Armenians in Erzurum and Trabzon to complement their houses in
Persia. Pope Innocent XII corresponded with both Krikor of Adana,
catholicos of Sis, and Nahabet, catholicos of Echmiadzin. He assured
Nahabet, 'although we are separated by long stretches of land
and sea, we can never forget you in our pastoral care nor be in-
attentive to your famous nation'. He promised to send Arakelian to
Echmiadzin as soon as possible so that he could give the catholicos
a complete exposition of the Catholic faith.[4]

In 1703 when Ahmet III came to power the officials of the
former regime of Sultan Mustafa II were replaced by those felt to
be loyal to the new sultan. The Armenian Patriarch Avediq was
deposed and imprisoned during the early months of Ahmet's
sultanate, but the *amiras* who belonged to Avediq's party soon
raised sufficient funds for a bribe, and he was restored. He returned
to office convinced that the Catholics among the Armenians, especially those employed as *dragomans* at the French embassy, were
responsible for his troubles, and Catholics were once more arrested,
fined and deprived of their property.

Charles de Ferriol, employing the king's influence and the king's
money, got Avediq removed and exiled to the island of Bozca Ada
(Tenedos). Subsequently, the ambassador's agents kidnapped the
deposed patriarch and put him aboard a ship for France; he was
brought to Marseille in chains. For the next three years he was a
captive in the monastery of St Michel, and thence was transferred
to the Bastille in Paris. Here the unfortunate man professed conversion to Catholicism, making an act of faith before the archbishop
of Paris. He was 'reordained' in the Latin rite and died in Paris
in July 1711.[5]

The treatment inflicted on Patriarch Avediq did not improve
relations between the Catholic Armenians and the national hierarchy; if anything de Ferriol's interference only widened the gap
between them. In 1707 Hovannes of Smyrna became patriarch,
and the persecution of Catholics recommenced with the arrest of
several bishops, forty priests and one hundred and eighty laymen.
Arakelian fled Istanbul to safety in Venice, but Kemurjian was

arrested. With him, eight other clerics suspected of Catholic conversion were brought before the Armenian *millet* court on charges of disturbing the nation's peace and of traitorous action against the sultan. Gomidas, spokesman for the group, asserted that they had indeed become Catholics, but not Franks. Catholicism meant religion, not nationality. His logic failed to convince the court and he and the eight others were taken to the court of a Turkish *kadi* and there presented as traitors. The accusation was upheld and, as was customary, their judge offered to remit the penalty to any who should accept Islam. Of the nine, eight weakened and agreed. Only Gomidas held firm, saying, 'I will not exchange my gold for your copper.' He was sentenced to death and on 4 November 1707 before a crowd of three thousand, which included his wife and children, was beheaded for his faith.[6]

The death of Gomidas caused such outrage in the Armenian community that de Ferriol prevailed upon the Porte to have Hovannes of Smyrna removed. This was accomplished and a moderate, Sahak of Apoutschek, became patriarch. Soon afterwards persecution of Catholics stopped.

A new French ambassador, Pierre des Alleurs, arrived in Istanbul in 1711, and at his insistence a plan to heal the schism within the Armenian community was drafted. This proposal called for the establishment of a separate Armenian Catholic *millet*, but the Ottoman authorities, fresh from a victory over the Russians, were in no mood to grant concessions which would enhance the position of Christians in Ottoman lands.

In 1715 the election of Hovannes Kolot to the Armenian patriarchate stabilized the situation of the church in Istanbul. Reforms were made in education and administration which considerably improved the church's condition. In addition to being a reformer Kolot was a vigorous proponent of the national church, within which he wanted to control the Catholic movement. To this end, he got authority from the Porte, then at war with Venice and Austria, to arrest any Armenian known to be a Catholic convert. Once more the prisons in Istanbul and the provinces were crowded with Catholic Armenians. The Jesuit stations in Trabzon and Erzurum were closed. Turkish troops brought in chains to the capital the leaders of the Catholic party, among them Bishops Apraham Ardzivian of Aleppo and Melkon Tasbasian of Mardin. They were imprisoned in the Bagno, where Bishop Melkon soon died as a result of his treatment; Ardzivian was later released.

Despite all the miseries of the persecution, Armenian Catholicism did not perish. In 1720, the Latin patriarchal vicar, Giovanni Battista Mauri, reported twenty thousand Armenian converts. Of that number five thousand attended the Latin churches in Galata exclusively, nine thousand went to both the Latin and the national churches, and six thousand more were secret Catholics, having privately professed Catholicism but never having attended the Latin churches. The latter disturbed Mauri, who thought their secrecy compromised their faith. He blamed their conduct upon Mekhitar and his disciples, who argued that a private profession of Catholicism was sufficient. Mauri dissented, ordering that all Armenians must publicly practise their faith.[7]

Once more the question, whether Oriental converts to Catholicism could continue to attend the Orthodox or Eastern Christian churches, was raised. The opinion of Roman theologians, that Catholics should make public profession of their faith no matter what the consequences, conflicted with the practice of many clergy in Istanbul. There, for example, no Armenian Catholic churches existed, so what was the convert to do? Mekhitar argued that his Catholic countrymen should not be expected to risk the charge of treason against the Ottomans by attending Latin churches. On the other hand, the Franciscan Custodian of the Holy Land, Lorenzo Cozza, urged Rome to speak out strongly against secrecy of conversion which, he claimed, scandalized the weak and encouraged the indifferent.[8]

Because of Mauri's objection to the secret Armenian Catholics and to the 1722 *firman* of Ahmet III which forbade conversions to Catholicism altogether, the Congregation for the Propagation of the Faith was asked to make a decision. The Roman authorities promised to be guided by a discussion held among Jesuit missionaries in Aleppo. Unfortunately the missionaries themselves could not agree, so, in a response of 9 July 1723, the Congregation left the question open. Oriental converts were simply told to consult the opinion of 'theologians, doctors, and missionaries who have lived in those areas for a long time'.[9]

In 1727 the Patriarch Hovannes met with the catholicos of Echmiadzin, Karapet III, to discuss the problem of Catholics among the Armenians. The result was a compromise: national church leaders would no longer condemn the Council of Chalcedon and Leo I in liturgical prayer or official teaching, and so Catholic Armenians, in good conscience, might attend the national churches.

Catholic Armenian leaders were quick to apply to Rome for permission to accept. Unsympathetically, Benedict XIII's advisers urged not only rejection of the request but also a definite prohibition of attendance by converts in national churches. The Congregation agreed and issued just such a decree on 5 July 1729. The Congregation also declared that such behaviour amounted to participation in false worship conducted by heretical ministers, that it opened the door to scandal, indifference and danger to the faith.

When the response became known, Patriarch Hovannes sought and obtained permission from the Porte authorities to station informers at the entrance of the Latin churches in Galata to report on Armenian worshippers. He further ordered a thorough examination to discover those with Catholic tendencies. These measures resulted in a new wave of arrests of Armenian Catholics.

The Marquis de Villeneuve then intervened, suggesting that the Catholic Armenians be permitted to purchase a church for their use. He assured the Ottoman government that his sovereign would guarantee the necessary funds up to sixty thousand *piastres*. Opposition followed at once, some of it from Latin missionaries who feared the loss of their best parishioners, and the project was abandoned.

After this setback, Villeneuve set about bettering his personal relations with Hovannes and the Armenian hierarchy. He feted the patriarch at the embassy and, with his family, paid an official visit to the Armenian patriarchal church. By January 1740 a new agreement, designed to ameliorate the position of the Armenian Catholics, was reached: Hovannes agreed that henceforth no objection would be made to any Armenian 'who wants to go to the church of our Latin brothers'.[10] No longer would the national church speak of Catholics as heretics nor condemn Pope Leo I. Both patriarch and ambassador hoped the resolution would allow the Armenian Catholics, in good conscience, to recognize the patriarch as their legitimate civil and religious head.

Their hopes were dashed; Rome refused to allow Armenian Catholics to recognize Hovannes as leader so long as he would not accept the pope as his. The compromise, like so many preceding it, fell apart. In 1741 when Hagop Nazlan, the new Armenian patriarch, appeared, the Catholics again took up the project of purchasing a place for their separate worship. They offered to buy the church of St Gregory in Galata, but Patriarch Hagop refused. News reaching Istanbul made it impossible to accede to such Catholic petitions, for in Aleppo Armenian Catholics had taken matters in their own hands, electing a catholicos and setting up their own hierarchy.

The Aleppan example persuaded Istanbul's Catholic community to press Rome for local leadership. For several years Istanbul's Armenians, impatient of patriarchal vicars, had argued that a native Armenian Catholic bishop would solve most of their difficulties. Naturally both Bishop Bona, then serving as vicar, and the Latin missionaries resisted this proposed emancipation of Armenians from Latin control and, in Rome, their voice proved the stronger. Indeed, Bona's authority increased when Pope Benedict XIV named him vicar apostolic of the East in 1742.[11]

This setback to Catholic Armenians, however, proved to be temporary. Within a few years Benedict XIV allowed them a vicar, Athanasius Merassian, an Armenian Catholic priest. It was presumed that he would receive episcopal consecration, but this was not to happen for many years because of the objections raised by Latin Catholics in Istanbul. It was only after a long wait, in 1759, that Merassian was consecrated bishop with the right to ordain priests for his community. On the other hand, he was not assigned a geographical area of jurisdiction nor was he allowed to determine policy independent of the Latin patriarchal vicar. At the time of his consecration, there were twelve thousand Armenian Catholics, served by twenty-eight clergy.[12]

Unfortunately Merassian and the then Latin vicar, Biagio Paoli, were often at odds over the direction of Istanbul's Catholic Armenians. Paoli insisted on having the final word in disputes; Bishop Athanasius believed that word should be his, especially on problems between his people and the national Armenian hierarchy. Charges and counter-charges went to Rome and finally, in February 1765, a special legate went out from Rome, but arbitration proved impossible. The Congregation for the Propagation of the Faith maintained that Latin bishops must hold uncontested primacy over all Catholics in Istanbul.[13]

That such arguments could go on within the Armenian Catholic church attests a relaxed attitude on the part of national church leaders concerning Catholics in their midst. True, Patriarch Hagop Nazlan did issue orders for the arrest of fifty Armenian Catholics caught attending Latin churches in 1761, but this action was exceptional. His successor Krikor III Pasmadjian was sympathetic to Catholics and, after resigning the patriarchate in 1776, made a profession of Catholic faith.

In the latter part of the eighteenth century, during the sultanates of Abdulhamit I and Selim III, renewed attempts by the Armenian Catholics to win their own ecclesiastical jurisdiction were more remarkable for perseverance than for success. Neither Rome nor the Porte helped, and in 1778, Bishop Athanasius Merassian once more sought Roman definition of his relationship with the patriarchal vicar, only to be put off. He resigned in frustration and left to live in retirement in Rome. As his successor, Andon Missirlian, a professor of moral theology, was appointed.

Meanwhile, Patriarch Zacaria of the Armenian national church sought to frighten Catholics by making arrests among clergy known to favour Catholicism. Thirty-five priests brought to the patriarchate for investigation professed themselves loyal Armenians – but refused to sign a document drawn up by the patriarch clarifying what was meant by 'loyal'. At the conclusion of his inquiry, Zacaria decreed that Catholic Armenians must consider themselves outside patriarchal jurisdiction and, therefore, excommunicated.

Hovannes Serposian, a well-known Armenian Catholic, responded to this challenge by an appeal to the grand vezir, Mehmet Zilifdar, for a separate Catholic *millet*, but not even an offer of a large sum of money moved the vezir. Several years later Serposian published a letter which he had sent to Rome urging Roman permission for Catholics to attend, and communicate in, national churches, thereby lessening the tension. Pope Pius VI submitted the matter to the Congregation for the Propagation of the Faith which, acting on its own past rulings, and on a dissent from the Cilician Catholic head, totally rejected Serposian's appeal.

In 1783 Archbishop Frachia reported to Rome that there were now twenty thousand Catholic Armenians in Istanbul and that, since they far outnumbered all other Catholic communities in the capital, they were his major concern. To care for them he could count on six priests, alumni of the Urban College, five Mekhitarists and four Lebanese clergy, as well as twenty-five Armenian convert priests from among the national clergy.[14]

THE FOUNDATION OF THE ARMENIAN CATHOLIC PATRIARCHATE

In 1718 the catholicos of the Armenians attached to Sis was Hovannes of Hadjin. He lived principally in Aleppo, and there he encountered

Western missionaries who persuaded him and several other prelates of his jurisdiction to unite their church with Rome. On this account the catholicos, and those of his clergy who were in sympathy with him, forwarded a profession of faith to Rome.

Three years later the Armenian Catholics of Aleppo elected their archbishop, Apraham Ardzivian, catholicos of the Catholic Armenian nation in Syria. Recognizing the trouble that might arise from such an illegal proceeding, Apraham sought to avoid the responsibility. Patriarch Hovannes in Istanbul, hearing of the election, declared it invalid and Hovannes of Hadjin, neutral until now, ordered Apraham into exile on a small island off the Lebanese coast near Tripoli.

The following year, in February 1722, Apraham escaped and took refuge with some Catholic Armenian monks from Aleppo who had settled in Lebanon after his exile. This community, following St Anthony's rule, was composed of four brothers of the Mouradian family, who, thanks to the generosity of the Maronites, had been able to settle on a small estate on the mountain at Kreim. In order to raise the money to construct a convent and a chapel for them, Apraham sold his property in Aleppo, and, on the Maronite patriarch's recommendation, Rome gave the foundation its approval.[15] Apraham wrote to the Congregation for the Propagation of the Faith praising the hospitality of the monastery's Maronite patrons: 'They have received me with every courtesy; they have given me lands and money with which I have consecrated a monastery dedicated to the Holy Saviour.'[16] Aleppan Catholics continued to regard Apraham as their leader despite the fact that he lived two hundred miles away. Neither the Ottoman officials nor the leaders of the Armenian *millet*, however, were willing to concede the legitimacy of his election.

In 1737 when Loukas Achabahian died, the Cilician catholicate became vacant. The synod's election of Loukas' brother Mikael gave Aleppan Catholics an excuse to reject his leadership on a charge of nepotism. The Catholics further argued that there was already a catholicos in the person of Apraham Ardzivian, and become so insistent that Apraham should return to his city that he agreed to come back on the assurance of French protection.

After his return in May 1740 Apraham established a church hierarchy. In the company of two Catholic Melkite prelates, he consecrated Hagop Hovsepian coadjutor for Aleppo and, shortly afterwards, Sahak Parseghian and Melkon Touhmanian as bishops for the Catholic Armenians of Syria and Cilicia. On 26 November 1740 a synod of the three newly consecrated bishops, forty priests and fourteen of the leading members of the lay community elected Apraham catholicos for a second time. The action was taken in his absence, for he had by this time returned to his more comfortable residence in Lebanon. Two years later he set off for Rome to seek the pope's blessing.

Apraham reached the Eternal City in August 1742 and was well received by Benedict XIV. A commission of the Congregation for the Propagation of the Faith heard evidence that the catholicate of Sis had become vacant, or at least that a 'heretic' now occupied it. Bishop Bona wrote from Istanbul urging the shakiness of Apraham's claims to Sis. How much the cardinals understood the situation is hard to determine, but the majority decided that Apraham should be recognized, a minority arguing that he had been elected by an illegal synod. On 26 November 1742 he made his profession of faith before the pope, eighteen cardinals and several refugee Armenian bishops. Then Benedict XIV himself placed the pallium on his shoulders and certified him 'patriarch' of the Armenians. Benedict's allocution included a statement that if, indeed, there had been some defect in Apraham's election, now, by the fulness of Petrine power, the pope had rectified it.[17]

Benedict wrote to the French ambassador in Istanbul to see if Apraham might be allowed to settle there, but the envoy replied that it was out of the question. Indeed both Patriarch Hagop Nazlan and Catholicos Mikael of Sis issued orders for his arrest should he come to Syria. Apraham, therefore, took ship to Alexandria and then returned to the monastery at Kreim whence he maintained contact with the Armenian Catholics through missionary monks. Meanwhile, since his jurisdiction included only the Armenians in the catholicate of Cilicia, Istanbul's Catholics remained under the vicar, Bishop Bona.

Apraham died on 1 October 1749, after requesting that the Armenian Catholic bishops consider Hagop Hovsepian of Aleppo to be his successor. Before the electoral synod met, the Maronite chieftains offered their Armenian guests a donation of land and money at Bzommar for a new monastery and patriarchal residence. This was readily accepted, and therefore when Hagop was elected, as Apraham had hoped he would be, he made his residence at Bzommar. Rome quickly confirmed Hagop's election and conferred the pallium. Apraham had added the name 'Peter' (in Armenian

Bedros) to his title, so Hagop asked to be known as Hagop Bedros II.[18]

After only three years in office, Hagop died, and the electoral synod chose a priest, Mikael Gasparian, to succeed him. There were some misgivings in Rome about his selection when it was learned that Mikael had been made bishop only after his patriarchal election. But these were resolved and Mikael Bedros III received recognition.

Several years later, a jurisdictional dispute broke out between Mikael Bedros and Istanbul's Catholic vicar. The patriarch notified the pope that he considered all Armenian Catholics to belong to his patriarchate and that he had appointed members of his clergy to Istanbul, Trabzon and Diyarbakir. Biagio Paoli, the Latin bishop, resisted this claim, arguing that Mikael's powers should be limited since Istanbul had a vicar. Mikael decided to visit Rome and present his case personally. He arrived on 30 April 1759 and made his appeal before a general meeting of the cardinals of the Congregation for the Propagation of the Faith. Unfortunately for the patriarch, the cardinals were unconvinced. They decided that his jurisdiction should be limited to the ancient lands of Sis; to Cilicia, Anatolia, Cappadocia and Syria. While the cardinals did not include Mesopotamia, Pope Benedict XIV added it to his authority when he approved the Congregation's decision. Mikael Bedros III returned to Lebanon disappointed but he and his successors continued to raise the issue that as patriarch of Armenian Catholics, the Bzommar patriarch and his hierarchy should govern all of the church.[19]

In other parts of the Ottoman Empire the fortunes of the Catholic Armenians prospered. In Ankara Catholic clergy held four out of seven churches, serving some four thousand men and women. The Mekhitarists in Erzurum counted twelve thousand Catholics, while Akhaltsikhe and Aleppo had four thousand in their communities. The single exception to this phenomenal growth occurred in the old Catholic homeland of Nakhichevan. Since this area had been the eighteenth-century battleground of Ottomans and Persians, Catholic life there had been in constant turmoil. The last of the Unitor monasteries was abandoned in 1745 and the archbishop of Nakhichevan, Domenico Salviani, fled to Rome where he died twenty years later. Only a handful of priests and people lingered amid the ruins of their once prosperous region. Of this remnant, the last survivors, about eight hundred people led by the priest Tomas Issaverdens, emigrated to Izmir. From here they dispatched letters to Rome and Versailles asking funds for a church and hospice. In a short time, the small community, integrated into the Latin Catholic church, had lost all corporate religious life of its own.[20]

The loyalty of Armenian Catholics to their faith is remarkable when one thinks of the dangers and difficulties this brought to them. They lived much as the early Christians in the Roman empire, never certain that their allegiance might not bring them loss of property, freedom or even life itself. Jurisdictional disputes between members of their own hierarchies must have pained them considerably since so many more important issues were at stake. Several times it appeared as though a compromise between their own *millet* authorities and the missionaries was at hand, but nothing was ever concluded – one more disappointment for a brave and courageous group.

13

The Near Eastern churches

THE MARONITES

At the close of the seventeenth century the Maronites numbered about seventy thousand people governed by a patriarch and a synod of seven bishops. French protection was provided by the consuls in Saida and Beirut who intervened on the Maronites' behalf with the Ottoman governor or the Druze chieftains.

The major event in Maronite history at this time had been monastic reform instituted by three Maronites of Aleppo – 'Abdallah Kar'ali, Jibra'il Hawa and Yusuf El-Betn – in 1695. Their congregation, influenced by the Aleppan Jesuits, departed considerably from Maronite monastic tradition, and began to suffer from divisive argument over the extent to which Western models should be followed. The more nationalistic members under Kar'ali left the monastery and established a new community, St Elija, where they became popularly known as the order of Maronite Aleppans. In 1700, the Aleppans received grudging recognition from the Maronite bishops.

In 1705 the synod elected Ya'kub 'Awad to the patriarchate – an unpopular choice. Many people, lay and clergy alike, found the new patriarch's leadership lacklustre. Eventually the faction opposing him gained the support of some Latin missionaries on Mt Lebanon, but Rome did not become aware of the patriarch's unpopularity until the Congregation for the Propagation of the Faith received word that a synod of Maronite bishops had accused 'Awad of several crimes, convicted and deposed him. The synod then chose an administrator, Yusuf Mobarak, to govern the church until a permanent replacement could be found.

Pope Clement XI, when informed of the problem, asked the Custodian of the Holy Land, Lorenzo Cozza, to investigate. Lorenzo's solution was to ask 'Awad to resign so that peace might be restored to the church. The synod then formally selected Yusuf Mobarak to succeed as patriarch, but the ousted 'Awad appealed to Rome, claiming that he had been deposed on false charges. His claim was supported by the French consul in Saida, so the Congregation for the Propagation of the Faith agreed to review the synodal actions. At the conclusion of its work, the prefect of the Congregation found Patriarch Ya'kub innocent and recommended that the pope reinstate him. On 30 June 1713, therefore, Pope Clement XI addressed to the Maronites an encyclical, *Nationem vestram*, reinstating 'Awad and declaring his prior resignation null and void. In January 1714 Ya'kub returned to Qannubin and resumed office. Despite internal problems during these years, the Maronite church continued to grow in numbers and influence. The conversion to Christianity of several Muslim and Druze families aided this growth immeasurably. Some Shehabs, among the most important Druze *shaykhs*, converted in 1711; another Druze clan, the Jumblatts, contributed to Maronite foundations in their territories.[1]

The difficult patriarchate of Ya'kub 'Awad ended with his death in February 1733. His successor was Yusuf al-Khazen, then holding the episcopal title of Ghosta. At the synod called for his election many churchmen demanded ecclesiastical reforms. They argued that ecclesiastical structure was not clearly defined and that there was a progressive Latinization in progress due to the influence of foreign missionaries and of Maronite students who returned to Lebanon after studies in Rome. The hierarchy contained several factions, and all of the meetings meant to bring harmony among them faltered. At last Patriarch Yusuf and the synod decided to ask for Roman intervention, requesting Clement XII to send a legate to Lebanon. At the time their own kinsman Yusuf al-Sim'ani (Joseph Assemani) was prefect of the Vatican Library; more a scholar than a politician, he was more at home in the West than the East, but the pope appointed him as his representative to straighten out Maronite affairs. Al-Sim'ani was given authority to summon a general synod in which all administrative and liturgical issues within the Maronite church were to be examined.

Arriving in Lebanon in June 1736, al-Sim'ani made the journey to Qannubin and there on 1 July read the communication from Rome to the assembled Maronite clergy. The synod was to open on 15 August at the monastery of Raifun. Al-Sim'ani spent the following weeks travelling about Mt Lebanon gathering support from the clergy and the *mouqaddamin* for the synod and the canons which he intended to introduce. Meanwhile Patriarch Yusuf made no preparations for the council, since his talks with al-Sim'ani had showed that Rome expected radical changes – which were not to his liking – to be made in the Maronite church. Another bishop, Iliyas Mohasseb of Akra, took the lead in forming a party to oppose any significant modifications in Maronite traditions.

A letter from Pierre Fromage, a Jesuit missionary in Lebanon, listed the matters considered to be abuses within the Maronite church. These included having double monasteries where monks and nuns lived side by side and shared the same church. (One of these, in fact, existed at the patriarchal residence.) A second abuse was the high charge required for chrism blessed by the patriarch. A third, that the Eucharist was not preserved in all Maronite churches, while still others lacked proper vestments and ornaments. Again, widowed priests were remarrying, contrary to the canons. Finally, Maronites in Aleppo had abandoned Syriac, their liturgical language, for the Arabic vernacular.[2]

Maronite reluctance to attend al-Sim'ani's council must have been considerable: a quorum was not achieved until 14 September, nearly a month after the official opening. Eight Maronite bishops, a smattering of chieftains, and several Latin clergy were the only people in attendance to hear the papal legate read the canons designed to activate the necessary church reform. These were patterned on the disciplinary legislation adopted by the Ruthenians at the council of Zamość in 1720, despite the obvious differences which existed between the Ruthenian and Maronite churches. When al-Sim'ani reached the canon which affected the distribution of chrism and forbade a payment in respect of it to the patriarch, Yusuf rose to protest and left the assembly.

When the council convened on the following day, Yusuf and three of the bishops refused to attend, thus halting the proceedings. Al-Sim'ani and the remaining bishops, accompanied by the Jesuits and Franciscans, repaired to the monastery of Saiyidat al-Luwayzah, where, through emissaries, negotiations between the two parties consumed the next ten days. At last, agreement was reached. The patriarch agreed to attend the synod provided he had the right to examine and confirm all the canons which were authorized by the assembly.

On 30 September the synod reconvened at al-Luwayzah, opening with an address by the Jesuit Fromage, after which deliberations began. Action was taken to set the number of bishops at eight and to establish for them diocesan jurisdictions based on territorial jurisdictions. A series of canons dealt with preaching, the censorship of books, days of fast and abstinence, and the administration of the sacraments. Liturgical changes required the use of unleavened bread in the Eucharist and the suppression of communion in both kinds for the laity. To express the correct belief on the procession of the Holy Spirit, the phrase 'and the Son' was to be added to the creed. The synod agreed that confirmation must be separated from baptism and administered only by a bishop. Double monasteries were forbidden and the sale of marriage dispensations was to stop. In effect, the canons of al-Luwayzah Latinized the Maronite church in a way which was quite opposed to the spirit of the Council of Florence; they were contrary to the countless protestations by Rome that the Eastern churches *must* preserve their traditions intact.[3]

By the time the council concluded on 2 October, fourteen Maronite prelates were in attendance along with two Melkite bishops and the Armenian Catholic bishop, Apraham Ardzivian. Of this number, ten of the Maronites, including Patriarch Yusuf, signed the Arabic version of the council's acts. To what extent the Maronite hierarchy understood the implication of their actions is unknown. Certainly many of the reforms, if such they were, still remained only on paper, one hundred years later. Yet al-Luwayzah's synod had been a partial success: for the first time in Maronite history a truly national assembly of clergy had met for three days and deliberated on a number of important issues.

Before leaving for Italy al-Sim'ani addressed a letter to the Maronite clergy informing them of the new legislation. He also wrote to Cardinal André-Hercule de Fleury announcing the successful conclusion of the synod and asking that French protection for the Maronites be reaffirmed by Louis XV. In addition, he sent a notice to monastic superiors that double monasteries could no longer exist and that monastic properties presently held by such institutions should be divided between the men and women. On his way home, he paused to visit the Maronites on Cyprus and in Egypt to inform them of the decisions of the Lebanese council.

Upon his arrival in Rome, al-Sim'ani submitted the Arabic original of the council's acts, with a Latin translation, to the Congregation for the Propagation of the Faith. A commission of cardinals was set up to examine the proceedings. Meanwhile, Iliyas Sa'ad, a Maronite priest, had arrived in Rome as a delegate from

Patriarch Yusuf, who announced that after examination by the Maronite bishops it was discovered that the Latin and Arabic texts were not in agreement and that therefore the ratification of al-Luwayzah's council should be delayed.[4]

While the issue remained unsettled, Clement XII died and Benedict XIV replaced him. Benedict appointed a second commission of review which, with a few slight emendations, urged the pope to approve the acts of the council, which he did on 1 September 1741. A later decree issued by Rome allowed the patriarch to recoup revenue lost from the distribution of chrism from other fees.[5]

Just after the confirmation of the synod and before any of its provisions could go into force, Yusuf died, on 13 May 1742. When the electoral synod met to choose a successor, the bishops registered their reaction to the Council of al-Luwayzah by electing to the patriarchate one of the synod's most outspoken critics, Iliyas Mohasseb. Two of the electors, the archbishops of Cyprus and of Tyre, were not present at the election, and they, aggrieved at the decision, set about consecrating two other bishops, summoning their own synod and there electing the archbishop of Cyprus, Tubya al-Khazen, as patriarch. Both candidates sent delegates to Rome to seek recognition by Benedict XIV.

The pope, once again troubled by a problem in the Maronite church, asked *Propaganda* to make a recommendation. After some study, a commission of the Congregation told the pope that they believed neither nominee should receive approbation and that the pope himself should appoint a patriarch. Not unwillingly, Benedict acted on this advice, naming Shim'un 'Awad, archbishop of Damascus and a former Roman student, to the office. Since Rome heretofore had never directly appointed a Maronite patriarch, the delicate task of placating Maronite sensitivities was entrusted to the Franciscan Custodian of the Holy Land, Giacomo de Lucca, who, with a pallium in his baggage, sought out Shim'un to inform him of his appointment. He invested him with the pallium and then set about persuading a Maronite synod, called for Harissa in early October 1743, to accept him. Giacomo was successful: the synod acclaimed Shim'un as patriarch.

Afterwards five of the bishops regretted their acceptance of Shim'un, withdrew their support from him and dispatched a letter to Rome saying that he was unacceptable. Naturally, Benedict XIV supported his man: he wrote to the bishops that they were damaging the church by refusing his authority and urged the dissenters to fall in line. Eventually, the hierarchy joined Shim'un and the threatened schism was avoided.[6]

While the question of the patriarchal succession was under debate still another problem arose. This involved the appearance in Lebanon of a Maronite nun from Aleppo, Anna Ajami, also known as Hendiye, who claimed to be a mystic and attracted a large following among her people as a living prophetess. Anna had come under Jesuit influence early in her spiritual life and had become greatly attracted to the devotion to the Sacred Heart of Jesus, a type of spirituality quite foreign to Maronite tradition. In her enthusiasm, she formed, at Bkerke, a congregation of nuns dedicated to this devotion. This group enjoyed a great deal of notoriety since Anna claimed, and thousands believed, that her spiritual allocutions came directly from Christ.

Anna's mystical experiences increased in number over the years and convinced her that she was united with the Trinity in a unique way. Her Jesuit advisers had second thoughts about Anna when her claims to a special Trinitarian relationship passed the bounds of theological propriety, but despite Jesuit reservations, Patriarch Shim'un and the majority of Maronite clergy grew more enthusiastic than ever over Anna's revelations.

When Shim'un learned that Anna had been reported to the authorities in Rome as a possible victim of self-delusion, he was so incensed that he forbade the Jesuits to have any further contact with the Maronites. He threatened to excommunicate any Maronite who attended Jesuit churches. Benedict XIV, alerted to the storm over Anna, put his faith in the Jesuits and wrote to Shim'un ordering the suppression of Anna's congregation, the prohibition of her writings, and her transfer to a convent of traditional Maronite nuns.

The pope appointed an Aleppan Franciscan, Desiderio da Casabasciana, to investigate the affair. From the middle of May until July 1752 the inquiry was conducted by the Franciscan. Contrary to expectations, it was Anna who convinced *him* that her experiences were authentic and that the attacks upon the Sacred Heart Congregation were unwarranted. The pope's attitude, therefore, became more tolerant and in a second letter to patriarch Shim'un he asked only that Anna be kept in a convent where she would be less apt to cause a commotion, and that she should have her spiritual directors chosen from more prudent men.[7]

A final problem arose to trouble the peace of the Maronites during this period when the Catholic Melkites questioned the sanctity of their founder, St Maron. The Melkites, including Patriarch Kyrillos VI, taunted the Maronites that Maron was in fact a heretic. The Maronites naturally resisted the charge and complained to Rome. Once more, Desiderio da Casabasciana was appointed to decide the issue. His sentiments were on the side of the Maronites and he wrote to Rome accordingly. Benedict XIV thereafter ruled that the Melkites must desist from their attack on Maron, admitting, however, that confusion was possible, due to the paucity of historical sources concerning the original saint and to incorrect identification of a later, and perhaps heretical, Maron.[8]

Despite the improved status of his people, Patriarch Shim'un 'Awad continued to have difficulties both with Rome and with his own clergy. Since the Ottoman sultans did not recognize the Maronite patriarch's office, he was at least free of vexation from that quarter – but not from Rome. *Propaganda*, dissatisfied because 'Awad had failed to implement the decisions of the al-Luwayzah synod (no diocesan structure had been set up, and several other canons legislated by the council remained a dead letter), continued to prod the patriarch. Shim'un, in response, called a synod for 1755. Although fifteen canons were adopted at this gathering, little new ground was broken except for Canon XII, which forbade Latin missionaries to interfere in Maronite affairs unless their assistance was requested.[9]

Shim'un died on 12 February 1756, leaving little concrete evidence that the Maronites whom he governed were any more enthusiastic than himself over changes in their traditions. His successor, Tubya al-Khazen, it will be recalled, had been chosen patriarch once before only to have Rome annul his candidacy. Tubya first called a synod, which proved as fruitless as its predecessors; then he announced his support for Anna Ajami. The Roman authorities, convinced that the Maronites should be concentrating on the task of bringing their ecclesiastical practice into conformity with Rome and quelling the fervour of Anna Ajami's supporters, were chagrined.

During Tubya's patriarchate, an unfortunate division arose within the Antonine monastic community. Those monks who were drawn principally from peasant families on Mt Lebanon had a view of monastic life different from that held by the brethren from Aleppo and other urban centres. The former cared little for book-learning but much for austerity – something unwelcome to city-bred monks. A dispute over this broke out upon the occasion of the election of an abbot who favoured the Aleppan party. The rigorists (Baladites) refused their obedience to him and sought to create a separate identity. Benedict XIV received the Baladite appeal for an autonomous organization but denied it, recommending, instead, greater efforts to resolve the differences.

The internal harmony Benedict sought was not to be, and eventually, under Pope Clement XIII, permission to split the order was granted on 19 July 1770. Into the Aleppan branch went sixty-one monks, ninety-one went to the Baladites. The monks established in St Isaiah's monastery had taken no part in the dispute and continued as before, so that after 1770 there were three congregations of Maronite monks, all following the rule of St Antony.[10]

When Yusuf Estphan was elected patriarch in 1766 on the death of Tubya al-Khazen, he took up residence in the Ghosta monastery, which he himself had founded, in Kisrawan. Here, in the heart of the Maronite homeland, the new patriarch felt more secure. When Yusuf sent to Rome for his pallium, Clement XIV used the occasion to remind him that several canons of the al-Luwayzah council remained unenforced and that the number of Maronite bishops still exceeded the limit authorized by Rome. In order to follow Rome's prescriptions, Yusuf called a synod to meet at Ghosta in 1768. Once more, all participants agreed that the canons should be enforced, but, by this time, a faction opposed to the patriarch had developed and its adherents wrote to both the Congregation for the Propagation of the Faith and to Clement XIV, asking for his deposition; however, Rome demurred from taking such radical action.

Patriarch Yusuf practised an ardent devotion to the Sacred Heart, which placed him among the supporters of Anna Ajami and her congregation. Despite Rome's disapproval, Anna's saintly reputation was unchallenged among her own people. In fact, she had become something of a heroine for having submitted to a series of investigations by Latin clerics, none of which had proven anything, as far as the Maronites were concerned. With all this in mind, Patriarch Yusuf commissioned Arsenius, archbishop of Damascus, to go to Rome in August 1774 in order to inform the church authorities there of the Lebanese situation. The archbishop appeared before the Congregation for the Propagation of the Faith but got little sympathy. The cardinals queried whether it was true that Patriarch Yusuf had gone on his knees to obtain Anna's blessing and if, indeed, her picture now hung in the patriarchal church? While Arsenius denied the rumours, he was obliged to admit that Yusuf had made the feast of the Sacred Heart a holy day of obligation for the Maronites, an action Anna had strongly promoted.

For three years, Arsenius waited for a promised audience with the pope, Pius VI, but in June 1779, instead of an invitation, he received word that the Congregation had suspended Patriarch Yusuf and had ordered him to report to Rome. In his stead, as administrator, Pius appointed the archbishop of Tripoli. Mikha'il al-Khazen, while a new investigation was made. Anna's Congregation of the Sacred Heart was to be dissolved; she was to retire and her writings were proscribed.

In Lebanon, Patriarch Yusuf received the news of his suspension in sorrow, but prepared to go to Rome to defend himself. When he arrived in Beirut, however, he fell sick and for over a month could not continue his journey. His doctors advised against the difficult trip to Rome, and when the worst was over, Yusuf went to Mt Carmel to recuperate.

The cardinals of *Propaganda*, convinced that Yusuf's illness was psychosomatic, saw his failure to appear as a prime opportunity to bring an end to the patriarch's tenure. They prodded the Maronite administrator to call a synod to the monastery of Maifuan. Many of the Maronite bishops were reluctant to go, and, when they did arrive, they levelled acrimonious charges and counter-charges. The majority held for Anna and the patriarch and were in no mood to abandon them; a small minority was equally convinced that Anna was a fraud and Yusuf her unwitting dupe.

The Congregation sent Yusuf Tian, a Maronite priest stationed in Rome, to ascertain the mood of the bishops. He returned at the end of the synod to report that sentiment was overwhelmingly in favour of Yusuf. His report changed the minds of the cardinals, and on 21 September 1784 the Congregation restored the patriarch to his office.[11]

The turbulence in the Orient caused by the French Revolution, Yusuf's death in April 1793, and Anna's in February 1798 brought this era to an end. Two short patriarchates followed Yusuf's; then Yusuf Tian, whom Rome trusted as one of its own, was elected to the office on 24 April 1796. He was there when Napoleon left Egypt in February 1799 for an attack on Syria. Before his assault, Napoleon wrote to the Maronite patriarch and to the civil head of Mt Lebanon, Amir Bashir al-Shehab II, that he was coming as friend and ally of the Christians and the Druzes. While the siege of Acre was in progress a Maronite delegation visited Napoleon but was careful to make no commitments to a French general representing a government which, at that very moment, was holding Pope Pius VI captive.[12]

THE MELKITE CATHOLICS

Few events in the history of the Christian Orient have had such lasting importance as those which led to a division in the Antiochene Melkite church in the early eighteenth century. A lasting schism developed within the church which resulted in rival hierarchies, both claiming to represent the authentic traditions of their church. On one side, the partisans of Rome believed in communion with the Western church; on the other, partisans of Constantinople urged union with the East as the sure guarantee of orthodoxy.

Already in 1701, the Roman authorities had agreed to permit Euthymios Saifi, head of the Western party and metropolitan of Sidon, to enjoy the title of bishop of Melkite Catholics. This conformed with the policy of the Congregation for the Propagation of the Faith to win over converts from the Oriental churches by allowing them their own clergy and ritual. The transition to Rome for Eastern Christians would amount only to recognition of papal primacy and adherence to the agreed formulas of the Council of Florence. Western missionaries were constantly reminded that they were in the Orient to make Eastern, not Latin, Catholics.

Euthymios Saifi, however, was enamoured of Latin ways and had made alterations in liturgical practices and in the laws of fasting and the canons regulating marriage, all designed to achieve closer conformity to Rome. In 1708, he sponsored the founding of a monastic community formed from his disciples. It was known as *Dair al-Mukhallis*, the Monastery of the Saviour. About the same time, two Melkite students, Gerasimos and Suleyman, began a foundation at Shuwair on the road from Beirut to Ba'labakk, dedicated to St John the Baptist. The monks in both communities followed the rule of St Basil, but modified by several Latin customs. Both served as major centres of the Catholic party among the Melkites.[13]

The Catholic current ran so strong in the early eighteenth century that the patriarch of Antioch, Kyrillos V al-Za'im, was always careful to keep on good terms with the Maronites, the Latin missionaries in Syria and the French consuls. Such was the impression the Jesuits made upon him that they suggested to Pope Clement XI that he write to Kyrillos inviting him to make a profession of

Catholic faith. The Pope complied, writing a letter on 9 January 1716 which was dispatched to Euthymios Saifi for delivery to Damascus, the patriarchal residence. While Kyrillos studied the papal letter and accompanying literature, one of his clerics reported him to the Ottoman authorities as having gone over to the 'Franks'. He was summoned before the paşa of Damascus and threatened with serious consequences if he even contemplated such an act. The paşa imprisoned him for several days until his community and the French consul raised enough money to secure his release. The incident did not change Kyrillos' mind. He signed the Catholic profession of faith which had accompanied Clement XI's letter and announced to his synod that he intended to send a delegation to Rome with gifts and his pastoral staff to confirm his decision to unite with the Western church. One other bishop, Gerasimos of Daydnayya, once the head of the Shuwair monastery, added his name to the profession.[14]

While Kyrillos held office, a rival Melkite group looked to another bishop, Athanasios III Dabbas, as their head. In order to end this division, Kyrillos and Athanasios had agreed between themselves that when Kyrillos died, Athanasios should succeed him. In 1720, therefore, when Kyrillos succumbed, Athanasios followed without difficulty. Before his succession, Athanasios had shown sympathy for Catholics, but, once in office, his attitude changed and he began looking for ways to limit Western influence on the Antiochene church. To this end, he journeyed to Istanbul late in the summer of 1722 to consult the Greek patriarch, Jeremias, himself a vigorous opponent of Catholicism. Jeremias had already excommunicated Euthymios Saifi for his Catholic activities. He had failed, however, to discourage Euthymios, who charged:

The Greek patriarchs for twenty years have never given up plotting our destruction, by imperial *firmans* sometimes condemning us to exile, at other times to life in prison, but Providence always saved us from their evil designs thanks to Kyrillos, the late patriarch, who had no use for their plots.[15]

Athanasios and the Greek synod agreed that all Catholics in the Oriental churches should be excommunicated. They sought from Ahmet III's government a *firman* which was issued on 14 September 1722, ordering that all Ottoman subjects in the Christian *millets* must remain there. Anyone violating the regulations would be subject to arrest as a traitor.

Two years after obtaining the ban on Catholic Melkites, Athanasios III died. He had groomed a successor, Sylvester, a Greek monk from Cyprus who shared the patriarch's antagonism toward the Catholics. On the other hand, the prohibition of Catholicism among the Melkites had failed and the partisans of the Western church were anxious to elect a Catholic candidate to the patriarchate. Their nominee was Seraphim Tanas, a native of Damascus and a nephew of Euthymios Saifi. Seraphim had been educated in the Urban College and was a monk of the Shuwair monastery. He had been ordained by his uncle on his return to the East and served on the staff of Patriarch Kyrillos al-Za'im until he had been imprisoned as a result of the *firman* of 1722.

The Catholic party of Damascus took the initiative when a synod of twenty-nine priests, two deacons and a number of lay leaders convened to elect Seraphim patriarch. There were no Melkite bishops in attendance, so the consecration of Seraphim posed a problem. Two bishops were known to support Seraphim: Neophytos Nasri of Sidon and Vasileos Finan of the Monastery of the Saviour. Together, these two consecrated a third, Euthymios Fadl, so that the three might form a synod to proceed to the acclamation of Seraphim as patriarch.

Thus, Seraphim became patriarch, taking the name Kyrillos VI, on 20 September 1724 in the cathedral of the Virgin Mary in Damascus. The paşa Ismail al-Azm was informed and asked to secure from Istanbul a *berat* confirming the election. With the request went a large sum of money to be put to use among the officials at the court.[16]

A week after Kyrillos VI became patriarch in Syria, the Constantinopolitan synod under Jeremias III nominated Sylvester of Cyprus as head of the Antiochene church. Melkite representatives attended the election, and gave their consent, although all previous patriarchs had been natives. As was expected, Sultan Ahmet's government gave its *berat* to Sylvester and his choice was the beginning of a succession of Greeks in the Antiochene patriarchate which lasted until the end of the nineteenth century.[17]

Sylvester took advantage of the support he had received from the Greek Orthodox, the Ottoman civil authorities and the Melkites of Aleppo, who resented the high-handed action of the Damascenes in holding the patriarchal elections without consulting them. As Sylvester approached Damascus, Kyrillos VI decided his position was vulnerable and he left the city for the safety of the Monastery of the Holy Saviour.

Sylvester sought the allegiance of all Syrian Melkites; partisans of Kyrillos were deposed and exiled, and all clergy were examined to ascertain their position on papal authority and on the Council of Florence. Those who showed pro-Roman tendencies were excommunicated. The community at Damascus was especially suspect; Sylvester's agents watched the Latin churches to report on Melkites who attended services there. But the attempts to destroy Catholicism came too late. Leading members of the Melkite church, both from conviction and from fear of losing the political, educational, and economic advantages gained by close association with the Western church and its French representatives in the East, refused to follow him. Even from a distance of hundreds of miles, Kyrillos still held the loyalty of many Melkites who resented Greek interference in their church's affairs.

Kyrillos was anxious to obtain recognition of his title from the pope, but lack of information in Rome delayed a quick decision. The Capuchin superior in Damascus defended Kyrillos' election as valid:

I do not understand why the Christians of Aleppo are not of the same mind as those of Damascus. Possibly heretics are more numerous than the Catholics and thus prefer Sylvester, a well-known heretic, compared to Kyrillos, of whom no one doubts his Catholicism.[18]

Benedict XIII named a special commission to examine the election of Kyrillos. The commission held seven sessions between 15 March and 5 July 1729 and decided that Kyrillos had been validly elected and should receive papal recognition. Acting upon this advice, Benedict XIII, in a letter dated 13 August 1729, certified Kyrillos' election to Antioch. He appointed a Carmelite legate, Dorotheos of the Holy Trinity, to obtain Kyrillos' signature on a profession of faith and on a second document which promised he would make no changes in the liturgy and traditions of his church. This implied that all of the modifications introduced into the Melkite liturgy by his uncle were to be cancelled.

Dorotheos arrived at the Monastery of the Holy Saviour in the following spring, and convoked a synod of the Catholic Melkites for 25 April 1730. All clergy who attended, along with the patriarch, signed a profession of faith. Dorotheos proclaimed the papal recognition of Kyrillos, but he had no pallium to confer. Rome was still unsure of the patriarch, and its doubts were confirmed when, within a year of his recognition, Kyrillos mitigated the rules of fast and abstinence for his church.[19]

During Benedict XIV's pontificate, Rome endeavoured to restrain the Melkite Catholic penchant for the abandonment of tradition, thus displaying an aptitude quite different from that taken toward the Maronites in the Council of al-Luwayzah. It was the Melkites themselves who wanted change, especially in the duration and severity of the fasts legislated by their church. On 24 December 1743 Benedict addressed a cautionary letter, *Demandatam caelitus*, to Patriarch Kyrillos VI in which he emphasized Rome's prerogative of having the final word on question of reforms:

Concerning the rites and customs of the Greek church as they have generally been understood, we decree that no one has the right or permission, no matter what his title, rank, authority or dignity, even if it is episcopal or patriarchal, to dare make any innovations or introduce any foreign customs that modify the integrity and exactness of the ritual.

Melkites were forbidden to transfer to the Latin rite without express permission from Rome, and missionaries who encouraged such moves were held guilty of serious transgression against canon law. With several minor exceptions, any innovations already started were to be halted.[20]

On the presumption that Kyrillos shared his sentiments, Benedict finally dispatched a pallium to him on 29 February 1744. Before investiture, Kyrillos had been required to renew his profession of the Catholic faith and to take an oath to uphold *Demandatam caelitus*.

Since Kyrillos could do little directly to supervise affairs in Syria, he busied himself with monastic questions. In 1736, he sought to merge the Monastery of the Holy Saviour, his own residence, with the community of St John the Baptist at Shuwair. The monks at Shuwair were hesitant: a three-day conference aimed at bringing the congregations under a common constitution failed, and the two decided to retain separate existence.[21]

In 1751, Kyrillos summoned a council of Melkite Catholics to meet at the Monastery of the Holy Saviour to review the status of the church. At the conclusion of the synod, the bishops adopted thirteen canons designed to improve ecclesiastical administration. Rome had not been consulted prior to the council, an omission which caused officials at the Congregation for the Propagation of the Faith to view its proceedings with misgivings. Patriarch Kyrillos, for his part, was vexed at Latin missionaries, whom he felt were too influential with the members of his church. It was his belief that

some Maronites were seeking to convert Melkites that started the
quarrel over the holiness of St Maron. During the course of this
dispute, Kyrillos tore up a picture of the Maronite founder, claiming
he was a heretic.

The major problem for Kyrillos was his exile from the Melkite
heartland where his rival, thanks to the Ottomans, held the cathedral
of Damascus. He grew frustrated over his impotence to assist the
Catholic Melkite clergy persecuted by Sylvester and his followers,
of whom the French consul at Saida testified: 'These men are
without faith and are full of anger at the Catholics upon whom they
descend with all the fury of their chief.'[22] Meanwhile, Kyrillos had to
accept the bitter fact that his presence in Damascus, or anywhere
else in Syria, would be impossible until the attitude of the Orthodox
Melkites should change. In 1759, still living in exile on Mt Lebanon,
he had reached the age of eighty. He was prepared to resign, yet
wanted to ensure the succession for one of his great-nephews,
Ignatios Jawhar. Most of the Melkite hierarchs resented this, for
Ignatios was only twenty-seven, not yet a bishop, and the choice
would be flagrant nepotism. When Kyrillos sought to call a synodal
election meant simply to confirm his choice, a majority of the eleven
Melkite bishops refused to appear. After two more attempts at
obtaining the necessary electors, a synodal quorum was achieved
and seven bishops cast their votes for Jawhar. He was duly consecrated and acclaimed patriarch under the name Athanasios. The
absent bishops, led by Maximos Hakim of Hieropolis, dispatched a
complaint to Rome contesting the validity of the election.

Propaganda ruled in favour of the dissidents, arguing that not
only was Athanasios' election invalid, but so, too, was Kyrillos'
resignation, for he had not sought Rome's permission. Both Athanasios and his electors were suspended from office. A Dominican
legate, Domenico Lanza, was commissioned to go to Lebanon and
announce Rome's decision to appoint Maximos Hakim patriarch
rather than call for a new election. When Lanza met with Athanasios, he sought to persuade him to resign, but was unsuccessful. He
then went to Shuwair monastery, where he informed Maximos
Hakim of Rome's appointment. Maximos was required to take a
long oath concerning his fidelity to the pope and was only then
invested in his office. Athanasios, when informed of what happened,
declared that he would not recognize Maximos, and Lanza then
excommunicated him.[23]

The double patriarchate caused confusion in the church over the following weeks, as both religious heads appointed their partisans to vacant offices and ran up significant debts in the struggle to sway Ottoman authorities. Then, on 28 November 1762, Maximos died. During his tenure of three months he had added the feast of Corpus Christi to the Melkite calendar, an action which shows how powerfully Latin influence played upon the Melkite Catholics.

The Melkite bishops, loyal to Maximos Hakim, chose Athanasios Dahan, bishop of Damascus, to succeed him. Athanasios adopted Theodosios V for his patriarchal name and easily obtained Roman recognition. He took up residence in the monastery of St Anthony at Karkafeh. Meantime, a Latin vicar was sent to Athanasios Jawhar in the hope of winning him over by offering him the bishopric of Sidon, but Jawhar refused. Instead, he summoned a council of his partisans which certified him as the true patriarch, and, as a result, he was once more excommunicated by Clement XIII on 11 September 1765. Three years later, Jawhar was at last reconciled with Rome, and the divisive struggle within the Catholic Melkite communion finally came to an end.[24]

Partly as a result of the Melkite controversy, Rome appointed a Latin apostolic vicar for Aleppo on 27 June 1762. His jurisdiction included the whole of the Near East and Cyprus, excepting only Palestine, where the Franciscan Custodian of the Holy Land retained his traditional authority. The first appointee was Arnard Bossu, a member of the Lazarists, who was given authority over Eastern Catholics, Latins and all religious superiors. He was also empowered, during times of persecution, to allow Eastern Catholics, on an individual basis, to have their children baptized and to be married and buried in the national churches. The general principle that Catholics could not participate in the sacraments of heretics and schismatics was kept intact, but, sensibly, dispensations could now be given. Bossu's major function was to bring peace to the Melkite church, but, after three years of frustration, he resigned his office and returned to the West. No one replaced him. The first attempt at establishing a Latin arbiter in the Near East had proven a failure.[25]

The close of the eighteenth century saw peace within the Catholic Melkite church, since Ignatios (Athanasios) Jawhar remained content with his bishopric of Sidon. In 1788, when Patriarch Theodosios VI died, Ignatios was elected patriarch, at last fulfilling his ambition. He chose the title Athanasios IV, and governed the Melkite church from the monastery of the Holy Saviour. There was some bitterness toward him in the monastery of Shuwair, as well as in Aleppo, where that city's bishop, Germanos Adam, had little respect for him. In October 1790 a synod of bishops issued canons which Shuwair thought prejudicial to its particular interests and upon which the community appealed to the pope for rectification. Germanos Adam himself went to Rome to present the case for Shuwair and obtained a successful resolution of the matter. After only five years as patriarch, Athanasios IV died, and many hoped that the controversies which plagued the church were at an end, but this was not to be. Attention now focused on Germanos Adam, the most vigorous bishop of the Catholic Melkites, and his doctrinal writings.

Adam had been born in Aleppo, had joined the monastic clergy and attended the Urban College. After returning to the East, he became bishop of Acre in 1774 and, three years later, metropolitan of Aleppo. Here he gathered into the episcopal residence a group of celibate priests to teach and minister to the Melkites of the city. Germanos wrote two books, *An Exposition of the Proofs for the Orthodox Faith* and *The Torch of Highest Knowledge or a Presentation on the Authority of the Church.* Neither was publicly circulated, but rumour had it that they contained questionable doctrine. The Latin missionaries in Aleppo did not like Adam – there were quarrels over property which had to be settled by litigation – but Rome's confidence in him was witnessed by his appointment to the presidency of a Maronite synod in 1790.[26]

During his trip to Italy on behalf of the Shuwair monastery, Adam came into contact with a number of bishops who were Jansenists, Gallicans, or both, and was especially taken by the ideas of an Italian, Scipione Ricci of Pistoia. When he returned to Aleppo, he began speaking of these subjects to members of his community. His thoughts were enthusiastically adopted by some of the clergy and a good portion of the laity in Aleppo. In July 1806 a sympathetic audience of Melkite bishops assembled at St Anthony's monastery of Karkafeh and heard Adam present his views on the church. In general, he urged that the Melkites should support a conciliar position, recognizing that a general council should take precedence over papal power and that Rome's primacy was more honorary than actual. A catechism he had written was recommended to the bishops to be used for popular instruction. In it, Adam stated that both the words of institution and the *Epiklesis*, the prayer summoning the Holy Spirit and found only in the Eastern liturgies, were both essential for the consecration of the bread and wine into the Body and Blood of Christ. Either because the bishops actually supported him or because they were ignorant of the consequences, the Melkite bishops, the Maronite patriarch, Yusuf Tian, who had been a guest at the synod, and even the Latin Apostolic Visitator, Luigi Gandolfi, signed the *acts* of the Karkafeh synod.

Soon afterward, some of the participants became aware of the discrepancies between the acts of the synod and Catholic doctrine. The Shuwair monks were nervous over what Karkafeh had done to strain relations between Rome and the Catholic Melkites. Long debates were held over the bishops' decisions and, to quiet a rising chorus of opponents, Adam agreed to amend that portion of his catechism which required an *Epiklesis* at all liturgies. Without this compromise, the Latin Mass would have had to be considered invalid.[27]

THE SYRIAN CATHOLICS

Since Syrian Catholics were converts from the Jacobite church, Ottoman law still regarded them as members of the Armenian *millet* which encompassed all of the monophysite subjects of the sultan. It is not surprising, therefore, that the persecution of Armenian Catholics in Istanbul early in the century affected the Syrians also. The Armenian Patriarch Ephrem persuaded the Turks that any Jacobite who had turned Catholic was an apostate and should be arrested, and the Syrian Catholic patriarch, Risqallah, was therefore imprisoned in Mardin, along with three of his bishops and several clergy. On a charge that he sought to change the religion of his nation, Risqallah was given eighty strokes as the first of his penalties.

In November 1701 Risqallah, one of the bishops and ten Syrian Catholic priests were chained together around the neck and ordered to leave for Adana. The French consul in Mardin begged the Turks to allow the patriarch, over sixty years of age, to have a horse, but his request was refused. The caravan moved off as scheduled, but by the end of the first day, Risqallah had collapsed. For the rest of the journey he was thrown across a horse and in that painful fashion arrived in Alexandretta. The French consul there was able to have the chains removed and the prisoners were then conveyed by a wagon. In Adana at last, the Syrian bishop died from the hardships of his journey, while the patriarch and priests were imprisoned in a dungeon. Throughout the winter, their situation remained unchanged, their only comfort being the realization that news of their plight had reached Versailles. Louis XIV personally ordered three hundred *piastres* to be used to assist the prisoners and wrote to the consul: 'You know it is our intention to protect them in every way.'[28]

In the spring, the paşa of Adana invited Risqallah to his quarters, welcomed him as a guest and served him coffee. When he returned to his cell, Risqallah became paralysed, and died on 12 April 1702, possibly from poison in his drink. The surviving Syrian clergy remained in prison until the overthrow of Sultan Mustafa II. Efforts to revive the church upon their release were fruitless and for the next few decades the Syrian Catholic community was practically extinct.

A rebirth of interest in Catholicism occurred in Aleppo among the Jacobites towards the end of the eighteenth century. At that time, the Jacobite bishop, Mikha'il Jarweh, converted to Catholicism and took a large number of his flock with him. The Franciscans in the Holy Land were suspicious of Jarweh and demanded an investigation into his sincerity. Once these misgivings were dismissed, in a letter of 22 June 1776, Pope Pius VI recognized him as a true Catholic.

Jarweh paid for his decision by a four-year imprisonment in a monastery, a stint in an Ottoman jail, and flights to avoid arrest which carried him as far away as Egypt and Cyprus. Somehow, in 1783, he managed to arrive at the synodal election called to replace the deceased Jacobite bishop in the monastery of Dair al-Za'fran. Only five bishops were in attendance, and Jarweh had strong support from the Latin missionaries of Mardin, the Chaldean patriarch, Yusuf IV, and the Catholic Armenians. After being so long a hunted fugitive, Jarweh was elected patriarch, taking the name Ignatius Mikha'il.

Unfortunately for the newly chosen patriarch, his well-known Catholic sympathies made him unacceptable to a large segment of the Syrian church. The bishops among his opposition held a second election and chose another patriarch named Matta. In the race to Istanbul to receive the *berat* of appointment, it was the partisans of Matta who arrived first and obtained recognition from Sultan Abdulhamit I's ministers. Instead of approbation, the unlucky patriarch Ignatius Mikha'il received a prison sentence.[29]

Eventually, sufficient funds were raised to ransom him, and Ignatius Mikha'il went off to Baghdad and subsequently to Mt Lebanon, ever the sanctuary of persecuted Catholics. At Sharfeh, he and a few followers lived in a monastery endowed for them by the Maronites and which Ignatius Mikha'il dedicated to Our Lady of Deliverance. He owned an ikon of Mary which had this title and which he had carried with him through all of his misfortunes. Pope Pius VI forwarded Ignatius Mikha'il a pallium and recognition as patriarch of the Syrians. By the time of his death in 1801, several bishops and congregations of Jacobites had joined his small community and so guaranteed the continued existence of the Syrian Catholic Church.[30]

THE CHALDEANS

The Chaldean church in the last decade of the seventeenth century witnessed some dramatic changes. The catholicoi of the Chaldeans, whose line had begun with the election of Yuhanna Sulaqa, lapsed into a Nestorian doctrinal position under Shim'un XIII. For several decades, communication with Rome had been intermittent, but after 1692, there was nothing. Shim'un XIII and his advisers were now located in the mountains of Kurdistan, in a village called Kudshannis, isolated religiously and culturally from the rest of the world.

Meanwhile, in Diyarbakir, which had its own Chaldean catholicos, the episcopal succession passed from Yusuf I to Yusuf II Sliba in 1691. Yusuf I, who had been 'patriarch' for ten years, chose his successor on his own initiative and consecrated him before retiring to Rome. The officials at the Congregation for the Propagation of the Faith were irritated because they had not been consulted on the choice of a successor or the manner of his election, and they delayed recognition of Yusuf II until 18 June 1696. By then, the vexations which he had suffered in trying to hold together the Chaldean church in Diyarbakir had earned him Rome's respect.

The majority of Chaldean Catholics fell to the Turkish Empire as a result of the wars against Persia at the end of Sultan Ahmet III's rule. Diyarbakir, seat of the catholicos, was a staging area for the Ottoman invasion, and this placed Yusuf II in a precarious position with enemies on all sides. By July 1708 his burdens became so heavy that he requested Roman authorities to allow him to resign and move to Italy. *Propaganda* purposely delayed a decision until it no longer had to make one, when Yusuf II was carried off by pestilence in 1713. Before his death, he chose a successor, just as he had himself received his appointment from Yusuf I. His nominee was the bishop of Mardin, Timotheus Maroghin, who took the name of Yusuf III.[31]

The new catholicos inherited all his predecessor's problems. The members of the Church of the East in Diyarbakir hounded the Chaldean clergy and eventually took the city cathedral from Yusuf. The Capuchin friars, the great patrons of the Chaldeans, closed their mission in Diyarbakir in 1726 and left for Europe, soon followed by Yusuf himself, who travelled first to Poland, then to Austria and finally to Rome. There he stayed, unaware of the embarrassment his travels had caused *Propaganda* officials.

While Yusuf III lived in exile in the West, the Chaldeans in Istanbul convinced Ottoman officials that they should separate their nation from the Church of the East. The Porte agreed that the Chaldeans were to hold the bishoprics of Diyarbakir and Mardin, while bishops of the Church of the East were assigned to Mosul and Aleppo.[32]

In the region about Mosul, despite its placement among the bishoprics of the Church of the East, the number of Catholics had considerably increased after 1700. The Capuchin missionaries were the impetus behind the Catholic movement so that even Al-Qosh, the village adjoining the monastic residence of the Iliyas line of catholicoi, had a Chaldean minority. Their cause was assisted by the conversion of a priest of the prominent Hormizd family, many of whose kinsmen felt influenced thereby to take the same step. In 1728, the Latin bishop of Babylon counted sixty thousand Catholics in his territories, the majority of whom were Chaldeans.[33]

Yusuf III continued in Roman exile so long as the Turks and Persians fought about Diyarbakir, and it was not until 1741 that he made the long journey home to resume leadership of the Chaldean people. For the next thirteen years he governed his church, until November 1754 when he chose his successor, Antun Galla. Since he too had made this choice without Rome's knowledge, *Propaganda* refused Galla his confirmation, so that Yusuf remained at the head of the church.

Meanwhile, the Discalced Carmelites of Baghdad had gained the good will of Yusuf's rival, the catholicos of the East, Iliyas XII, who lived in the monastery of Rabban Hormizd. In 1734, Iliyas wrote to Rome for the first time, speaking in broad terms of his good will toward the Western church. When the Latin bishop assigned to Persia, Emmanuel de Saint-Albert Balliet, actually took up residence in Baghdad in 1742, after many years in Hamadan, Iliyas was persuaded by him to compose a profession of Catholic faith to be sent to Rome. The Congregation, however, considered the statement lacked sufficient clarity, and so the establishment of formal relations between the churches was delayed.

On 23 January 1757, at the age of ninety-five, Patriarch Yusuf III died after forty-four years as head of the Chaldean church. Church representatives quickly voted to replace him with Lazarus Hindi, a former student of the Urban College, but until Rome was sure of the validity of his election, Hindi was recognized only as archbishop of Amida. After due investigation, Clement XIII, on 9 April 1759, dispatched his approval and sent him a pallium. Hindi, now entitled Yusuf IV, enjoyed a status unique among the other Eastern Catholic patriarchs, for he was able to go to Istanbul and receive a *berat* of appointment. The Ottomans looked more favourably upon Hindi than upon the other Catholic patriarchs who lived unrecognized and in exile. They wished to keep the Chaldeans loyal to the Porte, for they lived in the borderland between the Ottomans and Persians. In 1765, Hindi went to Rome to oversee the printing of the Chaldean liturgical books and gospels. He stayed for three years before returning to Diyarbakir.[34]

In 1771, as a result of the prodding of Yuhanna Hormizd, his nephew and bishop of Mosul who had leanings to Rome, Iliyas XII once again sent off a refurbished profession of his Catholic belief. This time Rome accepted his protestation of sincerity and he was brought into communion with the Catholic church.[35]

The remaining catholicos of the East, now Shim'un XVI, living in Kudshannis, also announced a conversion to Catholicism at this time, restoring his people to the Roman allegiance after decades of severed relations. At a secret consistory held on 17 June 1771 Pope Clement XIV announced with pleasure to the cardinals the details of a letter Shim'un had written him: 'he calls Mary mother of Christ and honours her as mother of God'. So by this date all three leaders of the old Church of the East had become Chaldeans, a situation doctrinally pleasing to the Catholic authorities, but administratively presenting them with a unique three-headed problem.

In 1778, Iliyas XII was carried off by plague and the usual familial tradition was activated. His nephew, I'so'yahb, was named catholicos, with the title Iliyas XIII. His legitimacy, however, was challenged by Yuhanna Hormizd, now openly a Catholic. He signed a profession of the Catholic faith to be sent to Rome, describing his conversion: 'I, Hanna, the undeserving, thought within myself that I would not walk in the way of my fathers, but would take refuge under the wings of the holy Catholic church and embrace the faith of the church of Rome and live therein...'[36] Following the lead of its bishop, the whole diocese of Mosul came into union with Rome, and Yuhanna Hormizd, ignoring his cousin Iliyas XIII, began speaking of himself as catholicos. He wrote to Rome asking to be confirmed in office, but the Congregation for the Propagation of the Faith pointed out there was an incumbent in the catholicate who, moreover, was in communion with Rome. Despite this rebuff, after 1780, Yuhanna applied for a *berat* from the sultan's government. The Porte responded affirmatively and bestowed patriarchal authority upon him.

In August, 1780 Yusuf IV submitted his resignation to the pope, announcing he had handed over his position to a nephew, Augustinus Hindi. Pius VI agreed to accept Yusuf's departure, but following *Propaganda*'s suggestion, Pius refused to allow the appointment of Augustinus. When Yusuf learned of the decision, he withdrew his resignation and held on in Diyarbakir. Difficulties soon arose. He was imprisoned by Ottoman officials for non-payment on a debt of twenty thousand *piastres*. He subsequently escaped, taking refuge with a friendly Kurdish chieftain, and then left for Istanbul where he boarded a ship for Italy. Yusuf came to Rome in March 1791, only to learn that the Congregation for the Propagation of the Faith had decided to act favourably on Yuhanna Hormizd's request to be named patriarch. Rome had not heard from Iliyas XIII and felt justified in taking this action. News that his rival was on the road to victory brought Yusuf IV to arms. He argued that he alone was patriarch of the Chaldeans. The cardinals of the Congregation sought a compromise. Both Yuhanna Hormizd and Yusuf IV would retain their titles and Yusuf's nephew, Augustinus, could expect to be the next bishop of Diyarbakir. Rome hoped, in fact, that Iliyas XIII would speak out so that neither Hormizd nor Hindi would be the major church figure in the East. This was not to be, however, for in 1804 Iliyas XIII died, leaving no nephews to inherit, and Yuhanna Hormizd in Mosul claimed that he alone was now patriarch; Augustinus Hindi, having succeeded his uncle in Diyarbakir in 1802, moved to Mardin and spoke of himself as 'Yusuf V'.[37]

Part of the confusion over leadership in the Chaldean community resulted from the failure of Latin clerics in the area to offer leadership to the church. In 1776, a Cistercian, Jean Baptiste Miroudot du Bourg, was named Latin bishop of Babylon, but never went to Baghdad. In 1791, he was suspended by Rome for having gone over to the side of the revolutionaries in France. Bishop du Bourg had sent his nephew to the Orient as vicar, but he proved quite incapable and, in fact, no Latin resident bishop was forthcoming until 1848.[38]

The eighteenth century closed much as it had begun for the Catholic Near Eastern churches. With the exception of the Chaldeans, who were well served by their geographical position, none of them enjoyed recognition from the sultan's government. In addition, family concerns and local jealousies brought constant crises every time a patriarch died. All of this made Roman authorities convinced that their intervention was called for, welcome or not. That the Ottoman government tolerated such actions can be explained only by the low profile the patriarchs kept, hidden away in monastic residences, and by the need to keep their French allies content.

14

Palestine and Egypt

THE HOLY LAND

During the rule of Süleyman II at the close of the seventeenth century, the Catholics made new gains in Palestine. This was largely a result of French insistence on a reopening of the question of owner-ship of the shrines in the Holy Land. Fazil Mustafa Köprülü Paşa, the vezir, at that moment successfully leading the Ottoman armies against the Habsburgs in the Balkans, sought to reassure Louis XIV, so as to keep his good will. For the same reason, the *divan*, the Sultan's advisory council, decided in favour of the Franciscans, and ordered the Orthodox to divest themselves of properties they had gained earlier in the century. To assure the permanence of the Latin victory, Louis XIV sent Sebastian Brémond to open a consulate in Jerusalem. However, in 1700, when Brémond arrived, he was faced at once with rioting Orthodox and Muslim crowds and was forced to retire from the city.

The Englishman Henry Maundrell and some companions, visiting Jerusalem after the Latins had returned to their stations in the Holy Places, found twelve friars living inside the Holy Sepulchre, organizing pilgrims and setting the schedules for all the Oriental church services. Conflict with the Greeks was, however, endemic and the Franciscan Father Custodian showed them 'a great scar upon his arm, which he told us was the mark of a wound given him by a sturdy Greek priest in one of these unholy wars'.[1]

A census of Catholics in the Holy Land taken in 1702 by the Franciscan superior demonstrates how few native Latins there were in the Catholic community. There were only two hundred in Jeru-salem, three hundred and fifteen in Bethlehem and ninety-five in Acre. Soon afterwards the number of foreign merchants from Western Europe began to increase, and this enabled the Franciscans to expand their missions. They built new churches in Damascus,

Acre and Latakia and in 1730, fulfilling a Franciscan dream of many years' standing, a small church at Nazareth. By 1730 one hundred and fifty-two Franciscans in twenty-one convents were distributed throughout the Holy Land. Since the number of Latin Catholics, in relation to the clergy, was so few, even the Congregation for the Propagation of the Faith cautioned the Franciscans about the number of missionaries sent to Palestine.[2]

In 1755 the Franciscans succeeded in obtaining sole possession of the church of St Mary in Gethsemane. This so upset the balance between the churches that the Greeks planned a counter-attack. Most of the Franciscans in Jerusalem were Italians and Spaniards, and lacked the sense of accommodation that French missionaries usually showed. They lived, in changing three-month shifts of ten, in a small dormitory in the Church of the Holy Sepulchre, and believed themselves secure. But on 2 April 1757, the Saturday before Palm Sunday, a crowd of a thousand Orthodox descended upon them. The friars took up defensive positions, building a barricade inside the church. For a time they held their own, but the superior numbers of the Easterners overcame their resistance; the Franciscans were thrown out of the Holy Sepulchre and later lost not only their church in Bethlehem but also the newly won church in Gethsemane. The local *kadi*, having received a 'gift' from the Greek side, confirmed the latter's victory, and despite vigorous protests by the French ambassador the Porte upheld the Greeks. Louis XV personally wrote to Mustafa III and sent eight hundred thousand francs to sway the grand vezir's feelings, but all in vain. The ambassador wrote to Versailles: 'Money, which is the great vehicle of this government, has not been spared on this occasion.'[3] The Turks in Jerusalem, according to Baron de Tott, were delighted to keep the Catholic–Orthodox struggle alive in the Holy Places, since this situation provided a constant flow of bribes from the Christian groups trying to hold the favour of Ottoman officials.[4]

In Istanbul the government drew up a document entitled 'The Status Quo in the Holy Places' which confirmed that the Latin monopoly was indeed forever gone and which defined the properties of each Christian group. The edict was specific even to establishing the number of lamps allowed to be burned at the shrines by Catholic and Orthodox and to delineating the cleaning obligations of each group. The latter assignment was very important, since, in Islamic courts, possession was often based on the right of physical maintenance. The Latins were allowed to return to the Holy Sepulchre on this claim, but were excluded completely from Bethlehem and Gethsemane. The triumphant Greeks also limited the rights of the Armenians, even seeking to oust them from St James' monastery, their most important establishment in Jerusalem.[5]

The Napoleonic invasion in 1799 had little effect on the church in Palestine. Napoleon had a worthy opponent in the paşa of Saida, Ahmet al-Jazzar, born a Bosnian Christian but converted to Islam. Ahmet al-Jazzar, governor of Acre, was sceptical of Napoleon's assurances of good will; he was strong enough to be practically independent of Istanbul's control and did not intend to lose his freedom of action. Napoleon took Jerusalem and the coastal cities easily enough, but when he came to Acre he found himself forced into a siege. Ahmet, well supplied by the British navy, held the French off successfully, and after three months Napoleon had to withdraw to Egypt.

During the French occupation the Franciscan friars remained strictly neutral, though had Napoleon represented Christian France their sentiments would doubtless have been different. Although a number of their friaries were used as hospitals, and some church supplies were taken by the army, the Franciscans and the Latin Catholics kept a discreet distance from the French general staff. On 11 September 1799 the British admiral Sidney Smith arrived at the Franciscan convent in Jerusalem and announced to the startled friars that the British king had taken them under his protection. This situation continued until the return of Ahmet al-Jazzar. Because of the war, the Latins in Palestine were impoverished throughout the next decade.[6]

EGYPT

In Egypt Catholic missionaries continued to expend much energy on conversions but their successes were few. In 1692 the French consul wrote a discouraging report:

They [the missionaries] have tried everything, but the only way of making a convert from the Copts is to take a child almost from birth and separate him entirely from his own people.[7]

This opinion was borne out by the situation at the Franciscan mission in Akhmim, where for five years the missionaries had laboured without gaining a single convert. Yet Akhmim became an apostolic vicariate for the missionaries in upper Egypt and Ethiopia, and in this same decade new Franciscan stations opened to serve the North African missions at Sousse, Benghazi and Derma.[8]

In 1711 a Jesuit missionary travelled throughout Egypt gathering information on every aspect of religious life, and reported his findings to his superiors in France. In general, he preferred the Copts to the Melkites because, despite their aversion for Westerners, he found them to be more honest and humble. Most Copts had no religious training outside of whatever they learned from the liturgy. Although their rejection of the Council of Chalcedon made them heretics in Catholic and Orthodox eyes, few Copts of the missionary's acquaintance had even heard of the Council. The Jesuit thought that the Copts did not like to talk with Latin missionaries for fear the Ottomans would believe they had gone over to the 'Franks'.

He was amazed at the severity of Coptic fasts, but discouraged over their failure to confess their sins; very few ever received the sacrament of Penance, and none received the Eucharist until they were seventeen or eighteen years old and ready to be married.

Melkite education seems also to have been poor. When the Jesuit called upon the Melkite patriarch, Samuel Kapasoulis – who welcomed him warmly – Kapasoulis confided that he thought that he was the only person in Egypt who had received an education except for the Latin missionaries. Since he had no knowledge of Arabic he could not preach to most of those who belonged to his church. He told him that he would like his church to join Rome but feared the reaction of the Turks.[9]

The life of Samuel Kapasoulis is an interesting one. A native of Chios, he grew up in an environment which included both Catholics and Orthodox. In 1679 he found employment as a cleric in the service of the patriarch of Alexandria. Later on he became a synodal bishop and on 22 January 1710 was chosen to become Melkite patriarch of Alexandria. Soon after assuming office, he contacted Lorenzo Cozza, Franciscan Custodian in the Holy Land, telling him of his desire to bring his church into communion with Rome. He signed a profession of faith before Cozza and the French consul in Cairo in June 1712. Clement XI received the news of his conversion and interpreted it incorrectly as meaning a corporate reunion of the whole Melkite church in Egypt. He accepted Samuel's profession of faith and forwarded a pallium. It was solemnly conferred on him by Cozza at the Franciscan convent in Cairo on 20 June 1715. By this time Samuel had several problems. A rival patriarch named Cosmas, who also flirted with Rome, had been chosen by a faction

of his church, and Seraphim Tanas, later to become the Catholic
Melkite patriarch of Antioch, told the Roman authorities that
Samuel was not to be trusted.

At the same time that Samuel was professing allegiance to the
papacy, two of his representatives, Arsenios, metropolitan of Thebais,
and Gennadios, an archimandrite of Alexandria, who had arrived
in England in 1714, were seeking alms from the Anglicans. They
secured £200 from Queen Anne and then travelled about the
country looking for more. Two years later they encountered the non-
juring Anglican clergy, those who refused to take the oath to the
House of Orange. Their leaders, Archibald Campbell and Thomas
Brett, urged the advantage of a union between themselves and the
Orthodox under the patronage of Peter the Great. This proposal
of the non-jurors was sent off to the East outlining their sentiments,
but Chrysanthos of Jerusalem, in response, pointed out the difficulties
of such an arrangement. Nothing came of the project, despite correspondence which included the patriarch of Constantinople nor, for
that matter, was anything more heard from Samuel Kapasoulis in
Rome once he had received his pallium.[10]

The greatest success the Latins scored at this period was the
conversion in 1740 of the Coptic bishop of Jerusalem, Anba Athanasius. His profession of faith was forwarded to Rome in the same
year and an enthusiastic Benedict XIV thought of placing him at
the head of a Catholic Coptic church similar to that of the Melkites
and Armenians. On 4 August 1741 the pope issued a letter explaining:

Since many faithful of the Coptic rite, both laity and clergy, for several
years have been illuminated by the light of truth, but must live under
heretical or schismatic bishops, it is right that they should have a
bishop.[11]

Athanasius wisely kept his residence in Jerusalem and named a
less conspicuous priest to be his vicar in Egypt, Yustos al-Maragi, a
native of Akhmim. The number of Coptic Catholics in Egypt was
very small and the best justification of the Latin presence in Egypt
was the number of Christian boys who had been recruited for
education in Rome, one of whom had been al-Maragi himself.
Another, Rufa'il al-Tukhi, was a Franciscan convert from Girgeh.
Both had gone to Rome in 1736, studied at the Urban College, had
been ordained and had returned to Egypt. After several years there,
al-Tukhi returned to Italy to edit the Coptic liturgical books, a task
which he seems to have enjoyed more than missionary work.

The Catholic Copts were often victims of popular prejudice as well as official harassment. It was not unknown for them to be accused of treason or for the Latin missionaries to be charged with kidnapping in their efforts to find Coptic boys to send to Rome. The priests among the Copts who became Catholic were allowed, by the Jesuits at least, to make private professions of faith and to continue to serve their congregations. In 1738 one report listed thirty-eight priests in that category.

In mid-century the movement waned. Archbishop Athanasius began to lose interest in Catholicism, and his relations with the Latin missionaries were strained. Rufa'il al-Tukhi returned to his native land in 1764 as bishop of Arsinoe, but his sojourn was a brief one, for he soon returned to Rome and the life of a scholar. Despite these setbacks Western church influence increased, for a large number of Catholic Melkites began immigrating into Egypt. Here they formed an active merchant class whose financial acumen was so appreciated that the Mamluk *shaykh*, Ali-Bey, transferred the collection of customs from the Jews to the Melkites.

THE NAPOLEONIC INVASION

At the end of the eighteenth century, the Egyptian world was shaken by an invasion from France led by Napoleon Bonaparte. It was meant to break Britain's links with India and its influence in the Near East; it certainly was no crusade for Christianity. In fact, Napoleon, in his pragmatic way, sought to convince the Muslims he was one of them and wanted their support, not that of the native Christian groups. Nevertheless he kept up contact with the Coptic leader Jirjis al-Gauhari and promised his people a better future if they would support the French. Copts and Melkites, on an individual basis, enrolled in the French forces, and a Coptic general recruited an all-Christian army of two thousand men to join the invaders. When Napoleon left Egypt he told General J. B. Kléber:

You know, citizen general, how I see the internal politics of Egypt: whatever you do, the Christians will always be our friends. They must be stopped from being too insolent, lest the Turks feel the same fanaticism against us as against the Christians, which would make them irreconcilable.[12]

Napoleon had little effect on the Catholic Coptic movement. Hopes for a hierarchy faded completely when the convert bishop of

Jerusalem, Athanasius, returned to his church. So far from naming episcopal successors, Rome appointed only priests, Yuhanna Farargi and Matta Righet, to lead the Catholic Coptic community. The successful attempt to form an Eastern Catholic church in Egypt would have to wait for more auspicious times.[13]

PART IV

From expansion to disaster

15

The Catholics of Istanbul from the nineteenth century to the proclamation of the Turkish Republic

THE STATUS OF THE CATHOLICS IN ISTANBUL

In 1807, the year of Mahmut II's accession to the sultanate, Giovanni Battista Fonto was vicar of the patriarchate, with his residence at the Holy Trinity cathedral. In 1808 Bishop Fonto took a census of Ottoman Catholics in his jurisdiction and found a total of thirty-two thousand people: of these eighteen hundred were Catholics of European background and five hundred were Latin Arabs from Aleppo. The Catholic Armenians made up the bulk of the total, approximately thirty thousand in number. In his vicariate, forty-two Latin priests, almost all from religious orders, and fifty Armenian priests served the congregations. In 1814 Vincenzo Corresi, a native of Chios and formerly the archbishop of Naxos, became coadjutor to Bishop Fonto and in 1816 he succeeded to the office of vicar, which he held until 1833.[1]

After 1815 and the Congress of Vienna, the Catholic church enjoyed a more stable condition. Once more a French Bourbon ruled in Paris and his ambassador could return to Istanbul and represent, not revolutionary nor Napoleonic, but Catholic France. The first of these Bourbon ambassadors, the Marquis de Rivière, was instructed by Louis XVIII that: 'He should especially take under his protection the Holy Places and all the Latin-rite institutions of the Levant.'[2] The ambassadors had difficulty in regaining the confidence of the Latin missionaries, especially those who were not French nationals, as well as of Ottoman bureaucrats who had lost faith in Paris after the events of the past two decades.

During the War of Greek Independence Mahmut was well aware that the French were aiding the Greek revolutionaries, so he made few concessions towards restoring their privileges. Turkish opinion became increasingly hostile to all Western Europeans in the capital after 1821. After the combined British, French and Russian fleet had sunk the Ottoman navy in Navarino Bay in October 1827, the sultan considered retaliation against his Christian subjects. His foreign minister, Pertew Efendi, had sent him a memorandum blaming the pope and the Catholic church for much of Ottoman distress and declaring that all Ottoman Catholics were at least suspect of treason. Persuaded by these charges, Mahmut initiated a persecution of all Catholics which lasted until the Treaty of Adrianople, signed in 1829, restored peace to the Near East.

This peace allowed the Armenian Catholics to form a separate *Katolik millet* and encouraged the Latins in the capital to seek an autonomous position as well. They had the support of Bishop Julien Hillereau, the first Frenchman to be appointed vicar of the patriarchate. In 1836 the Latins, mostly Italians, Spaniards, French, and Maltese who had emigrated to Istanbul during the Napoleonic wars, were allowed to choose an official to represent them before the Porte. He was to hold the title Director of the Latin Ottoman Chancery, but became more commonly known as the 'Latin consul'. The first to hold the office was Othon Varthaliti.

The Director's duties were the same as those of the patriarchs in the *millets*: to serve as intermediary between the government and the Latins, to act as judge in cases of dispute between Latins, and to issue certificates of nationality in matters of birth, marriage, death and foreign travel. He was generally subject to the Ottoman foreign affairs office. For practical purposes, the state of relations between him and the patriarchal vicar and between him and the French ambassador determined his usefulness.[3]

One community of Latins which arrived from Poland during this time still survives in present-day Turkey. The great Polish patriot, Prince Adam Czartorysky, purchased five hundred hectares of land in Thrace from the French Lazarists which he designed to be a haven for veterans of the Polish revolution of 1830. The town he sponsored was originally known as Adampol, the city of Prince Adam, but subsequently the Turkish population gave it the name Polonezköy, the village of the Poles.

Polish veterans and other nationalists sought to make their adopted country a replica of the homeland. They built a church and dedicated it to the Madonna of Czestochowa, patron of Poland; they set up a school which taught Polish history and culture, and they continued to prefer *wodka* over any local drink. During the second Polish revolution more settlers arrived and they, too, were confirmed in their lands by the sultan's government.[4]

Catholics in Istanbul enjoyed even greater freedom and influence once the *Tanzimat*, the Turkish reform movement, had begun during the sultanate of Abdulmecid. The first document of the *Tanzimat*, the *Hatti şerif of Gulhané* (the Rescript of the Rose Garden), which appeared on 3 November 1839, sought to enhance the Ottoman image in the eyes of its allies in Western Europe. Since public opinion in the West considered Ottoman treatment of its Christian subjects as a crucial issue blocking international accord, Reshid Paşa, the sultan's able adviser on the matter, saw to it that the Rescript firmly promised that all Ottoman subjects, both Christian and Muslim, would henceforth enjoy complete equality. Subsequent legislation provided that the same code of laws would apply to all, that trials would be public, that no advantage would be given to a Muslim citizen over a Christian, and that the armed forces would be open to all. Obviously such reforms meant abandoning the *Shari'a*, the holy law of Islam, and true Muslims were aghast at it. Their opposition brought about the downfall of Reshid Paşa, but he was later returned to office in other capacities.[5]

A crisis occurred early in 1853 when Russian and French interests in Palestine clashed over control of the churches there and both governments expected the Turks to favour their particular interests. It was the pressure exerted on Abdulmecid by Paris and St Petersburg that led, step by step, to the Crimean War, which began in October 1853 and continued for the next three years. When the Treaty of Paris concluded the conflict, the Russians had been humbled and the British and French were, for the moment, undisputed masters of Near Eastern affairs.

On 18 February 1856, just before the representatives of the powers met in Paris, the second document of the *Tanzimat*, the *Hatti humayun*, was issued. Like the Rescript of the Rose Garden, it was meant to demonstrate Ottoman sincerity in offering equality to the Christians. The *Hatti humayun* specified that 'all the privileges and spiritual immunities' of the churches would be respected and that individual Christians would enjoy all civil rights on the same level as Muslims. The old *millet* system was to be abandoned in favour of church government by an episcopal synod and a lay assembly. Each Christian community was to draw up a constitution for its own governance and submit it to the Porte for confirmation. The office of patriarch, now strictly a religious position, would be held for life. Fees and dues payable to the state were to be fixed and regulated by law. The *cizye*, the Christian poll-tax, had already been cancelled by a *firman* of 6 May 1855. The Rescript reaffirmed the right of Christians to bear arms and to serve in the armed forces but, since most were expected to resist conscription, the law provided for a *bedel* tax, by which one might purchase exemption. This secularization of Turkish government was primarily the work of West European ambassadors in Istanbul in cooperation with two new reformers, Ali Paşa and Fuad Paşa. The hearty dislike of its provisions by Muslim Turks made it extremely difficult to enforce. In Muslim eyes, Christian equality was impossible without loss of status for those who were true believers in the Prophet's message.[6]

CATHOLICS IN THE CAPITAL IN THE LATE NINETEENTH CENTURY

By the time of Bishop Julien Hillereau's death in 1855, the Ottoman Latin church was on the threshold of a new and brighter day. The primary reason for its growth was immigration: Catholics arriving from both Western Europe and the Balkans. When the immigrants arrived in Istanbul they found that religious personnel had preceded them and were offering a variety of religious services as well as schools of high quality. Such long-established orders as the Dominicans and Franciscans increased the number of their clergy in the Galatan churches and expanded their facilities; the Lazarists served three churches and maintained a college at Bebek; the Daughters of Charity, in Istanbul since 1842, had begun schools for girls there and in Izmir. In the same year a brother of the Christian Schools came to Istanbul to begin planning an institution which was later opened near Taksim. Italian Capuchins built a new church in 1845, followed shortly afterwards by the Sisters of Our Lady of Zion, whose purpose was to provide for the education of Istanbul's Christian women.[7]

Of all the Latin missionaries in Istanbul none was as well known as Eugène Boré. He had been a student of Oriental languages in Paris and a disciple of Félicité de Lamenais. In 1837 on a commission from the Academy of Inscriptions he had arrived in Istanbul to perfect his knowledge of Armenian and had become so engrossed in his task that he left the city for the Armenian cities of Azerbaijan, where he eventually settled, opening a school for Christians in Tabriz.

Over the next several years Boré passed back and forth between France and the Orient and was sent by Louis Napoleon Bonaparte to investigate the situation in the Holy Land on behalf of the French government. The results of his inquiry, later published in a book, *The Question of the Holy Places*, had a strong influence on French public opinion before the Crimean War.

For ten years Boré lived in the Lazarist college and finally, in January 1849, he joined the congregation; a year later he became director of the College of Bebek, a position which allowed him to be in the midst of Catholic Ottoman affairs for the next fifteen years.[8]

The flurry of missionary activity in the Orient delighted Pius IX, who had been elected to the papacy in 1846. His concern for the Catholics in Ottoman lands extended from his encouragement of the newly reopened Greek College in Rome to plans for a Latin patriarchate in Jerusalem. When his envoy, Bishop Innocenzo Ferrieri, arrived in Istanbul to conclude negotiations with Porte officials concerning the Jerusalem patriarchate, he brought with him an encyclical, *In suprema Petri Apostoli sede*, dated 8 January 1848, addressed to the heads of the Orthodox and Eastern Christian churches in Ottoman territory.

In this document, Pius recalled the past glories of the Eastern Christian churches and noted that tradition was now kept alive in the Eastern Catholic churches. He was distressed that not all Christians were in communion with Rome and with the shepherd whom Christ had appointed to lead his flock. He assured the Orientals that they had nothing to fear from union with Rome: the Eastern clergy would retain their positions, their rites would be kept intact, their canons unchanged: 'No burden will be imposed that is unnecessary; only the matters which divide the churches will be done away with.'[9]

The Greek Orthodox patriarch Anthimos IV and his synod, in conjunction with the Melkite patriarchs, were quick to reject Pius' letter. They prepared a counter-encyclical which listed fifteen points upon which the church of Rome was in heresy, and Anthimos claimed, 'The papacy has never ceased from disturbing the peaceful church of God, but everywhere sends out so-called missionaries, men of evil mind, "moving land and sea to make a single convert".' Instead of attacking the Orthodox faith in the East, the missionaries might better try to get rid of 'the heresies of the West'.[10] Pius' encyclical was called a plague to be avoided at all costs. A number of similar responses were made to the pope's encyclical by other Oriental churchmen. Obviously Rome had misjudged Eastern sentiment.

The Orthodox were encouraged in their stand by Protestants, whose numbers were growing as American and British missionaries arrived in Istanbul, in European Turkey and in Anatolia to set up schools and hospitals. The Presbyterian Eli Smith made known his agreement with Patriarch Anthimos about the Catholics in the Ottoman world: 'Unfortunately a [Protestant] missionary can hardly set his foot upon any spot in that field without encountering some sentinel of the "Mother of harlots" ready to challenge him and sound the alarm.'[11]

During Abdulaziz's rule from 1861 to 1876 the number of Latin Catholics in Istanbul increased considerably as the flow of Italians and other south Europeans to the Turkish capital continued. By 1872 the total stood at twenty-two thousand. At this time, the head of the church was the vicar of the patriarchate, Archbishop Paolo Brunoni, an able administrator when dealing with people, but afflicted with an ambitious building programme which put the church heavily in debt. He went to Rome to request larger subsidies, but instead he received an apparent promotion to the titular Latin patriarchate of Antioch, an appointment which removed him from the capital. In 1869 Rome appointed his successor, the Dutch Passionist Josef Pluym, vicar and apostolic administrator in Istanbul. Pluym had not been there a year when in June 1870 a fire destroyed his residence and all the archives of the Latin church in Istanbul. In 1870 he was awarded the title of apostolic delegate, but the Ottoman government refused to give him diplomatic status.[12]

A stream of Latin clergy and nuns poured into Istanbul and its environs during this period. In 1863 the Dominicans opened a house at Makriköy and the Capuchins a residence at San Stefano. The Franciscan Conventuals established a chapel at Büyükdere while the Christian Brothers opened a college in Kadiköy. Among the religious orders arriving for the first time were Polish Resurrectionists, Austrian Capuchins, and Assumptionists from France. Women religious were also well represented: Sister Oblates of the Assumption, Sisters of the Immaculate Conception of Ivrea and Franciscan Sisters of Genoa.

This tide continued into the sultanate of Abdulhamit II until every major Turkish city had Latin missionaries. The Austrian Lazarists and Daughters of Charity appeared in 1882 and the Christian Brothers added Salonica and Ankara to their list of establishments. The Marist Brothers set up a residence in 1893 and soon expanded into Syria and Egypt. The Salesians went first to the Holy Land and then to Istanbul, in 1904. The number of women's orders showed even more dramatic growth.[13]

The French Capuchins returned to the Orient in 1861, reassuming their role as chaplains of St Louis church attached to the French embassy. Here they began a seminary for the education of Eastern Catholics under the rigorous direction of the superior, Marcel of Montaille. The first term began in 1882 and the number of candidates sent by their bishops slowly grew until fifteen years later St Louis had fifty students. The Capuchins determined that the language of instruction should be exclusively French, and that the curriculum be structured so as to mirror the clerical education then offered in France. In 1892 the ordination of the first graduate initiated a small but steady stream of educated clergy for the Eastern churches which continues to the present day. The Capuchins also made plans for a school to train their own missionaries in the Orient; a site on Chios was first proposed, but an earthquake in 1881 discouraged construction there, and a new location was chosen near Izmir. The college, named the Oriental Institute, had places for sixty students. The first class opened with nineteen novices and grew to hold fifty-five in 1891, its most flourishing year. In addition to the Institute, the Capuchins staffed schools at Plovdiv in Bulgaria and a novitiate at San Stefano after 1894. These schools graduated fifty-two Capuchins for work in the East prior to the First World War.[14]

THE WANING OF FRENCH MISSIONS

Since 1870 the popes had protested at the establishment of an Italian national government in Rome by retreating into voluntary isolation within the Vatican walls. Neither Pope Pius IX nor Leo XIII recognized the Italian government; instead, despite the anti-clerical tone of members of the government of the French republic, both relied upon France for assistance to the Catholic missionaries in the Orient. Leo, through the Congregation for the Propagation of the Faith, had dispatched letters to the Catholic clergy in the Ottoman Empire urging them to lay all their diplomatic needs before French representatives. Italian officials were to receive only 'due respect'. By 1900, however, the Third Republic had turned ever more hostile to Catholics; many religious orders were disbanded by law. Then the French ambassador to Rome was recalled and the papal nuncio to France was expelled. In 1905 church and state were completely separated. Ironically, these moves against religious personnel in France were not duplicated in the Orient. For example, although the acceptance of novices was forbidden to most religious orders in France, exception was made for any congregation whose members were destined to teach in the schools of the foreign missions. Despite this dispensation the number of French religious in the missions declined from 2,150 in 1902 to 1,300 in 1912.[15]

During the sultanate of Abdulhamit II, from 1878 to 1905, the role of the apostolic delegate in Istanbul was enhanced. The Latin archbishop considerably overshadowed the civil heads of the Latin community, since the duties of the Latin consuls, after the *Tanzimat* legal reforms, had been assumed by the Ottoman bureaucracy, and the lay consuls' activities became more ceremonial than substantial. The apostolic delegate was responsible for supervising the eleven Latin Catholic parishes in existence in Galata and its environs. He also kept watch over the large number of educational institutions which now served several thousand students in the capital. In addition he was charged with the direction of the Catholic orders which were involved in staffing hospitals, orphanages and asylums. At that time there were eleven religious orders of men located in sixty-one houses, totalling five hundred and twenty-eight priests and brothers. Catholic women's orders numbered fifteen in fifty-four houses holding six hundred and seventy-four sisters. Thirty Catholic schools were in operation, extending from primary institutions to colleges. The money to operate these endeavours came from both private and public sources, mostly from France. By 1907 it was estimated that forty-five thousand Latin Catholics were living inside the apostolic delegate's territories.[16]

When the Ottomans entered the First World War in November 1914 the position of Catholics in Turkish territory was jeopardized by the government's lack of trust in its Christian subjects. The Capitulations with France which for centuries had provided protection to Catholics were cancelled early in the war, since France was now an enemy. Many missionaries in the outlying provinces were forced to leave, and church property was confiscated.

It was only in Istanbul that, thanks to the presence of German and Austrian representatives, allies of the Turks, Catholics enjoyed security. Even here, however, the number of Catholics declined precipitously. Istanbul was occupied in February 1919 by a French army led by General Frachet d'Espérey, who rode into the city on a white horse, his entry reminiscent of Mehmet II's in 1453. The

Christians cheered, the Muslim Turks did not. For several years the Allied forces, joined by a Greek army in the area about Izmir, kept a fragile peace in the Ottoman Empire. The foreign occupation allowed a few Catholic missions to reopen, but except in Istanbul, there were few Christians left to be served. When the Turkish Republic was proclaimed in 1923 the once flourishing Catholic community of the Ottoman world was but a shadow of its former self.

16

The Vatican Council,
the Eastern churches and the papacy

POPE PIUS IX

Pope Pius IX was the most ardent supporter of the centralization of ecclesiastical power in the papacy and the great advocate of Roman primacy and infallibility. This was, in part, a reaction to the European – especially the Italian – situation of the day; in part it stemmed from his own temperament. Without doubt, he thought the best kind of relationship between Rome and the Eastern Catholic churches was one in which the Orientals looked to Rome as children to father. He wanted every bit of administrative autonomy handed over to Rome. He passed more laws concerning the Eastern churches than any pontiff before him, in an effort to bring them into conformity with Western practice, and he seems to have believed that Eastern bishops, even the Orthodox hierarchy, would find Roman direction to their liking. In June 1862 Pius took the first step in securing control over the Eastern churches by establishing a special commission for Eastern Affairs within the Congregation for the Propagation of the Faith. The letter of foundation introduced at its inauguration announced that the commission's purpose was the preservation of the Eastern rites. It stated: 'The Holy See demands one thing only, that in these rites nothing be introduced which would be contrary to the Catholic faith, dangerous for souls or opposed to virtue.' The commission would act to promote Christian unity in the Orient and would be charged with gathering data on the condition of churches, monasteries, schools and other institutions of the Eastern Catholics.[1]

In 1864 Pius IX was considering calling a council of the Catholic church. Such an assembly, he believed, would strengthen the Western church and perhaps lead to better relations with the Orthodox and Eastern churches. He questioned the two Chief Latin prelates of the Orient, Paolo Brunoni, vicar apostolic in Istanbul, and Giuseppe

Valerga, patriarch of Jerusalem, on their opinions, and both replied that they would not expect any bishop outside the Catholic churches to attend. The Armenian Catholic archbishop, Andon Hassoun, suggested that letters be sent to all Eastern bishops, not to the patriarchs only. Ironically, while the matter was still under consideration, Pius issued the decree *Reversurus* for Armenian Catholics which, more than any previous display of Roman authority, frightened the Orthodox hierarchy in the East, since it effectively removed the administrative autonomy of that church.

It was Pius IX's intention to make *Reversurus* a model for the other Eastern Catholic churches, but instant intervention by the Maronite and Melkite patriarchs, then visiting in Rome, headed off that possibility. Only the smaller and weaker Chaldean and Syrian churches were endangered by its application. The pope's singling out of the Armenian Catholics was, without doubt, a result of the turbulence found in that church over the preceding decades.[2]

THE FIRST VATICAN COUNCIL

In May 1867, the pope summoned all Eastern Catholic patriarchs to Rome to discuss with him the effects the proposed assembly might have on their churches, and to participate at the installation of the Armenian patriarch. A preparatory commission for the council, entitled 'For the Missions and Churches of the Oriental Rite', was then set up. Cardinal Barnabo, prefect of the Congregation for the Propagation of the Faith, presided, but the real power in the commission was the secretary, Patriarch Valerga of Jerusalem. The commission met intermittently from September 1867 to May 1870.

During the early part of the commission's deliberations the Oriental bishops were allowed to submit memoranda embodying suggested changes for the betterment of the churches. Most of the recommendations were pastoral in nature and concerned the improvement of educational opportunities for both clergy and laity as well as ways to strengthen their spiritual values. Some complaints were lodged against foreign missionaries who ignored Eastern sensibilities and sought to convert the Orthodox to Latin Christianity.

Patriarch Valerga led the group that believed a uniform discipline should be established for all Eastern churches, a discipline conforming closely to the traditional practices of the West; he held for location of greater authority in the patriarchs and less in the episcopal synods. He believed that the general prohibition against change of rites was now obsolete and that greater freedom should be given to individuals who wanted to transfer. Finally he urged that the married clergy who served the Eastern Catholic churches should be phased out and celibacy required of the parish clergy.[3]

On 8 September 1868, with the time for the council drawing near, Pius IX sent 'to all bishops of the Eastern rite not in communion with the Apostolic See', a letter of invitation. Despite the address, the patriarchs were the primary recipients of this document, *Arcano divinae providentiae*, which appealed to the Oriental prelates for inter-church peace and harmony. The Vatican Council, according to the letter, would present a new opportunity for church unification, as the earlier Councils of Lyon and Florence had done; all divisions among the churches would vanish and the voices of Christian leaders would speak in unison.[4]

Apparently, since he was not given to empty gestures, Pius IX really believed his invitation would evoke a positive response. How he could have dreamt of such a thing after looking at the past history of the churches is difficult to explain. He was badly served by the officials in the Congregation for the Propagation of the Faith, who should have cautioned him against such undue optimism but did not.

Before the letters were dispatched to the Eastern hierarchs, the text fell into the hands of the editors of the *Giornale di Roma*, who published it, allowing correspondents and churchmen to comment on it; and when the papal legate, Giovanni Pitra, brought the invitation to the Phanar, Patriarch Anthimos VI returned it, remarking that he had already read it in the newspaper and had found that it expressed ideas quite unacceptable to Orthodox Christians. In Alexandria there was a similar response: an official of the Orthodox Melkite patriarchate claimed that prior publication of the contents made it impossible to discuss the matter. The Orthodox patriarchs of Antioch and Jerusalem were more polite, saying they could not act on the invitation without the consent of all the Eastern churches. The national Armenian patriarch in Istanbul asked for time to consult with the catholicos of Echmiadzin, who, in fact, never replied. The plan for Eastern Christian participation at the council proved a fiasco.[5]

The first Vatican Council opened on 10 December 1869 with six hundred and seventy-nine participants. Eastern Catholics were represented by Yusuf Audo for the Chaldeans, Andon Hassoun for the Armenians, Philipp 'Arqus for the Syrians and Gregorios Yusuf Sayyour for the Melkites. The Maronite patriarch, Bulus Massad, did not attend, but several bishops represented his church. Among the appointments announced at the assembly were those of the Latin patriarch, Valerga, and the Melkite patriarch, Gregorios Yusuf, both named to the executive commission of the council.

Although a definition of papal infallibility was not on the official agenda, it was soon evident that the question was of paramount interest to the pope, and since the issue was necessarily linked to that of papal primacy, it was of great concern for the Eastern Catholics too. Speaking at a commission session on 9 February 1870, Gregorios Yusuf argued that a promulgation of infallibility would make it much harder for Eastern Catholics to win over the Orthodox to communion with Rome. Of all aspects of Catholicism, Oriental Christians found the monarchical papacy the most difficult to accept. The patriarch spoke again when the debate on primacy was brought before a general session of the council, arguing that nothing beyond the narrow definition of the Council of Florence should be attempted.[6]

The Chaldean catholicos, Yusuf Audo, also took a stand against accenting Western church tradition to the detriment of the East. At the general session of 25 January on 'bishops, synods and vicars general', his statement was read in Latin by the archbishop of Sens. Audo commented: 'It appears that a plan is in the making to establish one and the same discipline for the Western and Eastern churches and to set up a uniform body of canon law for both.' He argued that this would be a serious mistake since the circumstances of the two churches were so dissimilar. In Mesopotamia,

Bishops, priests and people are, many of them, recent converts from Nestorianism; churches, schools and seminaries are absent, in many places Christians are massacred or forced into exile and their churches destroyed. Yet the Chaldeans are wonderfully faithful to their Catholic religion.

He pleaded, 'Judge therefore if it is possible to legislate for such a desolated church in the same way as for the flourishing churches of the West.' The East, he argued, knew its own ways best; local bishops meeting in synod legislated all that was necessary for the good order of the church. He himself, when consecrated, had promised to hand on to his successors all the rights and privileges of the office of catholicos; if he were now obliged to diminish those prerogatives, he would be violating his oath by doing so.[7]

The speech was a moderate plea for understanding, but an angered Pius IX summoned the Chaldean catholicos to the papal apartments that very evening and scolded him for his temerity at the council and for his failure, several years earlier, to consecrate two Chaldean bishops whom Rome had nominated. He told Yusuf that in view of his attitudes he might consider submitting his resignation. A refinement of *Reversurus* was then put before the catholicos for his acceptance; Audo left the Vatican well aware that if he intended to retain the catholicate, he would have to conform to papal requirements.

In the debate over promulgation of a definition of papal infallibility, the Eastern Catholic bishops found themselves in two camps. Patriarch Andon Hassoun and eleven Armenian bishops signed for the definition, as did seven Chaldeans. The anti-infallibilists, the so called 'minority party', included eight of the Melkite bishops. On 19 May Patriarch Gregorios Yusuf spoke against the declaration and, on the following day, Hassoun and 'Arqus were placed on the schedule to provide a rebuttal. Hassoun went so far as to suggest that the Melkite's position bordered on schism. In the vote of 13 July 1870 to bring the infallibility statement, which now included the definition on primacy, before the council, both Gregorios Yusuf and Yusuf Audo voted *non placet*, i.e. that it should not be done. Five days later they joined the other bishops of the minority party and left Rome rather than vote 'against the pope'. The Eastern Catholic prelates who remained, including most of the Armenians and two bishops for the Syrian delegation, voted on the final tally for the declaration which defined papal primacy and infallibility as part of the content of the Catholic faith.[8]

LEO XIII

Leo XIII, who followed Pius IX to the papacy in 1878, took an immense interest in the Eastern church. His active diplomacy envisaged an opening to the East which included a permanent Russian mission to the Vatican. While Pius had looked upon the church as a fortress to be preserved, Leo saw it as a more open community at the service of mankind. In his genuine concern for Eastern Catholics he felt that they would provide a bridge for union between the Orthodox and Rome. On the occasion of the anniversary of his episcopal consecration, 20 June 1894, the pope issued an apostolic letter, *Praeclara gratulationis*, addressed to the Orthodox and Eastern churches, inviting them into full communion with Rome. The tone of the document avoided anything negative, but its reception by Eastern hierarchs was no different from that they had accorded to similar letters before it.[9]

Following the apostolic letter, Leo invited the heads of the Eastern Catholic communities to Rome, to confer on ways to improve the condition of their churches. The meetings lasted from 24 October to 28 November 1894 and were concluded by the publication of a new statement on Eastern Catholics, *Orientalium dignitas*. This document stressed the importance to the universal church of the Oriental communities, and the security which they enjoyed because of their union with the papacy. In reply to charges that some Western missionaries were proselytizing among the Orthodox, Leo ruled that anyone doing so in the future would be automatically suspended, pointing out that:

It is more than ever the duty of our office to see to it that no injury be done them [Eastern Christians] by the imprudence of ministers of the gospel from Western lands whose zeal for the teaching of Christ sends them to the Eastern nations.[10]

Leo ordered every Latin church in the Orient to display a copy of the prohibition in its sacristy as a reminder to missionaries. Moreover, he encouraged Latin Catholics in the East who had transferred from another rite to return to their ancestral church. The concern of the pope was shared neither by the Roman curia nor by the members of *Propaganda*'s administration.

Anxious to improve the education of Eastern Catholic clergy, Leo opened a new Armenian College in Rome, and so as to revive the authentic spirit of the Greek College, ruled that only natives might enrol. The administration of the college was subsequently handed over to Belgian Benedictines. Leo also provided impetus for the foundation of Capuchin schools in the East and of the French Assumptionist college at Kadiköy. He encouraged the opening of St Anne's seminary for Melkites in Jerusalem and a Coptic Catholic College in Cairo. To spark interest in the Orient the pope sponsored the publication of a wide variety of new scholarly publications addressed to Western audiences: *Revue de l'Orient Chrétien, Revue des églises d'Orient, Echos d'Orient, Bessarione,* and *Oriens christianus.*

PIUS X, BENEDICT XV AND PIUS XI

When Pius X became pope a shift in Roman policy occurred, since the new incumbent in St Peter's Chair had his interests in the West. The Eastern Catholic churches were of interest only to the extent that they might show any independence from Roman direction. During the First World War the papacy could do little to protect or aid Catholics in the Ottoman Empire, yet activity concerning Eastern Catholics continued in Rome, for on 1 May 1917 Benedict XV established the Sacred Congregation for the Oriental Church, reserving the office of prefect of the congregation to himself; next in rank was a cardinal secretary, and there was a governing board of sixteen other cardinals. The staff, made up of both Latin and Eastern Catholics, was given competence over all those matters concerning the Oriental churches which were formerly handled by the Congregation for the Propagation of the Faith. Benedict also established the Pontifical Institute for Eastern Studies, which eventually became an autonomous branch of the Jesuit-run Gregorian University. An outstanding library was soon collected, and works on Eastern Christianity edited and published to an extent unequalled in any other institution of Europe.

The Code of Canon Law, inaugurated by Pope Pius X, appeared initially during the war years. Its monumental task of collecting and editing the laws of the Western church was completed only in 1917. The Eastern Catholic churches were specifically exempted from the Code, yet Canon CCLVII placed all persons, discipline and rites of Eastern Catholics under the jurisdiction of the Sacred Congregation for the Oriental Church – all of this done in a way which recognized no inconsistency in Rome's position.[11]

Perhaps this should not be surprising, since Roman attitudes towards both the Ottoman sultans and their Christian subjects had fluctuated considerably over the centuries. From hostility to friendship, from crusading bulls to welcoming Turkish delegations to Rome – all, at one time or another, reflected the policy of the curia. Pragmatic rather than ideological concerns were always paramount.

17

The Balkan churches

THE ALBANIANS

Ali Paşa's revolt against the central government in Istanbul was suppressed by the army of Mahmut II, and had little effect on the Catholic Albanians since Ali's power base was in the south, but when the last of the Bushatlis surrendered to the Ottoman army in 1831 all Albanian Catholics were returned to Ottoman political sovereignty. Most of the tribal chieftains continued to hold the loyalty of their subjects, but the clergy had more difficulty. The Englishman, William Hobhouse, passing through the northern mountainous area at this time, noted the growth of anti-clericalism among the people. This resulted from their fierce individualism, which caused them to resist clerical attempts to require exact fulfilment of church disciplinary laws. Hobhouse also observed that the only men in the country who did not carry rifles were the clergy, an omission quite unthinkable to Albanian men, who were always armed.[1]

Albania had an archbishop in Durrës and bishops in Lezhë, Shkodër and Pulaj. Lezhë was a town of five thousand served by a convent of Franciscans who believed the improbable tradition that St Francis himself had founded their community. Their convent was a site for pilgrimages and had been given the prerogative of ringing its bells. Certain northern Albanian tribes, the Clementi, the Doda, and the Mirdites, on whose mountain not a single Muslim lived, were still completely Catholic. Here stood the monastery of St Alexander, its abbot a man of great influence.

In 1846, four villages of Albanians living north of Skopje in Macedonia who had been crypto-Christians for decades took advantage of the religious guarantees provided by the *Hatti şerif*, threw off their Islamic pretence and publicly declared themselves Catholic. Needless to say, local Muslim officials were not prepared for such an eventuality and, ignoring the central government's laws, arrested many of the villagers and tortured the leaders. The British ambassador in Istanbul succeeded in getting Abdulmecid's government to take action on behalf of the Christians, and the survivors returned home, but the precedent established by this persecution made other crypto-Christians more cautious about renouncing their way of life.[2]

The reforms of the *Tanzimat* made little difference to those Catholic Albanians who paid no taxes to Istanbul, had never been without weapons and who followed their own laws. When they fought in the sultan's armies, it was on their own terms. Unfortunately Albanian individualism carried over into daily life, where the vendetta was accepted as more normal than peace. In a single year over a thousand people might be victims of assassination and hundreds of houses might be burned to the ground. The clergy tried to reduce the violence by establishing two periods of truce: from St Anthony's day (13 June), to All Saints (1 November), and from All Souls (2 November), to St Nicholas' Day (6 December).

The level of lay religious knowledge was very low despite clerical efforts to convince their flocks of its importance. Catholicism here was actually a 'tribal' religion and the emphasis was more on externals than any conversion of the spirit. To assist the clergy in their difficult task of religious education, in 1856 the Jesuits established a college in Shkodër, and several years later the Franciscans, traditional ministers to the Albanians, also set up a school of higher education in the same city.[3]

Matters were improved considerably for the Albanian Catholics during the sultanate of Abdulaziz thanks to growing educational opportunities. A visitor to Shkodër estimated that there were twelve thousand Catholics in the total population. The cathedral was set in an open field and the congregation was often so large that the overflow worshipped outside, where many Albanian men attended with rifles in hand. He noted that the dedication of the Albanian Catholics was evidenced by the wearing of many religious medals, observance of feast days and a feeling of hostility towards the members of all other religious communities.[4]

Catholic church leaders were active in the Albanian nationalist movement during the era of Abdulhamit II. The organ of nationalism was the Albanian League, which had been formed in June 1878 in response to the Congress of Berlin's awarding to Montenegro what was considered Albanian territory. The northern Catholic leaders, Ilyaz Paşa of the Mirdites and Hodo Paşa of the Shkodër area, attended a meeting of Albanians in Prizren organized to resist any loss of territory. Of all Catholic nationalists, the Franciscan Gjergj Fishta was the most active; a gifted poet, he wrote a poem on the struggle between the Albanians and Montenegrins, immortalizing the Albanian war leader, Ali Paşa of Gusinje, in an epic, *Lahute e Malcis* (Lute of the Mountain), which kept the national spirit alive even after the Ottomans had suppressed the Albanian League and arrested its leaders.

The Jesuit and Franciscan schools at Shkodër, supported by Austrian funds, were the only schools of higher learning in the country where classes were taught in Albanian. Here the future national leaders were trained to assume their roles once the country received its independence in 1913.[5]

In 1886 Shkodër became the metropolitan see of Albania, in charge of all other dioceses except Durrës. In 1907 Shkodër's province held a total Catholic population of twenty-eight thousand, while there were another twenty thousand in the Durrës diocese. In recognition of Mirdite loyalty, Rome allowed the abbot of St Alexander's monastery to hold certain episcopal powers and to oversee nearby parishes. Usually the bishops were foreigners, although the lower clergy were natives, and the Austrians, rather than the French, obtained the *berats* of Albanian bishops from Istanbul.

In 1913 Montenegro, hoping to add Shkodër to its own territories, attacked Albania and besieged the town; in April 1913, after six months of great suffering by the civilian population, Shkodër surrendered. The Catholic Albanians were decimated and much of their property destroyed. When a joint Italian–Austrian army reoccupied the town, there were few Catholics remaining in what had once been the most important centre of the Latin church in northern Albania.

BOSNIA AND HERCEGOVINA

By mid-century the largest number of Catholics in European Turkey lived in Bosnia and Hercegovina. Croatian emigrants added considerably to the core of native Latins who traditionally lived in these provinces. It was believed that one hundred and twenty-five thousand Latins lived in Bosnia and thirty-five thousand in Hercegovina. There was an archbishopric in Bar and an apostolic vicariate for Bosnia in Sarajevo, with a bishopric in Trebinje. An important Franciscan serving the Bosnian Catholics in the middle of the nineteenth century was Grga Martić, an early advocate of South Slavic unity whose works had been published in the newspapers of Ljudevit Gaj and Stanko Vraz. Martić was stationed in Sarajevo, where he cared for the city's Catholics and also served as official Franciscan representative to the Ottoman governor. He was a friend of the incumbent, Omar Paşa Latas, and was therefore able, with aid from his Austrian friends, to increase the size and quality of the Catholic mission in Bosnia.[6]

At the conclusion of the Congress of Berlin, Austria–Hungary was allowed to occupy Bosnia–Hercegovina in 1878. With the Habsburg army in control, on 5 July 1881, Pope Leo XIII expanded the Catholic hierarchy, establishing bishoprics in Banja Luka, Marcana and Mostar. At that time the Catholics were four hundred thousand strong, with forty-four secular priests and one hundred and sixty-five Franciscans ministering to them. The population continued to look to the Franciscans for spiritual guidance, more than to the secular clergy.[7]

THE BULGARIANS

In Bulgaria the commission entrusted to the Italian Passionist order had foundered for want of men and money, and, in 1834, Rome sent Redemptorists to take over the southern missions in Plovdiv and Sofia. The situation in Bulgaria steadily improved in the mid-nineteenth century. In 1841 the Capuchins arrived under the leadership of the able Andrea Canova of Garessio. He at once made his presence felt in all the Catholic communities, prodding the people to provide proper churches, to receive the sacraments, and to take a public stand for their faith. The Capuchins also began work in towns and villages where there were no Catholics. They would settle in these localities, building small chapels whose roofs were no more than tree branches covered with clay. Although at first these were easy targets for destruction by Muslim and Orthodox partisans who resented their presence, the persistence of the friars soon earned them respect. In March 1847 Canova, already apostolic vicar, was consecrated bishop. Subsequently, he commissioned the construction of a Latin cathedral in Plovdiv and thoughtfully dedicated it to St Louis of France, since its patrons were members of French missionary societies.[8]

While Bishop Canova was establishing a strong Catholic presence in the homeland during the 1850s, Bulgarians in Istanbul rose in revolt, not so much from a Catholic as from a nationalist spirit, to shake off Greek ecclesiastical domination. This was the first step in a struggle which would culminate in political independence from the Turks.

Early in 1853, a Bulgarian Orthodox bishop named Benjamin, living in Istanbul, had made a profession of Catholic faith to a missionary who had sent it on to Rome; the letter was intercepted, Benjamin was accused of becoming a Frank and, therefore, an apostate from his church. His punishment, meted out by a synod of Orthodox bishops, was enforced exile to a monastery near Samokov. Here he languished for several months until the Lazarists heard of his plight and informed the French ambassador. Soon the Ottoman government ordered Benjamin's release. He returned to Istanbul and spent the next few years attempting to persuade his countrymen to turn to Rome.

Later in the 1850s, there was a notable convert to Catholicism, Dragan Tsankov, a leading Bulgarian intellectual educated in Vienna. After moving to Istanbul in 1854, Tsankov began agitating among the Bulgarians to work for a free and independent state. One of his goals was to open a Bulgarian press in the Ottoman capital, but official intransigence prohibited this. Finally, thanks to the assistance of his friend, Eugène Boré, director of the college, he was invited to set up a press on the grounds of the Lazarist college in Bebek. In the spring of 1855, his newspaper, *Bulgaria*, appeared and, several months later, Tsankov told Boré that he wanted to convert to Catholicism. After instruction, he was admitted to the church and took a position teaching Bulgarian at Bebek. His conversion sparked others among Bulgarians in Istanbul. By 1859, dissatisfaction with the Greek patriarchate and disenchantment with Russia, after that nation's humiliation in the Crimean War, resulted in a widespread movement toward Catholicism in the city. It was bolstered by the example of the autonomous Armenian Catholic community in Istanbul.[9]

Opposition to the Greek hierarchy was not confined to Istanbul. Several Bulgarian parishes in Macedonia also opened discussions with local Latin clergy. In July 1859, representatives of the ten thousand Orthodox Bulgarians of Kilkis, a town about thirty miles north of Salonica, approached a Latin missionary and asked him to request papal permission for them to affiliate to the Catholic church while retaining their own rite. Their proposal was granted by the Roman authorities.

Throughout the autumn of 1859, Bulgarian separatists were frequent callers at the residence of the Latin vicar, Brunoni, and at the office of the Armenian Catholic patriarch, Hassoun. Hassoun was eager to enlist them, but at first entertained doubts about their motivation. Later he received word from the Congregation for the Propagation of the Faith that they should not be denied.

On 30 December 1860, a large number of Bulgarians entered the Catholic church. Two archimandrites, Josif Sokolski and Makariji Savov, and one hundred and twenty laymen were admitted after they had presented to Archbishop Brunoni and Patriarch Hassoun a petition with two thousand names. An act of union was read and a statement issued on behalf of the papacy saying that Bulgarian Catholics would have an autonomous hierarchy and that nothing more would be required of them beyond the stipulations for union between Eastern and Western Christians as provided by the Council of Florence. Archimandrite Makariji replied on behalf of the Bulgarians, after which Hassoun welcomed them into the Catholic patriarchate. The participants then moved to the church of St John Chrysostom where the *Te Deum*, a hymn of thanksgiving, was sung. In the course of the song, the two Bulgarian archimandrites approached the altar, handed over their professions of Catholic faith and exchanged the kiss of peace with the Latins.[10]

The Ottoman government had followed the Bulgarian Catholic movement from its inception and had put no obstacles in its path, believing, in this case, that the uniting of a portion of its Catholic subjects with Rome would actually be beneficial. They reasoned that, in turning to Rome, Bulgarian Catholics would cut themselves off from the influences of St Petersburg and of Athens. This estimate was proved correct when the Russian ambassador made a vigorous protest to the Turkish ministry. The government soon issued a *firman* recognizing the release of the Bulgarian Catholics from Greek jurisdiction and acknowledging their autonomy. Archimandrite Makariji was appointed religious head and Tsankov the civil leader of the Bulgarian Catholic community.

Archbishop Brunoni set up a 'Committee of the Bulgarian Union' to assist converts. The French ambassador and *Propaganda* provided funds to rent a house in Galata which was hurriedly converted into a church and, on Epiphany 1861, with five hundred people in attendance, the Bulgarian-rite Catholic Eucharist was offered there for the first time. Pope Pius IX was delighted with the news of the Bulgarian union, which was soon followed by similar favourable reports of conversions from Edirne, Monastir and Kazanluk. The pope issued another welcome to the Bulgarians on 21 January 1861 and privately wrote to Boré in Istanbul asking him to accompany the seventy-five-year-old Josif Sokolski to Rome, since he had decided to consecrate Sokolski archbishop. On 8 April 1861 at a ceremony in the Sistine Chapel, the pope personally consecrated the Bulgarian – an act he considered the first step toward corporate union between the whole Bulgarian Orthodox church and Rome, since sixty thousand Bulgarians were rumoured to be waiting to join the newly formed church. Sokolski was given the additional title of apostolic vicar of Bulgaria and was showered with gifts and good wishes before his return to Istanbul. Despite the pope's enthusiasm, some observers considered he had acted hastily in consecrating a new convert so quickly, and their opinion was soon to be confirmed.

On his return to Istanbul, Archbishop Sokolski made a triumphal entry into his community, where he was greeted by all the Bulgarians of the capital. The sultan's government quickly provided him with a *berat*. Then, to the shock of everyone, less than two months after taking office, Archbishop Sokolski disappeared. Several days later, a letter written by him from Odessa was published in Istanbul. In it, he announced that he had gone to Russia in order to return to the Orthodox faith. He urged the Bulgarian Catholics to follow his example and abandon the union. The letter, which was undoubtedly in Sokolski's handwriting, plunged the Bulgarian Catholic community into despair. The Latin missionaries could only shrug their shoulders. Archbishop Brunoni wrote at once to Rome about the defection of the archbishop upon whom so many hopes had rested.

It was not until several years later that the full story of Sokolski's disappearance became known. Apparently, the archbishop had received an invitation to visit the Russian ambassador at his residence in Büyükdere and had gone off to pay his respects. While there, he was asked to board a ship tied up at the dock to inspect it and, before he realized what was happening, the boat had left land and sailed off to Odessa. Agents of the Russian ambassador were responsible for the kidnapping and the letter sent in his name had been dictated by them. The archbishop was subsequently taken to Kiev and confined in the Monastery of the Caves where, some years later, he appeared briefly at an ordination. Interviewed at the time, he stated that he had never willingly abandoned the union and wanted to return to Istanbul, then wept as he said, 'It is impossible. I am in iron hands.' Still in Kiev, he died in 1879.[11]

Rome sought to salvage what it could of the Bulgarian Catholic church by appointing a Latin Catholic Bulgarian, Petur Arabazhiski of Plovdiv, to head the community. Arabazhiski went to Istanbul, received a *berat* from the sultan, but then had second thoughts about his appointment. He knew nothing of the Bulgarians' situation in Istanbul and he disliked the Eastern rite. At his consecration, he celebrated the Eucharist in the Roman rite and pointedly omitted preaching a sermon. His apathy did not bode well for the future of the church.

Several thousand converts now drifted back to Orthodoxy, so, in 1863, the bishop resigned and promoted his Ukrainian vicar to succeed him. The appointment was opposed by the remaining Bulgarian Catholics, who held out for a native. Rome agreed with them, so Raphail Popov, a Bulgarian priest, was nominated and consecrated bishop on 19 November 1865 but, by this time, Bulgarian-rite Catholics had diminished to a few hundred people.[12]

At this low point in the fortunes of Bulgarian Catholicism, a new religious order, the Augustinians of the Assumption, appeared to brighten the scene. The founder of this congregation, Emmanuel d'Alzon, had intended that the Assumptionists direct their attention to the Holy Land, but Pope Pius IX requested him to consider the mission in Bulgaria. D'Alzon went to the East to survey the situation and, in 1864, the Assumptionists opened a school in Plovdiv, the first of the order's foundations. Four years later, it was possible to establish a college in Edirne and eventually a seminary for training Bulgarian Catholic priests at Karacadağ.

While Istanbul's Bulgarian Catholics had all but disappeared, several villages in Macedonia and Thrace remained within the Catholic communion. Their allegiance to Rome was vigorously fought by the Russian minister to the Porte, Count Nikolai Ignatiev, who said:

In approaching the Bulgarians I told them that the dissolution of their nationality would be the inevitable result of union. I discredited Bishop Raphail in their eyes. I favoured the sending of young Bulgarians to Russian schools, and finally I spared nothing to obtain the return to Orthodoxy of the villages converted to Catholicism.[13]

In March 1870, Russian diplomatic moves contributed to the establishment of a Bulgarian exarchate, which secured the long-sought autonomy for the Orthodox and removed one of the major reasons for Bulgarian conversions to Catholicism.

In 1878, when Bulgaria got political independence, a majority of the Latin Catholics found themselves within the boundaries of the new nation, enjoying complete toleration. One Capuchin missionary, François Reynaudi, was so popular with his adopted countrymen that he was chosen president of the parliament for three sessions. Dragan Tsankov, the first leader of the movement towards Catholicism, served as prime minister in 1880 and 1883. He apparently remained a Catholic until his death, but no longer practised his religion.

From 1884 to 1894, Bulgarian-rite Catholicism enjoyed remarkable growth in areas where the Ottoman government and Greek hierarchy held on in Macedonia and Thrace. Sixty villages of Bulgarians came over to Rome at this time. Their bishop, Nil Izvorov, a convert from Orthodoxy, succeeded Raphail Popov and lived in Istanbul to represent the Bulgarian Catholics to the Ottoman government. During these years of expansion, Izvorov came under fire from the Bulgarian exarch, who argued, 'To become Catholic is to renounce being a Bulgarian.' This message had the desired effect; after 1894 the number of converts declined and Bishop Izvorov himself returned to the Orthodox church. The same transition was made by another convert Bulgarian Catholic bishop, Lazar Mladenov of Salonica, who led many of the Catholic villages of Macedonia back to Orthodoxy. Although he himself later returned to Catholicism, few of the former Catholics did.

The story of the Ottoman Empire's Bulgarian Catholics ends in a tragedy. The First and Second Balkan Wars proved disastrous for the Catholic villagers of Thrace and Macedonia. In 1912, there were twelve parishes and approximately three thousand people in Thrace, and twenty-seven parishes with over ten thousand members in Macedonia. During the First Balkan War, the Turkish army destroyed all the Thracian villages; only three hundred survivors managed to flee behind Bulgarian lines. In the course of the Second Balkan War, Greeks and Serbs wreaked havoc on the Catholics. Twelve parishes were completely destroyed by the invading Greek army and six were 'converted' to Orthodoxy. In 1914, only two thousand Catholic Bulgarians of Macedonian origin remained, refugees in Strumica.[14]

GREEK CATHOLICS AND THE REVOLUTION OF 1821

The overriding concern of the Catholic Greeks during the sultanate of Mahmut II was their position regarding the Greek revolution. As Christians and Greeks, many sympathized with the revolutionaries who sought freedom from Islamic rule, yet a majority feared what might happen to them in a state based upon Hellenic nationalism identified with the Orthodox faith. What the Catholics knew of the Phanariotes in Istanbul gave them little confidence in the security of Latin Christians in a state where this group of Greeks would play a leading role. They at least knew what to expect under continued Ottoman rule, where, despite other drawbacks, French protection blunted most negative effects. As a result, Greek revolutionaries seeking to enlist Catholics had little success. The known evil was preferred to the uncertainties of war against the Turks which, in the end, might indeed establish a Christian state, but one hostile to Catholicism.

The last few decades had, in fact, seen increased tension on the islands between Orthodox and Catholics. The Latins were sometimes the butt of popular preaching, and the pope was pictured as little better than the devil incarnate. It was sometimes easy for Orthodox clergy to charge that the Catholics were anti-national, since the actions of foreign missionaries and Roman-trained natives, as well as the usual appointment of Italian bishops to the Greek bishoprics, provided sufficient verification for their accusations.

When the Greek revolution commenced, its leadership in the provisional governments of the Peloponnesus sought to convince the sixteen thousand island Catholics that they had everything to gain by joining the national effort. For diplomatic reasons, since these governments were in desperate need of foreign support, every statement of the revolutionaries stressed that religious toleration would be promoted in the new Greece. In April 1822, Theodoros Negris, head of the government in Eastern Roumeli, wrote to Archbishop Andreas Veggetti of Naxos, inviting him to Corinth to discuss church affairs. Veggetti sought instruction from Rome, telling the prefect of the Congregation for the Propagation of the Faith of his invitation and of the verbal assurances he had received that union of the churches was a distinct possibility. If he were to go, Archbishop Veggetti would need a safe-conduct, secured from the Ottoman government by the French ambassador in Istanbul. Realistically, Veggetti wondered if this could be obtained. Rome replied that the

Congregation shared his suspicions concerning Turkish approval of his trip but instructed him that if, indeed, he went to Greece, negotiations on church unification should be based upon the decisions of the Council of Florence.[15]

In still another effort, the Greek revolutionary governments sent emissaries to Rome to enlist papal assistance. In moves reminiscent of the last Byzantine century, the Greeks presented their case to Roman authorities, but papal policy remained strictly neutral. From Rome's point of view, hardly ever favourable to revolution, the outcome of the Greek struggle was unpredictable, and a commitment to the Greek cause would risk damage to all other Catholic communities in the Ottoman state.

The popes did open the Papal States to refugees fleeing from Greece, and appropriated funds for their care. There were, of course, Catholic priests who wanted the revolt to succeed: Padre Paolo, the Italian Capuchin in Athens, gave Lord Byron, the British poet and Philhellene, a cross, and urged him to carry it with him in his fight against the 'infidels'.[16]

At the start of the revolution, the island of Naxos held but three hundred Catholics, governed by Archbishop Andreas Veggetti. His courage was a major influence in the events of the war. Early in the conflict a Greek ship from Ydra docked at Naxos with one hundred and eighty Turkish prisoners abroad. The captain wanted to leave them on the island where, he suggested, they could be used as labourers under the protection of the Orthodox and Catholic bishops. One party of extreme nationalists wanted the Turks killed and successfully began taking matters into their own hands. At this point, over the protests of much of the population, Archbishop Veggetti intervened, took all the Turks who had so far escaped death and lodged them in buildings owned by the Catholic church and protected by the French consul. The Orthodox then drew up a plan to attack the Catholics, who had, by now, barricaded themselves into the upper town of Naxos. The attack never materialized, however, and when a French ship came to the island, the Turks were put on board and their lives saved.

The archbishop's action made his position a precarious one throughout the conflict. When commissioners representing the Greek government landed on the island and sought to collect taxes from the Catholics, they were rebuffed, and this led to even more tension. Appeals for aid went to Rome from the Catholic leaders, who claimed they were caught between the 'Greeks' and the Turks.[17]

Their small numbers had not stopped the Latins on Naxos from pursuing an independent policy regarding the war, so it is not surprising that on Siros, where almost all the inhabitants were Catholic, and on Tinos, where Catholics were fifty per cent, opposition to the revolution was even stronger. The Latins continued to pay their taxes to Istanbul and would not cooperate with agents of the several Greek governments. Claiming French protection, the Catholic churches on the islands flew the *fleur-de-lis* of the Bourbons in their churchyards, and on Sundays the Latin clergy warned their parishioners to stand aloof from a war which was not of their making.

When fifteen hundred Greek troops arrived on Siros, the neutral stance of the Catholics became more difficult and, to their chagrin, there arrived on 'the Pope's island' numerous refugees, all Orthodox, who, for the first time in the island's recent history, made significant Orthodox settlements. The Latins and the Greek settlers were often at odds, and the Latin bishop, Luigi Blanci, had to serve as mediator. When at last a French ship arrived, the bishop asked the captain to remain as a guarantee of Catholic security. This was agreed to by Admiral de Rigny, French naval commander in the Aegean.[18]

When the Latins of Siros learned that the Great Powers, meeting in London to propose a treaty of peace, had drawn the boundaries of an independent Greece to include all the Catholic islands but Chios, they protested. In an appeal to Rome, the islanders on Siros lamented:

The Greeks have revolted against their sovereign. Three Christian powers have decided to make a portion of the country of Greece independent and we have learned with deep sorrow that our island is included in this part. We will be forced to abandon our homeland or to change our religion in order to live with people so intolerant.[19]

Their plea was fruitless; indeed the Catholic islands became part of Greece at the conclusion of the war, but, to the credit of the Greek leaders, the expected disaster did not occur and the Catholic communities soon flourished in the new Greek state.

The situation on Chios for both Catholics and Orthodox proved to be a tragic one as a result of the revolution. Naturally, both the Greeks and Turks hoped to hold Chios, since it was the most prosperous island of the Aegean. There was apparently little revolutionary sentiment among the natives, least of all among the eight hundred Catholics, who were too close to the Turkish mainland to be optimistic about an armed uprising on their island even if they had been so inclined. On neighbouring Samos, however, feelings ran high against the Turks, so that a raiding party from there landed on Chios in 1822, proclaiming that the inhabitants were now 'free'. As they crossed Chios, the Samians plundered Catholic households, believing correctly that the Latins were not on their side. As this was happening, news arrived of the sighting of the Ottoman fleet; the Samians hurried to their boats, leaving the hapless Chians alone to face the Turks. Although the Orthodox bishop attempted to explain what had happened, the Turks were uninterested. Several thousand Ottoman troops were put ashore to begin a massacre of the population. The bishop and many of his clergy were hanged; his residence and the Orthodox cathedral were burned to the ground. There was killing, plundering and burning all over the island. The Latins ran to their church of St Felix in the grounds of the French consulate. Here, the single French Capuchin safely harboured three hundred men, women and children.[20]

While the Catholic cathedral of St Nicholas had been burned along with the other buildings of Chios town, the churches in the villages, flying the French flag, were not damaged. In 1826, permission was given to rebuild the cathedral, but now there were problems of financing the construction. Pope Leo XII asked Archbishop Luigi Cardelli of Izmir to visit the island. He came in September 1826, received a good welcome, and reported to Rome that the Catholics numbered four hundred and fifty-six individuals. The clergy were still plentiful: thirteen secular priests, a Franciscan and a Capuchin were living on the island. In 1827, Chios was once again the scene of a Greek landing, and in the fighting which ensued, the Franciscan church of St Anthony was destroyed. The Catholic community, once more subject to military requisitions, was left penniless.[21]

When the war ended, the island of Chios, a shadow of its former self, remained in Ottoman hands. Both Orthodox and Catholic communities tried to rebuild, but were hampered by their poverty. A French Jesuit, Giles Henry, a colourful figure, arrived as chaplain to Bishop Ignazio Giustiniani. He later wrote a memoir of his early days on the island: on the one hand, he wrote: 'On my arrival in the East in 1830, I could not help condemning the animosity and the unjustified arrogance our clergy showed towards the Greeks.' On the other hand, he was upset to learn that the Latin clergy were expected to attend the funeral of the Orthodox bishop. He was convinced that 'the whole Orient is sick'. Church discipline was ignored by both priests and laity. He was especially distressed by those graduates of the Urban College who had come back to Chios to live with their families. They offered the Eucharist in their dining rooms, sometimes with women as servers, abandoning all sense of propriety.[22]

Only in Izmir did the Aegean Catholic church find a secure environment during the Greek revolution. Catholics increased sufficiently in numbers for Pope Pius VII to again appoint a resident archbishop, Luigi Cardelli, in March 1818. Cardelli's presence aroused resentment in some quarters, and his efforts at reform proved most unwelcome. Eventually he had to abandon Izmir for Rome after poison had been mixed with his Eucharistic wine.[23]

AFTER THE REVOLUTION

The loss of the Aegean islands to the new nation of Greece meant a serious decline in the number of Greek Catholics within the Ottoman empire. These were now to be found only among immigrants to Istanbul and Izmir and among the native Catholics on the island of Chios. There were a few Catholic Greeks on Crete also, but the single church on the island was used mainly for foreigners. The Lazarists kept a church open in Salonica but here, too, the congregation was generally made up of French or other West European merchant families.

Efforts were made by Rome to solidify the Catholic presence on Cyprus. A Maronite bishop took up residence on the island in 1848 to give support to the members of his church. Latin secular priests were later sent to the island from Jerusalem and an order of Catholic religious, the Sisters of St Joseph of the Apparition, staffed a school, hospital and pharmacy in Larnaca.

In Izmir, a new archbishop, Antonio Mussabini, had more success than his predecessor in bringing together the diverse elements of the city's Catholic population. With funds from the kingdom of Sardinia it was possible to expand to the island of Mitilini in 1846. The Christian Brothers began a school in Izmir in 1841 and, five years later, the Franciscans inaugurated a parish at Ayvali.

More letters of the Jesuit Giles Henry make it possible to form some idea of Catholic life on Chios at this time. Henry felt isolated and in a difficult position, for in the space of five years he had received only two letters from France. 'I find myself on Chios, a land soiled by the abominations of the Mohammedans, surrounded by Greek churches where the Body and Blood of the Saviour is consecrated in sacrilegious hands.' He regarded the Orthodox priests as 'vile slaves of the civil authority' who purchased their church offices. The upper classes of Chios were, he complained, all atheists after having received their education in France and Germany. Too many Catholics were forced by the lack of opportunity on the island to emigrate to Izmir or to Istanbul, where many fell away from the faith.

Henry had little use for the Italian bishops sent out to the Greek islands or the native secular priests who graduated from the Urban College. They were all caught up in the prevailing mood: 'The bishops and other students of *Propaganda*, instead of "propagating" religion are occupied in "propagating" plantations of orange and lemon groves.' In another letter, complaining that intellectual life on the island was nil, he said: 'The only thing anyone talks about here is oranges, lemons, olives, and almonds, and nothing else.' All books had been destroyed at the time of the massacre of 1822. Bishop Guistiniani was so poor he had to wear his father's coat, which he had inherited in 1821, but, despite the paucity of resources, he was still trying to complete the rebuilding of his cathedral.

The moral life of the Catholics of Chios, especially their public dancing, disturbed Henry. A general condemnation had been issued to stop this scandal, but many disregarded it. If repentant dancers came to confession, Henry imposed on them, as a fitting penance, that they should drink their coffee without sugar for a whole year. He applauded the island tradition that women be veiled in church and should enter and leave the building by a separate door. He had heard that at St Anthony's church, Istanbul's most fashionable, all restraint was abandoned since, in order to get to their places, women who attended Mass often passed between a line of men, sometimes actually touching them! The views expressed by Henry give an interesting insight into attitudes typically held by many of the Latin missionaries.[24]

During the sultanate of Abdulmecid, another missionary effort was made to attract the Greek Orthodox. In 1856, a Latin priest of Siros, Ioannis Hyacinth Marango, founded a congregation of the Byzantine rite for converts to Catholicism. He settled his group in Istanbul, taking advantage of the *Hatti humayun*'s guarantee of tolerance. Over the next decade, several followers joined him in his Congregation of the Most Holy Trinity, or in the women's branch, the Congregation of the Holy Family. Two former Orthodox bishops, Meletios of Drama and Veniamin, titular of Neapolis, affiliated themselves to Marango's movement. There was considerable opposition to the Congregation from the Orthodox hierarchy and even from Ottoman officials, so that any major gains were out of the question.[25]

THE GREEK CATHOLICS TO WORLD WAR I

The number of Greek Catholics in the mid-nineteenth-century Ottoman empire was very low: three hundred on Chios worshipping in two churches and perhaps another hundred in Istanbul from among immigrants to the capital. Since they were Latin-rite Catholics, they were assimilated into the larger European community there. The small mission of Ioannis Marango to the Orthodox still functioned but had no great success. Only on Crete was there some growth. By 1874 there were eight hundred natives and two thousand foreigners living on the island who were identified as Catholic. Hence, Pius IX named a bishop for the island, with residence in Candia.

Izmir continued to be the most important Catholic centre, with a bishop and four parishes in the city itself and four others located outside. In 1907, the Latins numbered sixteen hundred and there were, additionally, eight hundred Armenian Catholics. The Capuchin Institute located nearby provided an over-abundant supply of clergy.

The Catholics on Cyprus, under British administration since 1878, experienced a small revival when more foreigners came to the island. Nicosia held a church and Larnaca and Famagusta also had chapels. In all, the Latin church had almost a thousand members. The village of Louroujina, which had managed to survive as crypto-Christian from the start of the Turkish occupation, threw off its Islamic veneer as a result of the British occupation. Approximately twelve hundred people were thereby added to the Catholic communion. The Maronites on Cyprus numbered over a thousand people and supported several monasteries.[26]

The island of Rhodes, without a Catholic church since the Knights Hospitallers of St John had been expelled in 1523, received a Catholic mission once more in 1897 and a small church was built in the capital by the Franciscan Observants. But, while Catholicism was reviving on Rhodes, it was still in decline on Chios. Now less than three hundred people remained to testify that this was once a stronghold of Catholicism in the islands. As if to confirm the situation, the cathedral of St Nicholas was struck by an earthquake in 1881, and had to be rebuilt from donations raised in Western Europe. In 1911, the Italian army occupied Chios as a result of that country's war with the Turks.

The apostolate of Marango to convert the Orthodox Greeks to union with Rome did little more than survive. A periodical he began ran out of funds, and the Congregation for the Propagation of the Faith complained about the looseness in the rule of his religious orders. In 1878, Marango himself left the community and retired to Athens. He was succeeded by Polykarpos Anastasiadis, a convert from Halki, who struggled to hold the group together, but the task was always a difficult one.

Greater success was had among the Greeks in Kayseri in Anatolia, where several Orthodox families transferred to Catholicism, and in the town of Malkara in Thrace. In Malkara, one of the converts, Isaias Papadopoulos, began a school and attempted to form a Catholic religious community. In 1907, the Latin vicar of the patriarchate, on orders from Rome, appointed Papadopoulos to the office of vicar general for Catholics of the Greek rite, and in January 1912 he was raised to the episcopate. At the end of the First World War, the Catholic Greeks moved from the Ottoman Empire to an uncertain future in Salonica and Athens.[27]

The Balkan Catholic communities remained weak until such outside influences as the appearance of the Austrians in Bosnia–Hercegovina intervened to change their fortunes. A large increase in the number of missionaries from Western Europe, performing educational or charitable work in the heart of the area, broke down many of the prejudices against Catholicism. Converts were few, but attitudes were being changed, and a new and better day appeared to be approaching.

18

The Armenian Catholic community

PERSECUTION AND RESTORATION

The status of Catholic Armenians continued to be a source of contention when Sultan Mahmut II came to power. Although the Catholics had a vicar, he had recognition only from Rome and enjoyed no official position either in the Armenian *millet* or with Ottoman officials. Those Catholic Armenian clergy who were Mekhitarists or who came from Rome held foreign citizenship, which caused the Turks to be disgruntled. The laity still had to worship either in the Latin churches or in private homes, and in all civil matters had to refer to the national patriarch and his staff. The result was frustration and suspicion among all parties. Despite their questionable status, many Armenian Catholics, since they were better educated and frequently wealthier than other members of the *millet*, held positions in the Ottoman administration.

In 1816 the national patriarch, Boghos of Adrianople, had made one more in a long series of attempts to reconcile the Catholics to the *millet* by inviting their leaders to consultations with him. The Mekhitarists were sympathetic, but no other Catholic group showed interest. The alienation continued and even worsened when, in a number of Ottoman cities, especially Ankara and Trabzon, where there were large numbers of Catholics, ecclesiastical properties were fought over between the national church and the Catholics. Patriarch Boghos held a conference to examine the question, summoning the Catholic *amiras* and heads of the Armenian guilds, but it was unsuccessful.[1]

Contention in the Armenian community often resulted in personal tragedies. For example, the grand vezir, Halet Efendi, owed a large debt to the Duzian brothers, Catholic Armenians, in charge of the imperial mint. In order to escape the debt, which he was unable to pay, Halet Efendi accused the Duzians of embezzlement.

He dispatched soldiers to search and secure their homes and, in the investigation, they discovered the private Catholic chapels in which the Duzians worshipped. The possession of places of worship on private property was illegal, so Halet Efendi now had another charge to make against them. On 16 October 1819, one brother and a cousin were hanged in front of their houses; the other brothers were beheaded at the gate of the palace and their bodies left exposed. Throughout the empire, relatives of the Duzians were arrested and their property confiscated.[2]

Early in 1820, Sultan Mahmut told Patriarch Boghos he would like to have the Catholic problem solved once and for all. The simple solution the patriarch employed was to banish all known Armenian Catholic clergy. After this was done, Boghos, seeking the Catholics among the laity, drew up an oath for all Armenians in the *millet*: 'Whatsoever the Holy Orthodox Armenian Church accepts from the day of our holy Gregory the Illuminator until the present time, I accept, and whatsoever it rejects, I reject.' Despite the general tone of the document, many Catholics refused to take the oath and Boghos withdrew it, substituting instead the Nicene Creed. On this creed, at least, all Armenians were in agreement.

The Mekhitarists in Istanbul, led by their superior Mesrop, met with the Balian and Bezjian *amiras*. The Balian family was in charge of the sultan's architectural planning and the Bezjians' head, Haruntun, had succeeded the Duzian brothers at the mint and also headed the Armenian National Council of the *millet*. A compromise, entitled 'An Invitation to Love', was drawn up; it was promulgated on 18 April 1820 and was approved by Patriarch Boghos. The content of the statement resembled other attempts at agreement: the national church would omit from the liturgy its condemnation of Pope Leo I and the Council of Chalcedon if the Catholics returned to patriarchal jurisdiction. Seven of the ten Catholic clergy who were engaged in the discussion felt the document met their requirements. To demonstrate his good will, Patriarch Boghos ordained two known Catholics to the priesthood and confirmed, on 30 April, that the union of the Armenians was now a fact.

The euphoria, however, did not last. From the beginning, the compromise had principally been the work of the Mekhitarists and their partisans among the laity who were anxious to reach a settlement. The Armenian alumni of the Urban College had held aloof, as had Andon Missirlian, Catholic vicar of the Armenians attached to the Latin bishop's office.

During the summer, Patriarch Boghos lost some of his support when, without referral to the catholicos, he consecrated oil for the anointing of the sick. In August, even more damage was inflicted on the fragile compromise as the result of an incident in which a Catholic Armenian of Ankara, who worked as a shoemaker, placed a picture of Pope Pius VII in place of Gregory the Illuminator in an edition of the 'Invitation to Love'. When he showed this to the members of his guild they were angered by what they considered national apostasy. A crowd of shoemakers marched off to the patriarchal residence at Koum Kapou demanding an explanation from the patriarch. His representatives, who attempted to explain the patriarch's position, were shouted down; the crowd entered the building and plundered its contents while Boghos fled for safety. The tumult among the Armenians so angered the Turks that several leaders of the riot were killed and many prominent *amiras* exiled, including the Bezjians.

Patriarch Boghos was restored and sought to calm his critics by sending out of the city the Mekhitarists who had accepted his jurisdiction. Unfortunately, this resulted in their dissociation from the patriarch, for the Mekhitarists went to the Latin religious in Galata, asked to be taken in, and withdrew their support of the union with the national church.

For the next seven years, things remained quiet, for Haruntun Bezjian had returned to office and sought to keep the feuding Armenian factions apart. As president of the National Council, he even recommended the appointment of a Catholic representative, Andon Nurijian, to the executive board of the Council in 1827. However, it was in that same year that the Ottomans were dealt grave setbacks in the Greek revolutionary war. While two Catholic *amiras* close to Mahmut, Hagop and Hovsep Tenjerian, pointed out the loyalty of the Catholic population, Patriarch Karapet argued that he could not be sure of them, since the Catholics were friends of the 'Franks'.

After the battle of Navarino in late October, Mahmut expelled the foreign ambassadors, and on 8 January 1828 issued new restrictions on Europeans in Ottoman lands. All Catholic clergy were to be expelled and Patriarch Karapet was told that Armenian Catholics who lived in Galata among the Westerners were to be resettled in the centre of the capital where they could be kept under surveillance. Catholics who had emigrated to Istanbul and were not native born were ordered to return to their place of origin. In February, therefore, all known Catholic Armenians in Istanbul were evicted from their homes and given only tents for shelter in the midst of the capital or in Scutari while their houses and possessions were auctioned off. Ottoman soldiers rounded up the Catholics of Ankara in the middle of a cruel and bitterly cold winter to begin the trek to their homes without provision of food or adequate clothing. An estimated four hundred people, mostly children, died on the way despite assistance from the Latin Bishop Coressi and the European colony in Istanbul. Fear struck Armenian Catholics everywhere; many fled to Russia, the Greek islands or even Trieste. In a period of weeks, the Catholic Armenians, once a strong and wealthy group, were reduced to an impoverished and wandering existence.[3]

Then conditions rapidly improved for the Catholics, as a result of international developments. Russia had declared war against the Ottomans on 26 April 1828, forcing Mahmut to seek reconciliation with the French and, hence, to ease the persecution. Both French and Austrian ambassadors, urged on by Pope Leo XII, appealed to the sultan to stop his attack on the Catholics. The Treaty of Adrianople, signed on 14 September 1829, brought an end to the Russo-Turkish war and paved the way for a complete restoration of the Catholic Armenian community.

In January 1830 the French emissary, the Comte de Guilleminot, was able to write to Paris that the sultan had agreed not only to permit Armenian Catholics to return to their homes, but also to give them their own *millet* and patriarch, thus removing the cause of so much discontent. Negotiations in this matter were conducted by Bartolomeo Capellari, the future Pope Gregory XVI.[4]

On 5 January 1831, the *Katolik millet* was set up by an imperial *firman*. In it, Mahmut recounted how, from the time of his ancestors, the Catholics had had to live under Greek or Armenian patriarchs who held a religion different from theirs, and had had to frequent Frankish churches, a humiliating condition. Now, to assure their future well-being, they would be able 'to practise their religion in churches set apart for them without going to those of the Franks'. The Catholics would have as their civil head Patriarch Hagop Manuelian, who was to pay initially fifty thousand *aspers* to the treasury for his appointment and, henceforth, thirty-eight thousand *aspers* annually. All Catholics were to acknowledge him as their chief and his jurisdiction was to be on a par with that of all other patriarchs of the Empire.[5]

Manuelian was a priest who had come to office as a result of an

election by a council of Catholic Armenians. At the same time,
Rome recognized Andon Nurijian as archbishop-primate and was
unsure how to react to an independent patriarch. Nurijian enjoyed
independent status and reported directly to Rome. The fact that
the Ottomans considered Manuelian the elected head of the
Armenian Catholics, while Rome looked to Archbishop Nurijian,
was not the best of solutions, but both Ottoman law and Roman
practice had to be served.[6]

It must be said that, when it is considered how severe the 1828
persecution had been, over the next decade the progress of the
Armenian Catholic *millet* was remarkable. Archbishop Nurijian
reported in August 1834 that he counted forty-five thousand people
and fifty churches within his jurisdiction; a quarter of the members
had become Catholics since 1830. In Galata, the Catholics had a
Church of the Holy Saviour which Nurijian used for his cathedral.
Even Haruntun Bezjian, head of the Armenian National Council,
had been a major contributor to its furnishing.[7]

When Nurijian died, the *Katolik millet* nominated three candidates to succeed him and sent the list to Rome for the pope to
choose the one he felt would make the best archbishop. Pope Gregory
XVI, however, ignored the *millet*'s suggestions and unilaterally
appointed Boghos Marouchian on 9 April 1838.

During these years, Protestant missionaries travelling in the
Empire often noted the condition of Catholic Armenians in the
provinces. Eli Smith was in Izmir in 1830 and spoke of a Catholic
community of between two thousand and three thousand people,
some of them with roots in Nakhichevan. In 1830, they still had
no church but worshipped in the Latin Catholic churches. At Tokat
he found eight 'papal' Armenian families without any church or
even any clergy since the great persecution. Another missionary,
Horatio Southgate, was depressed by what he saw of the Christians
in Anatolia, especially by their servility to the Muslims. Very often
the native clergy would not communicate with him. He pictured,
for example, the sad state of Muş in 1838:

The streets are filthy, irregular and uneven with rivulets of dirty water
running through them. There are no covered bazars and the few stalls
which bear the name are ill-furnished and mean, without regularity of
display...The number of poor, insane and diseased persons is astonish-
ing. Boys and girls are seen running with a single rag, and often entirely
naked, through the streets. The Christians appear to be the most
thriving part of the population, but all complained of poverty.

The fifty Armenian Catholics of Muş were without a church building because it had been destroyed by partisans of the national church.[8]

The Armenian Catholics of Aleppo resented that they had been ignored when the decisions were made which led to the establishment of the *Katolik millet* and to the selection of its leaders. They had suffered during the persecution of 1828 as much as any group, yet were denied a voice in setting up the new agreement. Their own patriarch on Mt Lebanon would obviously be little competition for the patriarchate in the capital. As a result, there was a move among them towards forming an autonomous church in Aleppo (a tendency encouraged by the Austrian internuncio in Istanbul), but Rome would not hear of it. There were already too many administrative problems in the Eastern churches.

Throughout these years of alternating persecution and recognition of the Armenian Catholics, the patriarchs at Bzommar, Krikor Bedros V and Krikor Bedros VI, were able to avoid disruption because of the security they enjoyed in the Maronite community of Lebanon. The Aleppan demand for independence was the only serious difficulty requiring the attention of the patriarchs.[9]

THE ARMENIANS AFTER THE 'Hatti Şerif'

As a result of the *Hatti Şerif of Gulhané*, the Ottoman Armenians enjoyed many new privileges, among them the right to choose their own religious leaders. Since Rome feared that the National Council of the Catholic Armenians set up according to the rules of the *Hatti Şerif* expected to do just that, one of the goals of the Congregation for the Propagation of the Faith was to persuade Archbishop Marouchian to take a coadjutor with the right of succession. Although he expressed some reluctance, the archbishop accepted Rome's candidate for this office, Andon Hassoun, in 1842. His nomination was accomplished by presenting the civil leaders of the Armenian Catholic community with a *fait accompli*. On a visit to Rome, Marouchian presided at the consecration of Hassoun, thus avoiding the conflict which might have occurred if the episcopate had been conferred in Istanbul. Hassoun was sufficiently diplomatic to obtain the respect, if not the affection, of the Catholic Armenians in Istanbul. Proof of this was his election to the patriarchate of the *Katolik millet* in 1845, which made him civil head of the community. The following year, Archbishop Marouchian died, so Hassoun automatically became archbishop-primate. For the first time, the offices of archbishop and patriarch were both combined in the same person.

Nevertheless, Hassoun's concentration of power caused protests to go to Rome from twelve leading Catholic *amiras*. The recently elected Pope Pius IX was urged to make future provisions for broader participation by the National Council, the executive board of the Catholics, in the selection of Armenian religious leaders. Pius sent a representative, Innocenzo Ferrieri, to Istanbul for consultations; Ferrieri arrived on 16 January 1848, was greeted by Hassoun, and listened sympathetically to the archbishop-patriarch's account of the Armenian Catholic situation. Hassoun, like Pius IX, was an authoritarian, and found it difficult to work with the National Council. He convinced Ferrieri that to strengthen the ecclesiastical party among the Armenians it would be helpful to increase the number of bishoprics, and he offered the Roman legate his list of acceptable candidates. In an apparent gesture to the National Council, Hassoun then proceeded to relinquish his civil powers.[10]

After Ferrieri returned to Rome, Pope Pius IX acted on his advice, accepting Hassoun's point of view, and, on 30 April 1850, established bishoprics in Ankara, Artvin, Bursa, Erzurum, Trabzon and Isfahan in Persia. All of Hassoun's nominees were to be consecrated without consultation with the National Council.

When this news reached Istanbul there was strong reaction from the lay leaders of the *Katolik millet*, as well as from the Ottoman government. The Armenian church had a long tradition of participation by both clergy and laity in episcopal choices, so Rome's unilateral appointments were resented. For their part, Ottoman officials were upset at not having been advised on the expansion of the patriarchal boundaries. Since bishops were also Ottoman civil administrators, officials of the Porte felt they should have been consulted on the appointments. Understandably, the government announced that the new Armenian bishops would not be allowed to reside in their sees. This did not prevent Hassoun, however, from going ahead with the consecrations.

The fact that the Catholic Armenian patriarch of Cilicia, living at Bzommar in Lebanon, had also been ignored caused the incumbent there, Krikor Bedros VIII, to fear for the future of his church. Throughout the sultanates of the early nineteenth century the Lebanese patriarchs had been in a kind of limbo. They had been aggressive in dispatching monk–missionaries into the rest of the Ottoman world but had failed to impress upon the Roman authorities that what they did really mattered. Now, Krikor Bedros VIII, challenged by Rome's favouritism toward Istanbul, named several bishops himself and summoned a synod of the Cilician hierarchy to meet at Bzommar in 1851. At that time, the bishops attached to Cilician jurisdiction were seated in Adana, Mardin, Amasya, Maraş, Alexandria and Kayseri. It was Krikor's plan to add new sees in Baghdad, Killis and Damascus, all cities in his own territory, as well as in Tokat and Sivas which lay within the Istanbul province. This was a challenge to Istanbul's archbishop for primacy in deed, if not in title.

It is questionable whether the rash of Armenian Catholic episcopal appointees was necessary. Expansion there surely was: for example, Ankara's Armenian Catholics composed seventy-five per cent of the city's population. Tokat and Diyarbakir also had sizable Catholic parishes which were still growing. Perkenik, a village near Sivas, with a population of eighteen hundred people, was completely Catholic. Wherever there were bishops, some Catholics were, obviously, present but to justify doubling the number of bishoprics was problematical.

The synod at Bzommar, in addition to creating the new bishoprics, also adopted legislation which, for the most part, would have endeared the bishops to Rome. The Maronite council of al-Luwayzah provided a model for most of the canons. Some of the other issues were not so benign, among them the establishment of cathedral chapters of canons, an idea altogether novel to Armenian tradition. It was only in 1855, after a lengthy Roman examination had required emendations, that the council received approbation.[11]

Meanwhile, *Propaganda* was looking for ways to break the stalemate between the National Council and the Ottoman government on one side and Archbishop Hassoun and the hierarchy on the other. At length, the staff of the Congregation suggested a new method of choosing bishops. The patriarch would summon an assembly with equal numbers of clergy and laity which would nominate at least six, but not more than twelve, episcopal candidates. The hierarchy would then choose three names from this list, with at least one nominee from the monastic clergy. This list of three candidates would be forwarded to Rome where the final selection was to be made by the pope.

The Armenian Council, however, did not feel Rome had gone far enough. The lay leaders, influenced by the Mekhitarists who represented the national party among the Catholics, felt the choice of clergy should be made according to traditional patterns. On the other hand, partisans of the priests who were graduates of the Urban College were willing to allow Rome the deciding vote. A bitter contest developed over the issues, leading Pius IX to send a new communication to the Armenian Catholics on 2 February 1854. In this, the pope urged harmony among the factions, chastized the Mekhitarists, and forbade all polemical writing on the matter. Despite this admonition, the Catholic Armenians remained divided, and a continuous stream of letters passed back and forth between Rome and Istanbul. To the chagrin of many, in 1860, Archbishop Hassoun resumed the patriarchate, thus once again combining all authority in his own person.[12]

To add a further dimension to the church activities of the Armenians, the growth of Protestantism caused grave distress to both national and Catholic churches. In 1844, the patriarch, Matteos, forbade any Armenians to attend Protestant services, and in 1846 an Armenian priest was excommunicated for favouring the Evangelical ministers. Subsequently, a general campaign was launched against Armenian Protestants, but persecution did not lessen the number of converts. The British ambassador, Stratford Canning, obtained a *firman* from Abdulmecid's government in November 1847 which gave the Protestants autonomy and thus protected the Evangelical Church from further harassment. In 1850, Protestant Greeks and Syrians were included, and so a Protestant *millet* was created.

Protestant evangelization was remarkably successful in Istanbul and in all of the major cities of Anatolia. American and British missionaries were insistent on having native pastors and autonomous congregations. In a notable contrast with Catholic clerics from France or Italy, the Protestant clergy hardly ever assumed permanent pastoral responsibility for local congregations. Their stress on the importance of the local congregation's standing on its own feet, without expectation of continued foreign aid, goes far to explain their success.[13]

THE CATHOLIC ARMENIAN SCHISM

Political consciousness within the Armenian Catholic community was growing at the time when Pope Pius IX was attempting to appropriate to himself all the decision-making privileges of the Eastern churches. It was not long before a clash occurred. The first move was made by Rome upon the death of the Cilician Armenian patriarch of Bzommar, Krikor Bedros VIII, in January 1866. The Latin patriarch of Jerusalem, Valerga, acting with papal acquiescence, nominated an interim vicar solely on his own authority. Meanwhile, he let it be known to the Bzommar hierarchy that Roman officials would no longer tolerate a double-headed leadership in the Armenian Catholic hierarchy. The opportunity was now at hand to remove this problem. When the Cilician synod met on 18 September 1866 with Patriarch Valerga presiding, the bishops demonstrated their loyalties by unanimously nominating Andon Hassoun, archbishop-primate of Istanbul, as patriarch. The bishops further urged him to come to Lebanon for his installation. Hassoun, however, went instead to Rome in July 1867, where Pius IX invested him as Andon Bedros IX and gave him the pallium. His title was to be patriarch of Cilicia, but his residence remained in Istanbul.[14]

Twelve of the Armenian Catholic hierarchs came to Rome for the occasion, as did the Maronite and Melkite patriarchs. While the Armenians were there, Hassoun called a meeting to discuss the issues raised by Pius IX's preparation of the document *Reversurus* which made some dramatic changes in the traditions with which the Armenians were familiar. Despite some objections raised by the Armenian bishops, the pope promulgated *Reversurus* on 12 July 1867. After a section concerning Rome's historical successes in warding off heresy and schism, *Reversurus* argued that the Orient had suffered numerous defections from orthodoxy as a result of its fragile relations with the papacy and divisions within its own hierarchy. This condition would now be remedied because the Cilician patriarchate had been united with the Armenian Catholic primatial see and the pope had personally invested the incumbent. Henceforth, the Armenian patriarch would be enthroned only after having received Roman confirmation, and none of his powers could be used until he received the pallium. The patriarch would also be expected to visit Rome once every five years, like Latin bishops, so that he might report on the state of his church. The names of three candidates for the patriarchate were to be submitted to Rome by the hierarchial synod whenever a vacancy occurred in that office, and the final decision would be made by the pope. Bishops alone – priests and laity being excluded – were to submit candidates: Pius ordered that 'No one of the laity may be involved in the election, nor have the right to speak for any reason or pretext.'

Appointments to bishoprics could either be made directly by the Congregation for the Propagation of the Faith, or the synod of the Catholic Armenian bishops might forward three names of possible candidates for Rome's selection.[15]

Hassoun returned to Istanbul in August for his enthronement and for a *berat* from the government of Sultan Abdulaziz which would recognize his position. Patriarch Valerga came with him, acknowledging that some opposition to *Reversurus* might be expected. On 1 November, the day of Patriarch Andon's installation, *Reversurus* was promulgated to Istanbul's Armenian Catholic clergy and laity. Valerga sought to lessen recrimination by explaining that the laity might still submit names of ecclesiastical candidates to the bishops so long as they did not take part in the election itself. Plans were announced to summon a national assembly of Armenian Catholics to implement the requirements of *Reversurus*.

While opposition to the papal decree was muted in late 1867 because of the excitement attendant upon Hassoun's installation, by the end of the year considerable complaints were surfacing in Aleppo, especially within the monasteries of the Antonine monks. Spokesmen for these groups felt that the move of church leadership to Istanbul excluded them, and they resented the centralizing of their community's authority in the patriarch and the pope. They were not at all pleased with the new title given to Archbishop Brunoni in Istanbul, 'Apostolic Delegate for the Oriental Rites', nor did they accept the thesis of Pius IX which stated that the major duty of the Eastern patriarchs was to represent the authority of the popes to their communities.[16]

When the national assembly was convened in July 1869, the church was seriously divided between those who supported and those who rejected *Reversurus*. The arguments grew long and tedious as both sides sought to make a proper response to the papal directive. Some delegates, charging that Hassoun had allowed Armenian identity to be lost, called for his removal. Seventy-nine sessions were held by the assembly, but instead of compromising their differences, the two factions became even more divided. Hassoun decided to suspend the convention rather than risk further difficulties. The Vatican Council was approaching and the hierarchy would soon be leaving for Rome. A calmer atmosphere might prevail with the passage of time.

Opposition to Hassoun and *Reversurus* was led by the Abbot Placid Kasanjian, archbishop of Antioch and head of the Antonine

Congregation. He sent agents to Italy to present the point of view of those who believed *Reversurus* needed modification, apparently unaware how dim his prospects for success were in the Rome of Pius IX. Kasanjian attacked Hassoun as an authoritarian, causing endless troubles within the church because of his efforts to dominate it. He informed the pope that those who were in opposition to the changes in church administration remained good Catholics:

We declare that, at the same time, we are children devoted to St Gregory the Illuminator and faithful members of the Eastern Catholic Armenian church. We want to keep intact the rights, privileges and usages of our church, such as they have been passed to us by our fathers and enjoyed by us from the time of our ancestors.[17]

While the first sessions of Vatican I were in progress, a solution to the problems of the church was sought by Archbishop Basil Gasparian, vicar of Hassoun, and Josef Pluym, the Latin vicar of the patriarchate. Pope Pius IX wrote to Pluym in February 1870 that the Antonine monks were acting in a rebellious manner and were violating the laws of the church; he had received word that Abbot Placid no longer commemorated the pope's name in the liturgy. Therefore, Pius told Pluym to go to Lebanon and make a visitation of the Antonine monasteries so as to learn their disposition and to oust the abbot from office.

On the basis of the evidence he had gathered, on 31 March 1870 Pluym announced the suspension of all priests and religious acting in defiance of Patriarch Hassoun. The Antonines in Istanbul were particularly singled out. In late May, Pius IX stepped up the attack upon the dissenters when he addressed a letter to the Armenian Catholics complaining of the serious scandal afflicting their church. He chided the Antonines for becoming needlessly upset over a small number of changes which affected church discipline, but neither the faith nor the rites of the Armenian church. Pius argued that if the bishop of Rome, head of the universal church, could not make a decision on the proper administration of the churches united in the Catholic faith, where indeed did he have any authority?

The pope's arguments were vain, and by summer 1870 there were forty Armenian Catholic clergy in opposition to Rome and Patriarch Hassoun. How many laity were involved is difficult to ascertain. Finally, on 2 November, the pope excommunicated by name four bishops: Placid Kasanjian, Basil Gasparian, bishop of Cyprus, Hagop Bahdiarian of Diyarbakir and Ignatius Kalipjian of Amasya.

Also included in the censure were eighteen Antonines, twelve Mekhitarists, five monks from Bzommar and ten secular priests.

Up to this point the French government had consistently backed Patriarch Hassoun and the pro-papal party of the Armenian Catholics, but at this juncture, the Prussians' defeat of France put the ambassador of Louis Napoleon in a weak position in Istanbul, and, seeing French influence so much lessened, the opponents of Patriarch Hassoun obtained a cancellation of his *berat* from the Ottoman government. The dissenters then chose one of their own, Hagop Bahdiarian, as their religious head. For the moment, the Ottoman government withheld recognition, but this did not stop Bishop Hagop from taking the title Hagop Bedros IX and consecrating four additional bishops.[18]

Pius IX responded to the schism by sending his legate, Alessandro Franchi, to Istanbul in March 1871 to present the Roman case against Bahdiarian and his church. The foreign minister, Ali Paşa, was sympathetic to Franchi, but he died before the problem could be resolved and was succeeded by a friend of the schismatics. The result was that on 13 May 1871 Andon Hassoun was declared deposed and banished from the Ottoman Empire, and the Armenian Catholics were invited to elect a new patriarch. Instead of a single convention, there were two: the pro-Roman group chose Bishop Filikan of Bursa while the schismatics elected a priest, Hovannes Kupelian, to become patriarch. It was the latter who received recognition from the Porte. Kupelian lived in Istanbul while Bishop Hagop made his residence in Lebanon.

During the next several years a battle over bishoprics, properties and titles everywhere afflicted the Armenian church. From his exile, Hassoun, with the support of Piux IX, attempted to strengthen the loyalist party among the Armenian Catholics and to discourage support for the schismatics. New excommunications were levied: among the victims was the abbot of the Venetian Mekhitarists, who was deposed from office.

By February 1874 the recently appointed Latin apostolic delegate in Istanbul, Serafino Milani, prevailed upon the Ottoman government to grant recognition to the pro-Roman Armenian Catholics once more. They recovered several church properties, and Hassoun returned to Istanbul, though he did not resume the patriarchal office. Despite the lack of civil recognition, Patriarch Andon was the only Armenian prelate recognized by Rome, and each year more of the schismatic clergy and laity moved to support him.

Finally, Patriarch Kupelian sought reconciliation with the papacy in March 1879, resigned his office and left for Rome to promise his fidelity to Leo XIII. The pope accepted his apology with grace and the schism came to an end when the Ottoman government once more gave its recognition to Hassoun on 9 April 1879.

Within a few months the pope asked Hassoun, who still had many enemies, to come to Italy, where he was named a cardinal of the Roman church on 13 December 1880, the first Oriental Catholic to be so honoured since Bessarion. He never returned to Istanbul, but died in Rome in 1884. The only permanent effect of the schism was the loss of the Antonine monks, who returned to the national church. One of these, the noted author Malachai Ormanian, eventually became its patriarch.[19]

The successor to Andon Hassoun was Stepon Azarian, formerly bishop of Nicosia, who took the title Stepon Bedros X. During his patriarchate, nationalist and revolutionary movements gathered strength among the Armenians. Catholics were less involved in these groups than members of the national church or the Marxists among the Armenians. When the nationalist Armenakan party was formed in Van in 1885, its rules allowed only ethnic Armenians to belong but they could be of any religion since its members were banded together to 'win for the Armenians the right to rule over themselves through revolution'.[20] The reaction of Sultan Abdulhamit II to these societies was ruthless suppression. The Kurdish tribes became the principal agents in the Ottoman government's attempt to carry out the sultan's wishes. In Eastern Anatolia, defenceless Armenian villages became the object of raids which left only the dead and wounded, and smoking ruins where houses had once stood. The patriarch of the national church, Khoren Ashegian, protested to the Ottoman officials in vain. Khoren became further involved in the summer of 1890 when a leader of the revolutionary Hunchakian party read a manifesto in his church and forced him to join a march upon Abdulhamit's palace. The result was riot and the arrest of hundreds of people.

The worst was yet to come. In the summer of 1894, Kurdish militia attacked Armenians near Sassoun, killing at least ten thousand Christians. In 1896, a group of Armenians, in desperation, seized and burned the Ottoman bank in Galata, which prompted Abdulhamit to call for a general slaughter of Armenians in the Eastern provinces. Perhaps fifty thousand people died as a result. Entire villages were converted to Islam by force and their churches turned into mosques. Eighty thousand people were forced into exile with the loss of all their property. By the end of the year, only seven bishops of the national church out of a total of sixty-five were still in residence.[21]

The Catholic Armenians were not the immediate targets of Abdul-hamit's policies, but Kurds and Ottoman soldiers sent out to enforce the sultan's policies found it difficult to distinguish between Armenians of the national church and those who were Catholics. Usually, if they had sufficient time, the Catholics could flee to the French consulates in the larger cities or into the grounds of foreign missions. The Capuchins, for example, rescued five thousand Armenians in Diyarbakir alone. At Kharput, when Kurdish leaders demanded that the refugees be turned over, the French Capuchin superior told them: 'You can kill us, but you will not take our guests unless you pass over our corpses.'[22]

In more remote areas the Catholics were lost. The Catholic village of Telarmen was completely plundered. It would be impossible to be certain how many Catholics died, but Robert Davey estimated the number at between four and five thousand. The policy of Patriarch Stepon Azarian was to say nothing and do nothing to antagonize the Turks, but to act only in a humanitarian way to aid the refugees. The Turks were therefore to assume that no revolutionaries were found among the Catholics.[23]

The patriarch and Catholic bishops, during these years of national crisis, busied themselves with church affairs. In April 1888 a constitution was issued ignoring *Reversurus* and setting up a new procedure for the selection of the patriarch and the bishops. Upon a vacancy, the ecclesiastical and national assemblies were to nominate five candidates to the episcopal synod. The bishops were then expected to choose one of the five for patriarch. The patriarchal candidate's name was to be given to the sultan's government for the issuing of the *berat*. Rome was to be informed of the election and requested to confirm the nominee and send him a pallium. Bishops were to be selected by the patriarch from nominations made by the assemblies. Neither Pope Leo XIII nor the Congregation for the Propagation of the Faith accepted the constitution, and later Patriarch Stepon himself withdrew his support. When Patriarch Stepon died early in 1899, the electoral synod, rather than choosing his successor on its own authority, sent the names of five possible patriarchal candidates to Rome. Pope Leo XIII chose Boghos Emmanuelian from the list and confirmed him in office on 24 July

1899. Within a year a national council met in Kadiköy to attempt a solution to the church's problems. Both he and his successor, Patriarch Boghos Bedros XII Sabbagian, continued the policy of non-involvement in political affairs which they believed best for their church.[24]

The revolution of the Young Turks in 1907 allowed the Armenians a deceptive respite from their afflictions. The pause gave time to several lay leaders of the Catholic community to assail Patriarch Boghos Sabbagian as an unworthy prelate and demand that the government withdraw his *berat*. Division within the Catholic Armenian community was hardly new, yet Patriarch Boghos apparently had little taste for it. Over the next few years, the Armenian lay leaders persisted in attacking his authority, so that he finally submitted his resignation to Rome in August 1910. The Catholic National Council then assembled to submit names to the synod for a successor, and on 23 April 1910 unanimously chose Bulos Terzian, bishop of Adana, whose diocese had been devastated by massacres perpetrated by Kurds and Turks. Terzian was invested in office as Bulos Bedros XIII.[25]

Despite his initial popularity, many lay leaders soon found fault with Bulos' administration, and they raised against him the same complaints that had been directed against his predecessor. Because of the never-ending controversies within the church over the selection of bishops (there were then nine vacancies within the Armenian Catholic hierarchy), when Bulos left for Rome to receive his pallium, he presented his problems to the pope. Pius X told the patriarch he would make the appointments himself, choosing from a list of candidates approved by both *Propaganda* and the patriarch. The pope then summoned the Armenian Catholic bishops to Rome to confer on the difficulties facing their church.

On 15 October 1911, Patriarch Bulos opened the synod in Rome's Armenian Catholic church of St Nicholas de Tolentino with thirteen bishops present. Eleven were not there, for when news had reached Istanbul about plans to hold a council in Rome, Armenian Catholic dissenters had mounted a campaign to prevent their bishops from attending. The Ottoman government issued a decree to stop the bishops from going, but too late to prevent those who had already left for Italy. During the course of the council, many late-comers arrived, after a successful appeal to Turkish officials.

The problems discussed at this gathering demonstrated how ineffective *Reversurus* had been, since the bishops were required to take up the old questions of participation by the national council in the nomination of the bishops and patriarch, the title to church property, and the civil administration of the Armenian Catholic community. At the end of the meeting, the *Acts* of the council filled four hundred and sixty-seven pages. In the one thousand and nine canons, every imaginable subject was legislated upon, including doctrine, morality, worship and church administration. The tenor of the council's decrees reflect a desire of the church hierarchy to free itself from lay interference by turning even closer to Rome. The final documents were signed by Patriarch Bulos and eighteen of the Armenian Catholic bishops.[26]

While the council met in Rome, the Catholic National Council in Istanbul voted to oust the patriarch from office and, when Bulos returned to Istanbul, he found the doors to the patriarchate locked and a hostile crowd at the entrance. While the patriarch found a house in a nearby parish, a barrage of criticism was levelled against him in the press, and officials of the Turkish government let it be known that they would not oppose the election of a new patriarch.

On 31 March 1912 Sultan Mehmet V's government publicly announced that it would no longer recognize Bulos as patriarch because he had illegally held a synod outside Turkish borders and had consecrated bishops without obtaining government approval beforehand. A *locum tenens*, Bishop Hatchadourian of Malatia, was chosen by the national council, and he moved into the patriarchate. Rome then suspended him from office, but was unable to restore Bulos as long as the Turkish government supported a rival. Thus the Armenian Catholic church, with about 140,000 members, entered the period of the First World War with a deep division in its ranks. Each patriarch had his own partisans among the clergy and laity, and compromise seemed far away. Despite the fact that of all Armenians, Catholics were the most loyal to the Ottoman government, they were not to be spared the genocide which lay ahead.[27]

THE FIRST WORLD WAR AND THE ARMENIAN MASSACRE

Several months before the Empire entered the war, the Young Turk government had apparently decided to exterminate the entire Ottoman Armenian population. The towns of Eastern Anatolia were struck first: the Armenians were given a choice of conversion to Islam or exile. The agents of death then moved over all of Anatolia.

At first a distinction was made between Catholic Armenians and those who were members of the national church. Catholics also enjoyed foreign protection, a blessing not available to members of the national church. As the attack upon Armenian nationals continued, however, Turkish and Kurdish police made no distinction between the groups. Thus, in Ankara, home of sixteen thousand Catholic Armenians, the first expulsion order exempted the Catholics from deportation, but in late August 1915 all Catholic men were arrested and threatened with execution. Only the prompt intervention of the Austrian minister to Istanbul saved them. Later they were forced to leave their homes to go first to Konya and then to Adana. By the end of the war, the Ankaran Catholic community had been destroyed.[28]

Tales of the Armenian genocide are too numerous to recount, but a certain pattern soon emerged. First the able-bodied men of the national church were commanded to leave, later the women, then the Catholics and finally the elderly. While the men were usually executed shortly after deportation, women and children were put into caravans to be marched off to the deserts of northern Syria without sufficient food, water or clothing. On the way they were subjected to terribly harsh treatment. Thousands died of typhus. The Italian consul of Trabzon reported from his post:

It was a real extermination and slaughter of the innocents...The Armenian Catholics, who in the past had always been respected and excepted from the massacres and persecutions, were this time treated worse than any – again by order of the Central Government.

The attempts of foreign missionaries to intervene were often unavailing since most were Frenchmen. Latin priests and nuns were forced out of their stations, and the Armenian churches and schools were burned to the ground.[29]

At the end of the war over a million and a half Armenians were dead in this first genocide of the twentieth century. The toll among members of the national church was heaviest, but the Catholic Armenian church had practically been destroyed. Dead were the bishops of Adana, Ankara, Artvin, Bursa, Kayseri, Maraş, and Trabzon; one hundred and thirty priests, forty-seven nuns, and up to one hundred thousand people had been slain. The forty thousand Catholics who remained fled to Syria and Lebanon. Only the community of Istanbul was exempted. Hierarchical divisions faded before the overwhelming tragedy. On 27 August 1917, Patriarch

Bulos Terzian resigned and Hovannes Nasalian became *locum tenens*. The patriarchal office was not filled again until 1928.[30]

In assessing this period of Armenian Catholic history, the tragedy of the massacres is so overwhelming that it makes the bickering which plagued the church in the nineteenth and early twentieth centuries inconsequential. Yet there is something to be learned in the creation of the *Katolik millet*, for this demonstrated that the evolution of the Catholic Eastern churches was progressing in its relation with the Ottoman government. Unfortunately, factionalism persisted, complicated by Roman insistence that its solution rested in bringing the Armenians under stricter Western discipline. *Reversurus* attempted to rewrite the agreement between East and West made at the Council of Florence. In this regard it was a dangerous document, destroying the balance between Western and Eastern traditions, and placing one more hurdle in the way of church unity.

19

The Maronites after the reign of Mahmut II

MARONITES DURING MAHMUT II'S SULTANATE

For twenty-eight years of Mahmut's reign, from 1804 to 1832, Lebanese affairs were dominated by one man, Emir Bashir II Shehab, an adroit politician, able to maintain himself in power so long because he could combine political alliances with both the mountain chieftains and the Ottoman government. Though he professed himself a Druze he was suspected of being, secretly, a Christian.

Bashir's political longevity stands in sharp contrast to the short-lived tenures of the Maronite patriarchs. Of these latter, Yusuf Tian, elevated in 1796, resigned his office in 1809. He was followed by Yuhanna el-Helou, who was elected while Pius VII was still a prisoner of Napoleon and, though confirmed in the patriarchate, had to wait until 1814 before the pope could send him the pallium. By the time it came, Yuhanna had returned to the monastery of Qannubin, once the traditional residence of the patriarchate, which had been abandoned for several decades. As well as re-establishing the ancient residence, Yuhanna was of a mind to enforce the legislation against double monasteries which had been agreed upon at the 1736 council of al-Luwayzah; with Roman encouragement, he called a synod for 1818, and there the bishops once again agreed that men's and women's monasteries could not be placed side by side. Rome, of course, was delighted with the results and hastened to confirm a decision which reflected an almost-century-old church law. Any person not agreeing to the separation was subject to excommunication.[1]

The actual disestablishment of the double monasteries and the difficult decisions concerning division of properties took place under the patriarchate of Yusuf Habash, who came to the leadership of the church in May 1823. In addition to supervising the separations

Yusuf also enforced one other canon of al-Luwayzah, that which required bishops to reside in their dioceses. The Congregation for the Propagation of the Faith considered Yusuf a friend, and Pope Gregory XVI favoured the Maronites with an encyclical written 15 August 1832. Yusuf also enjoyed good relations with the Ottomans, though the Maronites had never sought *berats* for their bishops and patriarch. It was he who, for the first time, sent a representative to Istanbul to represent the Maronites before the government of the Porte.[2]

Not all was harmonious, however, for the patriarch was outraged by the appearance of American Presbyterians in Lebanon. William Goodell and Isaac Bird, the first of these missionaries, had settled in Beirut in 1823, and more Americans followed, setting up an Arabic press and opening a school. Yusuf threatened with excommunication any Maronite who should consort with the Protestants and, indeed, the first Maronite convert they gained was arrested, tortured, and died in prison for his convictions.[3]

In 1832 an Egyptian army, captained by Ibrahim Paşa, occupied Syria and Lebanon as part of Muhammad Ali's plans to create a Near Eastern empire centred around Cairo. Ibrahim wanted Christian support but had to balance this with traditional Muslim hostility towards Christian equality. He sought to recruit a thousand Maronites for his army, but his invitation was not welcomed by the Christians, who realized that it might very well open the door to conscription, something they dreaded. Patriarch Yusuf flatly announced that no Maronites were to be enlisted, and he warned Ibrahim that the Maronites would call for French assistance if he persisted. Ibrahim, who did not care for the traditional autonomy of the mountain inhabitants, took another tack. He ordered that the Maronites and the Druzes were not to be allowed to have weapons, and announced that taxes would be raised to three times their former level to pay for the government of Syria and Lebanon.

However, Ibrahim was favourably disposed to Catholics. Upon learning of the conversion of an Orthodox to Catholicism, he commented: 'I am very pleased to learn you have become a Catholic, for Catholics are more loyal to their sovereigns.'[4] Their loyalty was soon to be tested, for in 1838 the Druzes in Jabal Hawran rose in revolt against the Egyptians. Ibrahim then decided to arm the Maronites so that they could garrison Mt Lebanon while he took his Egyptian troops to quell the revolt. By the end of the year the Maronites had fifteen thousand men with rifles, something which gave them a position of strength they had never had before. A native Christian militia was a significant innovation in the Near East. The Druzes became angered at what the Egyptians had done, and rightly believed that it would be difficult ever again to impose the old landholding obligations upon the Maronite peasantry.

Foreign agents were also busy in Lebanon. A British Catholic, Richard Wood, had been sent by London to try to talk the Maronites into throwing off Ibrahim's rule. Wood contacted Patriarch Yusuf and spoke to him of England's influence with Mahmut II, which could be employed to gain political autonomy for the Maronites should they rise against Ibrahim. In April 1839 Mahmut II ordered the Turkish army into Syria, but Ibrahim won a great victory over the Turks at Besib. Further to strengthen his Christian following, Ibrahim then announced a policy of complete Christian–Muslim equality in his domain. It was at this point that Mahmut II died and, had it not been for the British conviction that the Ottoman Empire must be preserved at all costs, the Egyptian leader's Near Eastern policies might have opened a new and better era for Christians.

THE MARONITES UNDER ATTACK

When, with the reopening of the conflict between the Ottoman Empire and Egypt, a second Near East crisis arose, Lebanon was in ferment. The Maronites, one hundred and forty thousand strong, well armed, were now determined never again to be found defenceless. When the news came to Beirut that Maronite students in Cairo had been drafted by Muhammed Ali and that orders had been sent to Lebanon to disarm the Christians, the Maronite leaders were in a quandary. Emir Bashir II Shehab, true to his Egyptian alliance, ordered Maronites and Druzes alike to surrender their weapons, but the Maronite chieftains of Dair al-Kamar decided upon resistance and took a solemn oath to keep their rifles. The emir confronted them unsuccessfully, and in no time there was a full-blown revolt upon the mountain. The British, with their agents in Lebanon, intervened and landed troops on the coast to assist the Maronites. Later, Ottoman soldiers also arrived to help, and the combined armies were able to drive the Egyptians from Lebanon. Alas, once Ottoman rule had been reimposed, the Maronites found they had succeeded only in changing one master for another:

The Christians were everywhere reviled and insulted; in many places were assaulted in the bazaars; had their turbans torn off their heads and were compelled to resume their old distinctive garb of degradation.[5]

The Turks installed a loyalist Shebab, Bashir III Kassem, to replace Bashir II, whom the British had evacuated to Malta. The new emir was unable to gain support, however, so a number of other candidates came under consideration. Maronite Patriarch Yusuf insisted that only a Maronite emir would be acceptable; what he had in mind, actually, was the dismissal of Bashir III, which he hoped would open the way for Bashir II's return.

In September 1841, on the advice of his British and Turkish advisers, Bashir III established a Council of Twelve which, he intended, would assist in the administration of the mountain. The Druzes would have three seats on the council, Maronites the same number, and the other Christian and Muslim communities would supply the rest. But the Druzes, believing Bashir III was prejudiced against them, refused to participate; they were further angered by a document of Patriarch Yusuf, circulating in the Maronite villages, which urged Maronites to defy the authority of Druze landowners. Na'aman Bey Jumblatt, the Druze leader, made a personal visit to Patriarch Yusuf, but failed to get him to change his position. Maronites outnumbered Druzes; they had guns and French money to buy more, but the Druzes were armed too, and they feared that if the Maronites continued to reject their traditional leadership they would soon lose everything.

Accordingly, on 13 October, a Druze force attacked the Maronites of Dair al-Kamar and laid siege to the residence of Bashir III. The emir fled, the Christians were slaughtered and their homes were burned to the ground. Similar attacks were made on other Lebanese towns, and the Druzes were altogether successful since the Christians were caught off guard and the Ottoman army stationed on the mountain did nothing to defend them.

The Maronites turned to France for aid, asking Paris for men and arms as quickly as possible. The French consul at Beirut imposed a condition: foreign missionaries who had been urging the Maronites to resist the Druzes must be dismissed, and one of these, the Lithuanian Jesuit Maximilian Ryllo, was to be expelled from the country. The French then acted to salvage the Maronites – but only after twelve thousand people had been killed. In conjunction with Great Britain, Russia and the Porte, France proposed a peace plan which divided the country into two administrative regions, Maronite in the north and Druze in the south, each with local leaders. Since there were Maronites in the south and Druze villages in the north, the project could not please everyone, and, in response to the civil disorder which continued to plague the nation, Sultan Abdulmecid dispatched an army under Omar Paşa to restore order.

All through this time of tension Patriarch Yusuf moved about the country, rallying the Maronites and encouraging them to hold fast. He spent the winters in Kisrawan at Bkerke and the summers at Qannubin, which practice allowed him to meet with a good many of his people. He encouraged more foreign missionaries, especially the French to whom his church was so indebted, to come to Lebanon. Therefore the Lazarists, in 1844, expanded their Tripoli mission to Beirut, while the Daughters of Charity opened a girls' school in the town several years later. The Jesuits, already in Beirut, planned a seminary for Lebanon, which opened in 1845 in Ghazir. The old residence of Fakhr ad-Din was renovated and became St Francis Xavier College.[6]

When in May 1845 Patriarch Yusuf died, he was succeeded by another of the same name, Yusuf al-Khazen, former bishop of Damascus. Rome was anxious for him to call a synod to strengthen church discipline, but he delayed because of the tense political situation. Rome was especially disturbed at the Maronite clergy's custom of frequently hearing confessions outside church buildings, and also at the little that was being done to combat the Protestant missionaries now spreading out from Beirut to other parts of the country. Since Yusuf rejected the criticisms of *Propaganda*, the cardinals suspended him on 18 February 1851, and for the following three years the Maronites were without proper leadership. Finally, in November 1854, Bulus Massad, once a student in Rome, was elected patriarch by the Maronite synod. Dutifully he called the council Rome had requested, and there at Bkerke discussed new methods of enforcing the canons of al-Luwayzah. As leader of the whole Maronite community the patriarch tried to enlist all the heads of the church, both clerical and lay, in pressing for greater advantages for the peasantry. His aggressive spirit caused several outbreaks of violence against Druze tax-collectors in 1857.

In the early summer of 1860 the Druzes repeated their attack of nineteen years before on Dair al-Kamar. Once more they massacred the Christians and destroyed their property. The abbot of the local Maronite monastery was flayed alive, and the monks, after various tortures, were killed by impaling. The promising Jesuit school was burned to the ground. Still other attacks were made on the Maronites of Saida and Zahlah and in the latter city five French Jesuits were martyred. The war spilled over: in the next several weeks the Druzes attacked not only Maronites but all Christians, and extended their war beyond Lebanon to Damascus, which was the scene of a terrible massacre in 1860. In Damascus the twenty thousand Christians, successful merchants and craftsmen, had their own quarter, where Maronites made up only a portion of the total. The publication of the *Hatti humayun* had grated upon the sensibilities of a Muslim population which resented any change in Christian status, and the Muslims welcomed the news of Druze successes in Lebanon; when a rumour spread that the sultan had ordered the elimination of all who were not followers of Islam, the Muslim Damascenes were ready to obey.

On 9 July 1860 a swarm of angry rioters rushed into the Christian quarter killing, looting and burning. The defenceless population ran to what they thought was sanctuary in their churches, but turned out to be their doom. Five hundred Melkites were burned alive inside their church. At the Capuchin chapel, the eight friars put up a barricade but it was soon torn down and all were killed. The superior of the Franciscan mission was dragged before the altar of his church and asked if he would convert to Islam. He said he would not, so his head was cut off on the spot.

While the Ottoman governor did nothing to assist the Christians, an Algerian Muslim chieftain, 'Abd el-Kader, who was living in exile in Damascus, became their protector. He and his men saved the Lazarist priests and the Daughters of Charity with the four hundred orphans in their care. Not only did 'Abd el-Kader give hope to the survivors who found sanctuary in his residence, but he offered to ransom every Christian captive. After negotiating the return of several hundred people in this manner, he led the Christian survivors over the mountain to safety in Beirut. After three weeks of indiscriminate destruction the Damascus Christian quarter was demolished: ten thousand were dead and several thousand more wounded.[7]

When news of the massacre reached Paris, Napoleon III dispatched twelve thousand troops to the Orient to protect the Christians. Their presence effectively stopped the conflict in both Lebanon and Syria, and it enabled Maronite and Druze leaders to adopt a truce supervised by the French and Ottomans. In Lebanon 1860 had been a tragic year: fifteen thousand Maronites were dead and up to one hundred thousand homeless; one hundred and fifty villages were in ruins and two hundred and fifty churches, forty-eight monasteries and convents and twenty-eight schools lost.[8]

Over the next several months the ambassadors of the Great Powers and representatives of the Turkish government sought to find a permanent solution to the problems in Lebanon. The result of their deliberations was the Organic Statute of 9 June 1861, which gave autonomy to most of the Christian area of Lebanon. This region would have its own governor, the *mutesharrif*, chosen from the Empire's Catholic population and appointed by the sultan. He would have a council drawn from all of the religious denominations represented in the country. No Turkish army was to be stationed in Lebanon, no tribute was to be extracted and no conscription of its citizens permitted. After long centuries of subjection to Muslim rule, the Maronites were now to enjoy a favoured position within the Ottoman world.

THE MARONITES UNDER THE MUTESHARRIFS

The first *mutesharrif* was an Armenian Catholic, Karapet Artin Daud Paşa, who had enjoyed a distinguished career in the Ottoman civil service. He continued to serve his government well by rebuilding Lebanon and restoring confidence in its future by fair and equal treatment of all religious groups in the nation. His appointment began a tradition which lasted until the First World War, that the *mutesharrif* should never be a Lebanese.[9]

After 1869 the office was held by Nasri Franco, an Aleppan Catholic nominated by the Maronite patriarch, and then by Rustem Paşa, an Italian career diplomat in Ottoman service. Since he aimed to increase the powers of the central government, the Italian diplomat was not popular in Lebanon, and his moves were resisted by the Maronite village chieftains and clergy. It was at this time that the Maronites began emigrating to Europe, Egypt and the Americas, drawn to those places by the hope of better economic conditions than were available at home.

Throughout this whole period, Bulus Massad held the patriarchate. In 1867 he journeyed to Rome, probably the first Maronite head to do so, in order to assist at the installation of Andon Hassoun as Armenian Catholic patriarch and to consult with Pius IX. He was in Rome at the time *Reversurus* was issued, and so was able to protect his church from its provisions; then, after leaving Rome, he visited Paris to thank Napoleon III for France's assistance to his people. On his return journey he met with Sultan Abdulaziz, who lodged him in his palace and even fitted out a chapel for his use. At the time of the Vatican Council, the patriarch excused himself and was the only Eastern Catholic patriarch who did not attend, the small Maronite delegation of four bishops being led by Butrus Bostani, archbishop of Tyre and Sidon. No Arabic translation of the Council documents appeared until 1900; the Maronites obviously felt that what happened in Rome was of major concern only to the West.[10]

In 1866 the Protestant presence in Lebanon became yet more important with the foundation of the Syrian Protestant College, opened by David Bliss, an American missionary. It soon grew into one of the Near East's most important colleges: it was not till 1875 that a Catholic university opened in Beirut, the Jesuits having moved their college from Ghazir. This school, St Joseph's, along with the Syrian Protestant College, made Beirut the intellectual centre of Syria.[11]

THE MARONITES' PROGRESS AND PERSECUTION

The sultanate of Abdulhamit II was relatively a quiet time for the Maronites. The mountain chieftains were generally little troubled by conflicts between the *mutesharrif* and the Maronite bishops, and the community's stability increased with Patriarch Bulus Massad's thirty-six-year tenure of office, from 1854 until 1890. His successor, Yuhanna Hadj, ruled for nine years. After him, Butrus Iliyas Hoyek was chosen in January 1899; like Massad he also had an extraordinarily long term of office, for he died only in 1931.

The monasteries of the Maronites flourished as a result of the security provided by the government of the *mutesharrifs*. At the monastery of St Maron of Annaya a monk named Sharbel Makhlouf so devoted himself to prayer and works of charity that he was canonized by Pope Paul VI in October 1977, the first Maronite to be so honoured by the Roman church.

All this time interest in education increased among the Maronites. St Joseph's College was raised to the status of a pontifical university in 1883. It had a school of theology which provided Maronite and other Catholic churches of the East with opportunities never before available. Meanwhile, in 1891, in Rome, the Maronite College was refounded for those students who wanted to pursue their studies abroad.[12]

This was also the time when Lebanese Maronites assumed a leading role in the Arab nationalist movement. Thanks to their education, they were able to publish numerous tracts urging the Arabs to struggle against what was considered to be the oppression of Ottoman rule.

This florescence of the Maronite church with its nearly half a million members was withered by the circumstances of the First World War. Patriarch Butrus Iliyas found himself helpless to aid his people as Turkish armies razed their homes and villages were destroyed. Close to one hundred thousand Maronites died in the war – a number that would have been even higher had it not been for the protection of General Allenby's army, which arrived in Lebanon in September 1918 to fend off further attacks.[13]

It is understandable, given the events of the past century and a half, how the Maronites have become one of Christendom's most aggressive groups. Confronted by so many bloodbaths, the Maronite identity had to be accentuated – the rifle and the cross went hand in hand.

20

The Catholic Melkites

THE PATRIARCHATE OF MAXIMOS MAZLOUM

In the early nineteenth century the major problem facing the Catholic Melkite church was to find a way of dealing with the factions created by the activities of Germanos Adam. Patriarch Agapios II believed that a first, sure step would be better education for the clergy. A synodal decision of 1811 established a seminary approximately fifteen miles south of Beirut at 'Ayn Traz where a secular clergy might be formed. All parties in the church agreed that the seminary constituted a useful step, but the appointment of its rector renewed old conflicts, for Patriarch Agapios selected Bishop Maximos Mazloum for the post.

Maximos Mazloum had been one of the protégés of Germanos Adam, who had ordained him, associated him with his family of clerics in Aleppo, and brought him as his personal secretary to the synod of Karkafeh where Germanos won his most important victory. When Germanos died in 1809, a majority on the Melkite episcopal synod chose Maximos Mazloum to succeed him, but the minority opposed to Germanos and led by Ignatios Sarruf of Beirut immediately challenged the election and appealed to Rome over the head of the patriarch. Their remonstrance won over a majority of the Catholic Melkites in Aleppo so that Maximos was unable to take possession of his see.[1]

The contest over Maximos' election occurred while Rome was in turmoil and the pope a prisoner of Napoleon. The acting prefect of the Congregation for the Propagation of the Faith decided against Maximos, ruled that his appointment was invalid and suspended him from all episcopal functions. The Melkite synod was seriously disturbed by this high-handed decision, and Patriarch Agapios sent word that no administrator approved by Rome for Aleppo would receive synodal recognition. Although Maximos was still withheld from installation in Aleppo, his appointment to 'Ayn Traz was the clearest statement of confidence the synod majority could give him.[2]

Hardly had the new seminary opened when Agapios, Maximos' great friend, died early in 1812; and the election which followed brought Ignatios Sarruf, leader of the opposition, to office. Under Ignatios the church knew no peace and one party continued to battle against the other, the unrest culminating in Patriarch Ignatios' assassination on 6 November 1812. The synod delayed choosing a new patriarch until passions had calmed, and it was almost a year before the bishops met to elect the brother of the deceased Agapios II. He became Athanasios V Matar, and again Maximos Mazloum had a friend in the patriarchate, but Athanasios held office for only a year.

Weary of the controversy surrounding him, Maximos left for Rome to submit his resignation: recognizing that his association with Germanos Adam would be neither forgiven nor forgotten, he intended to stay in Italy. When Pope Pius VII issued a decree in 1816 condemning all of Adam's works, especially his catechism, it was obvious that Roman sentiment was not on Maximos' side. Shortly thereafter the seminary of 'Ayn Traz closed.[3]

While Maximos spent his days in exile, persecution against all Catholics broke out in Aleppo, a carry-over of the attack on Armenian Catholics in Istanbul. Catholic Melkites and Armenians were arrested, imprisoned or forced into exile. On 16 April 1818 nine prominent Melkite Catholics in Aleppo were martyred for their faith. Sultan Mahmut II ruled that Catholic Melkite clergy could not validly baptize, marry or witness wills. The Melkites of Damascus came under severe pressure to return to the Orthodox community.[4]

In the midst of these difficulties Pius VII decided to reconstitute the Latin see of Aleppo; in January 1818 he named the Italian Lazarist Luigi Gandolfi to the bishopric and appointed him apostolic vicar of Syria, Egypt and Arabia. His position enabled Rome to feel more confident in its view of the Near Eastern situation; in earlier years the Congregation for the Propagation of the Faith had frequently mistrusted information received when it came solely from Eastern Catholics. Henceforth, after Gandolfi, the Latin bishop of Aleppo served Rome as a listening post in the East.[5]

While the patriarchate was held by Ignatios V Kattan, successor to Athanasios, a dispute broke out at the Catholic Melkite monastery of Shuwair. Just as with the Maronite Antonines, the values prized by monks from Aleppo and other Near Eastern cities differed from those esteemed by religious from rustic homes who believed asceticism to be the most important part of monastic discipline. As with the Maronites, it was finally agreed that there should be two congregations: the Aleppan branch, *al-Halibiyin*, and the rural branch, *al-Baladiyin*.

By the time of the Egyptian invasion of Syria, persecution had reduced the Catholic Melkite population to only fifty thousand people centred in Damascus, Aleppo, Tyre and Beirut. The Aleppan community had lost over half its number in a single decade and things were no different in Damascus, where the Catholic Melkites had not a single church left.

In 1830, on the positive side, because of the creation of the *Katolik millet* the Melkites were no longer subject to the Orthodox hierarchy and were freed from paying taxes to support a church that considered them heretics. Even better days were ahead thanks to the tolerance of Ibrahim Paşa, happy to favour a group with local leadership over the Orthodox Melkites who looked ultimately to Istanbul. Several Melkites joined Ibrahim Paşa's bureaucracy and more were employed as tax collectors.[6]

Another development which aided the Catholic cause for all Syrian Christians, especially Melkites, resulted from the Jesuits' return to the Near East in 1831. Eastern Catholic bishops had hoped they would come sooner, but it was not until then that the Society felt strong enough to resume its work in the Orient. Pope Gregory XVI was responsible for commissioning two priests and a brother to go to 'Ayn Traz and reopen the Melkite seminary, and he sent Maximos Mazloum with them. Maximos had won support in Rome during his exile because of his numerous activities on behalf of his countrymen; he even counted the pope among his acquaintances. Yet before leaving for home, Maximos was required to make a long profession of faith to disarm critics who believed he still espoused the opinions of Germanos Adam.

At 'Ayn Traz the Jesuits and Maximos set about preparing students for the Melkite priesthood, but Maximos' personality was such that the quiet life of the scholar–teacher could not suit him for long. He tried, but failed, to obtain an appointment to the staff of Patriarch Ignatios and for the time being had to be content with his work at the seminary.

On 9 February 1833 Ignatios died. An electoral synod of the eight Catholic Melkite bishops met at the monastery of St George

Algarb under the eye of a Roman legate who announced before the balloting that *Propaganda* had ruled that Maximos Mazloum could not be a candidate and that, if elected, he would not receive Roman confirmation. Despite, or perhaps because of this warning, the synod on 4 April elected Maximos patriarch. The disgruntled Latin delegate left the monastery to report to Rome.[7]

Maximos lost no time in consolidating his own position; he rode to Dair el-Kamar, residence of Emir Bashir Shehab, to announce his election and seek confirmation, and the emir, impressed, was happy to oblige. He then began a tour of northern Syria, even entering Damascus, residence of the Orthodox Melkite patriarch. It was the first time anyone there had seen a Catholic Melkite patriarch, and the population was struck by his confidence. While he awaited Rome's response to his election, Maximos set about reforming his church. In 1835, in cooperation with two other bishops, he drew up a constitution for the Catholic Melkites and called a synod to meet at 'Ayn Traz to ratify it. Here twenty-nine canons designed to facilitate church administration and improve ministry were agreed upon. Roman officials were upset when they learned of the synod, since Maximos had not yet been confirmed nor been given a pallium.[8] Gregory XVI let his sentiments be known in an encyclical, *Melchitarum catholicorum synodus*, which surveyed once again the acts of the synod of Karkafeh. It was clear that Maximos' independence, more than the long-dead ideas of Germanos Adam, was the target of the encyclical. Only in 1836 and then with reluctance did Gregory XVI finally bestow the pallium. Though he trusted Maximos in Italy, Gregory was none too sure that in the distant East the new patriarch would properly represent Roman prerogatives. He was probably right, but to delay confirmation any longer would have too much strained relations between Rome and the Catholic Melkites.[9]

The Orthodox Melkites felt threatened by Maximos' activity and they struck back in May 1837 by obtaining a *firman* which forbade Catholic Melkite clergy to administer the sacraments to the Orthodox, and further stipulated that Catholic Melkite clerics had to change their headdress so that their costume would not resemble that of the Orthodox. They were ordered to wear 'Frankish' headgear or a square *kalemavkion*, rather than the round traditional stove-pipe hat of Oriental clergy, for in the Ottoman world, what one wore on one's head was a matter of considerable significance. Maximos rose to the occasion and a 'battle of the hats' commenced which carried on for several months. Finally, Istanbul decided that the Catholic Melkite *kalemavkion* was to be six-sided and that the priests's outer garment, the *kumbaz*, was to be violet or blue coloured.

Maximos turned this affair to his own advantage, arguing that if the Melkites were to be distinguished by their dress from all other Eastern Christians, they should also be distinguished by having their own *millet*, and by being no longer subject to the Armenian Catholic patriarch. The sultan accepted this logic, and on 31 October 1837 extended civil guarantees to all Catholic Melkites, though stopping short of creating a separate *millet*. Maximos' success spread its influence to Rome, which now became more sympathetic – so much so, in fact, that in 1838 he was allowed, in a personal grant, to add Alexandria and Jerusalem to his title, thus becoming 'Patriarch of Antioch, Alexandria, Jerusalem, and of all the East'. It was little more than a gesture, but its significance lay in its demonstration that Rome now recognized Maximos as the most energetic of the Eastern Catholic prelates.[10]

And indeed the patriarch's life of journeying made a sharp contrast to the usual secluded monastic life of Eastern Catholic patriarchs. Wherever he went, especially in Egypt, he encouraged the building of churches, being seriously concerned that Melkites should not have to attend Latin churches and so lose their traditions. The patriarch also named a vicar for Jerusalem, Meletios Fendeh, in one more move meant to expand the Catholic Melkite world. Once, in Cairo, he even accepted the challenge of a *shaykh* in the Al-Azhar to a debate with him on the question of the superiority of Islam or Christianity. When war broke out between Egypt and the Ottoman sultan in 1839 and the Maronites and Druzes were tempted to revolt against Ibrahim Paşa, Maximos was in Egypt. His situation was delicate since part of his community favoured the Turks and to make a statement favouring either party would have been risky; Maximos diplomatically remained neutral and booked passage on a ship for Rome. Upon his return Maximos, taking advantage of the *Hatti şerif* guarantees, moved his residence to Damascus, thus sharing the same patriarchal city with the Orthodox patriarch of Antioch. He continued to travel extensively, visiting Melkite churches throughout the Near East, meeting civil and religious officials and seeking ways to enlarge activity in his community.

In the five-year period from 1843 to 1848 Maximos accomplished the complete independence of his church. First recognized as a vicar of the Armenian Catholic patriarch, in 1846 he was named head of his own *millet*, and by a *berat* of 7 January 1848 became chief of the Catholic Melkite church, completely independent of any other ecclesiastical community in the Ottoman empire.[11]

One of his projects was to increase the number of Catholic Melkite bishops well beyond what the actual number of Melkites warranted. At mid-century, for possibly seventy thousand Melkites, there were thirteen bishops, many of them chosen from his own staff of secular priests rather than from among the monks, a matter causing friction between him and the more traditional church members. With some of these bishops, he later had difficulties: Makarios Samman of Diyarbakir went over to the Orthodox, and Athanasios Tutungi, rector of the 'Ayn Traz seminary and bishop of Tripoli, had a prolonged quarrel with him, which was fought in Rome as well as in the Orient. Maximos appointed a patriarchal vicar to Alexandria in addition to the one in Jerusalem and, to the chagrin of Catholics in Istanbul, also to the Ottoman capital, where he opened a church. He even tried to intervene in the administration of the monastic communities of the Holy Saviour and St John the Baptist at Shuwair, but not always with success.

In May 1849, Maximos summoned a synod to meet at the new patriarchal residence and church of the Catholic Melkites in Jerusalem. Here he presented the bishops with a list of canons which reflected his view of the church. Three bishops, led by Agapios Ri'ashi, bishop of Beirut, protested, accusing him of making too many innovations. Nevertheless, the majority agreed to his proposals and a copy of the acts was sent, for information only, to the Congregation for the Propagation of the Faith. Officials there took little time in deciding that they could never approve the synod's work, but rather than risk a quarrel, they withheld their decision until after the patriarch's death.[12]

The last few years of Maximos' life were marked by controversies with members of his church and with the authorities in Rome. These affairs left many people embittered, but all were ready to recognize, after his death in Cairo on 11 August 1855, that he had accomplished much for the Catholic Melkites. Maximos' was a strong personality and his desire to supervise all the church's affairs himself dismayed many churchmen. Yet without doubt his activities assured the civil and religious position of his church and made him the most outstanding Eastern Catholic prelate of the nineteenth century.

THE MELKITES SEEK AN IDENTITY

Before the election of a successor, in April 1856 the synod of Catholic Melkite bishops agreed to impose limits on patriarchal authority and adopted canons to prevent the rise of another Maximos. They chose Clement Bahouth, a monk of the Holy Saviour monastery and bishop of Acre, to replace him.

Clement had neither the strong personality nor the vision of his predecessor, so it was unfortunate that he was persuaded to issue a decree in January 1857 that the Melkite church calendar should conform to the Gregorian. He took this action on the advice of Archbishop Brunoni of Istanbul, without consulting other Melkite bishops, and so at once stirred up a hornet's nest. There is hardly any item Christians have fought over with greater emotion through the centuries than the calendar.[13]

Church officials in Rome suggested that a Melkite synod should meet under the presidency of Archbishop Brunoni, but Clement's efforts to summon the bishops for the task of calendar reform evoked even more hostility. Four of the thirteen, Agapios of Beirut, Theodosios of Sidon, Meletios of Ba'labakk and Vasileos of Zahlah, resigned rather than be party to the change. Clement was unable to cope with his opposition, so he too resigned, withdrew to the quiet of the Holy Saviour monastery and later went off to Egypt. Pope Pius IX, informed of what had happened, rejected Clement's resignation and ordered him to return to office, and he sent letters to the dissident bishops ordering them to accept the patriarch's authority. Those opposed to Clement wrote to Rome and Istanbul outlining the reasons for their views and urging the sultan to accept Clement's resignation and recognize a synod which might proceed to a new election. Parishes that followed the Julian calendar began to spring up among the Melkites, and when Clement came to Beirut he was forbidden entrance into the cathedral. There was even talk of a return by Catholics to the Orthodox patriarchate of Antioch. Then, in the midst of the controversy, the massacre of Christians in Damascus took place, and the issue of calendar reform became less important than the feeding and care of the survivors.[14]

Worn out by dissension, Patriarch Clement Bahouth submitted his resignation a second time in 1864, and this time, following the advice of Archbishop Valerga, Latin patriarch of Jerusalem, the pope accepted. The Melkite synod then elected Gregorios Yusuf Sayyour, Clement's successor at Acre. Gregorios had studied with the Jesuits in Ghazir and had later attended the Greek College in

Rome. His Latin training guaranteed his acceptance by the Congregation for the Propagation of the Faith.

Gregorios defused the calendar question by allowing each bishop freedom of choice. Like his Maronite counterpart, he was in Rome at the time *Reversurus* was promulgated and could persuade the pope that his church would be thrown into turmoil if its provisions should become law. With his bishops, including the former patriarch Clement, he attended the Vatican Council, and here, as has been seen, he intervened several times in the discussions about primacy and infallibility. Although he absented himself from the final vote on this issue, he sent a letter of acceptance to Rome in February 1871, saying that he would abide by the council decrees.[15]

Just as educational progress for the clergy played a dominant role among the Maronites during the late nineteenth century, so it did among the Catholic Melkites. The seminary of 'Ayn Traz again provided opportunities for clerical training, and the Greek College in Rome allowed exceptional students to earn higher degrees in theology. Still, Patriarch Gregorios Yusuf was not content and in June 1882 he cooperated with the White Fathers – a French religious order whose main mission was to Muslim North Africa – in making the church of St Anne in Jerusalem the site of a Melkite seminary. Despite efforts to preserve the Eastern culture of their students, the White Fathers introduced Western spirituality: celibacy was so encouraged that all of the seminary's alumni accepted it. In 1890 its first graduate was ordained, beginning a succession of educated Melkite clergy which did much to enhance the position of the church.[16]

In the late nineteenth century the Catholic Melkites benefited from an influx of Orthodox converts due to the growing antagonism between the Arab-speaking laity and their Greek hierarchy. It became possible to open new churches in Tripoli, Hims and a number of other towns in the Syrian Orient. When the Eucharistic Congress of 1893 was held in Jerusalem, Patriarch Gregorios was one of its leaders, and enjoyed the prominence given to the Catholic Melkites. In the following year he asked Pope Leo XIII to let him have jurisdiction over all Catholic Melkites throughout the world. The pope, however, granted him jurisdiction only over the members of his church in the Ottoman Empire, then estimated at 135,000 individuals. After leading his community for thirty-three years Gregorios Yusuf died in July 1897, and his successor, Butrus IV Geraygiry, was elected in February 1898 despite the objections of the Ottoman government and many of his own bishops. There was a long delay before his appointment was recognized in Istanbul.

Butrus came to office in the year when, with the ousting of Spyridon, Greek incumbent patriarch of Antioch, and the installation of a Syrian, Meletios Doumani, conflict between Arabs and Greeks in the Orthodox Melkite church reached its climax. Although Meletios did not receive recognition from the Phanar and the other Orthodox patriarchates, recognition was to be only a matter of time. While Butrus had no troubles concerning Arab–Greek hostility in his church, he believed it opportune to draw up new legislation to update church governance. The patriarch submitted proposals for reform which brought mixed reactions from his hierarchy. He left for Rome in 1899 to submit his changes to the Congregation for the Propagation of the Faith, but a rival delegation sent by clergy opposed to his proposals also appeared on the scene. The reforms were still pending at the time of his death in 1902.

At the electoral synod which followed, the metropolitan of Aleppo, Kyrillos Giha, was chosen patriarch unanimously, taking the name of Kyrillos VIII. A suggestion for a new council was introduced at the synod but a decision was postponed. In 1909 Patriarch Kyrillos reluctantly called a synod for Melkite Catholics at 'Ayn Traz to discuss updating the canons of the church. Pope Pius X wanted the synod to be held in Rome, but Melkite sensitivities did not permit that. As had happened before, the canons drafted by the bishops never received approbation, since the legislation was viewed in Rome as being too independent of papal direction.[17] Patriarch Kyrillos left for Egypt during the First World War and died there in 1916. During his absence he had been condemned to death for treason to the Ottoman government. His vicar, Bishop Vasileos Haggiar, was largely successful in saving the Melkites from the massacres which struck the other Syrian churches.

The figure of Maximos Mazloum towers over the Catholic Melkite church of this period. His leadership gained his church respect and admiration; his educational reforms provided the Melkites with the most learned clergy of the Orient. He also bequeathed to his church a sense of independence from the Roman curia, of which the interference in Melkite internal affairs was always resisted. The Catholic Melkites owe him a great debt for setting a pattern which struck a balance between Eastern and Western traditions and separated the essentials from the accidental in both.

21

Syrian Catholics and the Chaldean church

THE GAINING OF INDEPENDENCE

During the sultanate of Mahmut II the Syrian Catholic church
succeeded in winning over several more Jacobite bishops and clergy
to the Roman communion. Then, during the patriarchate of
Ignatius Butrus Jarweh, almost all the Jacobite communities of
Damascus and south Lebanon joined the Syrian Catholics, among
their number the bishops of Diyarbakir, Mosul, Homs and
Damascus. In Mosul, Catholics and Jacobites shared the same
churches but each with their own clergy.

In 1830, when the Catholic Armenians obtained recognition as
a *millet*, the Syrians were included, and so the former civil ties to
the Jacobite clergy were broken. Because of this new freedom,
Patriarch Ignatius Butrus left the monastery of Sharfeh in Lebanon
and moved to Aleppo where he was closer to his people and could
show potential converts that they need no longer fear government
sanctions or threats of reprisal from the Jacobite hierarchy.[1]

By 1830 the Syrians were about twenty per cent of Aleppo's
Catholic population and were the group upon whom foreign missionary influence worked most strongly. One missionary wrote in
1834 that the progress of Eastern Catholics was remarkable, but he
was cautious:

It should not, however, be thought that [Latin] missionaries in Syria
are useless. The weak dispositions which one observes to the obedience
to the Holy See manifests clearly how easily some Syrians can detach
themselves from the Catholic faith; and, if one did not place missionaries among them, there would be fears for their perseverance. . .[2]

His assessment was probably true. Similar sentiments prompted the
Jesuits to abandon the education of Melkite seminarians at 'Ayn
Traz, a rather narrow apostolate, and to concentrate, at Bikfaya, on
a retreat house for the clergy of all the Eastern Catholic churches.

Here, they hoped, clergy already active could be better formed and educated.[3]

When Mahmut died there were perhaps only fifteen thousand Syrian Catholics. The ratio of clergy to laity was very high: in addition to Patriarch Ignatius Butrus Jarweh the Syrians counted five bishops and sixty priests, although they were frequently too poor to have their own church buildings. The opening of a seminary at the monastery of Sharfeh in 1841 gave promise of a better educated clergy and after 1843 liturgical services improved when a Syriac missal was printed in Rome.

The Syrians continued to be included in the Armenian Catholic *millet* until 1845 when, by common consent, an agreement was reached with the Armenians to allow them autonomy. When Ignatius Butrus died, Antun Samhiri, a former Jacobite, succeeded him, having been elected on 30 November 1853 and taking the title Ignatius Antun. At the urging of Benoît Planchet, Latin apostolic delegate in Syria, he summoned a synod to review the condition of the church. At this gathering the church canons were reviewed and some changes made along Western lines; then, in a long overdue move, the number of fast days was reduced.[4]

Ignatius Antun then left for Rome, where the pope personally invested him in his office on 7 April 1854. Since its acts were still under study, no mention of the council was made. The patriarch afterwards went on a tour of France, Belgium and the Netherlands seeking funds for his church; his travels consumed the next two years and the Roman authorities were displeased; they wanted him back in the East. When he did return in 1858, he announced that his church would henceforth use the Gregorian calendar, and the Syrians were too dependent on Rome to argue.[5]

When Ignatius Antun died on 16 June 1864, Rome appointed Bishop Jirjis Shelhot of Aleppo to administer the church until the hierarchy could form an electoral synod, which in fact did not meet until May 1866, with the Latin apostolic pro-delegate presiding. When the Syrian bishops were told that Rome expected the new patriarch to live in Mardin, three potential candidates asked not to be considered, and Philipp 'Arqus, the bishop of Diyarbakir, was elected. Accompanied by two of his bishops, 'Arqus set off for Rome and confirmation in his office.

While in Rome 'Arqus was urged to reduce the number of bishops, which the Congregation for the Propagation of the Faith believed to be excessive. When the patriarch and six of his bishops later attended the Vatican Council they played a passive role, for 'Arqus was a poor leader, and he thought of resigning his office. However, he held on until his death in March 1874, and the more vigorous Jirjis Shelhot succeeded him. Two years later, in 1876, Jirjis formed a new religious congregation, the Brothers of Mar Ephraim. He also successfully directed the integration of several Jacobite prelates and communities into the Syrian Catholic church and improved the church's relations with Sultan Abdulhamit, who decorated him for his services to the Ottoman Empire.[6]

In 1888 Jirjis called a council of the clergy of his church to meet at Sharfeh to consider new canonical legislation. A substantial group of laws was enacted, largely reflecting the influence of Latin missionaries. Clerical celibacy was made mandatory for all Syrian clergy except convert Jacobites. Ignoring the requirements of *Reversurus*, the council provided for a direct election of the patriarch by the hierarchical synod. Rome was to be informed of the choice and a pallium sought from the pope. This council of the Syrian bishops received the approbation of *Propaganda*, since in Leo XIII's days, Congregation officials were less liable than their predecessors to read schism into simple demands for traditional autonomy.[7]

In 1898 Ephrem Rahmani followed Patriarch Cyrillus Benham Benni's four-year term in the patriarchate, after a contest between the rival factions within the church was settled. A man concerned with the education of his clergy, he encouraged ecclesiastical students to study either in Jerusalem, where Benedictines from Subiaco had opened a school, or in Mosul where Dominicans operated a college for Syrians and Chaldeans. Patriarch Ephrem preferred to live at Sharfeh in Lebanon; he later moved to Mardin, the heartland of the Jacobites.

Just before the First World War Syrian Catholics had grown to number one hundred thousand: Patriarch Ephrem had ten metropolitans and bishops in his jurisdiction in the major cities of the Near East. But the war was to devastate the church and cut its numbers by half. Since Syrian Catholics lived in the same general areas as the Armenians, they were caught up in the general upheaval. Thousands died of starvation, including six bishops and the entire congregation of Brothers of Mar Ephrem. The patriarch himself moved from Mardin to the relative safety of Beirut and there the residence of the Syrian Catholic patriarch has been located ever since.

THE CHALDEAN CHURCH IN CONFLICT

The administration of the Chaldean church was a serious problem at the beginning of the nineteenth century. At Mardin, Augustinus Hindi ruled the church as Yusuf V in the line of the Diyarbakir hierarchy, while Yuhanna Iliyas XIII, formerly Yuhanna Hormizd, lived in the episcopal residence of Mosul. Both claimed to represent the true line of Catholic Chaldean catholicoi, but in fact that line was now represented by Shim'un XVII, who lived in the remote mountain area of Kudshannis, and had lapsed into the traditional theology of the Church of the East, thus cutting himself off from communion with Rome. Partisans of the three catholicoi were unwilling to make compromises.

Rome did not recognize Yuhanna Hormizd as catholicos because the Congregation for the Propagation of the Faith considered his claims to office insufficient. Moreover, a large faction within his jurisdiction resisted his authority and even had him imprisoned for a while; this group directed numerous complaints to Rome over his decisions. Far removed from the scene and unable to judge the validity of these complaints, the Congregation thought it prudent to suspend him from episcopal functions on 26 June 1818. It was not until eight years later, and upon the recommendation of the Latin bishop of Babylon, that Yuhanna was restored to office.[8]

While Yuhanna's episcopate remained under a cloud, Jibra'il Denbo, a Chaldean from Mardin considerably influenced by the Franciscans, sought to form a new religious order. In March 1808, having now sufficient followers, he inaugurated the congregation of St Hormizdas by getting the monks of Rabban Hormizd to accept his leadership. This monastery had enjoyed a great deal of prestige, since for centuries it had been the residence of the Iliyas line of patriarchs; however, Denbo encountered great difficulty in reforming the traditional life of the monks and he went to Rome for guidance. There he laid part of the blame for his troubles on unnecessary interference by Yuhanna Hormizd, whom he considered unworthy to be a bishop. In fact, many of Yuhanna's troubles in Rome came from the reports given there by Jibra'il Denbo. When Yusuf V died in 1828, Denbo feared that Rome might relent from its opposition to Yuhanna Hormizd and he successfully headed off a move to recognize his opponent. *Propaganda* temporarily avoided the issue by delaying the appointment of a successor to Yusuf V. Actually Rome did not care much for either party but under the circumstances had to tolerate both. A compromise was finally hit on to placate both Denbo and Yuhanna: Denbo's monastic constitution for Rabban Hormizd would be approved and Yuhanna Hormizd would be recognized as Chaldean catholicos with residence in Mosul. In the process, the incumbent bishop of Mosul, Yusuf Audo, who belonged to the hierarchy of Diyarbakir, was transferred to Al-'Amadiyah, but conflict soon broke out which necessitated the sending of two apostolic visitors to attempt a reconciliation. Meanwhile, Jibra'il Denbo was removed from the scene: on a journey outside his monastery in May 1832 he and two companions were cut down by Kurdish raiders.[9]

For the next seven years, while Yuhanna Hormizd ruled the Chaldean church the Roman authorities kept close watch on him by establishing a Latin apostolic vicar to Mosul on a permanent basis. Just before his death Patriarch Yuhanna resigned his office to a 'guardian of the throne', Jirjis Butrus, bishop of Jezireh. The patriarch was seeking thus to break the tradition that a nephew of the patriarchal family should succeed, for he had an episcopal nephew – whom he considered of little promise – waiting in the wings. The catholicos died on 16 August 1838, and the synod, not without controversy, picked the bishop of Salamas, Niqula Zaya, as his successor. He was confirmed by Rome in April 1840, but insisted on making his residence in his see city in Persia.[10]

In 1820 an officer of the British East India Company, James Rich, an amateur archaeologist digging about the area of Baghdad, 'discovered' the Church of the East. Amazed, he announced to the world that he had discovered Assyrian Christians, a name thereafter, unfortunately, adopted by Europeans for the Christians of the Church of the East, and, even more regrettably, by members of the community themselves. Thus, to the Catholic misnomer 'Chaldean' was added the equally confusing title of 'Assyrian'. British and American missionaries were soon on the scene, distributing bibles and attempting to explain the catechism to their Christian auditors. One positive result of the Protestant presence among them was the calling of public attention to the plight of Christians who were often mercilessly exploited by the Kurds. The American Presbyterian Eli Smith, journeying throughout the Near East, met a Chaldean bishop at Khosrowa; he described him as 'an old man with a long Kurdish cape and a green turban and a ragged sheepskin pelisse'. Although he had been educated in Rome and knew something of the West his condition was now so poor that he could

not even entertain his visitor. His church was hot, dark, and hung
with shawls and Western pictures. Sheepskins and bits of cloth
covered the floor. Smith was distressed that the services were so
hurried and the bare-footed worshippers so casual. Both European
Catholics and American Protestants had little experience in accepting the values of traditional religion in the Near East.[11]

Neither the Chaldean Catholic church nor the Church of the
East, situated on the fringe of the Ottomans' Eastern border, ever
enjoyed peace for long. Both were too far from Istanbul to be given
even a minimum of protection against the rapacity of local governors
and the lawlessness of the Kurdish tribes. Only the presence of
Ottoman garrisons and their own riflemen ensured the Christians'
existence; when these were taken away, the Chaldeans and the
Christians of the East were left defenceless. In 1843 a Kurdish
leader, Beder Khan, bargained with the Porte to be allowed to
govern Kurdistan in return for a large sum of money paid to
Istanbul. As soon as the bargain was struck, the Khan allowed his
army to collect taxes from the Christian villages, as much as could
be obtained, and to destroy those that refused to pay. As a result,
ten thousand Christians were killed. The altars of the monastery at
Rabban Hormizd were overturned, its ikons defaced, and the monks'
cells used as stabling for the Kurds' horses. In the town of Al-Qosh
only a single church was left standing. Finally Istanbul took notice
of the atrocities and sent an army to rout Beder Khan, while in
France, as soon as the plight of the Christians became known, aid
was sent to be dispensed by Bishop Yusuf Audo.[12]

Catholicos Niqula postponed requesting a *berat* from the sultan
until 1844 when he left for Istanbul to meet civil and religious
leaders and discuss with them the position of the Chaldean church.
The Armenian Archbishop Boghos Marouchian promised to represent the church before the Ottoman government and to add to
his staff a Chaldean priest who would act as agent of the catholicos.
On his return to northern Iraq, Catholicos Niqula grew weary of his
responsibilities, resigned his office and returned to Persia, while the
Chaldean synod selected the most learned of their bishops, Yusuf
Audo, to serve in his place. Audo was confirmed by the pope on
11 September 1848 and a pallium was dispatched to him. In that
same month the Congregation for the Propagation of the Faith
raised the Latin see of Baghdad to an archbishopric, with a
suffragan in Persia at Isfahan.[13]

THE CATHOLICATE OF YUSUF AUDO

Catholicos Yusuf ruled a church of approximately thirty thousand people and eight bishops distributed on both sides of the Ottoman–Persian border. In a letter to a French missionary society written in 1853 he lamented the poverty of his church: 'We are surrounded by ruins on all sides.' Few of his people could read, he had no printed service books, and the majority of his clergy had received only the barest minimum of theological training: 'You ask me about the knowledge of our clergy; without books and seminaries what do you suppose?'[14]

In an attempt to improve church administration, Yusuf, in collaboration with the Jesuit Benoît Planchet, planned a council for Rabban Hormizd in 1853. Planchet, a veteran of the Near Eastern missions, had only recently been named by *Propaganda* as apostolic pro-delegate for Mesopotamia. He was the guiding spirit of the council's reforms.

The synod of eight bishops began deliberations on 12 June, using the canons of the Maronite council of al-Luwayzah as a model. The Latinizing of the Chaldean church was guaranteed. Questions concerning reserved sins and indulgences, for example, were written into the *acts*, although such matters were completely foreign to the Chaldeans. Baptism by immersion, a tradition which extended back to the foundation of the church, was prohibited in favour of the Latin practice of infusion. At the conclusion of its work, the council had produced twenty-two chapters of canons, and these were duly forwarded to Rome where a Franciscan *consultor* scrutinized them and decided that the few remaining glimmers of Chaldean autonomy were too great to admit of Roman confirmation. To Planchet's embarrassment the conciliar acts were never approved. While the council was in progress the Jesuit president had been named bishop and given the full title of apostolic delegate. He graciously requested Yusuf Audo to be his consecrator.[15]

Despite the church's problems – perhaps because of them – Catholicos Yusuf embarked, in the next few years, on an ambitious effort to have the Syro-Malabar church of India recognize his authority. He consecrated a bishop, Tuma Rokos, expressly for the task of journeying to India to organize the church there. Planchet recognized that Audo's ambition was reaching too far, but he set no restrictions in the way of the catholicos. In September 1859, while on his way to Rome, Planchet's caravan was attacked by

Kurds between Urfa and Diyarbakir. He attempted to escape but rode his horse into a canyon which had no exit. There he died, first hit by a bullet and then struck by a sword, and the Chaldean church had tragically lost one of the few Latins who understood its situation.[16]

The prefect of the Congregation for the Propagation of the Faith then appointed the Dominican Henri Amanton to Planchet's post in Mosul. Amanton had been told to stop the catholicos' Indian adventure, so he forbade Rokos to leave for Malabar. When the bishop left in spite of the prohibition, Amanton censured him along with Yusuf and the rest of the hierarchy. Catholicos Yusuf wrote two long encyclicals explaining his position and then left for Rome to present his case in person. He received a cool reception from *Propaganda* and from Pius IX, the latter reiterating his view that the Chaldean church should limit itself to Mesopotamia. The catholicos gave in, returned to Mosul and ordered Rokos home. Rokos, however, had warmed to his task and refused to leave India, and was, therefore, excommunicated. The whole controversy over the exact boundaries of the Chaldean patriarchate clouded the fortunes of the Chaldean church in India.[17]

The history of the Chaldeans was marked by turbulence during the middle part of the nineteenth century. In the Mosul area, Dominican missionaries often clashed with Chaldean clergy over matters coloured by the cultural differences of the personalities involved. Rome was generally apt to agree with the Western missionaries – a fact not lost on the Chaldeans. Eventually, in 1864, a newly consecrated Chaldean bishop deliberately omitted mention of the councils of Florence and Trent from his profession of faith, thus reflecting a spirit of independence which certainly did not sit well with Roman authorities.

In 1867 Jirjis Butrus, Chaldean bishop of Diyarbakir, died in Rome. The Congregation for the Propagation of the Faith not only claimed title to his benefices, but also told Catholicos Yusuf Audo to submit three names to Rome so that a new incumbent might be selected. The Roman authorities also wanted *Reversurus* to apply to the Chaldeans, but waited until 21 August 1869 to promulgate *Cum ecclesiastica disciplina*, which extended similar legislation to them. After some delay, Yusuf, remarkably restrained in his response, dutifully forwarded a list of seven possible candidates to Rome for the vacant dioceses of Diyarbakir and Mardin. From this number, the Congregation for the Propagation of the Faith made two choices, but by then Yusuf had had a change of heart and refused to invest them.[18]

The Chaldean delegation to the Vatican Council included Yusuf and seven bishops. At the Council Yusuf outspokenly criticized Pius IX's ambition to be declared primate and infallible head of the universal church. It was his speech on the subject which so angered the pope that Yusuf was actually given the choice of abdication or silence.

After leaving Rome before the vote on the constitution concerning papal authority, Yusuf went to Istanbul, where he visited Sultan Abdulaziz. He assured the Ottoman ruler that the Chaldean church would not accept any changes which lessened either its autonomy or its bonds to the Ottoman state. He also talked with the Armenian dissenters opposed to Patriarch Hassoun. Once home in his native country, he mulled over his position for many months, and finally, on 28 July 1872, he set out his acceptance of the conciliar decrees in a letter to Pius IX, the last of the Eastern Catholic leaders to do so. He really had no choice. Pius responded with a letter of congratulations, reminding the catholicos that nothing had really changed in the relations between Rome and the Chaldeans, and arguing that without strong church leadership schism and heresy flourished, citing the current impasse with the Armenian Catholic dissenters as an example.[19]

In the late spring of 1874, contrary to the stipulations of *Cum ecclesiastica disciplina*, Yusuf consecrated four new bishops without consulting Rome. The Dominicans in Mosul were quick to report what had happened. The Latin apostolic delegate sent him a stern reprimand and charged him with more interference in the church of Malabar, by sending troublesome clerics to assume authority there where they had no legitimate rights.

Early in 1875 the catholicos wrote to Rome defending his actions. He claimed he was the victim of slander by the Mosul Dominicans,

who never cease attacking my faith by saying that I am a rebel, schismatic, etc., in such a way that these outrages have provoked the anger of the people and have stirred up its national zeal and patriotism. I suffer all this in patience, out of respect for the Holy See, since I have done nothing that can give occasion for the least suspicion concerning the orthodoxy of my Catholic faith and my moral teaching. I have done no more than simply exercise my ordinary patriarchal power.

The consecration of the new bishops had been carried out with the

full support of his synod, clergy and people, following the traditions
of the church. As for Malabar, Yusuf claimed that the Roman popes
had always considered the limits of the catholicate of the East to
extend to China, Malabar and the Indies. Sending clergy to organize
the church in India was, therefore, in no way an innovation, but
simply a restoration of the authority of the catholicos.[20]

In reply Pius IX said Yusuf's letter had filled him 'with much
sorrow and grief'. Obviously, the pope lamented, Yusuf had lost
reverence for the Holy See and had forgotten his conversation with
the pope in Rome, since he was now giving support to a dissident
bishop in India. Several months later, on 1 March 1877, Yusuf
backed down: he sent his acceptance of the pope's orders to Rome,
and the Chaldean mission to Malabar was recalled; the Congregation for the Propagation of the Faith, then, in a generous gesture
meant to consolidate reconciliation, allowed him to send only one
name to Rome for each of the four vacant Chaldean bishoprics.
Yusuf died on 14 March 1878.[21]

A TIME OF GROWTH FOLLOWED BY DISASTER

On 28 February 1879 the electoral synod chose Iliyas Butrus Andly-
onan, bishop of Jezireh, as its next patriarch. Iliyas was a native of
Mosul who had studied at the Urban College. During his tenure he
was especially concerned to support the Dominican seminary at
Mosul which had been set up to train priests both for his church and
for the Syrian Catholics. He was also instrumental in publishing
Chaldean liturgical books and in establishing schools in the major
population centres. He died in June 1894, to be succeeded by his
vicar, 'Abd-Ishu' Kayyath, another Urban College alumnus. In
November 1899 Maniuel II Tuma was chosen patriarch. Rome
gave him the interesting title 'apostolic delegate of the Nestorians'
on 3 July 1902.[22]

During this period converts from the Church of the East, including two bishops with many of their clergy and people, continued
to pass over into Catholicism. A new women's religious order of
Chaldeans, the Congregation of Rabban Hormizd, was begun in
1908 to join a community previously sponsored by the Dominicans.

Before the First World War the Chaldean Catholics numbered
one hundred thousand people served by ten bishops: seven in the
Ottoman empire and three in Persia. At the end of the war
Catholicos Maniuel II Tuma could count only forty thousand

people and half of his bishops and clergy. The Chaldeans had become victims of the Turks as a result of their identification with the Church of the East, which was led into the war by Catholicos Benyamin Shim'un XIX Hanayeshu. At first Benyamin successfully fought the Kurds and Turks and believed a Russian victory was imminent. When the October revolution of Vladimir Ilyich Lenin and the Bolsheviks left his people without an ally, he and his army held on until he was murdered by conspirators. His people, left to their own devices, eventually settled in Iraq, Persia, and the United States. The huge losses suffered by the Church of the East left the Chaldeans as the only Eastern Catholic church numerically stronger than its Orthodox or Eastern Christian counterpart. Catholicos Maniuel Tuma successfully rebuilt his church in Iraq after the war and lived to be ninety-seven years of age.[23]

If for no other reason than their survival against such heavy odds, the Chaldean Christians are remarkable. They never enjoyed the same French concern for their interests in Istanbul, and were left to their own devices time after time. The fact that the sultans recognized them as a loyal community was without doubt a major factor in their continual efforts to find security, but many times the Turkish army arrived 'too little and too late'. For the Chaldeans, existence had to depend on themselves, and God.

22

The Catholics of the Holy Land and Egypt

THE HOLY SEPULCHRE CONTESTED

In 1808 a great fire once again struck the Church of the Holy Sepulchre, destroying the dome over the rotunda. Afterwards a bitter controversy arose over the question of which church should have the 'right' to make repairs. Since Catholic influence was in decline in Istanbul at this time, Mahmut II issued a *firman* in favour of the Orthodox, whose architect, during the process of restoration, demolished the Latin Chapel of the Angels and many of the tombs of the Latin Kings of Jerusalem.[1]

In 1829 the Armenians petitioned the sultan for access to the Holy Sepulchre and to the Church of the Nativity. The Porte agreed, and at the expense of the Franciscans the Armenians were allotted space and permitted to hold services. A Latin missionary, writing in 1831, commented that the Franciscan Custodian had spent the last ten years in Istanbul attempting to ward off attacks upon Latin holdings in Palestinian churches. The Turks stabled their horses on the roof above the Franciscan residence. He complained that the Franciscan dormitory was hot and stuffy in the summer and freezing in the winter, while along with the cold came floods. In despair he concluded, 'If the French government does not take effective measures, I think it will be impossible for the Latins to hold on to the possessions they still have.'[2]

The occupation of Palestine by Ibrahim Paşa's Egyptians in 1832 proved more helpful to the Franciscans than anything France was able to do. Ibrahim's tolerance allowed Christians greater freedom than any previous regime had permitted, and the tolls formerly required of pilgrims to the Holy Land were removed. This quiet enjoyment of new status was interrupted in 1834 by an earthquake which caused extensive damage to the Christian shrines and gave rise to the usual bickering over repairs. This time the French were in a stronger position in Istanbul, so the Franciscans were allowed to repair the Church of the Ascension on the Mount of Olives. But the Greek Orthodox succeeded in rebuffing both Latin and Armenian claims to work on the Holy Sepulchre and the Church of the Nativity and so enhanced their position in these churches.

Throughout the 1840s it would hardly have been Easter in the Holy Land if there was no fighting between Latins and the Greeks in Jerusalem and Bethlehem. The worst attack came in 1846, when Greek monks outwitted the Turkish guards and poured through the Holy Sepulchre church windows to attack the Franciscans. The following year in Bethlehem the silver aureole with its Latin inscription which surrounded the birthplace of Jesus mysteriously disappeared. The Franciscans had no doubt it had been pried off its marble slab by Greek clerics.[3]

ESTABLISHMENT OF THE LATIN PATRIARCHATE OF JERUSALEM

For different reasons both Pope Pius IX and Sultan Abdulmecid wanted to strengthen the position of the Latin church in the Holy Land. While the pope's motives were simple and obvious, those of the sultan were more complex. He feared that the appearance in 1843 of a Russian prelate in the Holy Land, followed shortly afterward by the arrival of an Anglican bishop, presented a potential threat to stability in Jerusalem: Abdulmecid wanted Latin influence, which he deemed less dangerous, to counteract it. Negotiations in Istanbul between representatives of Rome and the Porte led to the decision to establish a Latin patriarch in the Holy City. Naturally the Orthodox were displeased, but so too were the Franciscans, who were unsure how the appointment would affect them. Additionally, the French ambassador in Istanbul thought the presence of such a high-ranking Latin prelate in Jerusalem would make the protection of the French king superfluous. At the time of the announcement there were about four thousand Latin Catholics living permanently in Jerusalem while another hundred Western pilgrims were apt to be in the city at any given time.

To this church, small in numbers but large in prestige, Pius IX named Giuseppe Valerga on 28 July 1847, 'for the good of souls and the glory of the see of Jerusalem'. Valerga had been in the Near East for several years and Rome considered him an expert on the situation there. He was consecrated bishop by the pope himself in October.[4]

In Jerusalem Valerga joined the Franciscan custodian in negotiations which extended over the next several years. He was an active missionary for Latin rights in the Holy Places and for establishing schools. In 1849 he left for Europe to persuade the Catholic princes to put pressure upon the Ottoman government to restore Catholics to their former position in the Holy Sepulchre, the Church of the Nativity and Gethsemane. They had lost precedence to the Greeks in 1755, but the Franciscans had records which showed every inch of space that had once belonged in Latin hands. Valerga found a willing listener in Louis Napoleon, who was looking for a way to cement relations with French Catholics. Here was an issue ready made, and the French president sent Eugène Boré to Jerusalem to report on the situation. On the basis of Valerga's and Boré's information, the French ambassador in Istanbul, jointly with his colleagues from Austria, Belgium, Spain and Sardinia, submitted a request to the sultan's government urging the restoration of the lost Holy Places to Latin control. The government was warned by the Russians, on the other hand, that any tampering with the present order would be taken badly by the Tsar's government.

On 9 February 1852 the Ottoman government announced a revision of the *Status Quo* document then in force in Palestine. These amendments provided that henceforth the government would make all church repairs in the Holy Sepulchre; that the Franciscans might return to Gethsemane and share the church with the Greeks and Armenians, but would have no private chapel; and that the aureole of Bethlehem with its Latin inscription should be replaced. An Ottoman official, Afifi Bey, was dispatched to Palestine to oversee implementation of the order.

The Russians were so incensed over the affair that Tsar Nicholas I ordered the occupation of the Principalities of Moldavia and Wallachia in an effort to pressure the Turks into rescinding the project. The British and French, always suspicious of Russian moves in the Balkans, came to the support of the Turks, and the Crimean War began. The Paris peace conference of 1856, after the war, preserved the revisions of the *Status Quo*, and awarded the church of St Catherine in Bethlehem, adjacent to the Church of the Nativity, to the Franciscans. The *Hatti humayun*, which gave legal recognition to equal rights for Christians, added to the confidence among Catholics in the Holy Land, and the next few years saw rapid social and economic progress among the Latin population.[5]

The long patriarchate of Giuseppe Valerga ended with his death in 1872. By that time he had firmly established an activist role for his patriarchate. In the Holy Land the number of Catholics had reached seven thousand five hundred people, served by twelve new parishes, some of which were located in rural areas. A number of new religious orders had come to Palestine, increasing the number of schools and dispensaries. Valerga had also overseen the construction of a cathedral in Jerusalem for the patriarchate. His successor, Vincenzo Bracco, was installed in this church and ruled it for the next sixteen years.

THE EUCHARISTIC CONGRESS

Interest in Palestine was renewed towards the end of the century as the Great Powers sought to enhance their positions in this strategic part of the Near East. The French strove to ensure their position via endowments and grants to the Latin Catholics, while the St Petersburg government generously funded the Russian church in Jerusalem. In 1882 the Holy Land Society was formed to funnel money to the local Orthodox churches throughout Syria and Palestine and to provide scholarships for Arab Christians who wanted to study in Russia. The British, too, were interested in enhancing the Anglican archbishopric of Jerusalem and in keeping Palestine under surveillance, since it was so close to the Suez Canal. The Germans also entered the scene. In 1898 Kaiser Wilhelm II personally visited the Holy City and in his wake left both German Protestant and Catholic representatives. As for the Catholics, the most important result of the German emperor's visit was the placing of German Benedictines from Beuron in the Monastery of the Dormition on Mt Zion.[6]

An Assumptionist priest, Paul Bailly, had long been the director of French pilgrimages to the Holy Land when he suggested that a Eucharistic Congress be held in Jerusalem. It would, he believed, aid the Catholic churches of the Near East in a way unparalleled by any event since the Crusades, and fit in well with the plans of Leo XIII for increased Catholic activity there among Arab-speaking Christians. Rome agreed, and plans for the event were devised once the Ottoman authorities signified their approval. The congress began in August 1892 with the papal legate, Cardinal Benoît Langénieux, archbishop of Rheims, in charge. He shared the conduct of the religious celebrations with the Latin patriarch, Archbishop Piavi, and the Eastern Catholic hierarchy. When Cardinal Langénieux entered Jerusalem to inaugurate the proceedings, an honour

guard of Ottoman soldiers lined his path. Upon his arrival he
announced his intention:

I come as a man of peace; I come in the name of him whom history
calls the chief pacifier of modern times. It is he who sends me to give a
new proof of his sympathy and admiration for the Eastern churches,
which are the first-born daughters of the church of God.[7]

The Congress lasted for six days and was considered a great
success. Thirty bishops attended, both Latin and Eastern, although
only the Melkite patriarch, Gregorios Yusuf, appeared. The pope
had asked Langénieux before he left to ascertain the exact condition
of Catholicism in the East. From his experiences in the Orient,
Langénieux was later to report to Leo XIII that more had to be
done to prevent the Latinization of the Eastern Catholic churches
if there was to be union between Rome and the Orthodox and
Oriental churches. It was with this in mind that the pope issued
Praeclara gratulationis in 1894 and sent personal invitations to the
Eastern Catholic patriarchs to come to Rome.[8]

By 1907 the Catholic church in the Holy Land under the patriarchate had grown to seventeen thousand people, with two hundred
and fourteen religious and thirty-three secular priests. The Franciscan Custody, with a distinct organization, had twenty-two houses
in Palestine and three hundred and fourteen friars. There were
thirteen orders of sisters, mainly from France and Italy, working in
the Holy Land. The First World War brought difficult times to the
Latins of Palestine but these difficulties were minimal in comparison
to the disasters inflicted on Eastern Catholics.[9]

THE COPTIC CHURCH UNDER MUHAMMED ALI

The Catholic Church in Egypt made significant progress as a result
of Muhammed 'Ali's administration. Latin Catholics who emigrated
to Egypt – Maltese, Italians and Spaniards – easily doubled the
size of the church. When Muhammed 'Ali abolished the *cizye*, the
Christian poll tax, Egypt became highly attractive to Europeans
seeking their fortunes along the Nile. In recognition of the large
number of Latin emigrants, Rome set up a vicariate for Egypt on
17 May 1839, separating it from the Holy Land custody. The
Franciscan Perpetuo Guasco was appointed vicar, the first Latin
bishop ever sent to Egypt on a permanent basis.[10]

At the beginning of the nineteenth century the fortunes of the

Catholic Copts looked bleak. There were only several thousand at that time and they had no bishop, but, as expected, the period of Muhammed 'Ali dramatically changed their position. In fact, the French consul upon whom the Egyptian leader depended suggested that it would be to Muhammed 'Ali's advantage to encourage Patriarch Butrus VII to join the Roman communion. The idea impressed Muhammed 'Ali: he had a plan drawn up and, as a first step, he encouraged his Coptic secretary, Mu'allim Ghali, to convert to Catholicism. However, opinion showed that corporate reunion between Rome and the Coptic church under the current circumstances was not likely to succeed, and a new version of the project was therefore planned to set up a separate Coptic Catholic hierarchy which would, by its prominence, influence all the Copts towards Rome.

Pope Leo XII, informed of this proposal, was anxious to accommodate, and named Maximos Zuwayya to the patriarchate on 18 September 1824. The pope's letter said the patriarchate was in the hands of heretics, hence the need to appoint a Catholic incumbent. Maximos was consecrated by the Melkite patriarch Ignatios Kattan, but his attempt to lead large numbers of Copts into his community was largely unavailing. The Catholic Copts had to worship in the Franciscan churches, and most Egyptian Christians were uncomfortable in this foreign environment.[11]

EGYPT DURING THE PONTIFICATE OF PIUS IX

The Latin mission to Egypt remained the least productive of Catholic efforts in the Orient. The Franciscans confined themselves primarily to the foreign community of Western Catholics, and their progress in converting Copts was painfully slow. In fact, under Patriarch Kyrillos IV, there was something of a renaissance in native Egyptian Christianity which blunted any progress the Catholics had envisioned. The English Church Missionary Society and the American United Presbyterian Church were now working in Egypt with more zeal than the Franciscans. It was therefore with some surprise that the Franciscans in Egypt learned of Pius IX's decision in 1859 to send a resident Latin patriarch to Cairo. Since there was a Franciscan bishop already on the scene with hardly enough to do, it soon became evident that the patriarch was not needed, and the pope wisely withdrew him after seven years in Egypt.[12]

THE CATHOLIC COPTIC CHURCH REESTABLISHED

The five thousand Catholic Copts received an accomplished church-man for their community when Agapios Ibrahim Bshaî was named to head the church in February 1866. Bshaî had studied at the Urban College in Rome, but this did not mean that he had learned to like Latin ways. One opinion had it that 'he hated the missions and missionaries and everything connected with the Latin rite and Latinity'.[13] Obviously such sentiments were not well known in Rome when he was appointed apostolic vicar. When he went to Rome to attend the Vatican Council, a question was raised about his being seated, since he was only a titular bishop. He kept quiet during the deliberations, much as the Syrians did, and except for his recorded votes, contributed little. In Egypt, he was so often at odds with Latin missionaries, whom he believed unduly influenced native Copts to join their rite, that Rome had to send a legate to arbitrate between them. It was not to his liking that several more religious orders in Western Europe contemplated foundations in Egypt.

The Jesuits returned to Egypt in 1879 to open in Cairo the College of the Holy Family, a small school for the Catholic Copts – which lasted until 1907 – and set up missions in Alexandria and in al-Minya. In 1899 Leo XIII established a seminary for the Copts at Tanta as part of the continuing efforts to produce a better educated clergy.

A report on the status of the Catholic Copts in 1880 estimated their numbers at between five and six thousand, of which eight hundred and fifty were in Cairo, where progress was slow, and the rest in upper Egypt, where success was greater, the people being more 'inclined to Catholicism'. In all of Egypt, the Franciscans with their ten churches were the most numerous of the Catholic religious.[14]

In 1882 the British occupation of Egypt began, changing the political situation considerably and giving foreign missionaries a security which they had never before enjoyed. Slowly the Catholic Copts increased in numbers and influence, although British admin-istrators did little to help the Egyptian Christians, since they wanted to keep the good will of the larger Muslim community. In the last decade of the nineteenth century, Catholic Copts sought greater autonomy and a regular church organization, and in 1893 the Franciscans handed over their churches to them. A Coptic priest, Jirgis Makarios, went to Rome to convince the pope of the advantages of establishing a diocesan organization for Egypt. On 25 November 1895 Pope Leo XIII, responding to the interest within the Catholic Coptic group, divided the country into three dioceses with a patriarch of Alexandria heading the church. His residence, like that of the Coptic patriarch, was in Cairo. The other bishoprics were set up for al-Minya (Hermopolis Magna) and Tanta (Thebes). Jirgis Makarios was given a titular bishopric and named patriarchal vicar.[15]

Three years later Makarios summoned a synod of his two colleagues to draw up canons for the church. The Syrian council of Sharfeh was taken as the model, and Latin and papal wishes were easily incorporated into the legislation during the five months the bishops were in session. Clerical celibacy was introduced as mandatory, but ritual integrity was to be preserved: 'The Alexandrian rite is to be retained in all its purity, as it has been handed down by the holy fathers.' On the other hand, confirmation was now to be conferred by bishops only, and several other sacraments were nudged towards Latin practice. Apparently, what the bishops understood by ritual purity referred only to the Eucharist.[16]

Rome enthusiastically approved the council, and rewarded Makarios by nomination to the patriarchate on 19 June 1899. As Kyrillos II he sought recognition from the local *khedive* although there was some dispute whether his *berat* should not more properly come from Sultan Abdulhamit II. He looked for assistance from the Austrian court rather than trusting to the vagaries of the French Third Republic. Kyrillos became extremely active in promoting the interests of his community. He built new churches, set up a printing press and saw the number of Catholic Copts double. He enjoyed good relations with Leo XIII, but when Pius X became pope the situation changed. Pius' secretary of state, Cardinal Merry del Val, disapproved of the patriarch's activities, often carried out on his own initiative without consultation with the Latin bishop in Egypt. Pius ordered Kyrillos to come to Rome, and in May 1908 the patriarch was suspended from office. The bishop of Hermopolis, Yusuf Sedfaoui, became administrator of the church, and for the next forty years there were no patriarchal appointments. In 1910 the suspended Kyrillos converted to the Coptic church, and remained there for two years, but then returned to the Catholic church. It took many years for the Catholic Copts to recover after the loss of their patriarch: the wounds were not healed until after the Second World War.[17]

Conclusion

The Catholic experience in the Ottoman Empire was unique. No other region of the world presented the same kind of challenges or rewards. What made it so different was the fact that the Orient – the Balkans and the Near East region – was really the homeland of Christianity and hardly a stranger to Christ's message. Churches of great antiquity were to be found here with thousands of members despite centuries of Muslim rule. However, it was *not* the centre of Latin Catholic Christianity and this meant that Western Christians considered it a mission field.

The indigenous Catholic communities, the Bosnians, Albanians and Greek Catholics, were endangered by the Turkish advance in the fifteenth century, and the papacy felt that it must take action. This was translated into a call for a crusade. Although the summons to arms was usually ignored, no one can accuse the popes of the fifteenth century of apathy toward the defence of Christianity.

When it became obvious that military action was impossible, French diplomacy intervened. Ottoman Catholics enjoyed having an advocate at the Porte and although this protection was not effective in every instance, on the whole it did prove advantageous. The ability of the Maronites to hold their ground until the nineteenth century shows French protection at its best.

The Catholic communities also profited by receiving personnel to staff their parishes and funds for their schools. Catholic facilities offered the best educational opportunities in the Ottoman world. Moreover, the presence of French or Italian clergy in their midst gave them a broader horizon and links to Western Europe denied to the Orthodox and Eastern Christians.

On the other hand, the Latin missionaries' role among Eastern Christians was a divisive one. For half a millennium hundreds of missionaries laboured to convert Eastern Christians to the West European point of view on how the church was meant to be structured and serve as a means of salvation. In spite of long and arduous years spent at this task, in the end, even before the apocalyptic events of the First World War, it was obvious that only limited success had been attained and that the cost far outweighed the results.

The ultimate goal of the papacy and Catholic missionaries was a united Christian church, one in doctrine and moral teaching, and looking to the bishop of Rome as head of all believers. The Council of Florence was always in the mind of the Latins: union had occurred once and it could happen again. Most missionaries believed that if the leaders of the Eastern churches were convinced that they should sign a Catholic profession of faith it would only be a matter of time until the whole church was brought into corporate union with Rome.

Some Orthodox and Eastern Christian hierarchs were won over, but their communities did not follow them. The risks were too great, the advantages too intangible. Therefore the missionaries turned to making individual conversions. Every Eastern church had its malcontents, and professing allegiance to Rome was one way of settling differences. People were willing to convert for a great many other reasons: social, economic, the protection offered by France, greater educational opportunities and, of course, the conviction that becoming a Catholic meant following the will of Christ.

Unfortunately, in pursuing individual conversions the higher goal of corporate reunion had to be abandoned. Splinter churches were set up, joined to Rome, but their members were too few to influence the course of their original communities. The Turkish *millet* organization was also a major deterrent to conversion to Catholicism. Eastern Christians, in the view of the Turks, had become apostates to their communities – they had joined 'the Franks' and were no longer to be trusted.

The world was much simpler before the twentieth century. In the pre-industrial environment of the Ottoman Empire religious issues were clearer and missionaries had no second thoughts. While in the present ecumenical age much of what was accomplished appears of dubious value, such was not the case at that time. Catholics in the sultan's world believed in the superiority of their Christian religion. The papal goal of a united Christendom is a noble one and remains so: finding the best means of reaching it is still elusive, but the mission to the Ottoman world should be instructive for that purpose.

Notes

I OTTOMAN GAINS AND CATHOLIC RESPONSE

1 On the siege of Constantinople, see Steven Runciman, *The Fall of Constantinople, 1453* (Cambridge, 1965), and the articles in *Le cinq-centième anniversaire de la prise de Constantinople*, in *L'Hellénisme contemporain*, 2nd ser., VII (Athens, 1953). On Galata's history, see Lodovico Sauli, *Della Colonia dei Genovesi in Galata* (Turin, 1830); Roberto Lopez, *Storia della Colonie Genovesi nel Mediterraneo* (Bologna, 1938).

2 Laonicus Chalkokondylas, *De origine ac rebus gestis Turcorum*, vol. XLVIII of *Corpus scriptorum historiae byzantinae*, ed. B. G. Niebuhr *et al.* (50 vols., Bonn, 1828–97), Book 8, 400–1; Nicola Iorga, 'Le privilège de Mohammed II pour la villa de Péra', *Bulletin de l'Académie Roumaine, Section historique* (Bucharest, 1913), 11–13.

3 The Galatan churches were: St Francis, St Anne, St Anthony, St Benedict, St Catherine, St Claire, St George, St John the Baptist, St Michael, St Paul, St Dominic, St Nicholas, and St Sebastian.

4 Freddy Thiriet, *Regestes des délibérations du Sénat de Venise concernant la Romanie* (3 vols., Paris, 1959–61), III, 187–9; Nicola Iorga, *Notes et extraits pour servir à l'histoire des croisades au XVᵉ siècle* (6 vols., Paris and Bucharest, 1899–1915), IV, 63.

5 Aeneas to Nicholas V, Graz, 12 July 1453, in Pius II, *Opera quae extant omnia*, ed. M. Hopper (Basel, 1571), Ep. 162, 712–16.

6 C. Baronius and O. Raynaldus, eds., *Annales*, anno 1453 (38 vols., Lucca, 1738–59), XXVIII, no. 9.

7 Isidoros' work is in J. P. Migne, *Patrologiae cursus completus, series graeca* (161 vols. in 166, Paris, 1857–66), CLIX, cols. 954–8; Leonardo of Chios, *Historia Constantinopolitanae urbis a Mahumete II captae*, in Migne, *PG*, CLIX, cols. 923–44.

8 The letter, dated 23 July 1453, is in Iorga, *Notes et extraits*, II, 518–19.

9 W. Heyd, *Histoire du commerce du Levant au moyen âge* (2 vols., new edn, Leipzig, 1885–6), II, 316–17. Venice had a treaty with

314

Mehmet II from 10 September 1451, promising peace and friendship. See G. M. Thomas and R. Predelli, eds., *Diplomatarium Veneto-Levantium sive acta et diplomata res Venetas, Graecas atque Levantis illustrantia* (2 vols., Venice, 1880–99), II, 382–4. The papal response has been studied in detail in Kenneth M. Setton, *The Papacy and the Levant, 1204–1571, vol. II: The Fifteenth Century* (Philadelphia, 1978), 138–60.

10 Baronius and Raynaldus, eds., *Annales*, anno 1454, XXIX, nos. 1–5; C. Marinescu, 'Le pape Nicolas V et son attitude envers l'empire byzantin', *Bulletin de l'Institut Archéologique Bulgare*, X (1936), 336–9; G. B. Picotti, 'Sulle Navi Papali in Oriente al Tempo della Caduta de Constantinopoli', *Nuovo Archivio Veneto*, ser. 3, XXII, 1 (1911), 413–53.

11 Baronius and Raynaldus, *Annales*, anno 1455, XXIX, nos. 12 and 19.

12 P. Paschini, 'La Flotta di Callixto III', *Archivio della Società Romana di Storia Patria*, LIII–LV (1930–2), 181–2; Ludwig Pastor, *History of the Popes from the Close of the Middle Ages*, ed. F. I. Antrobus (40 vols., St Louis, 1938–57), II, 371–6.

13 On the council, see Else Hocks, *Pius II und der Halbmond* (Freiburg, 1941), 101–30.

14 Kritovoulos, *History of Mehmed the Conqueror*, ed. C. T. Riggs (Princeton, 1954), Book 3, 137–9; Chalkokondylas, *De origine*, Book 10, 521.

15 Pastor, *History of the Popes*, III, 326.

16 Massimo Petrocchi, *La Politica della Santa Sede di Fronte all' Invasione Ottomana, 1444–1718* (Naples, 1955), 42–3; Aziz Atiya, *The Crusade in the Later Middle Ages* (2nd edn, New York, 1970), 228.

17 Pastor, *History of the Popes*, III, 249–52; L. Mohler, *Kardinal Bessarion als Theologe, Humanist und Staatesman* (3 vols., Paderborn, 1923–42), I, 304–76 and 416–29. Thomas' other daughter, Helen, became queen of Serbia. One son, Andreas, assumed his father's title and lived in Italy as pretender, the other, Manuel, went to Istanbul and converted to Islam. Bessarion lies buried in Rome's church of the Holy Apostles. The patriarchate of Constantinople, which Bessarion had filled since the death of Isidoros, now was given to a nephew of Pope Sixtus, Pietro Riario. Henceforth, Latin prelates held the office as titulars.

18 Heyd, *Histoire de commerce*, II, 382–407; N. Iorga, *Byzance après Byzance* (Bucharest, 1935), 46–7.

19 Dorothy Vaughan, *Europe and the Turk, 1350–1700* (Liverpool, 1954), 83ff.; Eric Brockman, *The Two Sieges of Rhodes, 1480–1522* (London, 1962), 90–9.

20 Franz Babinger, *Mehmet der Eroberer und seine Zeit* (Munich, 1953), 431ff.

21 Louis Thuasne, *Djem-Sultan, fils de Mohammed II, frère de*

Bayezid II, 1459–1495 (Paris, 1892), 57–98; Sydney N. Fisher, *The Foreign Relations of Turkey, 1481–1512*, vol. xxx, no. 1 of *Illinois Studies in the Social Sciences* (Urbana, 1948), 17–21.

22 Baronius and Raynaldus, *Annales*, anno 1490, xxx, nos. 1–4.

23 A. Mancini, 'Sulla corrispondenza fra Bajazet II e Innocenzo VIII', *Studi Storici* (Pisa, 1905), 103, quoting *Le Storie de' Suoi Tempi dal 1475 al 1510* of da Foligno (Rome, 1883), ii, 26.

24 All of the correspondence is in Heinrich Heldenheimer, 'Die Korrespondenz Sultan Bajazet II mit Papst Alexander VI', *Zeitschrift für Kirchengeschichte*, v, 4 (1882), 511–73.

25 Fisher, *Foreign Relations*, i, 49–51; Heyd, *Histoire du commerce*, ii, 331.

26 On Constantinople's population, see Robert Mantran, *Istanbul dans la second moitié du XVIIe siècle* (Paris, 1962), 44.

27 Franz Miklosich and Josef Müller, *Acta et diplomata graeca medii aevi sacra et profana* (6 vols., Vienna, 1860–90), v, 281–5.

28 J. N. Karmiris, Τὰ δογματικὰ καὶ συμβολικὰ μνημεῖα τῆς Ὀρθόδοξου Καθολικῆς Ἐκκλησίας (The dogmatic and credal statements of the Orthodox Catholic Church) (2 vols., Athens, 1952–3), ii, 987–9; G. A. Rallis and M. Potlis, Σύνταγμα τῶν θείων καὶ ἱερῶν κανόνων Collection of the divine and holy canons) (6 vols., Athens, 1852–9), v, 143; Steven Runciman, *The Great Church in Captivity* (Cambridge, 1968), 228–9.

29 J. Martin, 'Le Saint-Siège et la question d'Orient au seizième siècle: projets de croisade sous le règne de Léon X', *Revue d' histoire diplomatique*, xxx (1916), 35–9.

30 Letter of 14 February 1526 in Henri Mathieu, *La Turquie et ses différents peuples* (2 vols., Paris, 1857), i, 135.

31 On the relations between the Protestant movement and the Ottoman advance into Europe see Stephen Fischer-Galati, *Ottoman Imperialism and German Protestantism* (Cambridge, 1959); Carl M. Kortepeter, *Ottoman Imperialism during the Reformation: Europe and the Caucasus* (New York, 1972).

32 Ernest Charrière, *Négociations de la France dans le Levant* (4 vols., Paris, 1848–60), i, 129–31. Pilgrims to Jerusalem were under the official protection of the consuls of Genoa and Venice.

33 Charrière, *Négociations*, i, 255–8 and 283–94; François Rey, *De la protection diplomatique et consulaire dans les échelles du Levant et de Barbarie* (Paris, 1889), 116–20.

34 Nicolas de Nicolay, *Le Navigationi et Viaggi nella Turchia* (Anversa, 1576), 133–9; Francesco Sansovino, *Dell' historia Universale dell' Origine et Imperio de Turchi* (3 vols., Venice, 1560), i, 67.

35 E. Dalleggio d'Alessio, 'Les origines dominicaines du couvent des SS. Pierre-et-Paul à Galata; un texte definitif', *Echos d'Orient*, xxix, 4 (1930), 459–60.

36 Philip of Cyprus, *Chronicon ecclesiae Graecae* (Leipzig, 1687), 413–15; Runciman, *The Great Church*, 230. Patriarch Joasaph also contacted the Lutherans at Wittenburg. He sent a deacon, Demetrios Myzos, there for information, and Philip Melanchthon talked with him and gave him a copy of the Confession of Augsburg for the patriarch. No response was made to this overture. Paduan graduates who became Orthodox hierarchs include Meletios Pegas, Maximos Margounios and Gabriel Severos.

37 Rocco da Cesinale Cocchia, *Storia delle Missioni dei Cappuccini* (3 vols., Paris, 1867), I, 40–54.

2 THE OTTOMAN ATTACK UPON CATHOLICS IN THE BALKANS AND GREECE

1 Bariša Krekić, *Dubrovnik in the Fourteenth and Fifteenth Centuries* (Norman, 1972), 138–43; Nicolaas Biegman, *The Turco-Ragusan Relationship* (The Hague, 1967), 22–4.

2 Kritovoulos, *History of Mehmed the Conqueror*, Book 2, 88–103 and 111–13; Chalkokondylas, *De origine*, Book 8, 424–6.

3 L. von Thallóczy et al., eds., *Acta et diplomata res Albaniae mediae aetatis illustrantia* (2 vols., Vienna, 1913–18), II, 361–80; M. Šufflay, 'Die Kirchenzustande in Vortürkischen Albanien', *Illyrisch-albanische Forschungen*, ed. L. von Thallóczy (2 vols., Munich, 1916), I, 190–218.

4 Joseph von Hammer-Purgstall, *Geschichte des osmanischen Reiches* (10 vols., Pest, 1834–6), I, 459–61; Kristo Frasheri, *History of Albania* (Tiranë, 1964), 66–86; Ignatius Darrino, *Acta albaniae vaticana*, vol. CCLXVI of *Studi e Testi* (Vatican City, 1971), 60.

5 J. Fine, *The Bosnian Church: A New Interpretation* (New York, 1975), 275–95, 333–9; François de Sessevalle, *Histoire générale de l'ordre de Saint François* (2 pts, Paris, 1935), I, pt 1, 672–90.

6 Dominic Mandić, 'Borba Katolice Crkve za Opstanak u Bosni i Hercegovini', in *Etnicka povijest Bosne i Hercegovine* (Rome, 1967), 56–7. Zvijezdović died in 1498 and lies buried in the Church of the Holy Spirit in Foiniza. The convent at Jajce transferred its famous relic, the body of St Luke, to Venice.

7 Baronius and Raynaldus, *Annales*, anno 1465, XXIX, nos. 22–5. Andreas has been beatified by the Catholic church. There is a conflict over Andreas' origins and his faith raised by Orthodox scholars. See Dalleggio d'Alessio, 'Un néo-martyr catholique à Constantinople, André de Chio (1465)' *Mémorial Louis Petit, Archives de l'orient chrétien*, I (Bucharest, 1948), 64–77.

8 Doukas, *Decline and Fall of Byzantium to the Ottoman Turks*, ed. Henry J. Magoulias (Detroit, 1975), Book 3, 246; Miklosich and Müller, *Acta et diplomata*, III, 291.

9 Giorgio Fedalto, *La Chiesa Latina in Oriente* (2 vols., Verona, 1973–6), II, 51–4.

10 Bessarion, *Orationes de gravissimis periculis, quae reipublicae christianae a Turca iam tum impendere providebat* (Rome, 1543), n.p.

11 Hammer-Purgstall, *Geschichte*, I, 495ff.; Babinger, *Mehmed der Eroberer*, 301ff.

12 Philipp Loncier, *Chronicorum turcicorum* (Frankfort, 1584), 66–72; Brockman, *The Two Sieges*, 111–55.

13 Charrière, *Négociations*, I, 132–46; Petrocchi, *La Politica della Santa Sede*, 62.

14 Demetrios P. Paschalis, Ἡ δυτικὴ ἐκκλησία εἰς τὰς Κυκλάδας ἐπὶ Φραγοκρατίας καὶ Τουρκοκρατίας (The western church in the Cyclades during Frankish and Turkish rule) (Athens, 1948), 9–17.

15 William Miller, *The Latins in the Levant* (Cambridge, 1908), 570–649; Georg Hofmann, *Vescovadi Cattolici della Grecia: Naxos*, vol. 115 of *Orientalia Christiana Analecta* (Rome, 1938), 10–11.

16 Heinrich Kretschmayr, *Geschichte von Venedig* (3 vols., Gotha, 1905–34), III, 21–31; see also Julien de la Gravière, *Doria et Barberousses* (Paris, 1886).

17 Albert Lefaivre, *Les Magyars pendant la domination ottomane en Hongrie, 1526–1722* (2 vols., Paris, 1902), I, 20–33; Hans Pfeffermann, *Die Zusammenarbeit der Renaissancepäpste mit den Türken* (Winterthur, 1946), 182–91.

18 Ogier Ghiselin de Busbeq, *Legationis turcicae epistolae quatuor* (Basel, 1740), 16 and 99; Lajos Fekete, 'La Vie de Budapest sous la domination turque, 1541–1686', *Journal of World History*, VIII, 3 (1964), 527–9.

19 Ernle Bradford, *The Shield and the Sword: The Knights of St John, Jerusalem, Rhodes and Malta* (New York, 1973), 140–75; Fernand Braudel, *La Méditerranée et le monde méditerranéen à l'époque de Philippe II* (2 vols., 2nd edn, Paris, 1966), I, 843–50.

20 Philip Argenti, *The Occupation of Chios by the Genoese and their Administration of the Island, 1346–1566* (3 vols., Cambridge, 1958), I, 364–8.

3 THE CATHOLICS OF ARMENIA AND SYRIA COME UNDER OTTOMAN RULE

1 Echmiadzin, once one of the ancient seats of the catholicate, had been reconstituted in 1441 when the incumbent of Sis grudgingly allowed the Armenians in the Caucasus to elect their own head. Akhtamar's catholicate began as a schism in 1114, and Jerusalem's in 1311.

2 A. Balgy, *Historia doctrinae catholicae inter Armenos unionisque eorum cum Ecclesia Romana in Concilio Florentino* (Vienna, 1878), 163–6; Donat Vernier, *Histoire du patriarcat arménien catholique* (Paris, 1891), 272; Pierre Dib, 'Une mission en Orient sous le

pontificat de Pie IV', *Revue de l'Orient chrétien*, XIX (1914), 24–32, 266–77.

3 The opinion that the Melkites were in communion with Rome is strongly held by Basile Homsy, *Les Capitulations et la protection des chrétiens au Proche-Orient au XVIᵉ, XVIIᵉ et XVIIIᵉ siècles* (Paris, 1956), 350–61. He argues that the Antiochenes spoke of the pope in Rome as 'patriarch of the Melkites'. The name for the church comes from the Semitic word for 'king', for the Melkites supported the theology of the Byzantine emperor. See also Joseph Nasrallah, 'Le patriarcat d'Antioche, est-il resté, après 1054, en communion avec Rome?' *Istina*, XXI (1976), 374–411.

4 For early Maronite history, see Pierre Dib, *Histoire de l'Eglise maronite* (2 vols., Beirut, 1962); Charles Frazee, 'The Maronite Middle Ages', *Eastern Churches Review*, X, 1–2 (1978), 88–100, and Kamal S. Salibi, 'The Maronite Church in the Middle Ages and its Union with Rome', *Oriens christianus*, XLII (1958), 92–105.

5 On Gryphon, see Henri Lammens, 'Frère Gryphon et le Liban au XVᵉ siècle', *Revue de l'Orient chrétien*, IV (1900), 83–9; René Ristelhueber, *Les Traditions françaises au Liban* (Paris, 1918), 74–92.

6 Tobias Anaissi, *Bullarium maronitarum* (Rome, 1911), 25–35; Joseph Hajjar, *Les Chrétiens uniates du Proche-Orient* (Paris, 1962), 202–3.

7 Ernest Honigmann, *Le couvent de Barsauma et la patriarcat Jacobite d'Antioche et de Syrie*, Vol. VII of *Corpus scriptorum christianorum orientalia, subsidia* (Louvain, 1954), 176; Jean Chanin, 'Les patriarches de l'Eglise syrienne catholique', *Echos d'Orient*, I, 6 (1898), 201–3.

8 Dib, *Histoire de l'Église maronite*, I, 132–3; Anaissi, *Bullarium maronitarum*, 65–70.

9 For the history of the Church of the East, see Eugene Tisserant, 'Église nestorienne' in the *Dictionnaire de théologie catholique* (15 vols., Paris, 1899–1962) XI, pt 1, cols. 158–223.

10 Wilhelm de Vries, *Rom und die Patriarchate des Ostens* (Freiburg, 1963), 77–9; Joseph A. Assemani, *De catholicis seu patriarchis Chaldaeorum et Nestorianorum commentarius* (Rome, 1775), 215; Joseph Simone Assemani, *Bibliotheca orientalis* (4 vols., Rome, 1719–28), I, 523–34. Sulaqa's full biography is in J. M. Vosté, 'Mar Johannan Sulaqa: premier patriarche des Chaldéens', *Angelicum*, VIII (1931), 187–234.

11 Samuel Giamil, *Genuinae relationes inter Sedem Apostolicam et Assyrorum Orientalium seu Chaldaeorum ecclesiam* (Rome, 1902), 31–67; J. S. Assemani, *Bibliotheca orientalis*, I, 536–42.

4 THE OTTOMAN ADVANCE INTO PALESTINE AND SYRIA

1 Leonhard Lemmens, *Die Franziskaner im Heiligen Lande, 1335–1552* (Munster, 1925), 61–78; Martiniano Roncaglia, *Storia della Provincia di Terra Santa* (Cairo, 1954), 11–16; Francis Quaresimus, *Historica, theologica, et moralis Terrae Sanctae elucidatio*, ed. Cyprian de Tarviso (2 vols., Antwerp, 1639), gives a minute description of the work of the Franciscans in I, 257–58; 475–86. Vol. II describes the places of pilgrimage.

2 Marcellino da Civezza, *Storia Universale delle Missioni Francescane* (11 vols., Rome and Florence, 1857–95), VII, 377–89. Pilgrim literature is immense. Much has been gathered and published by the Palestine Pilgrim Text Society. An examination of this material is found in S. C. Chew, *The Crescent and the Rose* (New York, 1937), 56–93.

3 Girolamo Golubovich, *Biblioteca Bio-Bibliografica della Terra Santa e dell'Oriente Francescano* (new series, 14 vols., Quaracchi, 1921–1933), VI, 113–18.

4 E. L. Butcher, *The Story of the Church of Egypt* (2 vols., London, 1897), II, 236–44.

5 The document was signed by the pope, 20 cardinals, 30 bishops and 11 abbots for the West. Andreah alone signed for the Copts – a heady experience. Francis Rogers, *The Quest for Eastern Christians* (Minneapolis, 1962), 40-1.

6 Joseph Gill, *The Council of Florence* (Cambridge, 1959), 321–3.

7 Rey, *De la protection diplomatique*, 112–13; F. Charles-Roux, *France et chrétiens d'Orient* (Paris, 1939), 27–30.

8 Account of William Lithgow, *Rare Adventures* (London, 1632), 246, quoted in Chew, *The Crescent and the Rose*, 77; Uriel Heyd, ed., *Ottoman Documents on Palestine, 1552–1615* (Oxford, 1960), 177–8.

9 U. Heyd, *Ottoman Documents*, 182.

10 Otto F. A. Meinardus, *Christian Egypt, Ancient and Modern* (Cairo, 1965), 14ff.

5 THE GROWTH OF FRENCH INFLUENCE IN ISTANBUL

1 J. de Testa, *Recueil des traités de la Porte ottomane avec les puissances étrangères* (8 vols., Paris, 1864–94), I, 91–6; André Bruneau, *Traditions et politique de la France au Levant* (Paris, 1932), 29.

2 Roger C. Anderson, *Naval Wars in the Levant, 1559–1853* (Liverpool, 1952), 51–4; Hammer-Purgstall, *Geschichte des osmanischen Reiches*, II, 419–25; Petrocchi, *La Politica della Santa Sede*, 73–5.

3 Hyacinthe Hecquard, *Histoire et description de la Haute Albanie ou Ghégarie* (Paris, 1858), 31–2.

4 P. Rodotá, *Dell' Origine, Progresso, e Stato Presente del Rito Greco in Italia* (3 vols., Rome, 1758), III, 146–9; V. Peri, 'La

Congregazione dei Greci (1573)', *Studia Gratiana*, XIII (1967), 129–256. Gregory XIII also put all the Greek monasteries in Italy and Spain into the 'Basilian Order' under a single abbot. This order survives today in the monastery of Grottoferrata outside Rome. On the college, see P. DeMeester, *Le Collège Pontifical grec de Rome* (Rome, 1910).

5 Quoted in Aloys Pichler, *Geschichte der kirchlichen Trennung zwischen dem Orient und Occident* (2 vols., Munich, 1864–5), I, 461. See also E. Benz, *Wittenberg und Byzanz* (Marburg, 1948), 73ff.

6 The account of Cedulini is to be found in Adolf Gottlob, 'Die lateinischen Kirchengemeiden in der Türkei und ihre Visitation durch Petrus Cedulini, Bischof von Nona, 1580–81', *Historisches Jahrbuch der Görresgesellschaft*, VI, 1 (1885), 42–72. See also Georg Hofmann, *Il Vicariato Apostolico di Constantinopoli, 1453–1830*, vol. CIII of *Orientalia Christiana Analecta* (Rome, 1935), 15–17. Jeremias' correspondence with the papacy is contained in Georg Hofmann, *Griechische Patriarchen und Römische Päpste*, vol. XV, no. 52 of *Orientalia Christiana* (Rome, 1929).

7 Gottlob, 'Die lateinischen Kirchengemeiden', 49.

8 'Mr Harrie Cavendish, His Journey To and From Constantinople, 1589 by Fox, his Servant', ed. A. C. Wood, in *Camden Miscellany of the Offices of the Royal Historical Society*, XVII (1940), 16.

9 Stephan Gerlach, *Stephan Gerlachs des Aelteren Tagebuch* (Frankfort-am-Main, 1674), 40–5. St Michael's church had been destroyed by this time, probably by fire. St Mary was handed over to the Franciscan Observants in 1584 by Clara Bartolda Draperis, patron of the church. See François Belin, *Histoire de la latinité de Constantinople* (2nd edn., Paris, 1894), 196–9, 272.

10 Mancinelli's account has been published in part by Pietro Pirri, 'Lo Stato della Chiesa ortodossa di Constantinopli e le sue Tendenze verso Roma in una Memoria del P. Giulio Mancinelli, S.I.', in *Miscellanea Pietro Fumasioni-Biondi*, 1 (Rome, 1947), 79–104.

11 Cuthbert Hess, *The Capuchins* (2 vols., London, 1928), I, 373–5; Cocchia, *Storia delle Missioni*, I, 55–69. Giuseppe later worked in southern Italy. He was canonized a saint in 1746.

12 Abel's story is to be found in *Une Mission religieuse en Orient au XVIᵉ siècle*, trans. Adolphe d'Avril (Paris, 1866). See also G. Levi della Vida, *Documenti Intorno alla Relazioni delle Chiese Orientali con la S. Sede durante il Pontificato di Gregorio XIII*, vol. CXLIII of *Studi e Testi* (Vatican City, 1948), 2–8.

13 Wilhelm de Vries, 'Dreihundert Jahre syrisch-katholische Hierarchie', *Ostkirchliche Studien*, V, 2 (1956), 137–57; Levi della Vida, *Documenti*, 50–1.

14 Giamil, *Genuinae relationes*, 89–90, 108–15; Giuseppe Beltrami,

La Chiesa Caldea nel secolo dell' Unione, vol. XXIX, no. 83 of *Orientalia Christiana* (Rome, 1933), 68–76.

15 Abel, *Mission religieuse*, 36–7. See also Vernier, *Histoire du patriarcat arménien catholique*, 269. Sis then had twenty-four bishoprics and twenty monasteries in its jurisdiction. Gheuart Alishanian, *Sissouan, ou l'Arméno-Cilicie* (Venice, 1897), 262–3.

16 M. A. van den Oudenrijn, 'Uniters et Dominicains d'Arménie', *Oriens christianus*, XL (1956), 94.

17 Letter of 26 September 1584 in A. Rabbath, ed., *Documents inédits pour servir à l'histoire du christianisme en Orient* (2 vols., Paris, 1905–21), I, 193–6.

18. Levi della Vida, *Documenti*, 114–67; Butcher, *The Story of the Church of Egypt*, II, 250–1.

19 The incident is recounted in T. G. Djuvara, *Cent projets de partage de la Turquie, 1281–1913* (Paris, 1914), 133–7.

20 De Testa, *Recueil des traités*, I, 141. De Brèves was an Orientalist of some note. He bought a press using the Arabic alphabet and took it back to France with him on his return.

21 *Ibid.*, IX, 26.

22 Belin, *Histoire*, 351. A list of vicars general from 1559 is to be found in R. Janin, *La géographie ecclésiastique de l'empire byzantin* (3 vols., Paris, 1953), III, 741.

23 Pierre Lescalopier, 'Voyage faict par moy', quoted in Braudel, *La Méditerranée et le monde méditerranéen*, II, 349–50.

24 George Sandys, *A Relation of a Journey begun An. Dom. 1610 Containing a Description of the Turkish Empire, of Aegypt, of the Holy Land, and of the Remote Parts of Italy, and Ilands adjoining* (London, 1621), 85. Sandys also recounts (p. 86) the conversion of an Italian Franciscan to Protestantism. He fled to the house of the English ambassador who encouraged him to go to England. At length the Venetian authorities took him away and confined him to a galley.

25 Letter of de Canillac to a brother in France, 30 October 1610, in Auguste Carayon, ed., *Relations inédites des missions de la Compagnie de Jésus à Constantinople et dans le Levant au XVIIIᵉ siècle* (Paris, 1864), 1–57; Gabriel de Mun, 'L'introduction des Jésuites à Constantinople sous le règne d'Achmet Iᵉʳ, 1603–17', *Revue des questions historiques*, new ser. XXX (1903), 163–71.

26 Letter of de Canillac, n.p., 1612, in Carayon, *Relations inédites*, 62.

27 Louis de Moranvilliers to M. de Sancy, n.p., 27 January 1617, in Carayon, *Relations inédites*, 88; Mun, 'L'introduction des Jésuits', 171.

28 Gerard Tongas, *Les Relations de la France avec l'Empire Ottoman durant la première moitié du XVIIᵉ siècle et l'ambassade à Constantinople de Philippe de Harlay, Comte de Césy, 1619–1640*

(Toulouse, 1942), 12ff.; Antoine de La Croix, *La Turquie chrétienne: état present des nations et églises grecque, arménienne, et
maronite en Turquie* (Paris, 1695), pref., b. On Loukaris, see
C. Papadopoulos, Κύριλλος Λούκαρις (Kyrillos Loukaris), 2nd
edn (Athens, 1939).

29 Quoted in Georg Hofmann, *Griechische Patriarchen und Römische
Päpste*, vol. xv, no. 52 of *Orientalia Christiana* (Rome, 1929),
44–6.

30 Thomas Roe to Dr Williams, bishop of Lincoln, Constantinople,
29 April 1622, in Thomas Roe, *The Negotiations of Sir Thomas
Roe in his Embassy to the Ottoman Porte from the Year 1621 to
1628 Inclusive* (London, 1740), 36.

31 Paul Rycaut to the archbishop of Canterbury, Constantinople,
18 March 1622, in Paul Rycaut, *The Present State of the Greek
and Armenian Churches* (London, 1679), 134.

32 Quoted by Roe in a letter to Sir Dudley Carleton, Constantinople,
14 October 1623 in Roe, *The Negotiations*, 184–5.

33 Victor L. Tapié, *La France de Louis XIII et Richelieu* (Paris,
1952), 101–12; Gustave Fagniez, *Le Père Joseph et Richelieu, 1577–
1638* (2 vols., Paris, 1894), I, 31–59; Hilaire de Barenton, *La France
catholique en Orient* (Paris, 1902), 55. See also Vaughan, *Europe
and the Turk*, 215–36, and St Papadopoulos, Ἡ κίνηση τὸυ Δουκά
του Νεβερ, Καρόλου Γονζαγα γιά τὴν ἀπελευθερώση τῶν Βαλκανικῶν
λαῶν, *1603–1625* (The action of the Duke of Nevers, Charles
Gonzagà, for the liberation of the Balkan people (Thessalouika,
1966), 110ff.

34 The report of his journey has been published in Pacifique de
Provins, *Le Voyage de Perse*, ed. Godefrey de Paris and Hilaire de
Wingene (Assisi, 1939). On his life, see Godefrey de Paris, *Un
Grand Missionaire oublié, le P. Pacifique de Provins, capucin*
(Assisi, 1935).

35 Guillaume de Vaumas, 'L'Activité missionaire du P. Joseph de
Paris', *Revue d'histoire des missions*, xv (1938), 336–59.

36 Césy to M. de Marillac, 4 October 1626, in Tongas, *Les Relations
de la France*, 79.

6 THE MISSIONS COME UNDER THE CONGREGATION FOR THE PROPAGATION OF THE FAITH

1 Raphael de Martinis, *Juris pontificii de propaganda fide, pars
prima* (7 vols., Rome, 1888–97), I, 1–3; Alphons Mulders, *Missionsgeschichte* (Regensburg, 1960), 263–74.

2 J. Krajcar, 'The Greek College under the Jesuits for the First
Time', *Orientalia Christiana Periodica*, xxxi (1965), 86.

3 Rodotá, *Dell'Origine*. See also George Every, *Misunderstanding
between East and West*, vol. 4 of *Ecumenical Studies in History*

(London, 1965), 20–1. Allatios wrote on Ancient Greek and Byzantine subjects as well as church affairs. In his lifetime he produced over fifty-five books in addition to shorter essays and monographs.

4 *Collectanea S. Congregatione de Propaganda Fide* (2 vols., Rome, 1907), I, 11, no. 34.

5 Quoted in Ignazio da Seggiano, 'Documenti Indediti sull' Apostolato dei Minori Cappuccini nel Vicino Oriente, 1623–83', *Collectanea Franciscana*, XVIII (1948), 27.

6 De Martinis, *Juris pontificii*, I, 170–1.

7 Tongas, *Les Relations de la France*, 132ff.; Paulos Gregoriou, Σχέσεις Καθολικῶν καὶ 'Ορθοδόξων (Relations between Catholics and Orthodox) (Athens, 1958), 220–1.

8 Janin, *La Géographie ecclésiastique*, III, 678.

9 Philaretos Bapheides, 'Εκκλησιαστικὴ ἱστορία ἀπὸ τοῦ Κυρίου 'Ημῶν 'Ιησοῦ Χριστοῦ μέχρι τῶν καθ' ἡμᾶς χρόνων (Church history from Our Lord Jesus Christ until our own Times) (3 vols., Constantinople, 1912), III, 761; Pichler, *Geschichte der kirchlichen Trennung*, I, 469ff.

10 Hofmann, *Il Vicariato Apostolico*, 42–66; Leonhard Lemmens, *Hierarchia latina orientis, 1622–1922*, vol. 1 of *Orientalia Christiana* (Rome, 1923), 270–71.

11 Sir Henry Blount, *A Voyage into the Levant* (London, 1636), 109–10; Louis Gedoyn, *Journal et correspondance de Gedoyn 'le Turc', consul de France à Alep, 1623–5* (Paris, 1909), 74.

12 Evliya Çelebi, *Narrative of Travels in Europe, Asia and Africa in the Seventeenth Century*, trans. Joseph von Hammer (2 vols. in 1, London, 1834–50), II, 49–52.

13 Quoted in François Rey, *De la protection diplomatique*, 306.

14 Césy to Louis XIII, Constantinople, 4 March 1629, in Tongas, *Les Relations de la France*, 36.

15 Basile Homsy, *Les Capitulations*, 244.

16 Mauri's report is in Hofmann, *Il Vicariato Apostolico*, 18–19; G. B. Cervellini, ed., 'Relazioni da Constantinopoli del Vicario Patriarcale Angelo Petricca, 1636–39', *Bessarione*, XXVIII (1912), 15–33.

17 Paul Rycaut, *The Present State of the Ottoman Empire* (London, 1668), 28.

18 Lemmens, *Hierarchia latina*, 271.

19 Belin, *Histoire de la latinité*, 355.

20 Charles-Roux, *France et chrétiens*, 51.

21 Mantran, *Istanbul dans la second moitié du XVIIᵉ siècle*, 36; Belin, *Histoire de la latinité*, 273; A. Palmieri, 'Dagli archivi dei Conventuali de Constantinopoli', *Bessarione*, IX (1901), 132.

22 P. Bruno, 'Ambassadeurs de France et capucins français à Constantinople d'après le journal du P. Thomas de Paris', *Études franciscaines*, XXIX (1913), 408–12.

23 The details of this matter are in Bruno, 'Ambassadeurs de France', xxx, 387–91.

24 Quoted in Homsy, *Les Capitulations*, 252. See also César Famin, *Histoire de la rivalité et du protectorat des Eglises chrétiennes en Orient* (Paris, 1853), 24–40.

25 Charles-Roux, *France et chrétiens*, 57; A. Schopoff, *Les Réformes et la protection des chrétiens en Turquie, 1673–1904* (Paris, 1904), 3ff. The French colony in Istanbul reached twenty-four merchant houses and four Genevan, of whom thirty-one members were Calvinists. The Genoese turned over their interests to the French ambassador during this period.

7 THE BALKANS AND GREECE

1 The incident is recounted in Nicolaas Biegman, *The Turko-Ragusan Relationship*, 44.

2 A. Theiner and F. Miklosich, *Monumenta spectantia ad unionem ecclesiarum graecae et romanae* (Vienna, 1872), 57–60; Stavro Skendi, 'Religion in Albania during the Ottoman Rule', *Sudöst-Forschungen*, xv (1956), 323.

3 Fulvio Cordignano, *Geografia ecclesiastica dell'Albania dagli ultimi decenni del secolo XVI ella metà del secolo XVII*, vol. xxxvi of *Orientalia Christiana* (Rome, 1934), 237–43; Cirillo Karalevskij, 'La Missione Greco-Cattolica della Cimara nell'Epiro nei Secoli XVI–XVII', *Bessarione*, xxxix (1913), 173–75.

4 Gottlob, 'Die latinischen Kirchengemeiden', 42–72.

5 Georg Stadtmüller, 'Die Visitationsreise des Erzbischofs Marino Bizzi', *Serta Monacensia* (1952), 184–99; Kurnoslav Draganović, 'Izvješce apostolskog vizitatora Petra Masarechija o prilikama katoličkih naroda u Bugarskoj, Srbiji, Srijemu, Slavoniji i Bosni, g. 1623 i 1624', *Starine*, xxxix (1938), 2–10, Srećko M. Džaja, *Katolici u Bosni i Zapadnoj Hercegovini na prijelazu iz 18 v 19. stoljeće*, vol. 2 of *Analecta Croatica Christiana* (Zagreb, 1971), 47ff.

6 Luigi Villari, *The Republic of Ragusa: An Episode of the Turkish Conquest* (London, 1904), 298–321; Francis W. Carter, *Dubrovnik (Ragusa), A Classic City-State* (New York, 1972), 338–46.

7 De Martinis, *Juris pontificii*, i, 279.

8 Georg Hofmann, *Byzantinische Bischöfe und Rom*, vol. xxii, no. 70 of *Orientalia Christiana* (Rome, 1931), 132–4.

9 Gottlob, 'Die latinischen Kirchengemeiden', 51–2.

10 Ivan Dujčev, *Il Cattolicesimo in Bulgaria nel secolo XVII*, vol. cxi of *Orientalia Christiana Analecta* (Rome, 1937), 12–18, 32–4.

11 Clemente da Terzorio, *Le Missioni dei Minori Cappuccini. Sunto Storico* (10 vols., Rome, 1913–38), i, 387ff; de Martinis, *Juris pontificii*, i, 323.

12 Hofmann, *Naxos*, 11–25; William Miller, *Essays on the Latin Orient* (Cambridge, 1921), 173.

13 John Hackett, *A History of the Orthodox Church of Cyprus* (London, 1901), 157–9, 589–92; George Hill, *A History of Cyprus* (4 vols., Cambridge 1940–52) III, 765–837.

14 Letter of Cardinal de Rambouillet to Charles IX, Rome, 12 May 1570, in Charrière, *Négociations de la France*, III, 112.

15 Angelo Calepio, *Cronografia*, quoted in Hackett, *Orthodox Church*, 188.

16 R. Janin, 'Chypre (Église de)', in *Dictionnaire d'histoire et de géographie ecclésiastique* (15 vols., Paris, 1912–62), XII, col. 814.

17 Hofmann, *Naxos*, 396.

18 Césy to Louis XIII, Constantinople, 30 May 1627, quoted in Rey, *De la protection diplomatique*, 355.

19 Hofmann, *Naxos*, 34ff.

20 V. Laurent, ed., 'Relation de ce qui s'est passé en la résidence des pères de la Compagnie de Jésus établie à Naxie la 26 septembre de l'année 1627', *Echos d'Orient*, XXXIII (1934), 218–26, 354–75 and XXXIV (1935), 97–105, 179–204, 350–67, 472–80.

21 Philip Argenti, *Religious Minorities of Chios* (Cambridge, 1970), 216–22.

22 Marcellino de Civezza, *Storia Universale*, VII, 3, 512–13; Argenti, *Religious Minorities*, 225–27.

23 Baron Henrion, *Histoire générale des missions catholiques depuis le XIIIᵉ siècle jusqu' à nos jours* (2 vols., Paris, 1846–7), II, 254–6.

24 Rycaut, *The Present State of the Greek and Armenian Churches*, 340–9; Robert de Dreux, *Voyage en Turquie et en Grèce du R. P. Robert de Dreux, 1665–1669*, H. Pernot, ed. (Paris, 1925), 66.

25 Miklosich and Müller, *Acta et diplomata*, VI, 421ff.; de Terzorio, *Le Missioni dei Minori*, VI, 352–65.

26 Sophronius Petrides, 'Le vénérable Jean-André Carga, évêque latin de Syra, 1560–1617', *Revue de l'Orient chrétien*, V (1900), 407–44; Hofmann, *Syros*, 9–23

27 Visite, I, 538–9, Archivio della S. Congregazione di Propaganda, quoted in Georg Hofmann, 'La Chisea Cattolica in Grecia, 1600–1830', *Orientalia Christiana Periodica*, II (Rome, 1936), 405.

28 Hofmann, *Thera*, 10–11.

29 Rey, *De la protection diplomatique*, 356–7.

30 *Collectanea S. Congregatione de Propaganda Fide* I, 53 and 69.

31 Apostolos E. Bacalopoulos, *The Greek Nation, 1453–1669*, trans. Ian and Phania Moles (New Brunswick, 1976), 86–90.

32 Girolamo Dandini, *Missione Apostolica al Patriarca e Maroniti del Monte Libano* (Cesena, 1656), 15.

33 Ubaldo Mannucci, 'Contributi Documentarii per la Storia della Distruzione degli Episcopati Latini in Oriente nei secoli XVI e XVII', *Bessarione*, XXX (1914), 97–101; Paul Hidiroglu, *Das religiöse Leben auf Kreta nach Ewlijā Čelebi* (Leiden, 1969), 22 and 27, notes.

34 Dandini, *Missione Apostolica*, 23.

35 Lemmens, *Hierarchia latina*, 291–2.

36 Letter of Blaiseau, Chalkis, 2 January 1642, in Carayon, *Relations inédites*, 120–1.

37 Letter of Blaiseau in Carayon, *Relations inédites*, 123–38; Demetrios Sicilianos, *Old and New Athens*, trans. R. Liddell (London, 1960), 168.

38 Da Terzorio, *Le Missioni dei Minori*, IV, 366; Chrysostomos Papadopoulos, 'Η ἐκκλησία 'Αθηνῶν (The Church of Athens) (Athens, 1928), 48; Le Comte de Laborde, *Athènes aux XVᵉ, XVIᵉ, et XVIIᵉ siècles* (2 vols., Paris, 1854), I, 74–8.

39 Jacques-Paul Babin, *Relation de l'état présent de la ville d' Athènes* (Lyon, 1674), 16–17.

40 Basil Sphyroeras, 'Οι 'έλληνες ἐπὶ Τουρκοκρατίας (The Greeks during the Turkish Rule) (Athens, 1971), 144–7; Laborde, *Athènes*, II, 194–7.

41 The complete story of Rome's activities on Mt Athos is to be found in the two works of Georg Hofmann, *Rom und der Athos-Klöster*, vol. VIII of *Orientalia Christiana Analecta* (Rome, 1926), and *Rom und der Athos*, vol. CXLII of *Orientalia Christiana Analecta* (Rome, 1954).

42 In 1728 the Greeks did not participate in the Corsican revolt and the natives took reprisals upon them. Many left for Ajaccio in 1731 to avoid further trouble. In 1768 Corsica was annexed by France and the governor of the island settled the Greeks in Cargese, where they have remained to the present. T. Xanthopoulos, 'La colonie grecque catholique de Cargèse en Corse', *Echos d'Orient* v, 1 (1901), 33–8; Adrian Fortescue, *The Uniate Eastern Churches: The Byzantine Rite in Italy, Sicily, Syria and Egypt* (London, 1923), 143 and 169–71.

8 THE ORIENT AND THE LATIN MISSIONS

1 Henrion, *Histoire générale*, II, 253.

2 Letter of P. Tarillon, n.d., in Abbé Orse, Giraud and Saint Aroman, *Actes des apôtres modernes, ou missions catholiques: voyages des missionaires dans toutes les parties du monde* (4 vols., Paris, 18—), II, 137; Carayon, *Relations inédites*, 159; Dreux, *Voyage en Turquie*, 67.

3 Vernier, *Histoire patriarcat arménien*, 276–7; Basilio Talantian, 'Il Primato di Pietro e del Papa nella Chiesa Armena', *Centro Franciscano Studia Orientalia Christiana*, v (Cairo, 1960), 267.

4 Jean Mécérian, *Histoire et institutions de l'Église arménienne* (Beirut, 1965), 298.

5 Gerlach, *Aelteren Tagebuch*, 184–6; Avedis K. Sanjian, *Armenian Communities of Syria in Ottoman Times* (Cambridge, 1965), 230.

6 'Lettera di Ciriaco d'Erivan, Patriarca Armeno di Constantinopoli

(1641–2) scritta al Papa Urbana VIII e la sua Professione di Fede', *Bessarione*, XXXIV (1918), 120–3; Talantian, 'Il primato di Pietro', 263.

7 Jean-Baptiste Tavernier, *Les six voyages qu'il a faits en Turquie, en Perse, et aux Indies* (Paris, 1678), 150.

8 A. Balgy, *Historia doctrinae*, 175.

9 Rycaut, *The Present State of the Greek and Armenian Churches*, 447–57.

10 P. Monier to P. Fleurian, *Lettres édifiantes et curieuses des missions étrangères* (new edn, 5 vols., Toulouse, 1810), III, 71–2; Jacques Villotte, *Voyage d'un missionaire de la Compagnie de Jésus en Turquie, en Perse, en Armenie, en Arabie, et en Barbarie* (Paris, 1730), 141.

11 J. Queyrot to a Jesuit, 28 February 1631, in Rabbath, *Documents inédits*, I, 380; Georges Goyau, 'Une capitale missionaire du Levant: Alep dans la première moitié du XVIIe siècle', *Revue d'histoire des missions*, XI (1934), 161–86.

12 Joseph Besson, *La Syrie et la Terre Sainte au XVIIe siècle*, ed. Auguste Carayon (new edn, Paris, 1862), 49–65; Homsy, *Les Capitulations*, 372–3.

13 Quoted in Goyau, 'Une capitale missionaire', 166.

14 Lemmens, *Hierarchia latina*, 225–7, 296–7.

15 Relation of N. Pouresson, 1652, in Rabbath, *Documents inédits*, I, 54–6; Georges Goyau, 'Le rôle religieux du consul François Picquet dans Alep, 1652–62', *Revue d'histoire des missions*, XII (1935), 161–98; 'Mission at Aleppo', in Rabbath, *Documents inédits*, I, 452–4.

16 'Relation of the consul of Aleppo', in Rabbath, *Documents inédits*, I, 94–102.

17 Letter of the patriarchs, 11 February 1663, in Rabbath, *Documents inédits*, I, 468; da Terzorio, *Le Missioni dei Minori*, V, 58–64.

18 Goyau, 'Le rôle religieux', 181.

19 Nacchi to M. A. Tamburini, in Orse *et al.*, *Actes*, I, 168; Relation of Jean Amieu, 1650, in Rabbath, *Documents inédits*, I, 396.

20 Nacchi to Tamburini, in Orse *et al.*, *Actes*, I, 197–210; V. Grumel, 'Macaire, patriarche d'Antioche, 1642–72', *Echos d'Orient*, XXVIII, 1 (1928), 68–77; François Tournebize, 'Le catholicisme à Alep au XVIIe siècle, 1625–1703', *Études*, CXXXIV (1913), 358–60.

21 The letter of Caraffa is in Rabbath, *Documents inédits*, I, 140–41; Anaissi, *Bullarium maronitarum*, 70–5; Dib, *Histoire de l'Église maronite*, I, 135.

22 The acts of the council are in Rabbath, *Documents inédits*, I, 152–69. See also Charles de Clercq, ed., *Conciles des Orientaux catholiques*, vol. XI, pts 1 and 2 of C. J. Hefele, *Histoire des conciles* (11 vols., Paris, 1949–52), pt 1, 12–13.

23 See Anaissi, *Bullarium maronitarum*, 81–103 for the constitution of the college.

24 Dandini, *Missione Apostolica*, 3.

25 De Clercq, *Conciles*, pt 1, 19–21; Dandini, *Missione Apostolica*, 86–105.

26 Kamal S. Salibi, *The Modern History of Lebanon* (New York, 1965), 123ff.; Marcellino da Civezza, *Storia Universale*, III, 16–18.

27 J. C. Hurewitz, *Diplomacy in the Near and Middle East: A Documentary Record, 1535–1914* (2 vols., Princeton, 1956), I, 24.

28 Besson, *La Syrie*, 39–41; J. Crétineau-Joly, *Histoire religieuse, politique et littéraire de la Compagnie de Jésus* (2nd edn, 6 vols., Paris, 1845–6), I, 214.

29 Kamal S. Salibi, *Maronite Historians of Medieval Lebanon* (Beirut, 1959), 92–5.

30 Quoted in Dib, *Histoire*, I, 160–1.

31 Assemani, *Bibliotheca orientalis*, II, 457–8; Tisserant, 'Eglise chaldéenne', 230–3.

32 Adolphe d'Avril, *La Chaldée chrétienne* (Paris, 1864), 15ff.

33 Aboulahad of Amid, 'Les origines du patriarcat Chaldéen: vie de Mar Youssef Ier, patriarch des Chaldéens', ed. J. B. Chabot, *Revue de l'Orient chrétien*, I, 2 (1896), 71.

34 Albert Lampart, *Ein Märtyrer der Union mit Rom: Joseph I (1681–96) Patriarch der Chaldäer* (Einseideln, 1966), 85ff.; Assemani, *Bibliotheca orientalis*, I, 242; Samuel Giamil, *Genuinae relationes*, 205–13.

9 PALESTINE, EGYPT AND NORTH AFRICA

1 Quoted in Golubovich, *Biblioteca Bio-Bibliografica*, N.S. (14 vols., Quaracchi, 1921–33), I, 364.

2 Orders to the *kadi* of Jerusalem, September 1609 and January 1611, in Uriel Heyd, ed., *Ottoman Documents*, 184.

3 Louis XIII to Césy, Paris, 26 May 1620, in Rabbath, *Documents inédits*, I, 331; Charles-Roux, *France et chrétiens*, 37.

4 Girolamo Golubovich, 'La question de Luoghi Santi nel Periodo degli Anni 1620–1638', *Archivium Franciscanum Historicum*, XIV (1921), 213ff.

5 The controversy may be traced in detail in Golubovich, *Biblioteca Bio-Bibliografica*, N.S., VII, 230–51 and VIII, 1–20, 319–21.

6 *Ibid.*, VIII, 90–1.

7 Quoted in Teddy Kollek and Moshe Pearlman, *Pilgrims to the Holy Land* (Jerusalem, 1971), 178.

8 Rycaut, *The Present State of the Greek and Armenian Churches*, 349–51. The scene of the Holy Fire is also described in La Croix, *La Turquie chrétienne*, 40.

9 Sandys, *A Relation of a Journey*, 110; Vincenzo Buiri, *L'Unione*

della Chiesa Copta con Roma sotto Clemente VIII, 1592–1605, vol. XXIII, no. 72 of *Orientalia Christiana* (Rome, 1931), 111–12.

10 Hess, *The Capuchins*, I, 383; Meinardus, *Christian Egypt*, 405.
11 J. M. Wansleben, *The Present State of Egypt, or a New Relation of a Late Voyage into that Kingdom, 1672–73*, trans. M. D. and B. D. (London, 1678), 151–74.
12 The lengthy correspondence between Rome and Yuhanna is covered in J. P. Trossen, *Les relations du Patriarche Copte Jean XVI avec Rome, 1676–1718* (Luxembourg, 1948). See also Giacomo d'Albano, *Historia della Missione Francescana in Alto-Egitto, Fungi, Etiopia, 1686–1720*, ed G. Giamberardini (Cairo, 1961), 52–62.
13 Georges Goyau, *La France missionaire dans les cinq parties du monde* (2 vols., Paris, 1948), II, 39ff. and by the same author, 'Le Christianisme sur les côtes barbaresques jusqu'au XIXe siècle', *Revue d'histoire des missions*, VII (1930), 39–40; Joseph Sanita, 'Libya' in vol. II of *Historia missionum Ordinis Fratrum Minorum* (3 vols., Rome, 1967–8), 61–4.

10 THE EIGHTEENTH CENTURY IN ISTANBUL

1 Famin, *Histoire de la rivalité*, 235–6; Joseph Lammeyer, *Das französische Protektorat über die Christen im Orient* (Leipzig, 1919), 86–7.
2 Belin, *Histoire de la latinité*, 354–6; E. Dalleggio d'Alessio, 'Recherches sur l'histoire de la latinité de Constantinople: Nomenclature des églises latines de Galata', *Echos d'Orient*, XXV, 1 (1926), 29–30; Hofmann, *Il Vicariato Apostolico*, 19.
3 Marquis de Bonnac, *Mémoire historique sur l'ambassade de France à Constantinople*, ed. Charles Schefer (Paris, 1894), 189.
4 M. de Bonnac to Louis XV, Constantinople, 9 June 1723, in Rabbath, ed., *Documents inédits*, I, 545–7; Homsy, *Les Capitulations*, 392–5.
5 Villeneuve to the Comte de Marenpas, 1731, in Rey, *De la protection diplomatique*, 338.
6 Homsy, *Les Capitulations*, 256.
7 Father Tarillon's letter to Msgr Pontchartrain, 'On the present condition of the Jesuit fathers in Greece', Constantinople, 4 March 1714, in Orse *et al.*, *Actes*, II, 124ff.
8 'Relation of the establishment and progress of the Salonica mission', Orse *et al.*, *Actes*, II, 244–78.
9 H. L. Hofmann, 'De Benedicti XIV latinisationibus in constitutione "Esti pastoralis" et "Intermulta"', *Ephemerides Juris Canonici*, IV, 1 (1948), 11–26.
10 Benedict XIV, 'Esti pastoralis', in *Bullarium*, vol. 15 of *Opera Omnia* (17 vols., new edn, Prati, 1845), 197–212.

11 De Martinis, ed., *Juris pontificii*, III, 597–620 contains the document.
12 Belin, *Histoire de la latinité*, 268. Outside Istanbul there were Latin churches at Gallipoli, Bandirma and Tekir dag (Rodosto), where Prince Rakoczy was buried.
13 Anon., 'Letter of a missionary from Damascus', in Orse *et al.*, *Actes*, II, 44–5.
14 Ignatius Mouradgea d'Ohsson, *Tableau général de l'Empire ottoman* (8 vols., Paris, 1788–1824), IV, 428–30.
15 On the role of Auxentios see the work by Kallistos Ware, *Eustratios Argenti: A Study of the Greek Church Under Turkish Rule* (Oxford, 1964).
16 François de Tott, *Mémoires du Baron de Tott sur les Turcs et les Tartares* (2 vols., Paris, 1785), I, 82.
17 Sergios Makarios, Ὑπομνήματα ἐκκλησιαστικῆς ἱστορίας (Memoirs of Church History), in C. Sathas, ed., Μεσαιωνικὴ βιβλιοθήκη (7 vols., Venice, 1872), III, 201–10.
18 Karmiris, Τὰ δογματικὰ, I, 989–91. The *Oros* has never officially been revoked although since 1900 the practice of rebaptism has generally not been followed.
19 Makarios, Ὑπομνήματα, 210ff.; de Tott, *Mémoires*, I, 83–5.
20 Barenton, *La France catholique en Orient*, 179–89.
21 Pastor, *History*, XXXVIII, 113.
22 Letter of Saint-Priest is in Rabbath, *Documents inédits*, II, 602.
23 Charles-Roux, *France et chrétiens*, 93–6.
24 Barenton, *La France catholique*, 226–33.
25 Quoted in Charles-Roux, *France et chrétiens*, 108.

11 THE BALKANS AFTER THE PEACE OF KARLOWITZ

1 The acts are in Joannes D. Mansi, ed., *Sacrorum conciliorum nova et amplissima collectio* (53 vols., Graz, 1961), XXXV, cols, 1375–1436. See also Georg Stadtmüller, 'Das albanische National Konzil von Jahre 1703', *Orientalia Christiana Periodica*, XXI (1956), 68–74.
2 Hofmann, 'La Chiesa Cattolica', II, 176–7; Minas Nurikhan, *The Life and Times of Abbot Mekhitar, 1660–1750*, trans. John McQuillan (Venice, 1915), 323ff. Mekhitar and his community were given the island of San Lazaro in the Venetian lagoon by the Senate. Here a monastery was built which still exists as a centre of Armenian learning and publishing. The monks adopted the rule of St Benedict.
3 Testa, *Recueil des traités*, I, 218.
4 Villari, *Republic of Ragusa*, 329–30, 382–416.
5 Cordignano, *Geografia ecclesiastica*, 325ff.; Skendi, 'Religion in Albania', XV, 323.
6 Charles Fabrèques, 'L'Église latine en Bulgarie', *Echos d'Orient*, VII, 4 (1904), 207.

7 Joseph Pitton de Tournefort, *Relation d'un voyage du Levant* (2 vols., Paris, 1717), II, 22–4, 165.

8 Demetrios Cantemir, *The History of the Growth and Decay of the Ottoman Empire*, trans. N. Tindal (London, 1734), pt 2, book 4, 391ff. This whole incident is described in great detail in Philip Argenti, *The Occupation of Chios by the Venetians, 1694* (London, 1935).

9 Quoted in Orse *et al.*, *Actes*, II, 144. See also *Nouveaux mémoires de missions de la Compagnie de Jésus dans le Levant* (4 vols., Paris, 1715–24), I, 60–7.

10 Quoted in Orse *et al.*, *Actes*, II, 144.

11 Cantemir, *The History*, 395, note 400; Philip Argenti, *Religious Minorities*, 207–8 and 221–8; Tournefort, *Relation d'un voyage*, II, 49–50.

12 Hofmann, *Tinos*, 21–3; Carayon, *Missions des Jesuites*, 65–6.

13 Barenton, *La France catholique*, 175–9; Hofmann, *Naxos*, 42–3.

14 Père Tarillon, 'Voyage to Constantinople', in Orse *et al.*, *Actes*, II, 144.

15 Report of Msgr Castelli in Hofmann, *Chios*, 24–5.

16 *Ibid.*, pp. 25–6; Argenti, *Religious Minorities*, 313–26.

17 Hofmann, 'La Chisea Cattolica', 410ff.

18 Hofmann, *Naxos*, 26, and *Tinos*, 30–8.

19 Letter of 2 July 1793, in Archivio della S. Congregazione di Propaganda, quoted in Pastor, *History*, XXXIX, 386ff.

20 Marie Gabriel Choiseul-Gouffier, *Voyage pittoresque de la Grèce* (2 vols., Paris, 1782–1824), I, 34–5, 48.

21 Da Terzorio, *Le Missioni dei Minori*, II, 267–78.

12 THE CATHOLIC ARMENIANS

1 Report of David of St Charles, in Hofmann, *Il Vicariato Apostolico*, 78–83.

2 H. Riondel, *Une Page tragique de l'histoire religieuse du Levant: Le Bienheureux Gomidas de Constantinople, prêtre arménien et martyr, 1656–1707* (Paris, 1929), 27–33; Nurikhan, *The Life and Times of Abbot Mekhitar*, 28ff.

3 Mécérian, *Histoire et institutions*, 333ff.

4 Innocent XII to Nahab(i)et, Rome, 3 May 1698, in de Martinis, *Juris pontificii*, II, 183–4. Innocent wrote several letters to the shah of Iran interceding for Armenian Christians.

5 Charles Frazee, 'The Formation of the Armenian Catholic Community in the Ottoman Empire', *Eastern Churches Review*, VII, 2 (1975), 149–63.

6 Letters of Ferriol to the Ministry of Louis XIV, Constantinople, 3 July 1706, 4 November 1707, 8 November 1707, in Rabbath, *Documents inédits*, II, 126–30.

7 Report of Mauri, 28 March 1721 in Archivio della S. Congregazione di Propaganda, Scritture riferite, vol. 632: quoted in Hofmann, *Il Vicariato Apostolico*, 95–102.

8 Golubovich, *Biblioteca Bio-Bibliografica*, N.S., IV, 119.

9 *Collectanea S. Congregatione*, I, 99–101.

10 Archivio della S. Congregazione di Propaganda: Cong. Armeni, XVII, 785–6, quoted in Mesrob J. Terzian, *Le Patriarcat de Cilicie et les Arméniens catholiques, 1740–1812* (Beirut, 1955), 27.

11 Archivio di S. Congregazione di Propaganda: Cong. Armeni, XCVII, 94–5, quoted in Terzian, *Le Patriarcat*, 53.

12 Instructions to Bona, and Benedict XIV to Cardinal de Tenecin, Rome, 4 August 1745, in Emilia Morelli, *Le Lettere di Benedetto XIV al Cardinal de Tencin* (2 vols., Rome, 1955), I, 259–63; de Martinis, *Juris pontificii*, 232.

13 Stato della Nazione Armena de Constantinopoli, Cong., part. an. 1757, vol. 122, fos. 197–200: quoted in Terzian, *Le Patriarcat*, 47–57.

14 Relation of Frachia in Archivio della S. Congregazione di Propaganda, Scritture riferite: quoted in Hofmann, *Il Vicariato Apostolico*, 206–20. The Mekhitarists had an internal dispute in 1773. Several left Venice for Trieste where Maria Theresa provided them with a monastery; later they moved to Vienna.

15 Vernier, *Histoire du patriarcat arménien*, 272. The community was known as the Antonines.

16 Quoted in Mécérian, *Histoire*, 322.

17 De Martinis, *Juris pontificii*, III, 83–5; Benedict XIV to Cardinal de Tenecin, Rome, 30 November 1742, in Émile de Heeckerin, *Correspondance de Benoît XIV, 1745–55* (2 vols, in 1, Paris, 1912), I, 14–16.

18 Mécérian, *Histoire*, 323. The rule of the monastery of Antonines of Bzommar was approved by Rome only in 1838.

19 Archivio della S. Congregazione di Propaganda: Cong. Armeni, XIII, 407–8: quoted in Terzian, *Le Patriarcat*, 153 and 155–61.

20 Mécérian, *Histoire*, 122.

13 THE NEAR EASTERN CHURCHES

1 Anaissi, *Bullarium maronitarum*, 186–95; de Martinis, *Juris pontificii*, II, 95–8; Georges-Joseph Mahfoud, *L'Organisation monastique dans l'Église maronite* (Beirut, 1967), 130ff.

2 P. Fromage to Le Camus, Tripoli, 15 October 1736, in Orse *et al.*, *Actes*, I, 136–63.

3 The acts of the council are in Mansi, *Sacrorum conciliorum*, XXXVIII, cols. 7–334; de Clercq, *Conciles*, pt 1, 215–71.

4 Assemani to Cardinal de Fleury, 15 October 1736, in Rabbath, *Documents inédits*; de Clercq, *Conciles*, pt 1, 271ff.

5 Anaissi, *Bullarium maronitarum*, 251–5.
6 Letter of Benedict XIV to Maronite bishops, Rome, 20 July 1746, in Anaissi, *Bullarium maronitarum*, 329–33.
7 De Martinis, *Juris pontificii*, III, 482–3; Dib, *Histoire*, I, 195–6.
8 De Martinis, *Juris pontificii*, III, 550–4; see also J. Saba, 'Entre Melkites et Maronites au XVIIIᵉ siècle', *Echos d'Orient*, XVI (1913), 409–23, 536–48.
9 De Clercq, *Conciles*, pt I, 277–80.
10 Mahfoud, *L'Organisation monastique*, 146–7.
11 De Martinis, *Juris pontificii*, IV, 241–5; 326–7.
12 Charles-Roux, *France et chrétiens*, 602–7.
13 Paul Bacel, 'La congrégation des Basiliens Chouerites: les origines, organisation et développements', *Echos d'Orient*, VI, 3 and 4 (1903), 175–82, 242–8.
14 Antoine Nacchi, 'Voyage to Aleppo', in Orse *et al.*, *Actes*, I, 182–5.
15 Quoted in Homsy, *Les Capitulations*, 384. Euthymios died in Damascus in December 1723, after enduring many sufferings for his Catholic faith.
16 Letter of D'Andrezel to M. de Maurepas, Constantinople, 22 October 1724; letter of a Capuchin father, Damascus, 30 October 1724; letter of the consul of Aleppo to the Ministry, 5 March 1725, in Rabbath, *Documents inédits*, II, 566–73.
17 Robert M. Haddad, *Syrian Christians in a Muslim Society* (Princeton, 1970), 55ff.; Rashid Haddad, 'Sources (Hellènes) de la controverse dans l'Église melchite au XVIIIᵉ siècle', *Actes du premier congrès international des études balkaniques et sud-est européens* (Sofia, 1969), IV, 499–505.
18 Ambrose of Rennes to a Capuchin Father at Aleppo, Damascus, December 1724, in Rabbath, *Documents inédits*, II, 569.
19 De Martinis, *Juris pontificii*, II, 414; de Clercq, *Conciles*, pt 2, 135.
20 De Martinis, *Juris pontificii*, III, 124–30. See also Cyril Karalevskij, *Histoire des patriarcats melchites* (2 vols., Rome, 1910–11), II, 4.
21 Pope Clement IX had confirmed the rule of Shuwair in September 1739, and gave them the church of St Maria in Dominica in Rome for a college.
22 M. Lane to Count Castellane, Saida 1745, in Orse *et al.*, *Actes*, II, 1.
23 Letter of Clement XIII to Maximos, Rome, 1 August 1760, in de Martinis, *Juris pontificii*, IV, 49–51.
24 De Clercq, *Conciles*, pt I, 149–55; Letter of Clement to Ignatios, Rome, 11 September 1765, in de Martinis, *Juris pontificii*, IV, 119–21, 152–3.
25 Lemmens, *Hierarchia latina*, 297. On this question see W. de Vries, 'Das Problem der "communicatio in sacris cum dissentibus" in Nahen Osten zur Zeit der Union (17 and 18 Jahrhundert)',

Ostkirchliche Studien, VI I (1957), 81–106; English translation in *Concilium*, IV, I (1965), 18–40.

26 Paul Bacel, 'L'Église melkite au XVIIIe siècle', *Echos d'Orient*, XV, 2 (1913), 44–56, 134–43.

27 Karalevskij, *Histoire des patriarcats*, II, 1–5.

28 Relation of the consul at Aleppo, 12 November 1701, and letter of Louis XIV to de Ferriol, Paris, 1702, in Rabbath, *Documents inédits*, I, 113–14, 117.

29 L. Cheiko, 'Autobiographie du Patriarche Ignace-Michel Djaroue', *Revue de l'Orient chrétien*, VI (1901), 379–401.

30 Assemani, *De catholicis*, 243.

31 Giamil, *Genuinae relationes*, 213ff.

32 Assemani, *De catholicis*, 244; Tisserant, 'Église chaldéenne', XI, 250.

33 J. M. Fiey, *Mossoul chrétienne* (Beirut, 1959), 60–1.

34 Giamil, *Genuinae relationes*, 384–5; Assemani, *Bibliotheca orientalis*, II, pt 1, 578–84.

35 J. M. Fiey, *Assyrie chrétienne*, vol. XLII of *Recherches publiées sous la direction de L'Institut de lettres orientales de Beyrouth*, 48.

36 Quoted in Fiey, *Mossoul chrétienne*, 59.

37 Stephane Bello, *La Congrégation de S. Hormisdas et l'Église chaldéenne dans la première moitié du XIX siècle*, vol. 122 of *Orientalia Christiana Analecta* (Rome, 1939), 7–13.

38 Lemmens, *Hierarchia latina*, 277–89.

14 PALESTINE AND EGYPT

1 Henry Maundrell, 'The Journey of Henry Maundrell from Aleppo to Jerusalem, A.D. 1697', in Thomas Wright, ed., *Early Travels in Palestine* (London, 1848), 442–3.

2 Golubovich, *Biblioteca Bio-Bibliografica*, I, 290–1 and II, 11–16; Joseph Hajjar, 'La question religieuse en Orient au déclin de l'Empire ottoman, 1683–1814', *Istina*, XIII, 2 (1968), 167–72.

3 De Vergennes to Duc de Choiseul, Constantinople, 7 March 1757, in Golubovich, *Biblioteca Bio-bibliografica*, II, 164–7.

4 Tott, *Mémoires du Baron de Tott*, II, 92–3.

5 Marcellino da Civezza, *Storia universale*, III, 75–7.

6 Moshe Sharon, 'Palestine Under the Mamlukes and the Ottoman Empire, 1291–1918', in Michael Avi-Yonah, ed., *A History of the Holy Land* (Jerusalem, 1969), 286–9.

7 Quoted in Butcher, *The Story of the Church of Egypt*, II, 287.

8 Ildefonso da Palermo, *Cronaca della Missione Francescana dell' Alto Egitto: 1719—39*, ed. Gabriele Giamberardini (Cairo, 1962), 5; Sanita, 'Libya', 65.

9 De Bernat to Fleuriau, Cairo, 20 July 1711, in *Lettres édifiantes*, IV, 329–92.

10 Georg Hofmann, 'Griechische Patriarchen und Römische Päpste', vol. xxxvi of *Orientalia Christiana Analecta* (Rome, 1934), 86–96.

11 De Martinis, *Juris pontificii*, iii, 30–1; Angelo Colombo, *Le Origini della Gerarchia della Chiesa Copta Cattolica nel Secolo XVIII*, vol. cxl of *Orientalia Christiana Analecta* (Rome, 1953), 158–61.

12 Quoted in Norman Daniel, *Islam, Europe and Empire* (Edinburgh, 1966), 104.

13 Colombo, *Le Origini della Gerarchia*, 241–2.

15 THE CATHOLICS OF ISTANBUL FROM THE NINETEENTH
CENTURY TO THE PROCLAMATION OF THE TURKISH
REPUBLIC

1 Report of Fonto, in Archivio della S. Congregazione di Propaganda, Scritture non riferite; Romania, vol. xxii: quoted in Hofmann, *Il Vicariato Apostolico*, 30.

2 Quoted in Charles-Roux, *France et chrétiens*, 123–5.

3 A. Trannoy, 'La nation latine de Constantinople,' *Echos d'Orient*, xv, 3 (1912), 252; Richard Davey, *The Sultan and His Subjects* (2 vols., London, 1897), ii, 74; Eugène Boré, *Correspondance et mémoires d'un voyageur en Orient* (2 vols., Paris, 1840), i, 163.

4 M. Kukiel, *Czartoryski and European Unity, 1770–1861* (Princeton, 1955), 248.

5 Schopoff, *Les réformes*, 17–24. The text of the *Hatti şerif* is in Hurewitz, *Diplomacy in the Near and Middle East*, i, 113–16.

6 The *Hatti Humayun* is in Hurewitz, *Diplomacy in the Near and Middle East*, i, 149–53.

7 Henrion, *Histoire générale*, ii, 637; 'Les Frères des Écoles Chrétiennes en Orient', *Bessarione*, ix (1901), 151; da Terzorio, *Le Missoni*, i, 138. Hillerau had a new cathedral constructed in 1846.

8 Gérard van Winsen, 'La Vie et les travaux d'Eugène Boré, 1809–1878', *Neue Zeitschrift für Missionwissenschaft*, xxxiv, 2 (1978), 81–9.

9 The text of the letter is in Pius IX, *Acta SS. D. N. Pii P. P. IX* (8 vols., Rome, 1865), i, 78–92.

10 Ἐγκύκλιος τῆς μιᾶς, ἁγίας, καθολικῆς καὶ ἀποστολικῆς ἐκκλησίας ἐπιστολὴ πρὸς τοὺς ἀπανταχοῦ Ὀρθοδόξους (An encyclical letter of the one, holy, catholic, and apostolic church to the Orthodox everywhere) (Constantinople, 1948), 13–14.

11 Eli Smith and H. G. O. Dwight, *Missionary Researches in Armenia* (London, 1834), 210.

12 Lemmens, *Hierarchia latina*, 273–6; Graf E. von Mülinen, *Die lateinische Kirche im Türkischen Reiche* (Berlin, 1903), 33.

13 Barenton, *La France catholique*, 242–64.

14 J. B. Piolet, *La France au dehors: les missions catholiques françaises au XIXᵉ siècle* (6 vols., Paris, 1901–3), i, 81–94; Heinrich

Gelzer, *Geistliches und Weltliches aus dem türkisch-griechischen Orient* (Leipzig, 1900), 139–47.

15 Charles-Roux, *France et chrétiens*, 225–40. See also Louis Le Fur, *Le Protectorat de la France sur les catholiques d'Orient et la reprise de nos relations avec le Saint-Siège* (Paris, 1927).

16 *Missiones catholicae cura S. Congregationis de Propaganda Fide descriptae* (Rome, 1907), 139–40.

16 THE VATICAN COUNCIL, THE EASTERN CHURCHES AND THE PAPACY

1 Quoted in Adrian Fortescue, *The Uniate Eastern Churches: The Byzantine Rite in Italy, Sicily, Syria and Egypt* (London, 1923), 38. The constitution of the congregation is to be found in de Martinis, *Juris pontificii*, VII, 1, 367–72.

2 Gabriel Giamberardini, *Impegni del Concilio Vaticano I per l'Oriente Cristiano e Relazioni della Chiesa Egiziana*, vol. 17 of *Spicilegium Pontificii Athenaei Antoniani* (Rome, 1970), 116–19.

3 The *acta* of the commission are to be found in Mansi, *Sacrorum conciliorum*, XLIX, cols. 985–1162. The composition of the commission is discussed in Hajjar, *Les Chrétiens uniates*, 292–3.

4 De Martinis, *Juris Pontificii*, VII, 2, 21–2.

5 Giamberardini, *Impegni del Concilio*, 94–130; Cuthbert Butler, *The Vatican Council* (2 vols., London, 1930), I, 93–5.

6 Mansi, *Sacrorum conciliorum*, LI, 687.

7 Butler, *Vatican Council*, I, 224–6; II, 150.

8 August Hasler, *Pius IX, Päpstliche Unfehlbarkeit und I Vatikanum*, vol. XII of *Päpste und Papsttum* (2 vols., Stuttgart, 1977), 116–17, 180–99; Hajjar, *Les Chrétiens uniates*, 301–6. The former Melkite patriarch Clement Bahouth voted in favour of promulgation.

9 Roger Aubert, *Le Saint-Siège et l'union des églises* (Brussels, 1947), 31–4, quoting *Lettres apostoliques de SS. Léon XIII*, IV, 6–31. Leo's Eastern policy has been studied in great detail by Joseph Hajjar, *Le Vatican – la France et le catholicisme oriental (1878–1914)* (Paris, 1979), 17–79.

10 Quoted in Fortescue, *Uniate Eastern Churches*, 40.

11 *Codex juris canonici* (Rome, 1919), C. 257, para. 1.

17 THE BALKAN CHURCHES

1 John C. Broughton (Baron Hobhouse), *Journey Through Albania and Other Provinces of Turkey in Europe and Asia to Constantinople During The Years 1809 and 1810* (London, 1813), 146–8.

2 Stavro Skendi, 'Crypto-Christianity in the Balkan Area Under the Ottomans', *Slavic Review*, XXVI, 2 (1967), 239.

3 Hecquard, *Histoire et description de la Haute Albanie*, 36–59,

177–97, 215–25; Frédéric Gibert, *Les Pays d'Albanie et leur histoire* (Paris, 1914), 15–23.
4 Skendi, 'Religion in Albania', 317.
5 Mülinen, *Die lateinische Kirche*, 31–2; *Missiones catholicae*, 127–33.
6 Ilija Kecmanović, 'Bildnis eines bosnischen Franziskaners', *Südost Forschungen*, xv (1956), 402–7.
7 *Missiones catholicae*, 107–16.
8 R. F. O'Connor, 'The Capuchin Mission in Bulgaria and Reunion With Rome', *American Catholic Quarterly Review*, xliii (1918), 209–14.
9 Ivan Sofranov, *Histoire du mouvement bulgare vers l'Église catholique au XIX siècle* (Rome, 1960), 40–66. The Bulgarian Orthodox church had come under Greek domination after the suppression of the Orchid archbishopric in 1767.
10 Giorgio Eldarov, 'Die Union der Bulgaren mit Rom', *Ostkirchliche Studien*, x, 1 (1961), 5–8; Adolphe d'Avril, *La Bulgarie chrétienne* (Paris, 1861), 79–83.
11 Crescent Armanet, 'Le Mouvement des Bulgares vers Rome en 1860', *Echos d'Orient*, xii, 6 (1909), 355–61; Charles Fabrèques, 'Le Vicariat apostolique bulgare de Thrace', *Echos d'Orient*, vi, 1 (1904), 36–7.
12 De Martinis, *Juris pontificii*, viii, 258.
13 Quoted in Thomas Meininger, *Ignatiev and the Establishment of the Bulgarian Exarchate* (Madison, 1970), 24–5.
14 Orazio Premoli, *Contemporary Church History, 1900–1925* (London, 1932), 255–6; R. Janin, 'L'Église catholique en Turquie d'Europe', *Echos d'Orient*, xvi, 3 (1913), 236–42.
15 Negris to Veggetti, Corinth, 14 April 1822, and S. C. for the Propagation of the Faith to Veggetti, Rome, 4 July 1822, quoted in Georg Hofmann, *Das Papsttum und der Griechische Freiheitskampf*, vol. cxxxvi of *Orientalia Christiana Analecta* (Rome, 1952), 72–8.
16 The incident is contained in Robert Walsh, *A Residence in Constantinople*(2 vols., London, 1836), i, 128.
17 *Ibid.*, i, 187–92.
18 Maxime Raybaud, *Mémoires sur la Grèce* (2 vols., Paris, 1824–5), ii, 124–6, 144; François C. Pouqueville, *Histoire de la régénération de la Grèce* (4 vols., 2nd edn, Paris, 1825), iv, 186.
19 Quoted in *Courrière de Smyrne*, 22 March 1829.
20 Report of Céleste Étienne David to Vicomte de Chateaubriand, Chios, 14 June 1824, quoted in Philip Argenti, ed., *The Massacres of Chios Described in Contemporary Diplomatic Reports* (London, 1932), 82–4.
21 Pope Leo XII to Cardelli, Rome, 19 September 1826, in de Martinis, *Juris pontificii*, iv, 679; Hofmann, *Chios*, 29–30; Argenti, *Religious Minorities*, 223–30. The Catholic bishop, Francesco

Xavier Dragopolis, was not on the island at the time of the massacre and did not return to Chios.

22 Letter of Henry in Auguste Carayon, ed., *Missions des Jésuites dans l'archipel grec*, vol. XXI of *Relations inédites concernant la Compagnie de Jésus* (Poitiers, 1869), 66, 143–60.

23 Lemmens, *Hierarchia latina*, 254. Henry tells about the attempt on the bishop's life.

24 Giles Henry to Fathers of Lyon Province, 8 February 1846, and to Henri de Prunières, 14 January 1848, in Carayon, *Relations inédites*, 31–47, 131–63.

25 *Oriente Cattolico: Cenni Storici e Statistiche* (Vatican City, 1962), 124–5; Wilhelm de Vries, *Die christliche Osten in Geschichte und Gegenwart*, vol. XII, new ser., of *Das Östliche Christentum* (Würzburg, 1951), 129–30.

26 *Missiones catholicae*, 141; R. M. Dawkins, 'The Crypto-Christians of Turkey', *Byzantion*, VIII (1933), 256.

27 *Oriente Cattolico*, 315.

18 THE ARMENIAN CATHOLIC COMMUNITY

1 Leon Arpee, *A History of Armenian Christianity from the Beginning to Our Own Time* (New York, 1946), 256ff.

2 Leon Arpee, *The Armenian Awakening: A History of the Armenian Church, 1820–1860* (Chicago, 1909), 40–7.

3 Walsh, *A Residence in Constantinople*, II, 430; Report of Coressi in Archivio della S. Congregazione di Propaganda, Scritture riferite, Cong. Armeni, vol. XXXIII, 267, in Hofmann, *Il Vicariato Apostolico*, 30–2.

4 Charles-Roux, *France et chrétiens*, 128.

5 The imperil *firman* is given in its entirety in Walsh, *A Residence in Constantinople*, II, appendix, 531ff.

6 Several thousand Armenian Catholics of Akhaltsikhe were transferred to Russia as a result of the treaty which concluded the war in 1828.

7 Report of Nurijian to the editor of *Annales de la Propagation de la foi*, VII (1834), 306–7.

8 Smith and Dwight, *Missionary Researches*, 3, 44, 66 and 257; Horatio Southgate, *Narrative of a Tour Through Armenia, Kurdistan, Persia and Mesopotamia* (2 vols., New York, 1840), I, 202–40.

9 Abdolonyme Ubicini, *Lettres sur la Turquie* (2 vols., 2nd edn, Paris, 1835), II, 325–7.

10 Mécérian, *Histoire*, 135ff; de Martinis, *Juris pontificii*, VII, 1, 93–5.

11 Mansi, *Sacrorum conciliorum*, XL, 783–90; de Clercq, *Conciles*, pt 2, 508–19.

12 De Martinis, *Juris pontificii*, VII, 1, 232; Vernier, *Histoire du patriarcat arménien*, 312–14.

13 Leo G. Byrne, *The Great Ambassador* (Columbus, 1964), 162–72; Arpee, *The Armenian Awakening*, 93–171, discusses the growth of Protestantism in detail.

14 Mansi, *Sacrorum conciliorum*, XL, cols, 941–52, 991–3, 1026–32; de Clercq, *Conciles*, pt 2, 524.

15 *Reversurus* is found in de Martinis, *Juris pontificii*, VI, 1, 453–9.

16 Sesostris Sidarouss, *Des patriarcats: les patriarcats dans l'empire ottoman et spécialement en Egypt* (Paris, 1907), 44; de Clercq, *Conciles*, pt 2, 536–7; de Martinis, *Juris pontificii*, VII, 2, 7–8.

17 Quoted in Mansi, *Sacrorum conciliorum*, XL, 1039–42.

18 De Martinis, *Juris pontificii*, VII, 2, 62–74, 84–6, 110–13, 132–61.

19 From their origins in the eighteenth century, the Antonines had been extremely active in spreading the Catholic Armenian faith. All but a handful were now gone. See Mécérian, *Histoire*, 324.

20 Louise Nalbandian, *The Armenian Revolutionary Movement* (Berkeley, 1963), 80–98, 104–18, 151–63.

21 Richard Hovannisian, *Armenia on the Road to Independence* (Berkeley, 1967), 36; Sarkis Atamian, *The Armenian Community* (New York, 1955), 51–130. In 1891 a Kurdish militia, the *Hamidieh*, was formed to prey on the Armenian Christians.

22 Charles-Roux, *France et chrétiens*, 250–1; Barenton, *La France catholique*, 280–2.

23 Johannes Lepsius, *Armenia and Europe: An Indictment*, ed. J. Rendel Harris (London, 1897), 12; Davey, *The Sultan*, II, 195.

24 De Clercq, *Conciles*, 721–56; Vernier, *Histoire du patriarcat arménien*, 321; 'Reglements généraux des Arméniens catholiques', *Revue de l'Orient chrétien*, IV (1899), 306–13.

25 De Clercq, *Conciles*, 755, 881–5.

26 *Acta et decreta concilii nationalis Armenorum Romae habiti ad Sancti Nicolai Tolentinatis, 1913* (Rome, 1914).

27 'Chronique', *Echos d'Orient*, XV, 2 (1912), 63–7; XV, 3, 260; Jean Mécérian, *Le Genocide du peuple arménien* (Beirut, 1965), 47; Jean Naslian, *Les Mémoirs sur les événements politico-religieux en Proche-Orient de 1914 à 1928* (2 vols., Vienna, 1955), I, 3–35; Stanford and Ezel Shaw believe from their investigations of archival material that the Ottoman government had no determined policy to exterminate the Armenians. See *History of the Ottoman Empire and Modern Turkey* (Cambridge, 1977), II, 315–71.

28 Johannes Lepsius, *Le Rapport secret sur les massacres d'Arménie* (Paris, 1918), 10–19, 133–41; 'Statements of a traveler, Ankara, August, 1915' and report of Dr D., 8 September 1915, in Viscount Bryce, *The Treatment of Armenians in the Ottoman Empire, 1915–1916* (London, 1916), 382 and 421.

29 Report of G. Gorrini, Italian consul at Trabzon, in *Il Messaggero*,

25 August 1915, published in Bryce, *Treatment*, 286. The Catholics of Trabzon were eventually taken out to sea and drowned.
30 Naslian, *Les Mémoirs*, I, 147–63; *Germany, Turkey and Armenia: A Selection of Documentary Evidence Relating to the Armenian Atrocities From German and Other Sources* (London, 1917), 18–19; Clarence Ussher, 'The Armenian Atrocities and the Jihad', *Moslem World*, VI (1916), 140–3.

19 THE MARONITES AFTER THE REIGN OF MAHMUT II

1 Iliya Harik, *Politics and Change in a Traditional Society: Lebanon 1711–1845* (Princeton, 1868), 87–9; Anaissi, *Bullarium maronitarum*, 480–6.
2 De Martinis, *Juris pontificii*, V, 49–55; Mahfoud, *L'Organisation monastique*, 315.
3 James T. Addison, *The Christian Approach to the Moslem* (New York, 1942), 113–17.
4 Fr Eusebius to the editor of *Annales de la Propagation de la foi*, VII (1834), 341. See also Charles H. Churchill, *The Druzes and the Maronites Under Turkish Rule from 1840 to 1860* (London, 1862), 28–9.
5 Churchill, *The Druzes*, 34.
6 Dib, *Histoire*, I, 349–466; Charles Fabrèques, 'Le seminaire St François-Xavier', *Echos d'Orient*, VI, 7 (1903), 272–4; Michel-Marie Jullien, *La Nouvelle mission de la Compagnie de Jésus en Syrie, 1831–95* (2 vols., Tours, 1898), I, 133–49.
7 Churchill, *The Druzes*, 157–218; Laurent Saint-Aignan, *La Terre Sainte, Syrie, Egypte et Isthme de Suez* (Paris, 1868), 64–76.
8 Salibi, *Modern History*, 107.
9 Hajjar, *Les Chrétiens uniates*, 266; Moshe Ma'oz, *Ottoman Reform in Syria and Palestine, 1840–1861: The Impact of the Tanzimat on Politics and Society* (Oxford, 1968), 190.
10 Dib, *Histoire*, I, 226–8; de Clercq, *Conciles*, pt 2, 682.
11 Barenton, *La France catholique*, 294; Addison, *The Christian Approach*, 116–18.
12 Jullien, *La Nouvelle Mission*, II, 47–8. An Arabic printing press was begun in 1871 to disseminate Catholic literature.
13 Salibi, *Modern History*, 158–62.

20 THE CATHOLIC MELKITES

1 Karalevskij, *Histoire des patriarcats*, II, 7–23.
2 A biography of Maximos has been written by Joseph Hajjar, *Un Lutteur infatigable, le patriarche Maxime III Mazloum* (Harissa, 1957).
3 Fortescue, *The Uniate Eastern Churches*, 209.

4 'Extracts from a Diary of a Carmelite from Aleppo', in Rabbath, *Documents inédits*, II, 57.
5 Lemmens, *Hierarchia latina*, 297–8.
6 Karalevskij, *Histoire des patriarcats*, II, 24–48.
7 Cyril (Charon) Karalevskij, 'Les Debuts du patriarcat de Maximos III Mazloum, 1833–35', *Echos d'Orient*, IX, I (1906), 11–12.
8 De Martinis, 'Le Concile melchite de Ain-Traz', *Echos d'Orient*, IX, 4 (1906), 199–213.
9 De Martinis, *Juris pontificii*, V, 130–1, 150.
10 Fortescue, *The Uniate Eastern Churches*, 216.
11 Karalevskij, *Histoire des patriarcats*, II, 140–2.
12 De Clercq, *Conciles*, pt 2, 390–414; Hajjar, *Les Chrétiens uniates*, 283–8.
13 De Martinis, *Juris pontificii*, VII, 1, 293, 306–7, 318.
14 *Missiones catholicae*, 161; de Martinis, *Juris pontificii*, VII, 1, 287, 297, 427.
15 Hajjar, *Les Chrétiens uniates*, 288–9.
16 G. C. Anawati, 'The Roman Catholic Church and Churches in Communion with Rome', in A. J. Arberry, ed., *Religion in the Middle East* (2 vols., London, 1969), I, 394. Sultan Abdulmecid had given St Anne's, a church dating from the period of the Crusades, to the government of France at the conclusion of the Crimean War.
17 De Clercq, *Conciles*, pt 1, 784–5.

21 SYRIAN CATHOLICS AND THE CHALDEAN CHURCH

1 Donald Attwater, *The Christian Churches of the East* (2 vols., rev. edn, Milwaukee, 1947–8), II, 227. Patriarch Ignatius Butrus received his pallium on 28 February 1828. De Martinis, *Juris pontificii*, VI, 690.
2 Fr Eusebius to editor of *Annales de la Propagation de la foi*, VII (1834), 340.
3 Jullien, *La Nouvelle Mission*, I, 2–23.
4 De Martinis, *Juris pontificii*, VII, 1, 287 and 297.
5 Charles-Roux, *France et chrétiens*, 168.
6 De Martinis, *Juris pontificii*, VII, 1, 372 and 440–2; de Clercq, *Conciles*, pt 2, 586–98; Roger Aubert, *Le Pontificat de Pie IX, 1846–78*, vol. 21 of *Histoire de l'Église depuis ses origines jusqu'à nos jours*, ed. A. Fliche and V. Martin (Paris, 1952), 422.
7 De Clercq, *Conciles*, pt 1, 627; Adrian Fortescue, *The Lesser Eastern Churches* (London, 1913), 338.
8 Tisserant, 'Église chaldéene', cols. 242–3; de Martinis, *Juris pontificii*, IV, 564–6.
9 Bello, *La Congregation de S. Hormisdas*, 16–17, 86–107.

10 De Martinis, *Juris pontificii*, IV, 727–8; V, 121–3; Giamil, *Genuinae relationes*, 394–8; George P. Badger, *The Nestorians and their Rituals* (2 vols., London, 1852), I, 174–5.

11 Smith and Dwight, *Missionary Researches*, 357–8; Justin Perkins, ed., *Historical Sketch of the Mission to the Nestorians by Thomas Laurie of the Assyrian Mission* (New York, 1862), 8.

12 Aubrey Vine, *The Nestorian Churches* (London, 1937), 177; Avril, *La Chaldée chrétienne*, 60–2, 85.

13 De Martinis, *Juris pontificii*, VII, 1, 78–81.

14 *Annales de la société orientale pour l'union de tous les chrétiens d'Orient* (Paris, 1853) quoted in Avril, *La Chaldée chrétienne* 83; see also Giamil, *Genuinae relationes*, 407–14.

15 *Actes du Synode Chaldéen célébré au couvent de Rabban Hormizd près d'Alqoche du 7 au 21 juin, 1853*, ed. J. M. Vosté (Vatican City, 1942).

16 Letter of P. Angelo da Villarrubia to Chatry de LaFosse, Urfa, 7 October 1859 in Orse *et al.*, *Actes*, I, 149–62.

17 Giamil, *Genuinae relationes*, 424–9, 433–4; de Martinis, *Juris pontificii*, VIII, 252–5.

18 Tisserant, 'Église chaldéenne', cols. 245–54; de Martinis, *Juris pontificii*, VII, 2, 25–7, 32–5.

19 De Martinis, *Juris pontificii*, VII, 2, 162–4.

20 *Ibid.*, VII, 2, 276–8.

21 *Ibid.*, VII, 2, 278–83.

22 Giamil, *Genuinae relationes*, 438–56. In 1886 the archbishop of Canterbury inaugurated a 'Mission to the Assyrians' which was meant to strengthen the catholicate of Shim'un XXII at Kudshannis.

23 *Missiones catholicae*, 158–9; W. C. Emhardt and George Lamsa, *The Oldest Christian People* (New York, 1926), 108–11; Vine, *The Nestorian Churches*, 185; J. Tfinkdji, 'L'Église chaldéenne catholique', in *Annuaire pontifical catholique*, ed. A. Battandier (Paris, 1913), 807–14; John Joseph, *The Nestorians and their Muslim Neighbors* (Princeton, 1961), 131–44.

22 THE CATHOLICS OF THE HOLY LAND AND EGYPT

1 Famin, *Histoire de la rivalité*, 367–70; Golubovich, *Biblioteca Bio-Bibliografica*, N.S., II, 248–9.

2 P. Possou to M. Étienne, Damascus, 15 July 1831, in Orse *et al.*, *Actes* I, 62.

3 Famin, *Histoire de la rivalité*, 69.

4 Lemmens, *Hierarchia latina*, 303; Mülinen, *Die lateinische Kirche*, 35–6.

5 Edouard Driault and Michel l'Heritier, *Histoire diplomatique de la Grèce* (5 vols., Paris, 1925), II, 373; Bernard Collin, *Les Lieux saints* (Paris, 1962), 51.

6 Christopher Hollis and Ronald Brownrigg, *Holy Places* (New York, 1969), 94; C. H. Malik, 'The Orthodox Church', in A. J. Arberry, ed., *Religion in the Middle East*, I, 311, comments: 'But for the Russian Orthodox Church, Orthodoxy would have been an orphan. The churches of the West came to it as something alien; they wanted to change and convert it. Russian Orthodoxy came to it as bone of its bones and flesh of its flesh.'

7 Quoted in Fortescue, *The Uniate Eastern Churches*, 39.

8 J. Hajjar, 'A propos du Congrès eucharistique de Jérusalem (1893)', *Revue d'histoire ecclésiastique*, LXXIV (1978), 650–64; Jean Monval, *Les Assomptionists* (Paris, 1939), 103–4; Langénieux's report is given in full in Hajjar, *Le Vatican–La France*, 535–47.

9 *Missiones catholicae*, 165.

10 Lemmens, *Hierarchia latina*, 20; de Martinis, *Juris pontificii*, V, 178.

11 Aziz Atiya, *History of Eastern Christianity* (Notre Dame, 1968), 112; de Martinis, *Juris pontificii*, IV, 649.

12 Atiya, *History*, 113; Sidarouss, *Des patriarcats*, 35.

13 Quoted in Giamberardini, *Impegni*, 149.

14 Barenton, *La France catholique*, 295ff.; 'Relazione sulla stato della Chiesa Copta nell'immediato periodo post conciliare', in Gabriel Giamberardini, *Impegni*, 235–40.

15 'Lo Stato Presente dei Copti Cattolici', *Bessarione*, II, 17–18 (1897), 338–9.

16 De Clercq, *Conciles*, II, 757–80; Giamberardini, *Impegni*, 156–7. *Impegni*, 156–7.

17 Sidarouss, *Des patriarcats*, 105–7; Makarios died in Beirut in 1922. Only in 1947 did Rome appoint a new Coptic patriarch, Mark Khouzan.

Bibliography

GENERAL WORKS ON OTTOMAN HISTORY AND THE
CHRISTIAN CHURCHES

Abel, Leonard, *Une Mission religieuse en Orient au XVIᵉ siècle.* Trans. Adolphe d'Avril, Paris, 1866.

Addison, James T., *The Christian Approach to the Moslem.* New York, 1942.

Allatius, Leo, *De ecclesiae occidentalis et orientalis perpetua consensione.* Cologne, 1648.

Amantos Konstantinos, Οἱ προνομιακοὶ ὁρισμοὶ του Μουσουλμανισμοῦ ὑπὲρ τῶν χριστιανῶν', Ἑλληνικά, ix (1936), 103–66.

Anawati, G. C. 'The Roman Catholic Church and Churches in Communion with Rome'. In A. J. Arberry, ed., *Religion in the Middle East* (2 vols., London, 1969), i, 347–422.

Anderson, Roger C., *Naval Wars in the Levant, 1559–1853.* Liverpool, 1952.

Anderson, Rufus, *History of the Missions of the American Board of Commissioners for Foreign Missions to the Oriental Churches.* 2 vols., Boston, 1872.

Annales de la Propagation de la foi: recueil périodique des lettres des évêques et des missionaires des missions des deux mondes. 102 vols., Paris, 1824–1930.

Annuario Pontificio. Vatican City, 1912–23.

Arberry, A. J., ed., *Religion in the Middle East.* 2 vols., London, 1969.

Ardoin, Alexandre, 'La mission de Tunis, Bône et Constantine des Augustins déchaussés de France', *Revue d'histoire des missions,* xvi (1939), 540–53.

Assemani, Joseph Simone, *Bibliotheca orientalis.* 4 vols., Rome, 1719–28.

Atiya, Aziz S., *The Crusade in the Later Middle Ages.* 2nd edn, New York, 1970.

History of Eastern Christianity. Notre Dame, 1968.

Attwater, Donald, *The Christian Churches of the East.* 2 vols., rev. edn, Milwaukee, 1947–8.

Aubert, Roger, *Le Saint-Siège et l'union des Églises.* Brussels, 1947.

Le Pontificat de Pie IX, 1846–78. Vol. xxi of *Histoire de l'Église depuis ses origines jusqu' à nos jours*, ed. A. Fliche and V. Martin. Paris, 1952.

Avril, Adolphe d', *Documents relatifs aux Églises d'Orient et à leurs rapports avec Rome*. Paris, 1885.

Babinger, Franz, *Mehmet der Eroberer und seine Zeit*. Munich, 1953. (English trans. ed. William Hickman, Princeton, 1978.)

'Mehmet II der Eroberer und Italien', *Byzantion*, xxi (1951), 127–70.

Bangert, William, *A History of the Jesuits*. St Louis, 1972.

Barenton, Hilaire de, *La France catholique en Orient*. Paris, 1902.

Baronius, Caesare, and O. Raynoldus, eds., *Annales ecclesiastici*. 38 vols., Lucca, 1738–59.

Barozzi, Niccolò, and Guglielmo Berchet, *Le Relazioni degli Stati Europei: lettere el Senato dagli Ambasciatori Veneziani nel Secolo decimosettimo*. Vol. v, *Turchia*. Venice, 1871.

Benedictus XIV, *Opera Omnia* (new edn, 17 vols., Prati, 1845), Vol. xv: *Bullarium*.

Blount, Sir Henry, *A Voyage into the Levant*. London, 1636.

Bonnac, Marquis de (Jean Louis d'Usson), *Mémoire historique sur l'ambassade de France à Constantinople*, ed. Charles Schefer. Paris, 1894.

Boré, Eugène, *Correspondance et mémoires d'un voyageur en Orient*. 2 vols., Paris, 1840.

Braudel, Fernand, *La Méditerranée et le monde méditerranéen à l'époque de Philippe II*. 2nd edn, Paris, 1966. (English trans. Siân Reynolds, New York, 1972.)

Breuning, Hans-Jacob, *Orientalische Reyss dess Edlen und Vesten Hanns Jacob Breuning...* Strasbourg, 1612.

Broughton, John C. (Baron Hobhouse), *Journey through Albania and Other Provinces of Turkey in Europe and Asia to Constantinople during the Years 1809 and 1810*. London, 1813.

Bruneau, André, *Traditions et politique de la France au Levant*. Paris, 1932.

Bruno, P. 'Ambassadeurs de France et capucins français à Constantinople d'après le journal du P. Thomas de Paris', *Études franciscaines*, xxix (1913), 232–59, 394–413, 618–31; xxx (1914), 192–202, 401–14, 611–26; xxxi (1915), 164–76, 388–402, 530–50.

Buckhardt, John L., *Travels in Syria and the Holy Land*. London, 1822.

Busbecq, Ogier Ghiselin de, *Legationis turcicae epistolae quatuor*. Basel, 1740. (English translation by Charles Forster and F. Daniell, 2 vols., London, 1881.)

Butler, Cuthbert, *The Vatican Council*. 2 vols., London, 1930.

Buwler, H., *Papers Relating to the Condition of Christians in Turkey*. London, 1861.

Byrne, Leo G., *The Great Ambassador* [Stratford Canning]. Columbus, 1964.

Cambridge History of Islam, ed. P. M. Holt *et al.* 2 vols., Cambridge, 1970.

Campbell, John, and Philip Sherrard, *Modern Greece*. New York, 1968.

Campbell, Thomas J., *The Jesuits, 1534–1921*. 2 vols., London, 1921.

Cantemir, Demetrios, *The History of the Growth and Decay of the Ottoman Empire*, trans. N. Tindal. London, 1734.

Cassels, Lavender, *The Struggle for the Ottoman Empire, 1717–40*. New York, 1967.

Cavendish, Harrie, 'Mr Harrie Cavendish, his Journey to and from Constantinople, 1589, by Fox, his Servant', 1–25, ed. A. C. Wood. Vol. XVII of *Camden Miscellany of the Offices of the Royal Historical Society*, London, 1940.

Çelebi, Evliya, *Narrative of Travels in Europe, Asia and Africa in the Seventeenth Century*, trans. Joseph von Hammer. 2 vols. in 1, London, 1834–50.

Centro Francescano di Studi Orientali Cristiani. *Il Primato e l'Unione delle Chiese nel Medio Oriente: Collectanea, Studi, Documenti, Bibliografia*. No. 5 of *Studia Orientalia Christiana*. Cairo, 1960.

Chambers, D. S., *The Imperial Age of Venice, 1380–1580*. London, 1970.

Charles-Roux, F., *France et chrétiens d'Orient*. Paris, 1939.

Charrière, Ernest, *Négociations de la France dans le Levant*. 4 vols., Paris, 1848–60.

Chateaubriand, François A., *Itinéraire de Paris à Jérusalem*. New edn, Paris, 1968.

Chew, Samuel C., *The Crescent and the Rose*. New York, 1937.

Choiseul-Gouffier, Marie Gabriel, *Voyage pittoresque de la Grèce*. 2 vols., Paris, 1782–1824.

Clemente da Terzorio, *Le Missioni dei Minori Cappuccini. Sunto Storico*. 10 vols., Rome, 1913–38.

Cocchia, Rocco da Cesinale, *Storia delle Missioni dei Cappuccini*. 3 vols., Paris, 1867.

Codex juris canonici, Rome, 1919.

Coles, Paul, *The Ottoman Impact on Europe*. New York, 1968.

Collectanea S. Congregatione de Propaganda Fide. 2 vols., Rome, 1907.

Contarini, M. Paulo, *Diario del Viaggio da Venezia a Constantinopoli di M. Paulo Contarini che andava Bailo per le Republica Veneta alla Porta Ottomana nel 1580*. Venice, 1856.

Crétineau-Jolly, J., *Histoire religieuse, politique et littéraire de la Compagnie de Jésus*. 2nd edn, 6 vols., Paris, 1845–6.

Dakin, Douglas, *The Greek Struggle for Independence, 1821–1833*. Berkeley, 1973.

The Unification of Greece, 1770–1923. London, 1972.

Daniel, Norman, *Islam and the West*. Edinburgh, 1960.

Islam, Europe and Empire. Edinburgh, 1966.

Davey, Richard, *The Sultan and His Subjects*. 2 vols., London, 1897.

Davison, Roderic H., *Turkey*. Englewood Cliffs, 1968.

Reform in the Ottoman Empire, 1856–76. Princeton, 1963.

Dawkins, R. M., 'The Crypto-Christians of Turkey', *Byzantion*, VIII (1933), 247–75.

De Clercq, Charles, ed., *Conciles des Orientaux catholiques*. Vol. XI, pts 1 and 2 of C. J. Hefele, *Histoire des conciles*. Paris, 1949–52.

Delacroix, Simon, ed., *Histoire universelle des missions catholiques*. 4 vols., Paris, 1956–9.

De Rouen, Victor, *Histoire universelle des missions franciscaines*. Paris, 1898.

Descamps, Baron, *Histoire générale comparée des missions*. Paris, 1932.

Djuvara, T. G., *Cent projets de partage de la Turquie, 1281–1913*. Paris, 1914.

Dreux, Robert de, *Voyage en Turquie et en Grèce du R. P. Robert de Dreux, 1665–1669*, ed. H. Pernot. Paris, 1925.

Driault, Edouard, and Michel L'Héritier, *Histoire diplomatique de la Grèce*. 5 vols., Paris, 1925.

Duchesne, Louis, *Églises séparées*. Paris, 1905.

Ebersolt, Jean, *Constantinople byzantine et les voyageurs du Levant*. Paris, 1918.

Edelby, Neophytos, 'L'origine des jurisdictions confessionnelles en terre d'Islam', *Proche-Orient chrétien*, I, 3 (1952), 192–208.

Eliot, Sir Charles (Odysseus), *Turkey in Europe*. 2nd edn, London, 1908.

Etteldorf, Raymond, *The Catholic Church in the Middle East*. New York, 1959.

Eversley, Lord, *The Turkish Empire from 1288–1914*. 3rd edn, London, 1924.

Every, George, *Misunderstanding between East and West*. No. 4 of *Ecumenical Studies in History*. London, 1965.

Fagniez, Gustave, *Le Père Joseph et Richelieu, 1577–1638*. 2 vols., Paris, 1894.

Famin, César, *Histoire de la rivalité et du protectorat des Églises chrétiennes en Orient*. Paris, 1853.

Fattal, Antoine, *Le Statut légal des non-musulmans en pays d'Islam*. Beirut, 1958.

Fedalto, Giorgio, *La Chisea Latina in Oriente*. 2 vols., Verona, 1973–6.

Fidelle relation de l'horrible embrasement. Lyon, 1633.

Finlay, George, *History of Greece*, ed. H. F. Tozer. 7 vols., Oxford, 1877.

Fischer-Galati, Stephen, *Ottoman Imperialism and German Protestantism*. Cambridge, 1959.

Fischer, Sydney N., *The Foreign Relations of Turkey, 1481–1512.* Vol. xxx, no. 1, of *Illinois Studies in the Social Sciences.* Urbana, 1948.

'Ottoman Feudalism and Its Influence upon the Balkans', *Historian*, xv (1952), 3–22.

Fleuriau d'Armenonville, F. C., *Nouveaux mémoires des missions de la Compagnie de Jésus dans le Levant.* 2 vols., Paris, 1717.

Fortescue, Adrian, *The Uniate Eastern Churches: The Byzantine Rite in Italy, Sicily, Syria and Egypt.* London, 1923.

The Lesser Eastern Churches. London, 1913.

Fouqueray, Henri, *Histoire de la Compagnie de Jésus en France des origines à la suppression, 1528–1762.* 5 vols., Paris, 1910–21.

Missions de l'Assomption en Orient, 1862–1924. Lyons, 1925.

'Les Frères des Écoles Chrétiennes en Orient', *Bessarione*, ix (1901), 150–60.

Gabriel de Chinon, *Relations nouvelles du Levant.* Lyon, 1621.

Gams, Pius B., *Series episcoporum ecclesiae catholicae.* Regensburg, 1873.

Gelzer, Heinrich, *Geistliches und Weltliches aus dem türkisch-griechischen Orient.* Leipzig, 1900.

Giamberardini, Gabriele, *Impegni del Concilio Vaticano I per l'Oriente Cristiano e Relazioni della Chiesa Egiziana.* Vol. xvii of *Spicilegium Pontificii Athenaei Antoniani.* Rome, 1970.

Gibb, H. A. R., and Harold Bowen, *Islamic Society and the West.* 2 vols. in 1, London, 1951–7.

Giese, F., 'Die geschichtlichen Grundlagen für die Stellung der christlichen Untertanen im osmanischen Reiche', *Der Islam*, xix (1931), 264–77.

Gill, Joseph, *The Council of Florence.* Cambridge, 1959.

Godefroy de Paris, *Un Grand Missionnaire oublié, le P. Pacifique de Provins, capucin.* Assisi, 1935.

Gottlob, Adolf, 'Die lateinischen Kirchengemeiden in der Türkei und ihre Visitation durch Petrus Cedulini, Bischof von Nona, 1580–1581', *Historisches Jahrbuch der Görresgesellschaft*, vi, 1 (1885), 42–72.

Goyau, G., 'Le Christianisme sur les côtes barbaresques jusqu'au XIXᵉ siècle', *Revue d'histoire des missions*, vii (1930), 8–48.

La France missionaire dans les cinq parties du monde. 2 vols., Paris, 1948.

Gravière, Julien de la, *Doria et Barberousse.* Paris, 1886.

Grousset, René, *L'Empire du Levant: histoire de la question d'Orient.* Paris, 1948.

Guglielmotti, Alberto, *Storia della marina pontificia.* 2 vols., Rome, 1886.

Hajjar, Joseph, 'La question religieuse en Orient au déclin de l'Empire ottoman, 1683–1814', *Istina*, xiii, 2 (1968), 153–236.

Le Vatican – La France et le Catholicisme oriental. Paris, 1979.

Les Chrétiens uniates du Proche-Orient. Paris, 1962.

Hammer-Purgstall, Joseph von, *Geschichte des osmanischen Reiches.* 10 vols., Pest, 1834–6.

Hasler, August, *Pius IX, Päpstliche Unfehlbarkeit und I Vatikanum* (2 vols.). Vol. XII of *Päpste und päpsttum.* Stuttgart, 1977.

Hasluck, Frederick, *Christianity and Islam under the Sultans,* ed. Margaret Hasluck. 2 vols., Oxford, 1929.

Hayles, E. E. Y., *Pio Nono.* London, 1956.

Revolution and Papacy, 1769–1846. London, 1960.

Heeckerin, Émile de, *Correspondance de Benôit XIV, 1742–1755.* 2 vols. in 1, Paris, 1912.

Hefele, Karl Joseph von, *Histoire des conciles d'après les documents originaux.* 10 vols., French trans. H. Le Clercq, Paris, 1907–52.

Heiler, Friedrich, *Altkirchliche Autonomie und päpstlicher Zentralismus.* Munich, 1941.

Heldenheimer, Heinrich, 'Die Korrespondenz Sultan Bajazet II mit Papst Alexander VI', *Zeitschrift für Kirchengeschichte,* V, 4 (1882), 511–73.

Henrion, Baron Mathieu, *Histoire générale de l'Église.* 8 vols., Paris, 1835.

Histoire générale des missions catholiques depuis le XIIIe siècle jusqu'à nos jours. 2 vols., Paris, 1846–7.

Hergenröther, Joseph, and Johann Peter Kirsch, *Handbuch der allgemeinen Kirchengeschichte.* 4 vols., Freiburg, 1911–17.

Hess, Father Cuthbert, *The Capuchins.* 2 vols., London, 1928.

Heyd, W., *Histoire du commerce du Levant au moyen âge.* New edn, 2 vols., Leipzig, 1885–6.

Historia missionum Ordinis Fratrum Minorum. 3 vols., Rome, 1967–8.

Hitti, Philip K., *History of the Arabs.* 7th edn, New York, 1960.

Hocks, Else, *Pius II und der Halbmond.* Freiburg, 1941.

Holland, Henry, *Travels in the Ionian Isles, Albania, Thessaly, Macedonia, etc. during the Years 1812 and 1813.* London, 1819.

Homsy, Basile, *Les Capitulations et la protection des chrétiens au Proche-Orient au XVIe, XVIIe, XVIIIe siècles.* Paris, 1956.

Hurewitz, J. C., *Diplomacy in the Near and Middle East: A Documentary Record, 1535–1914.* 2 vols., Princeton, 1956.

Ignazio da Seggiano, 'Documenti Inediti sull' Apostolato dei Minori Cappuccini nel Vicino Oriente, 1623–83', *Collectanea Franciscana,* XVIII (1948), 118–224.

L'Opera dei Cappuccini per L'Unione dei Cristiani nel Vicino Oriente durante il secolo XVIII. Vol. CLXIII of *Orientalia Christiana Analecta.* Rome, 1962.

Inalcik, Halil, 'Imtiyazat'. In *Encyclopedia of Islam* (new edn, Leiden, 1945), III, 1178–89.

'Mehmed the Conqueror (1432–1481) and His Time', *Speculum,* xxv (1960), 408–27.

The Ottoman Empire: The Classical Age, 1300–1600. Trans. N. Itzkowitz and C. Imber, New York, 1973.

'Ottoman Methods of Conquest', *Studia Islamica,* ɪɪ (1954), 103–30.

Iorga, Nicola, *Geschichte des osmanischen Reiches.* 5 vols., Gotha, 1908–13.

Notes et extraits pour servir à l'histoire des croisades au XVᵉ siècle. 6 vols., Paris and Bucharest, 1899–1915.

Itzkowitz, Norman, 'Eighteenth-Century Ottoman Realities', *Studia Islamica,* xvɪ (1963), 73–94.

Janin, R., 'L'Église catholique en Turquie d'Europe', *Echos d'Orient,* xvɪ, 3 (1913), 236–42.

Les Églises orientales et les rites orientaux. Paris, 1955.

Jelavich, Charles and Barbara, eds., *The Balkans in Transition: Essays on the Development of Balkan Life and Politics Since the Eighteenth Century.* Berkeley, 1963.

Jugie, Martin, *Theologia dogmatica Christianorum Orientalium ab Ecclesia Catholica dissidentium.* 5 vols., Paris, 1926–35.

Jullien, Michel-Marie, *La Nouvelle mission de la Compagnie de Jésus en Syrie, 1831–95.* 2 vols., Tours, 1898.

Karpat, Kemal, *An Inquiry into the Social Foundations of Nationalism in the Ottoman State: From Social Estates to Classes, From Millets to Nations.* No. 39 of *Research Monographs of the Center of International Studies,* Princeton, 1973.

ed., *The Ottoman State and Its Place in World History.* Leiden, 1977.

Kienitz, Friedrich K., *Städte unter dem Halbmond.* Munich, 1973.

Király, Béla, *Tolerance and Movements of Religious Dissent in Eastern Europe.* New York, 1975.

Kirşehiroqlu, E., *Turkiye' misyoner faaliyetleri.* Istanbul, 1963.

Kissling, H. J., et al., *The Muslim World.* Trans. F. R. C. Bagley, 4 vols., Leiden, 1969.

Knolles, Richard, *The General Historie of the Turkes from the first beginning of that nation to the rising of the Othoman familie with all the notable expeditions of the Christian princes against them.* 3rd edn, London, 1621.

Kortepeter, Carl M., *Ottoman Imperialism during the Reformation: Europe and the Caucasus.* New York, 1972.

Kretschmayr, Heinrich, *Geschichte von Venedig.* 3 vols., Gotha, 1905–34.

Kritovoulos, *History of Mehmed the Conqueror.* Trans. Charles T. Riggs, Princeton, 1954.

Kukiel, M., *Czartoryski and European Unity, 1770–1861.* Princeton, 1955.

La Jonquière, A. de, *Histoire de l'Empire ottoman.* 2nd edn, 2 vols., Paris, 1914.

Lamanskii, Vladimir, *Secrets d'état de Venise*. 2 vols., St Petersburg, 1884.

Lammeyer, Joseph, *Das französische Protektorat über die Christen im Orient*. Leipzig, 1919.

La Mottraye, Aubry de, *Voyages du Sr. A. de la Mottraye en Europe, Asie et Afrique*. 2 vols., The Hague, 1727.

Lane, Frederic C., *Venice, a Maritime Republic*. Baltimore, 1973.

Lane-Poole, Stanley, *The Story of the Barbary Corsairs*. New York, 1890.

Turkey. London, 1888.

Lanessan, J. L. de, *Les Missions et leur protectorat*. Paris, 1907.

Lanne, Emmanuel, 'La Conception post-tridentine de la Primauté et l'origine des Églises unies', *Irenikon*, LII, 1 (1979), 5–33.

Le Fur, Louis, *Le protectorat de la France sur les catholiques d'Orient et la reprise de nos relations avec le Saint-Siège*. Paris, 1927.

Legrand, Émile, *Relation de l'établissement des P. P. de la Compagnie de Jésus en Levant*. Paris, 1869.

Lemmens, Leonhard, *Geschichte der Franziskanermissionen*. Munster-in-Westfalen, 1929.

Hierarchia latina Orientis, 1622–1922. Orientalia Christiana, 1 (1923), 225–93, and II (1924), 265–313.

Le Quien, Michael, *Oriens Christianus*. 3 vols., Paris, 1740.

Leroy, Jules, *Moines et monastères du Proche-Orient*. Paris, 1958. (English trans. Peter Collin, London, 1963.)

Lettres édifiantes et curieuses des missions étrangères. New edn, 5 vols., Toulouse, 1810.

Levi della Vida, G., *Documenti Intorno alla Relazioni della Chiese Orientali con la S. Sede durante il Pontificato di Gregorio XIII*. Vol. CXLIII of *Studi e Testi*. Vatican City, 1948.

Lewis, Bernard, *The Emergence of Modern Turkey*. 2nd edn, London, 1968.

'Some Reflections on the Decline of the Ottoman Empire', *Studia Islamica*, IX (1958), 111–27.

Lewis, Geoffrey, *Turkey*. 3rd edn, New York, 1965.

Loenertz, Raymond, 'Documents pour servir à l'histoire de la province dominicaine de Grèce, 1474–1669', *Archivium Fratrum Praedicatorum*, XIV (1944), 72–115.

Loncier, Philipp, *Chronicorum turcicorum*. Frankfort, 1584.

Lopez, Roberto, *Storia delle Colonie Genovesi nel Mediterraneo*. Bologna, 1938.

Luebeck, Konrad, 'Die Katholische Orientmission'. In *Vereinsschrift der Görresgesellich, 1916–19*. Cologne, 1917.

Lybyer, Albert H., *The Government of the Ottoman Empire in the Time of Suleiman the Magnificent*. Cambridge, 1913.

Maloney, George, *A History of Orthodox Theology since 1453*. Belmont, Mass., 1976.

Mancini, A., 'Sulla corrispondenza fra Bajazet II e Innocenzo VIII'. In *Studi Storici* (Pisa, 1905), 103–11.

Mansi, Joannes D., ed., *Sacrorum conciliorum nova et amplissima collectio.* Florence, 1759–1927; new edn, 53 vols., Graz, 1961.

Mantran, Robert, *Istanbul dans la seconde moitié du XVIIe siècle.* Paris, 1962.

La Vie quotidienne à Constantinople au temps de Soliman le Magnifique. Paris, 1965.

Marcellino da Civezza, *Storia Universale delle Missione Francescane.* 11 vols., Rome and Florence, 1857–95.

Marriott, J. A. R., *The Eastern Question: an Historical Study in European Diplomacy.* 4th edn, Oxford, 1940.

Martin, J., 'Le Saint-Siège et la question d'Orient au seizième siècle: projets de croisade sous le règne de Léon X', *Revue d'histoire diplomatique,* xxx (1916), 35–56.

Martinis, Raphael de, *Juris pontificii de propaganda fide, pars prima.* 7 vols., Rome, 1888–97.

Mathieu, Henri, *La Turquie et ses différents peuples. 2 vols., Paris,* 1857.

Maundrell, Henry, 'The Journey of Henry Maundrell from Aleppo to Jerusalem, A.D. 1697'. In Thomas Wright, ed., *Early Travels in Palestine.* London, 1848.

McNeill, William H., *Europe's Steppe Frontier, 1500–1800.* Chicago, 1964.

Venice, the Hinge of Europe, 1081–1797. Chicago, 1974.

Medlin, William K., and Christos Patrinelis, *Renaissance Influences and Religious Reforms in Russia.* Geneva, 1971.

Merriman, Roger, *Suleiman the Magnificent, 1520–1566.* Cambridge, 1944.

Michel, P., 'Les missions latines en Orient', *Revue de l'Orient chrétien,* i (1896), 88–123, 379–95; ii (1897), 94–119, 176–218.

Migne, J. P., *Patrologiae cursus completus, series graeca,* 161 vols. in 166, Paris, 1857–66.

Miklosich, Franz, and Josef Müller, *Acta et diplomata graeca medii aevi sacra et profana.* 6 vols., Vienna, 1860–90.

Miller, William, *Essays on the Latin Orient.* Cambridge, 1921.

The Latins in the Levant. Cambridge, 1908.

Milon, A., *Mémoires de la Congrégation de la Mission (Lazaristes).* New edn, 3 vols., Paris, 1911–12.

Missiones catholicae cura S. Congregationis de Propaganda Fide descriptae. Rome, 1907.

Mitchell, Rosamund J., *The Laurels and the Tiara: Pope Pius II, 1458–64.* London, 1962.

Montagu, Mary W., *The Complete Letters,* ed. Robert Halsband. 3 vols., Oxford, 1965–7.

Monval, Jean, *Les Assomptionistes.* Paris, 1939.

Morelli, Emilia, *Le Lettere di Benedetto XIV al Cardinal de Tenecin.*
2 vols., Rome, 1955.
Mouradgea d'Ohsson, Ignatius, *Tableau général de l'Empire ottoman.*
8 vols., Paris, 1788–1824.
Mouravieff, A. N., *A History of the Church of Russia.* Trans. R. W.
Blackmore, Oxford, 1842.
Mulders, Alphons, *Missionsgeschichte.* Regensburg, 1960.
Mülinen, Graf E. von, *Die lateinische Kirche im Türkischen Reiche.*
Berlin, 1903.
Musset, Henri, *Histoire du christianisme spécialement en Orient de
1789 à nos jours.* 3 vols., Harissa/Jerusalem, 1948–9.
Neale, John M., *History of the Holy Eastern Church.* 2 vols., London,
1847.
Nicolay, Nicolas de, *Le Navigationi e Viaggi nella Turchia.* Anversa,
1576.
*Nouveaux mémoires des missions de la Compagnie de Jésus dans le
Levant.* 4 vols., Paris, 1715–24.
'L'Ordine di S. Domenico a Constantinopoli', *Bessarione*, IV (1899),
413–24.
Oriente Cattolico: Cenni Storici e Statistiche. Vatican City, 1962, new
edn, 1974.
Orse, Abbé, Giraud and Saint-Aroman, *Actes des apôtres modernes,
ou missions catholiques: voyages des missionaires dans toutes les
parties du monde.* 4 vols., Paris, 18—.
Özoran, B. R., 'Turks and the Greek Orthodox Churches', *Cultura
Turkika*, II, 1 (1965), 28–41.
Pacifique de Provins, *Le Voyage de Perse*, ed. Godefroy de Paris and
Hilaire de Wingene. Assisi, 1939.
Pallis, A. A., *In the Days of the Janissaries.* London, 1951.
Papasogli, Giorgio, *Innocenzo XI, 1611–1689.* Rome, 1956.
Paschini, P., 'La flotta di Callisto III', *Archivo della Società romana
di Storia Patria*, LIII–LV (1930–2), 177–254.
Pastor, Ludwig, *History of the Popes from the Close of the Middle
Ages*, ed. Frederick I. Antrobus, R. F. Kerr, Ernest Graf, E. F.
Peeler. 2nd edn, 40 vols., St Louis, 1938–57.
Patelos, Constantin G., 'Aux origines dogmatiques de l'Uniatisme:
un texte ignoré', *Revue d'histoire ecclésiastique*, LXXIII, 2, (1978),
334–48.
Pertusi, Agostino, ed., *Venezia e il Levante fino al secolo xv*, 2 vols.,
Florence, 1973.
Petrocchi, Massimo, *La Politica della Santa Sede di Fronte all' In-
vasione Ottomana, 1444–1718.* Naples, 1955.
Pfeffermann, Hans, *Die Zusammenarbeit der Renaissancepäpste mit
den Türken.* Winterthur, 1946.
Pichler, Aloys, *Geschichte der kirchlichen Trennung zwischen dem
Orient und Occident.* 2 vols., Munich, 1864–5.

Piolet, J. B., *La France au dehors: les missions catholiques françaises au XIXe siècle*. 6 vols., Paris, 1901–3.

Pirri, Pietro, 'Lo Stato della Chiesa ortodossa di Constantinopoli e le sue Tendenze verso Roma in una Memoria del P. Giulio Mancinelli, S. I.', *Miscellanea Pietro Fumasoni Biondi*. 1 (Rome, 1947), 79–104.

Pitcher, Donald, *An Historical Geography of the Ottoman Empire from the Earliest Times to the End of the Sixteenth Century*. Leiden, 1972.

Pius II, Pope, *Lettera A Maometto II*, ed. Giuseppe Toffanis. Naples, 1953.

Opera quae extant omnia, ed. M. Hopper. Basel, 1571.

Pius IX, *Acta SS. D.N. Pii P.P. IX*. 8 vols., Rome, 1865.

Pobladura, Melchior, *Historia generalis Ordinis Fratrum Minorum Cappucinorum*. 3 vols., Rome, 1947–51.

Premoli, Orazio, *Contemporary Church History, 1900–1925*. Authorized translation, London, 1932.

Puryear, Vernon J., *France and the Levant from the Bourbon Restoration to the Peace of Kutiah*. Vol. xxvii of *The University of California Publications in History*. Berkeley and Los Angeles, 1941.

Rabbath, A., ed., *Documents inédits pour servir à l'histoire du christianisme en Orient*. 2 vols., Paris, 1905–21.

Rallis, G. A. and M. Potlis, Σύνταγμα τῶν θείων καὶ ἱερῶν κανώνων. 6 vols., Athens, 1852–9.

Rey, François, *De la protection diplomatique et consulaire dans les échelles du Levant et de Barbarie*. Paris, 1889.

Roe, Thomas, *The Negotiations of Sir Thomas Roe in his Embassy to the Ottoman Porte from the Year 1621 to 1628 Inclusive*. London, 1740.

Rogers, Francis, *The Quest for Eastern Christians*. Minneapolis, 1962.

Romain, S., *Storia documentata di Venezia*. 10 vols., Venice, 1855–61.

Rondot, Pierre, *Les Chrétiens d'Orient*. Paris, 1955.

Rycaut, Paul, *The Present State of the Ottoman Empire*. London, 1688.

Sachar, Howard, *The Emergence of the Middle East, 1914–24*. New York, 1969.

Saint-Priest, M. le Comte de, *Mémoires sur l'ambassade de France en Turquie et sur le commerce des Français dans le Levant par M. le Comte de Saint-Priest*, ed. Charles Schefer. Paris, 1877.

Sanderson, John, *The Travels of John Sanderson in the Levant, 1584–1602*. Vol. lxvii of the Hakluyt Society, 2nd ser., London, 1931.

Sandys, George, *A Relation of a Journey begun An. Dom. 1610 Containing a Description of the Turkish Empire, of Aegypt, of the*

Holy Land, of the Remote Parts of Italy, and Ilands adjoining. London, 1621.

Sansovino, Francesco, *Dell'historia Universale dell'Origine et Imperio de Turchi.* 3 vols., Venice, 1560.

Schevill, F., *History of the Balkan Peninsula from the Earliest Times to the Present Day.* New York, 1922.

Schmidlin, Joseph, *Katholische Missionsgeschichte.* Steyl, 1924. (English trans. Matthias Braun, Techny, Ill., 1933).

Papstgeschichte der neuesten Zeit. 3 vols., Munich, 1933–6.

Schopoff, A., *Les Réformes et la protection des chrétiens en Turquie, 1673–1904.* Paris, 1904.

Schwoebel, Robert, *The Shadow of the Crescent: The Renaissance Image of the Turk, 1453–1517.* Nieuwkoop, 1967.

Scott, Sidney, *The Eastern Churches and the Papacy.* London, 1928.

Sessevalle, François de, *Histoire générale de l'ordre de Saint François,* I, 2 pts, Paris, 1935.

Setton, Kenneth M., *The Papacy and the Levant, 1204–1571.* Vol. I: *The Thirteenth and Fourteenth Centuries,* Philadelphia, 1976; vol. II: *The Fifteenth Century* Philadelphia, 1978.

Shaw, F. E., *American Contacts with the Eastern Churches.* Chicago, 1937.

Shaw, Stanford J., *History of the Ottoman Empire and Modern Turkey.* 2 vols., Cambridge, 1976–7. (Vol. II jointly authored with Ezel Shaw.)

'The Aims and Achievements of Ottoman Rule in the Balkans', *Slavic Review,* XXI, 4 (1962), 617–22.

Between Old and New: The Ottoman Empire under Selim III, 1789–1807. Cambridge, 1971.

Sherrard, Philip. *Greek East and Latin West.* London, 1959.

Sidarouss, Sesostris, *Des patriarcats: les patriarcats dans l'Empire ottoman et spécialement en Egypte.* Paris, 1907.

Silbernagel, Isidor, *Verfassung und gegenwärtiger Bestant sämmtlicher Kirchen des Orients.* Landshut, 1865.

Smit, Giovanni, *Roma e l'Oriente Cristiano; l'Azione dei Papi per l'Unità della Chiesa.* Rome, 1944.

Smith, Eli, and H. G. O. Dwight, *Missionary Researches in Armenia.* London, 1834.

Smith, Thomas, *Remarks upon the Manners, Religion and Government of the Turks.* London, 1678.

Southgate, Horatio, *Narrative of a Tour through Armenia, Kurdistan, Persia, and Mesopotamia.* 2 vols., New York, 1840.

Spinka, Matthew, *A History of Christianity in the Balkans.* Chicago, 1933.

Spuler, Bertold, *Gegenwartslage der Ostkirchen.* Frankfurt am Main, 1968.

Stadtmüller, Georg, *Geschichte Südosteuropas.* Munich, 1950.

Stavrianos, L. S., *The Balkans since 1453.* New York, 1958.

Stoye, John, *The Siege of Vienna.* New York, 1965.

Stripling, George W., *The Ottoman Turks and the Arabs, 1511–1574.* Vol. xxvi, no. 4, of *Illinois Studies in the Social Sciences.* Urbana, 1942.

Sugar, Peter, *Southeastern Europe under Ottoman Rule, 1354–1804.* Vol. v of *A History of East Central Europe.* Seattle, 1977.

Sugar, Peter, and Ivo J. Lederer, eds., *Nationalism in Eastern Europe.* Seattle, 1969.

Tapié, Victor L., *La France de Louis XIII et Richelieu.* Paris, 1952.

Tavernier, Jean Baptiste, *Les Six Voyages qu'il a faits en Turquie, en Perse, et aux Indes.* Paris, 1678.

Testa, J. de, *Recueil des traités de la Porte ottomane avec les puissances étrangères.* 8 vols., Paris, 1864–94.

Theiner, Augustin, and Franz Miklosich, *Monumenta spectantia ad unionem ecclesiarum graecae et romanae.* Vienna, 1872.

Thiriet, Freddy, *Régestes des délibérations du Sénat de Venise concernant la Romanie.* 3 vols., Paris, 1959–61.

Thomas, George M., and R. Predelli, *Diplomatarium Veneto-Levantium; sive acta et diplomata res Venetas, Graecas atque Levantis illustrantia.* 2 vols., Venice, 1880–99.

Thornton, Thomas, *The Present State of Turkey.* 2 vols., London, 1809.

Thuasne, Louis, *Djem-Sultan, fils de Mohammed II, frère de Bayezid II, 1459–1495.* Paris, 1892.

Tongas, Gérard, *Les Relations de la France avec l'Empire ottoman durant la première moitié du XVIIᵉ siècle et l'ambassade à Constantinople de Philippe de Harlay, Comte de Césy, 1619–1640.* Toulouse, 1942.

Tott, François de, *Mémoires du Baron de Tott sur les Turcs et les Tartares.* 2 vols., Paris, 1785.

Tournefort, Joseph Pitton de, *Relation d'un voyage du Levant.* 2 vols., Paris, 1717.

Tritton, A. S., *The Caliphs and their Non-Muslim Subjects.* London, 1930.

Ubicini, Abdolonyme, *Lettres sur la Turquie.* 2nd edn, 2 vols., Paris, 1853.

Ursu, J., *La Politique orientale de François Ier, 1515–47.* Paris, 1908.

Vandal, Albert, *Une Ambassade française en Orient sous Louis XV* (Marquis de Villeneuve). Paris, 1887.

Vat, Odulfo van der, *Die Anfänge der Franziskaner-missionen und ihre Weiterentwicklung in Nahen Orient und in den mohammedanischen Ländern wahrend des 13. Jahrhunderts.* Werl in West., 1934.

Vaughan, Dorothy, *Europe and the Turk, A Pattern of Alliances, 1350–1800.* Liverpool, 1954.

Vaumas, Guillaume de, 'L'Activité missionaire du P. Joseph de Paris', *Revue d'histoire des missions*, xv (1938), 336–59.

Villote, Jacques, *Voyage d'un missionaire de la Compagnie de Jésus en Turquie, en Perse, en Arménie, en Arabie, et en Barbarie*. Paris, 1730.

Vogel, Franz J., *Rom und die Ostkirchen*. Zurich, 1959.

Volney, Jean-François, *Voyage en Egypte et en Syrie, 1783–85*. 2nd edn, 2 vols., Paris, 1825.

Vosté, J., 'Missio duorum fratrum Melitensium O. P. in Orientem saec. XVI et relatio, nunc primum edita, eorum quae in istis regionibus gesserunt', *Analecta Ordinis Praedicatorum*, XXXIII (1925), 261–78.

Vries, Wilhelm de, *Cattolicismo e Problemi nel Prossimo Oriente*. Rome, 1944.

Der christliche Osten in Geschichte und Gegenwart. Vol. XII, new ser., of *Das Östliche Christentum*. Würzburg, 1951.

' "Communicatio in sacris": An Historical Study of the Problem of Liturgical Services in Common with Eastern Christians Separated from Rome', *Concilium*, IV 1 (1965), 18–40.

'The Origin of the Eastern Patriarchates and Their Relationship to the Power of the Pope', *One in Christ*, II, 1 (1966), 50–69.

'The Primacy of Rome as Seen by the Eastern Church', *Diakonia*, VI, 3 (1971), 221–31.

Rom und die Patriarchate des Ostens. Freiburg, 1963.

Vucinich, Wayne S., 'The Nature of Balkan Society under Ottoman Rule', *Slavic Review*, XXI, 4 (1962), 597–616.

Walsh, Robert, *A Residence in Constantinople*. 2 vols., London, 1836.

Walther, Paulus, *Itinerarium in Terram Sanctam et ad Sanctam Catharinam*, ed. M. Sollwek. Stuttgart, 1892.

Winsen, Gerard Van, 'La Vie et les travaux d'Eugène Boré, 1809–1878', *Neue Zeitschrift für Missionswissenschaft*, XXXIV, 2 (1978), 81–91.

Wittek, Paul, *The Rise of the Ottoman Empire*. London, 1938.

Zakythinos, D. A., *The Making of Modern Greece from Byzantium to Independence*. Trans. K. R. Johnstone, London, 1976.

Zananiri, Gaston, *Catholicisme oriental*. Paris, 1966.

Papes et patriarches. Paris, 1962.

Zeiller, Jacques, 'La Société de St Vincent de Paul dans le Levant et le Sud-est européen', *Revue d'histoire des missions*, X (1933), 1–24.

Zeine, N., *The Emergence of Arab Nationalism*. Beirut, 1966.

Zinkeisen, J. W., *Geschichte des osmanischen Reiches in Europa*. 7 vols., Gotha–Hamburg, 1840–63.

ALBANIA AND ALBANIAN CATHOLICS

Bartl, Peter, *Der Westbalkan zwischen spanischer Monarchie und osmanischen Reich*. Vol. 14 of *Albanische Forschungen*, Wiesbaden, 1974.

Quellen und Materialien zur albanischen Geschichte im 17. und 18. Jahrhundert. Vol. 15 of *Albanische Forschungen*, Wiesbaden, 1975.

Borgia, N., *I Monaci Basiliani d'Italia in Albania*, 2 vols., Rome, 1935–42.

Boucart, Jacques, *L'Albanie et les Albanais*. Paris, 1921.

Camillis, Jean, 'Lettre inédite du R. P. Jean de Camillis de Chio sur la mission de la Chimère'. In Emile Legrand, ed., *Revue de l'Orient chrétien*, IV (1896), 58–67.

Chekrezi, Constantine, *Albania, Past and Present*. New York, 1918.

Cordignano, Fulvio, *Geografia ecclesiastica dell' Albania dagli ultimi decenni del secolo XVI ella metà del secolo XVII*. Vol. XXXVI of *Orientalia Christiana*. Rome, 1934.

Darrino, Ignatius, *Acta albaniae vaticana*. Vol. CCLXVI of *Studi e Testi*. Vatican City, 1971.

Frasheri, Kristo, *History of Albania*. Tiranë, 1964.

Gegaj, A., *L'Albanie et l'invasion turque au XVe siècle*. Louvain, 1937.

Gibert, Frédéric, *Les Pays d'Albanie et leur histoire*. Paris, 1914.

Hecquard, Hyacinthe, *Histoire et description de la Haute Albanie ou Ghégarie*. Paris, 1858.

Ippen, Theodor, 'Das religiöse Protektorat Österreich-Ungarns in der Türkei', *Die Kultur*, III (1902), 295–310.

Karalevskij, Cirillo, 'La Missione Greco-Cattolica della Cimara nell' Epiro nei Secoli XVI–XVII', *Bessarione*, XXIX (1913), 170–97.

Noli, Fan, *George Castrioti Scanderbeg*. New York, 1947.

Petrotta, G., 'Il Cattolicesimo nei Balcani: Albania', *La Tradizione*, I (1928), 165–203.

Skendi, Stavro, *The Albanian National Awakening, 1878–1912*. Princeton, 1967.

'Crypto-Christianity in the Balkan Area under the Ottomans', *Slavic Review*, XXVI, 2 (1967), 227–46.

'Religion in Albania during the Ottoman Rule', *Sudöst Forschungen*, XV (1956), 311–27.

Stadtmüller, Georg, 'Das albanische National Konzil von Jahre 1703', *Orientalia Christiana Periodica*, XXI (1956), 68–74.

'Die Islamisierung bei den Albanern', *Jahrbücher für Geschichte Osteuropas*, III (1955), 404–29.

Šufflay, Milan, 'Die Kirchenzustande in vortürkischen Albanien'. In *Illyrisch-albanische Forschungen*, ed. Ludwig von Thallóczy. 2 vols., Munich, 1916.

Thallóczy, Ludwig von, *et al.*, eds., *Acta et diplomata res Albaniae mediae aetatis illustrantia.* 2 vols., Vienna, 1913–18.

ARMENIA AND ARMENIAN CATHOLICS

Acta et decreta concilii nationalis Armenorum Romae habiti ad Sancti Nicolai Tolentinatis, 1913. Rome, 1914.
Alishanian, Gheuart, *Sissouan, ou l'Arméno-Cilicie.* Venice, 1897.
Arpee, Leon, *The Armenian Awakening: A History of the Armenian Church, 1820–1860.* Chicago, 1909.
A History of Armenian Christianity from the Beginning to Our Own Time. New York, 1946.
Atamian, Sarkis, *The Armenian Community.* New York, 1955.
Balgy, A., *Historia doctrinae catholicae inter Armenos unionisque eorum cum Ecclesia Romana in Concilio Florentino.* Vienna, 1878.
Bryce, Viscount, *The Treatment of Armenians in the Ottoman Empire, 1915–1916.* London, 1916.
'Chronique', *Echos d'Orient*, xv, 2 (1912), 63–7.
Dulaurier, E., *Histoire, dogmes, traditions et liturgie de l'Église arménienne orientale.* 2nd edn, Paris, 1857.
Fleurian, Thomas C., *Estat présent de l'Arménie.* Paris, 1694.
Frazee, Charles, 'The Formation of the Armenian Catholic Community in the Ottoman Empire', *Eastern Churches Review*, VII, 2 (1975), 149–69.
Fortescue, E. F. K., *The Armenian Church.* London, 1872.
Galano, Clemente, *Conciliationis ecclesiae Armenae cum Romana.* 3 vols., Rome, 1690.
Germany, Turkey and Armenia: a Selection of Documentary Evidence relating to the Armenian Atrocities from German and Other Sources. London, 1917.
Hovannisian, Richard, *Armenia on the Road to Independence.* Berkeley, 1967.
'The Armenian Question in the Ottoman Empire', *East European Quarterly*, VI, 1 (1972), 1–26.
Lepsius, Johannes, *Armenia and Europe: An Indictment*, ed. J. Rendel Harris. London, 1897.
Le Rapport secret sur les massacres d'Arménie. Paris, 1918.
'Lettera di Ciriaco d'Erivan, Patriarca Armeno di Constantinopoli (1641–42) scritta al Papa Urbana VIII e la sua Professione di Fede', *Bessarione*, XXXIV (1918), 120–3.
Mécérian, Jean, *Le Génocide du peuple arménien.* Beirut, 1965.
Histoire et institutions de l'Église arménienne. Vol. 30 of *Recherches publiées sous la direction de l'Institut de Lettres Orientales de Beyrouth.* Beirut, 1965.

Nalbandian, Louise, *The Armenian Revolutionary Movement*. Berkeley, 1963.
Naslian, Jean, *Les Mémoires sur les évenements politico-religieux en Proche-Orient de 1914 à 1928*. 2 vols., Vienna, 1955.
Nurikhan, Minas, *The Life and Times of Abbot Mekhitar, 1660–1750*. Trans. John McQuillan, Venice, 1915.
Ormanian, Maghak'ia, *The Church of Armenia*. 2nd edn, London, 1955.
Le Vatican et les Arméniens. Rome, 1873.
Oudenrijn, M. A. van den, 'Uniteurs et Dominicains d'Arménie', *Oriens christianus*, XL (1956), 94–112.
Pasdermadjian, H., *Histoire de l'Arménie*. 2nd edn, Paris, 1964.
Petit, L., 'Arménie'. In *Dictionnaire de théologie catholique*, I, cols. 1888–1968.
'Règlements généraux des Arméniens catholiques', *Revue de l'Orient chrétien*, IV (1899), 305–17.
Riondel, H., *Une Page tragique de l'histoire religieuse du Levant: Le Bienheureux Gomidas de Constantinople, prêtre arménien et martyr, 1656–1707*. Paris, 1929.
Sanjian, Avedis K., *Armenian Communities of Syria in Ottoman Times*. Cambridge, 1965.
Talantian, Basilio, 'Il Primato di Pietro e del Papa nella Chiesa Armena', *Centro Franciscano Studia Orientalia Christiana*, V (Cairo, 1960), 217–352.
Terzian, Mesrob J., *Le Patriarcat de Cilicie et les Arméniens catholiques, 1740–1812*. Beirut, 1955.
Tournebize, H. F., 'Ardzivian, Abraham', *Dictionnaire d'histoire et géographie ecclésiastique*, IV, cols. 183–6.
'Arménie', *ibid.*, cols. 290–391.
Histoire politique et religieuse de l'Arménie. Paris, 1910.
Urquhart, D., *Le Patriarche Hassoun*. London, 1872.
Ussher, Clarence, 'The Armenian Atrocities and the Jihad', *Moslem World*, VI (1916), 140–3.
Vandal, Albert, *Les Arméniens et la réforme de la Turquie*. Paris, 1897.
Vernier, Donat, *Histoire du patriarcat arménien catholique*. Paris, 1891.

BOSNIA, DUBROVNIK AND SOUTH SLAV CATHOLICS

Benković, Ambrozije, *Naselja Bosne i Hercegovine sa Katoličkim stanouništvom: Katoličke Župe Bosne i Hercegovine*. Djakovo, 1966.
Biegman, Nicolaas, *The Turco-Ragusan Relationship*. The Hague, 1967.
Bjelovučić, Harriet, *The Ragusan Republic: Victim of Napoleon and Its Own Conservatism*. Leiden, 1970.

Božić, Ivan, *Dubrovniki Turska u XIV i XV Veku.* Belgrade, 1952.

Carter, Francis W., *Dubrovnik, a Classic City-State.* New York, 1972.

Dimevsksi, S., 'Katoličkite misioneri vo Makedonija za Ilindenskoto Vostanie', *Glasnik na Institutot za Nacionalina Istorija*, VII, 1 (1963), 233–46.

'Nekoi podatoci od arhivot na S. Congregation de la Propaganda', *Glasnik na Institutot za Nacionalina Istorija*, IV, 1–2 (1960), 277–303.

Draganović, Krunoslav, ed., *Croazia sacra.* Rome, 1943.

'Izvješće apostolskog vizitatora Petra Masarechija o prilikama katoličkih naroda u Bugarskoj, Srbiji, Srijemu, Slavoniji i Bosni. g. 1623 i 1624', *Starine*, XXXIX (1938), 1–48.

Džaja, Srećko M., *Katolici u Bosni i Zapadnoj Hercegovini na prijelazu iz 18. u 19. stoljeće.* Vol. II of *Analecta Croatica Christiana.* Zagreb, 1971.

Dujčev, Ivan, ed., *Avvisi di Ragusa: Documenti sull' Impero Turco nel secolo XVII et sulla Guerra di Candia.* Rome, 1935.

Fekete, Lajos, 'La Vie de Budapest sous la domination turque, 1541–1686', *Journal of World History*, VIII, 3 (1964), 525–47.

Fine, J. A., *The Bosnian Church: A New Interpretation.* New York, 1975.

Grafenaver, Bogo, *et al.*, *Historija Naroda Jugoslavije.* 2 vols., Belgrade–Zagreb, 1953–9.

Hadrovics, L., *Le Peuple serbe et son église sous la domination turque.* Paris, 1947.

Kecmanović, Ilija, 'Bildnis eines bosnischen Franziskaners', *Südöst Forschungen*, XV (1956), 402–26.

Krekić, Bariša, *Dubrovnik in the Fourteenth and Fifteenth Centuries.* Norman, 1972.

Lefaivre, Albert, *Les Magyars pendant la domination ottomane en Hongrie, 1526–1722.* 2 vols., Paris, 1902.

Mandić, Dominic, 'Borba Katolice Crkve za Opstanak u Bosni i Hercegovini', *Etnička povijest Bosne i Hercegovine.* Rome, 1967.

Marković, Ivan, *Gli Slaveni i pape.* Zagreb, 1903.

Mousset, Jean, *La Serbie et son église.* Paris, 1938.

Okiç, M. Tayyib, 'Les Kristians de Bosnie d'après des documents turcs inédits', *Südöst Forschungen*, XIX (1960), 108–33.

Radonić, Jovan, *Rimska Kurija i Juzhnoslovenske Zemle od XVI do XIX veka.* Belgrade, 1950.

Sinor, Denis, *History of Hungary.* London, 1959.

Stadtmüller, Georg, 'Die Visitationsreise des Erzbischofs Marino Bizzi', *Serta Monacensia* (1952), 184–99.

Villari, Luigi, *The Republic of Ragusa: An Episode of the Turkish Conquest.* London, 1904.

Vinaver, Vuk, *Dubrovnik i Turska u XVIII Veku.* Belgrade, 1960.

Bibliography

BULGARIA AND BULGARIAN CATHOLICS

Armanet, Crescent, 'Le Mouvement des Bulgares vers Rome en 1860', *Echos d'Orient*, xii, 6 (1909), 355–61; xiii, 3 (1910), 101–10.

Avril, Adolphe d', *La Bulgarie chrétienne*. Paris, 1861.

'Chronique', *Echos d'Orient*, v, 5 (1902), 307.

Cvetkova, Bistra, 'La Situation internationale et la peuple bulgare à la fin du XVIe et le début du XVIIe siècle', *East European Quarterly*, vi, 3 (1972), 321–36.

Dujčev, Ivan, *Il Cattolicesimo in Bulgaria nel secolo XVII Secondo i Processi Informativi sulla Nomina dei Vescovi Cattolici*. Vol. cxi of *Orientalia Christiana Analecta*. Rome, 1937.

Eldarov, Giorgio, 'Die Union der Bulgaren mit Rom', *Ostkirchliche Studien*, x, 1 (1961), 13–27.

Fabrèques, Charles, 'L'Église latine en Bulgarie', *Echos d'Orient*, vii, 4 (1904), 207–10.

'Le Vicariat apostolique bulgare de Thrace', *Echos d'Orient*, vi, 1 (1904), 35–9; 2, 80–4.

Hayak, Alois, *Bulgarien unter der Türkenherrschaft*. Berlin, 1925.

Meininger, Thomas, *Ignatiev and the Establishment of the Bulgarian Exarchate*. Madison, 1970.

O'Connor, R. F., 'The Capuchin Mission in Bulgaria and Reunion with Rome', *American Catholic Quarterly Review*, xliii (1918), 205–27.

Sofranov, Ivan, *Histoire du mouvement bulgare vers l'Église catholique au XIXe siècle*. Rome, 1960.

THE CHALDEANS AND CHURCH OF THE EAST

Aboulahad of Amid, 'Les Origines du patriarcat Chaldéen: vie de Mar Youssef Ier, patriarch des Chaldéens'. In J. B. Chabot, ed., *Revue de l'Orient chrétien*, i, 2 (1896), 66–90.

Actes du Synode Chaldéen celébré au couvent de Rabban Hormizd près d'Alqoche du 7 au 21 juin 1853, ed. J. M. Vosté. Vatican City, 1942.

Assemani, Joseph A., *De catholicis seu patriarchis Chaldaeorum et Nestorianorum commentarius*. Rome, 1775.

Avril, Adolphe d', *La Chaldée chrétienne*. Paris, 1864.

Badger, George P., *The Nestorians and Their Rituals*. 2 vols., London, 1852.

Bello, Stephane, *La Congrégation de S. Hormisdas et l'Église chaldéenne dans la première moitié du XIXe siècle*. Vol. cxxii of *Orientalia Christiana Analecta*. Rome, 1939.

Beltrami, Giuseppe, *La Chisea Caldea nel secolo dell' Unione*. Vol. xxix, no. 83, of *Orientalia Christiana*. Rome, 1933.

Boré, Eugène, 'De la vie religieuse chez les Chaldéens', *Annales de philosophie chrétienne*, xxv (1842), 405–24; xxvi (1843), 57–71, 214–32, 313–21; xxxvii (1844), 31–48, 95–125.

Emhardt, W. C., and George Lamsa, *The Oldest Christian People*. New York, 1926.

Fiey, J. M., *Assyrie chrétienne*. Vols. xxii, xxiii and xlii of *Recherches publiées sous la direction de l'Institut de lettres orientales de Beyrouth*. Beirut, 1965–8.

Mossoul chrétienne. Beirut, 1959.

Giamil, Samuel, *Genuinae relationes inter Sedem Apostolicam et Assyrorum Orientalium seu Chaldaeorum ecclesiam*. Rome, 1902.

Gollancz, Hermann, *Chronicle of Events between the Years 1623 and 1733 relating to the Settlement of the Order of Carmelites in Mesopotamia*. Oxford, 1927.

Goormachtigh, B. M., 'Historia missionis Ordinis Praedictorum in Mesopotamia et Kurdistano ab exordiis ad hodierna tempora', *Analecta Sacri Ordinis Fratrum Praedicatorum*, Rome, 1896–7, ii, 79–88, 141–58, 197–214, 533–45; iii, 271–83, 405–19.

Gulik, W. Van, 'Die Konsistorialakten über die Begründung des uniert-chaldäischen Patriarchates von Mosul unter Papst Julius III', *Oriens christianus*, iv (1904), 261–77.

Joseph, John, *The Nestorians and their Muslim Neighbors*. Princeton, 1961.

Khayyath, Georgius, *Syri Orientales, seu Chaldaei, Nestoriani et romanorum pontificum primatus*. Rome, 1870.

Lampart, Albert, *Ein Märtyrer der Union mit Rom: Joseph I (1681–96), Patriarch der Chaldäer*. Einsiedeln, 1966.

Lemmens, Leonhard, 'Relationes inter nationem Chaldaeorum et custodiam Terrae Sanctae, 1551–1629', *Archivium Franciscanum Historiam*, xix (1926), 17–28.

Mauroy, Hubert de, 'Chrétiens en Iran', *Proche-Orient chrétien*, xxiv, 2 (1974), 138–62.

Perkins, Justin, ed., *Historical Sketch of the Mission to the Nestorians by Thomas Laurie of the Assyrian Mission*. New York, 1862.

Ratel, A., 'L'Église nestorienne en Turquie et en Perse', *Echos d'Orient*, vi, 5 and 6 (1904), 285–92, 348–52.

Strothmann, R., 'Heutiges Orient christentum und Schicksal des Assyrer', *Zeitschrift für Kirchengeschichte*, lv (1936), 17–82.

Tfinkdji, J., 'l'Église chaldéenne catholique', in *Annuaire pontifical catholique*, ed. A. Battandier. Paris, 1913.

Tisserant, Eugène, 'Église nestorienne', and 'Église chaldéenne'. In *Dictionnaire de théologie catholique*, xi, pt 1, cols. 158–223, 224–323.

Vine, Aubrey, *The Nestorian Churches*. London, 1937.

Vosté, J. M., 'Mar Johannan Soulaqa: premier patriarche des Chaldéens', *Angelicum*, viii (1931), 187–234.

Waterfield, Robin E., *Christians in Persia*. New York, 1973.

Wigram, W. A., *The Assyrians and Their Neighbours.* London, 1929.
Yuhannan, Abraham, *The Death of a Nation.* New York, 1916.

EGYPT AND COPTIC CATHOLICS

Basetti-Sani, Giulio, 'Documenti per la Storia del Christianismo in Egitto', *Studi Francescani*, L (1953), 65–95.
Buiri, Vincenzo, *L'Unione della Chiesa Copta con Roma sotto Clemente VIII, 1592–1605.* Vol. XXIII, no. 72, of *Orientalia Christiana* (1931), 105–264.
Butcher, E. L., *The Story of the Church of Egypt.* 2 vols., London, 1897.
Colombo, Angelo, *Le Origini della Gerarchia della Chiesa Copta Cattolica nel Secolo XVIII.* Vol. CXL of *Orientalia Christiana Analecta.* Rome, 1953.
d'Albano, Giacomo, *Historia della Missione Francescana in Alto Egitto, Fungi, Etiopia, 1686–1720*, ed. Gabriele Giamberardini. Cairo, 1961.
Faivre, J., 'Alexandrie'. In *Dictionnaire d'histoire et géographie ecclésiastique*, II, cols. 362–9.
Hardy, Edward, *Christian Egypt, Church and People.* New York, 1952.
Ildefonso da Palermo, *Cronaca della Missione Francescana dell' Alto Egitto, 1719–39*, ed. Gabriele Giamberardini. Cairo, 1962.
Levi della Vida, Giorgio, *Documenti Intorno alla Relazioni delle Chiese Orientali con la S. Sede durante il Pontificato di Gregorio XIII.* Vol. CXLIII of *Studi e Testi.* Vatican City, 1948.
'Lo Stato Presente dei Copti Cattolici', *Bessarione*, II, 17–18 (1897) 338–56.
Meinardus, Otto F. A., *Christian Egypt, Ancient and Modern.* Cairo, 1965.
Papadopoulos, Chrysostomos, Ἱστορία τῆς ἐκκλησίας Ἀλεξανδρείας. Alexandria, 1935.
Synodus Alexandrina Coptorum habita Cairi in Aegypto. Rome, 1898.
Trossen, J. P., *Les Relations du Patriarche copte Jean XVI avec Rome, 1676–1718.* Luxembourg, 1948.
Wakin, E., *A Lonely Minority.* New York, 1963.
Wansleben, J. M., *Nouvelle Relation en forme de journal d'un voyage fait en Egypte.* Paris, 1678. (English trans. M. D. and B. D., London, 1678.)
Wiet, G., 'Kibt'. *Encyclopedia of Islam*, II, 2, 990–1002.
Worrell, W. H., *A Short Account of the Copts.* Ann Arbor, 1945.

GREECE, ISTANBUL AND THE GREEK CATHOLICS

Amantos, Konstantinos, Σχέσις Ἑλλήνων καὶ Τουρκῶν ἀπὸ τοῦ ἐνδεκάτου αἰῶνος μέχρι τοῦ 1821. Athens, 1955.

Argenti, Philip, *Diplomatic Archive of Chios, 1577–1841.* 2 vols., Cambridge, 1954.
The Massacres of Chios Described in Contemporary Diplomatic Reports. London, 1932.
The Occupation of Chios by the Genoese and their Administration of the Island, 1346–1566. 3 vols., Cambridge, 1958.
The Occupation of Chios by the Venetians, 1694. London, 1935.
Religious Minorities of Chios. Cambridge, 1970.
Babin, Jacques P., *Relation de l'état présent de la ville d'Athènes.* Lyon, 1674.
Bacalopoulos, Apostolos E., *The Greek Nation, 1453–1669,* trans. Ian and Phania Moles. New Brunswick, 1976.
Bapheides, Philaretos, Ἐκκλησιαστικὴ ἱστορία ἀπὸ τοῦ Κυρίου Ἡμῶν Ἰησόυ Χριστοῦ μέχρι τῶν καθ' ἡμας χρόνων. 3 vols., Constantinople, 1912.
Barbaro, Nicolo, *Diary of the Siege of Constantinople. 1453,* trans. J. R. Jones. New York, 1969.
Belin, François, *Histoire de la latinité de Constantinople.* 2nd edn, Paris, 1894.
Benz, E., *Wittenberg und Byzance.* Marburg 1948.
Bessarion, Archbishop of Nicaea, *Orationes de gravissimis periculis, quae reipublicae christianae a Turca iam tum impendere providebat.* Rome, 1543.
Bradford, Ernle, *The Shield and the Sword: the Knights of St John, Jerusalem, Rhodes and Malta.* New York, 1973.
Bréhier, Louis, 'Bessarion'. In *Dictionnaire d'histoire et géographie ecclésiastique,* VIII, cols. 1181–99.
Brockman, Eric, *The Two Sieges of Rhodes, 1480–1522.* London, 1962.
Calian, C. S., 'Cyril Lucaris, the Patriarch Who Failed', *Journal of Ecumenical Studies,* X, 2 (1973), 319–36.
Caneve, Giuseppe, 'La Missione dei Padri Minori Conventuali di San Francesco in Constantinopoli', *Bessarione,* III (1898), 294–98.
Carayon, Auguste, *Missions des Jésuites dans l'archipel grec.* Vol. XXI of *Relations inédites concernant la Compagnie de Jésus.* Poitiers, 1869.
Relations inédites des missions de la Compagnie de Jésus à Constantinople et dans le Levant au XVIIIᵉ siècle. Paris, 1894.
Cervellini, G. B., ed., 'Relazione de Constantinopoli del Vicario patriarcale Angelo Petricca, 1636–39', *Bessarione,* XXVIII (1912), 15–33.
Chalkokondylas, Laonicus, *De origine ac rebus gestis Turcorum.* Vol. 48 of *Corpus scriptorum historiae byzantinae,* ed. B. G. Niebuhr et al., Bonn, 1845.
Cinq-centième anniversaire de la prise de Constantinople. In *L'Hellénisme contemporain,* 2nd ser., VII, Athens, 1953.
Cobham, Claude D., *The Patriarchs of Constantinople.* Cambridge, 1911.

Courrière de Smyrne, 22 March, 1829.

Crusius, Martin [Martin Kraus], *Germanogreciae*. Basle, 1585.

Turcograeciae, libri octo. Basel, 1584.

Dalleggio d'Alessio, E., "Ερευναι περὶ τῶν Λατινικῶν ἐκκλησιῶν καὶ μονῶν τῶν 'Αθηνῶν ἐπὶ Τουρκοκρατίας. Athens, 1964.

'Galata et la souveraineté de Byzance', *Revue des études byzantines*, XIX (1961), 315–27.

Ἡ Λατινικὴ ἐκκλησία 'Αθηνῶν. Athens, 1962.

'Les Origines dominicaines du couvent des SS. Pierre-et-Paul à Galata; un texte définitif', *Echos d'Orient*, XXIX, 4 (1930), 459–74.

'Recherches sur l'histoire de la latinité de Constantinople: Nomenclature des eglises latines de Galata', *Echos d'Orient*, XXIII, 4 (1924), 448–60; XXV, 1, 3 (1926) 21–41, 308–15.

'Traité entre les Génois de Galata et Mehmed II (juin, 1453): versions et commentaires', *Echos d'Orient*, XXXIX, 1 (1940), 161–75.

'Un Néo-martyr catholique à Constantinople, André de Chio (1465)', *Mémorial Louis Petit, Archives de l'Orient chrétien*, I (Bucharest, 1948), 64–77.

DeMeester, Placide, *Le Collège Pontifical grec de Rome*. Rome, 1910.

Doukas, *Decline and Fall of Byzantium to the Ottoman Turks*. ed. Henry J. Magoulias. Detroit, 1975.

Dugit, M. E., *Naxos et les établissements latins de l'Archipel*. Paris, 1874.

'Εγκύκλιος τῆς Μιᾶς, 'Αγίας, Καθολικῆς, καὶ 'Αποστολικῆς 'Εκκλησίας 'Επιστολὴ πρὸς τοὺς ἁπανταχοῦ 'Ορθοδόξους. Constantinople, 1848.

Evert-Kappesowa, H., 'La Tiare ou le turban', *Byzantino-slavica*, XVI (1953), 245–57.

Fernau, F., *Patriarchen am Goldenen Horn*. Opladen, 1967.

Finlay, George, *History of Greece*, ed. H. F. Tozer. 7 vols., Oxford, 1877.

Fleuriau d'Armenonville, F. C., *État des missions de Grèce présenté à NN. SS. les Archevêques, Evêques, et Députés du Clergé de France en 1695*. Paris, 1695.

Gerlach, Stephan, *Stephan Gerlachs des Aelteren Tagebuch*. Frankfort-am-Main, 1674.

Gerola, Giuseppe, 'Topografia delle Chiese della Città di Candia', *Bessarione*, XXXIV (1918), 99–119.

Gregoriou, Paulos, Σχέσεις Καθολικῶν καὶ 'Ορθοδόξων. Athens, 1958.

Hackett, John, *A History of the Orthodox Church of Cyprus*. London, 1901.

Hadjiantonios, G. A., *Protestant Patriarch*. Richmond, 1971.

Hidiroglu, Paul, *Das religiöse Leben auf Kreta nach Ewlijā Čelebi*. Leiden, 1969.

Hill, George, *A History of Cyprus*. 4 vols., Cambridge, 1940–52.

Hoffmann, H. L., 'De Benedicti XIV latinisationibus in constitutione "Esti pastoralis" et "Intermulta"', *Ephemerides Juris Canonici*, IV, I (1948), 9–54.

Hofmann, Georg, 'Apostolato dei Gesuiti nell' Oriente Greco', *Orientalia Christiana Periodica*, I (1935), 139–63.

'Byzantinische Bischöfe und Rom'. Vol. XXII, no. 70, of *Orientalia Christiana*, Rome, 1931, 132–54.

'La Chiesa Cattolica in Grecia, 1600–1830', *Orientalia Christiana Periodica*, II, 1–2 (Rome, 1936), 164–90, 395–436.

'Griechische Patriarchen und Römische Päpste'. *Orientalia Christiana*, XIII (1928); XV (1929); XIX (1930); XX (1930); XXV (1932); XXX (1933); XXXVI (1934).

Das Papsttum und der Griechische Freiheitskampf. Vol. CXXXVI of *Orientalia Christiana Analecta*. Rome, 1952.

Rom und der Athosklöster. Vol. VIII of *Orientalia Christiana Analecta*. Rome, 1926.

Rom und der Athos. Vol. CXLII of *Orientalia Christiana Analecta*. Rome, 1954.

Vescovadi Cattolici della Grecia: Chios. Vol. XCII of *Orientalia Christiana Analecta* (Rome, 1934); Vol. CVII, *Tinos* (Rome, 1936); Vol. CXII, *Syros* (Rome, 1937); Vol. CXV, *Naxos* (Rome, 1938); Vol. CXXX, *Thera* (Rome, 1941).

Il Vicariato Apostolico di Constantinopoli, 1453–1830. Vol. CIII, *Orientalia Christiana Analecta*. Rome, 1935.

'Wie stand es mit der Frage der Kircheneinheit auf Kreta', *Orientalia Christiana Periodica*, X (1944), 91–115.

Iorga, Nicola, *Byzance après Byzance*. Bucharest, 1935.

'Le Privilège de Mohammed II pour la ville de Péra', *Bulletin de la section historique, Académie Roumaine*, I (1913), 11–32.

Janin, R., *Constantinople byzantine*. Paris, 1950.

La Géographie ecclésiastique de l'empire byzantin, vol. III. Paris, 1953.

'Chypre, (Église de)', *Dictionnaire d'histoire et de géographie ecclésiastique*, XII, cols. 791–819.

'Le Patriarcat grec', *Dictionnaire d'histoire et de géographie ecclésiastique*, XII, cols. 629–754.

'Les Sanctuaires des colonies latines à Constantinople', *Revue des études byzantines*, IV (1946), 163–77.

Karalevskij, Cirilo, 'L'Instruzione di Clemente VIII "Super aliquibus ritibus graecorum" (1595) e le Congregazioni per la Riforma dei Greci', *Bessarione*, XXXIX (1913), 344–65.

Karmiris, Ioannis, Τὰ δογματικὰ καὶ συμβολικὰ μνημεῖα τῆς Ὀρθοδόξου Καθολικῆς Ἐκκλησίας. 2 vols., Athens, 1952–3.

Karolidis, Paulos, Ἱστορία τῆς Ἑλλάδος ἀπὸ τῆς ὑπὸ τῶν Ὀθωμανῶν ἁλώσεως τῆς Κωνσταντινουπόλεως μέχρι τῆς βασιλείας Γεωργίου τοῦ Α'. Athens, 1925.

Krajcar, J., 'The Greek College under the Jesuits for the First Time', *Orientalia Christiana Periodica*, XXXI (1965), 85–118.

Kritovoulos, *History of Mehmed the Conqueror*, ed. Charles Riggs. Princeton, 1954.

Kyriakos, Anastasios, *Geschichte der Orientalischen Kirchen von 1453–1898*, ed. Erwin Rausch. Leipzig, 1902.

Laborde, Le Comte de, *Athènes aux XVe, XVIe, et XVIIe siècles*. 2 vols., Paris, 1854.

La Croix, Sieur Antoine de, *La Turquie chrétienne: état présent des nations et églises grecques, arméniennes et maronites en Turquie*. Paris, 1695.

Laskaris, Stamatios T., Ἡ Καθολικὴ Ἐκκλησία ἐν Ἑλλάδι. Athens, 1924.

Laurent, V., ed., 'Relation de ce qui s'est passé en la residence des pères de la Compagnie de Jésus establie à Naxie le 26 septembre de l'année 1627', *Echos d'Orient*, XXXIII (1934), 218–26, 354–75; XXXIV (1935), 97–105, 179–204, 350–67, 472–80.

Lebon, G., 'Silhouettes de missionaires du Levant: Jacques Cachod', *Revue d'histoire des missions*, XIV (1936), 52–66.

Legrand, Émile, *Bibliographie helléniques ou description raisonnée des ouvrages publiés en grec par des Grecs au XVe et XVIe siècles*. 4 vols., Paris, 1885–1906.

Bibliographie helléniques ou description raisonnée des ouvrages publiés en grec par des Grecs au XVIIe siècle. 5 vols., Paris, 1894–1903.

Relations de l'établissement des p. p. de la Compagnie de Jésus en Levant. Paris, 1869.

Leonardo of Chios, *Historia Constantinopolitanae urbis a Mahumete II captae*. Vol. CLIX of *Patrologiae cursus completus, series graeca*, ed. J. P. Migne. 161 vols. in 166, Paris, 1857–66, 923–44.

Loenertz, R. J., 'Les établissements dominicains de Péra–Constantinople', *Echos d'Orient*, XXXIV, 3 (1935), 336–47.

'Pour la biographie du cardinal Bessarion', *Orientalia Christiana Periodica*, X (1944), 116–49.

Makraios, Sergios, Ὑπομνήματα Ἐκκλησιαστικῆς Ἱστορίας. In C. Sathas, ed., Μεσαιωνικὴ βιβλιοθήκη, III, Venice, 1872.

Mannucci, Ubaldo, 'Contributi Documentarii per le Storia della Distruzione degli Episcopati Latini in Oriente nei Secoli XVIe, XVIIe', *Bessarione*, XXX (1914), 97–128.

Marinescu, C., 'L'Ile de Rhodes au XVIe siècle et l'ordre de Saint-Jean de Jerusalem d'après des documents inédits', *Miscellanea Giovanni Mercati*, v, vol. CXXV of *Studi e Testi*, Vatican City, 1946.

'Le Pape Nicolas V et son attitude envers l'empire byzantin', *Bulletin de l'Institut Archéologique Bulgare*, X (1936), 331–42.

Mas-Latrie, L. de, 'Patriarches Latins de Constantinople', *Revue de l'Orient latin*, III (1895), 433–56.
Mohler, L. de, *Kardinal Bessarion als Theologe, Humanist und Staatesmann*. 3 vols., Paderborn, 1923–42.
Mun, Gabriel de, 'L'Introduction des Jésuites à Constantinople sous le règne d'Achmet Ier, 1603–17', *Revue des questions historiques*, XXX, new ser. (1903), 163–71.
Palmieri, A., 'Chypre', *Dictionnaire de théologie catholique*, II, 2424–72.
'Dagli archivi dei Conventuali in Constantinopoli', *Bessarione*, VIII (1900), 492–520; IX (1901), 128–43.
Pantazopoulos, Nikolaos, *Church and Law in the Balkan Peninsula during the Ottoman Rule*. Thessaloniki, 1967.
Papadopoullos, Theodore H., *Studies and Documents relating to the History of the Greek Church and People under Turkish Domination*. Brussels, 1952.
Papadopoullos, Chrysostomos, Ἡ Ἐκκλησία Ἀθηνῶν. Athens, 1928.
Ἡ Ἐκκλησία Κύπρου ἐπὶ Τουρκοκρατίας *1571–1878*. Athens, 1929.
Ἱστορία τῆς Ἐκκλησίας τῆς Ἑλλάδος. Athens, 1920.
Ἱστορία τῆς Ἐκκλησίας Ἱεροσολυμῶν. 2nd edn, Athens, 1970.
Κύριλλος Λούκαρις. 2nd edn, Athens, 1939.
Papadopoulos, St., Ἡ κίνηση τοῦ Δουκᾶ τοῦ Νεβέρ Καρόλου Γονζάγα γιὰ τὴν ἀπελευθερώση τῶν βαλκανικῶν λαῶν *1603–1624*. Thessaloniki, 1966.
Paparrigopoulos, Konstantinos, Ἱστορία τοῦ Ἑλληνικοῦ Ἔθνους. 7 vols., Athens, 1932.
Pargoire, J., 'Constantinople: les dernières églises franques', *Echos d'Orient*, IX, 5 (1906), 300–8.
Paschalis, Demetrios, Ἡ δυτικὴ ἐκκλησία εἰς τὰς Κυκλάδας ἐπὶ Φραγκοκρατίας καὶ Τουρκοκρατίας. Athens, 1948.
Λατίνοι ἐπίσκοποι Ἀνδροῦ *1208–1710*. Athens, 1927.
Paton, James, ed., *The Venetians in Athens, 1687–88, from the 'Istoria' of Cristoforo Ivanovich*. Cambridge, 1940.
Pears, Edwin, *The Destruction of the Greek Empire and the Story of the Capture of Constantinople by the Turks*. London, 1903.
Peri, V., 'La Congregazione dei Greci (1573)', *Studia Gratiana*, XIII (1967), 129–256.
Petit, Louis, 'Jérémie II Tranos', in *Dictionnaire de théologie catholique*, VIII, 886–94.
Petrides, Sophronius, 'Le Vénérable Jean-André Carga, évêque latin de Syra', *Revue de l'Orient chrétien*, V (1900), 407–44.
Philip of Cyprus, *Chronicon ecclesiae graecae*. Leipzig, 1687.
Phrantzes, Georgios, *Chronicon*. Vol. XIX of *Corpus scriptorum historiae byzantinae*, ed. B. G. Niebuhr *et al*. Bonn, 1838.
Picotti, G. B., 'Sulle Navi Papali in Oriente al Tempo della Caduta

de Constantinopoli', *Nuovo Archivio Veneto*, ser. 3, XXII (1911) 413–53.

Pouqueville, François C., *Histoire de la régénération de la Grèce*. 2nd edn, 4 vols., Paris, 1825.

Raybaud, Maxime, *Mémoires sur la Grèce*. 2 vols., Paris, 1824–5.

Rodotá, Pietro P., *Dell'Origine, Progresso, e Stato Presente del Rito Greco in Italia*. 3 vols., Rome, 1758.

Roth, C. *The House of Nasi: Doña Gracia*. Philadelphia, 1948.

The House of Nasi: The Duke of Naxos. Philadelphia, 1948.

Runciman, Steven, *The Fall of Constantinople, 1453*. Cambridge, 1965.

The Great Church in Captivity. Cambridge, 1968.

Rycaut, Paul, *The Present State of the Greek and Armenian Churches*. London, 1679.

Salaville, Sévérien, 'Le Nouvel Évêque Grec-Catholique', *Echos d'Orient*, XV, 1 (1912), 64–5.

Sarou, A. K., Ἡερὶ μεικτῶν ναῶν ὀρθοδόξων καὶ καθολικῶν ἐν Χίω', Ἐπετηρὶς Ἑταιρείας Βυζαντινῶν, XIX (1949), 194–208.

Sauli, Lodovico, *Della Colonia dei Genovesi in Galata*. Turin, 1831.

Setton, Kenneth M., *A History of the Crusades*: Vol. III, *The Fourteenth and Fifteenth Centuries*, ed. Harry Hazard. Madison, 1975.

'The Latins in Greece and the Aegean from the Fourth Crusade to the End of the Middle Ages'. In the *Cambridge Medieval History*: Vol. IV, pt 1, *Byzantium and its Neighbours*, ed. Joan Hussey (Cambridge, 1966), 389–430.

Sicilianos, Demetrios, *Old and New Athens*, trans. R. Liddell. London, 1960.

Sigalas, A. von, 'Die griechische Insel Syros in ethnischer und religiöser Hinsicht in der byzantinischen und neueren Zeit', *Ostkirchliche Studien*, VI, 1 (1958), 85–92.

Simopoulos, Kyriakos, Ξένοι ταξιδιῶτες στὴν Ἑλλάδα. 2 vols., Athens, 1970–3.

Sphyroeras, Vasilios, Οἱ Ἕλληνες ἐπὶ Τουρκοκρατίας. Athens, 1971.

Stephanides, Vasileios, Ἐκκλησιαστικὴ ἱστορία ἀπ'ἀρχῆς μέχρι σήμερον. Athens, 1948.

Stergelles, Aristeides, Τὰ δημοσιεύματα τῶν Ἑλλήνων σπουδαστῶν τοῦ Πανεπιστημίου τῆς Πάδοβας τὸν 17° καὶ 18° αἱ. Athens, 1970.

Tomadakis, N. B., 'Répercussion immédiate de la prise de Constantinople'. In *L'Hellénisme contemporain*, 2nd ser., VII (1953), *Le Cinq-centième anniversaire de la prise de Constantinople*, 55–69.

Trannoy, A., 'La Nation latine de Constantinople', *Echos d'Orient*, XV, 3 (1912), 246–57.

Tsirpanlis, Z., Τὸ Ἑλληνικὸ Κολλέγιο τῆς Ρώμης καὶ οἱ μαθητές του

(*1576–1700*), Ἀνάλεκτα βλατάδων, 327, Thessalonika, 1980.

Vailhé, S., 'Église de Constantinople: l'ancien patriarcat latin', *Dictionnaire de théologie catholique*, III, 1500–15.

Vaporis, Nomikos, *Post-Byzantine Ecclesiastical Personalities*. Brookline, 1978.

Ware, Kallistos, *Eustratios Argenti: A Study of the Greek Church under Turkish Rule*. Oxford, 1964.

'Orthodox and Catholics in the Seventeenth Century: Schism or Intercommunion?' In *Schism, Heresy and Religious Protest*, ed. Derek Baker. Vol. XI of *Studies in Church History*, Cambridge, 1972, 259–77.

Xanthopoulos, T., 'La Colonie grecque catholique de Cargèse en Corse', *Echos d'Orient*, V, 1 (1901), 33–8.

PALESTINE AND THE SYRIAN CHURCHES

Anaissi, Tobias, *Bullarium maronitarum*. Rome, 1911.

Aviau de Piolant, Comtesse, *Au pays des Maronites*. 4th edn, Paris, 1882.

Bacel, Paul, 'La Congrégation des Basiliens Chouerites: les origines, organisations et développements', *Echos d'Orient*, VI, 3, 4 (1903), 175–82, 242–48.

'L'Élgise melkite au XVIIIe siècle', *Echos d'Orient*, XV, 2 (1913), 44–56, 134–43.

'Les Innovations liturgiques chez les Grecs Melchites au XVIIIe siècle', *Echos d'Orient*, IX, 1 (1906), 4–10.

Besson, Giuseppe [Joseph], *Soria santa*. Rome, 1662. (French edition, *La Syrie et la Terre Sainte au XVIIe siècle*, ed. Auguste Carayon, Paris, 1862.)

Bliss, Daniel, *The Religions of Modern Syria and Palestine*. New York, 1912.

Chanin, Jean, 'Les Patriarches de l'Église syrienne catholique', *Echos d'Orient*, I, 6 (1898), 201–3.

Cheiko, L., 'Autobiographie du Patriarche Ignace-Michel Djaroue', *Revue de l'Orient chrétien*, VI (1901), 379–401.

Churchill, Charles H., *The Druzes and the Maronites under Turkish Rule from 1840 to 1860*. London, 1862.

Collin, Bernardin, *Les Lieux saints*. Paris, 1962.

Dandini, Girolamo, *Missione Apostolica al Patriarca e Maronite del Monte Libano*. Cesena, 1656.

DeWitt, Robert M., ed., *The Massacres in Syria*. New York, 1860.

Dib, Pierre. *Histoire de l'Église maronite*. 2 vols., Beirut, 1962.

'Une Mission en Orient sous le pontificat de Pie IV', *Revue de l'Orient chrétienne*, XIX (1914), 24–32, 266–77.

Etheridge, J. W., *The Syrian Churches*. London, 1846.

Fabrèques, Charles, 'Le Séminaire St François-Xavier', *Echos d'Orient*, VI, 2 (1903), 272–4.

Frazee, Charles, 'The Maronite Middle Ages', *Eastern Churches Review*, X, 1–2 (1978), 88–100.

Gedoyn, Louis, *Journal et correspondance de Gedoyn 'le Turc'*, *consul de France à Alep, 1623–25*. Paris, 1909.

Ghabriel, Michel A., *Histoire de l'Église Syriaque-maronite d'Antioche*. 2 vols. in 3, Ba'abda, 1900–4.

Al-Ghaziri, B. G., *Rome et l'Église syrienne-maronite, 517–1531*. Beirut, 1906.

Golubovich, Girolamo, *Biblioteca Bio-Bibliografica della Terra Santa e dell' Oriente Francescano, 1215–1400*. 3 vols., 1st series, Quaracchi, 1906–27.

New Series, 14 vols., Quaracchi, 1921–33.

'La question de Luoghi Santi nel Periodo degli Anni 1620–38', *Archivium Franciscanum Historicum*, XIV (1921), 209–42, 461–97.

Goyau, Georges, 'Une Capitale missionaire du Levant: Alep dans la première moitié du XVIIe siécle', *Revue d'histoire des missions*, XI (1934), 161–86.

'Le Rôle religieux du consul François Picquet dans Alep, 1652–62', *Revue d'histoire des missions*, XII (1935), 161–98.

Graf, Georg, *Geschichte der christlichen arabischen Literatur*. Vol. IV, no. 147, of *Studi e Testi*, Vatican City, 1951.

Grumel, V., 'Macaire, patriarche d'Antioche, 1642–72', *Echos d'Orient*, XXVIII, 1 (1928), 68–77.

Haddad, Rashid, 'Sources (Hellènes) de la controverse dans l'Église melchite au XVIIIe siècle'. In *Actes du premier congrès internationale des études balkaniques et sud-est européennes*, IV, Sofia, 1969, 499–505.

Haddad, Robert M., *Syrian Christians in a Muslim Society*. Princeton, 1970.

Hajjar, Joseph, 'L'Activité latinisante du Lazariste Nicolas Gaudez en Syrie', *Revue d'histoire ecclésiastique*, LXXV, 1 (1980), 40–83.

L'Apostolat des missionaires latins dans le Proche-Orient selon les directives romaines. Jerusalem, 1956.

'A propos du Congrès eucharistique de Jerusalem (1893): la politique orientale de Léon XIII', *Revue d'histoire ecclésiastique*, LXXIII, 3–4 (1978), 650–64.

Le Christianisme en Orient – Études d'histoire contemporaine (1648–1968). Beirut, 1971.

L'Europe et les destinées du Proche-Orient (1815–1848). Paris, 1970.

Un Lutteur infatigable, le patriarche Maximos III Mazloum. Harissa, 1957.

Hambye, E. R., 'The Syrian Quadrilateral Today', *Eastern Churches Quarterly*, XIV (1962), 336–59.

Harik, Iliya, *Politics and Change in a Traditional Society*: *Lebanon, 1711–1845*. Princeton, 1968.

Hess, Clyde G. and Herbert L. Bodman, 'Confessionalism and Feudality in Lebanese Politics', *Middle East Journal*, VIII, 1 (1954), 10–26.

Heyd, Uriel, ed., *Ottoman Documents on Palestine, 1552–1615*. Oxford, 1960.

Hitti, Philip K., *History of Syria including Lebanon and Palestine*. New York, 1951.

Lebanon in History. London, 1957.

Hollis, Christopher and Ronald Brownrigg, *Holy Places*. New York, 1969.

Honigmann, Ernest, *Le Couvent de Barsauma et le patriarcat Jacobite d'Antioche et de Syrie*. Vol. VII of *Corpus scriptorum christianorum orientalia, subsidia*. Louvain, 1954.

Hopwood, Derek, *The Russian Presence in Syria and Palestine, 1843–1914: Church and Politics in the Near East*. New York, 1969.

Karalevskij, Cyril [Charon], 'Antioche', *Dictionnaire d'histoire et géographie ecclésiastique*, III, 635–703.

'Le Concile melkite de Aïn-Traz', *Echos d'Orient*, IX, 4 (1906), 195–213.

'Les Débuts du patriarcat de Maximos III Mazloum, 1833–35', *Echos d'Orient*, IX, 1 (1906), 11–26.

'L'Église grecque melkite catholique', *Echos d'Orient*, IV (1900–1), 268–75, 325–33; V (1901–2), 18–25, 82–9, 141–7, 203–7, 264–9, 332–42; VI (1903), 16–23, 113–17, 199–206, 298–306, 379–85; VII (1904), 21–7.

Histoire des patriarcats melkites. 2 vols., Rome, 1910–11.

Kollek, Teddy and Moshe Pearlman, *Pilgrims to the Holy Land*. Jerusalem, 1971.

Lammens, Henri, 'Frère Gryphon et le Liban au XVe siècle', *Revue de l'Orient chrétien*, IV (1900), 68–104.

La Syrie. 2 vols., Beirut, 1921.

Lemmens, Leonhard, *Die Franziskaner im Heiligen Lande, 1335–1552*. Munster, 1925.

Mahfoud, Georges-Joseph, *L'Organisation monastique dans l'Église maronite*. Beirut, 1967.

Ma'oz, Moshe, *Ottoman Reform in Syria and Palestine, 1840–1861: the Impact of the Tanzimat on Politics and Society*. Oxford, 1968.

Martinis, Raphael de, 'Le concile melchite de Ain-Traz', *Echos d'Orient*, IX, 4 (1906), 199–213.

Nasrallah, Joseph, 'Le Patriarcat d'Antioche, est il resté, après 1054, en communion avec Rome?' *Istina*, XXI (1976), 374–411.

Papadopoulos, Chrysostomos, Ἱστορία τῆς Ἐκκλησίας Ἀντιοχείας. Alexandria, 1951.

Parkes, James, *A History of Palestine from 135 A.D. to Modern Times*. New York, 1949.

Parry, Oswald, *Six Months in a Syrian Monastery*. London, 1895.

Piana, C., *La Custodia di Terra Santa negli Anni 1762–67*. Cairo, 1956.

Polk, William R., *The Opening of South Lebanon, 1774–1840*. Cambridge, Mass., 1963.

Quaresimus, Francis, *Historica, theologica et moralis Terrae Sanctae elucidatio*, ed. Cypriano da Tarviso. 2 vols., Antwerp, 1639.

Raphael, P., *The Role of the Maronites in the Return of the Oriental Churches*. Youngstown, 1946.

Ristelhueber, René, *Les Traditions françaises au Liban*. Paris, 1918.

Roncaglia, Martiniano, *Storia della Provincia di Terra Santa*. Cairo, 1954.

Saba, J., 'Entre Melkites et Maronites au XVIIIe siècle', *Echos d'Orient*, XVI (1913), 409–23, 536–48.

Saint-Aignan, Laurent, *La Terre Sainte, Syrie, Egypte et Isthme de Suez*. Paris, 1868.

Salibi, Kamal S., 'The Maronite Church in the Middle Ages and its Union with Rome', *Oriens christianus*, XLII (1958), 92–105.

Maronite Historians of Medieval Lebanon. Beirut, 1959.

'The Maronites of Lebanon under Frankish and Mamluk Rule, 1099–1516', *Arabica*, IV (1957), 288–303.

The Modern History of Lebanon. New York, 1965.

Sauvaget, J., *Alep: essai sur le développement d'une grande ville syrienne des origines au milieu du XIXe siècle*. Vol. XXXVI of *Bibliothèque archéologique et historique. Services des Antiquités. Haut Commissariat de l'état français en Syrie et au Liban*. Paris, 1941.

Sharon, Moshe, 'Palestine under the Mamlukes and the Ottoman Empire, 1291–1918'. In Michael Avi-Yonah, ed., *A History of the Holy Land*. Jerusalem, 1969.

Spuler, Bertold, 'Die west-syrische (monophysitische) Kirche unter der Islam', *Saeculum*, IX (1958), 322–44.

Stavrou, Theofanis, *Russian Interests in Palestine 1882–1914*. Thessaloniki, 1963.

Synodi melchitarum. Vol. XLVI of J. P. Mansi, ed., *Sacrorum conciliorum nova et amplissima collectio*. Paris, 1911.

Tournebize, François, 'Le Catholicisme à Alep au XVIIe siècle, 1625–1703', *Études*, CXXXIV, 1 (1913), 351–70.

Vailhé, S., 'Antioche', *Dictionnaire de théologie catholique*, I, 1416–33.

Vries, Wilhelm de, 'Dreihundert Jahre syrisch-katholische Hierarchie', *Ostkirchliche Studien*, V, 2 (1956), 137–57.

Der Kirchen Begriff der von Rom getrennten Syrer. Vol. CXLV of *Orientalia Christiana Analecta*, Rome, 1955.

Zaide, Ignace, 'Église syrienne', *Dictionnaire de théologie catholique*, XIV, 3018–88.

Index